John Richard Turner Eaton

Permanence of Christianity : considered in eight lectures preached before the University of Oxford in the year MDCCCLXXII

John Richard Turner Eaton

Permanence of Christianity : considered in eight lectures preached before the University of Oxford in the year MDCCCLXXII

ISBN/EAN: 9783337263485

Printed in Europe, USA, Canada, Australia, Japan

Cover: Foto ©Lupo / pixelio.de

More available books at **www.hansebooks.com**

The Permanence of Christianity

CONSIDERED IN EIGHT LECTURES
PREACHED BEFORE THE UNIVERSITY OF OXFORD IN THE
YEAR MDCCCLXXII

On the Foundation of the late Rev. John Bampton, M.A.

BY

JOHN RICHARD TURNER EATON, M.A.

LATE FELLOW AND TUTOR OF MERTON COLLEGE ; RECTOR OF LAPWORTH, WARWICKSHIRE ;
HONORARY CANON OF WORCESTER CATHEDRAL.

RIVINGTONS
London : Oxford : Cambridge
MDCCCLXXIII

TO THE RIGHT REVEREND

HENRY

LORD BISHOP OF WORCESTER

THESE LECTURES ARE

𝔇𝔢𝔡𝔦𝔠𝔞𝔱𝔢𝔡

WITH SINCERE RESPECT.

EXTRACT

FROM THE LAST WILL AND TESTAMENT

OF THE LATE

REV. JOHN BAMPTON,

CANON OF SALISBURY.

—— "I give and bequeath my Lands and Estates to the
"Chancellor, Masters, and Scholars of the University of
"Oxford for ever, to have and to hold all and singular the
"said Lands or Estates upon trust, and to the intents and
"purposes hereinafter mentioned; that is to say, I will and
"appoint that the Vice-Chancellor of the University of
"Oxford for the time being shall take and receive all the
"rents, issues, and profits thereof, and (after all taxes, repa-
"rations, and necessary deductions made) that he pay all the
"remainder to the endowment of eight Divinity Lecture
"Sermons, to be established for ever in the said University,
"and to be performed in the manner following:

"I direct and appoint, that, upon the First Tuesday in
"Easter Term, a Lecturer may be yearly chosen by the
"Heads of Colleges only, and by no others, in the room
"adjoining to the Printing-House, between the hours of
"ten in the morning and two in the afternoon, to preach
"eight Divinity Lecture Sermons, the year following, at
"St. Mary's in Oxford, between the commencement of the
"last month in Lent Term, and the end of the third week
"in Act Term.

EXTRACT FROM CANON BAMPTON'S WILL.

"Also I direct and appoint, that the eight Divinity Lecture Sermons shall be preached upon either of the following subjects—to confirm and establish the Christian faith, and to confute all heretics and schismatics—upon the divine authority of the holy Scriptures—upon the authority of the writings of the primitive Fathers, as to the faith and practice of the primitive Church—upon the Divinity of our Lord and Saviour Jesus Christ—upon the Divinity of the Holy Ghost—upon the Articles of the Christian Faith, as comprehended in the Apostles' and Nicene Creed.

"Also I direct, that thirty copies of the eight Divinity Lecture Sermons shall be always printed, within two months after they are preached; and one copy shall be given to the Chancellor of the University, and one copy to the Head of every College, and one copy to the Mayor of the city of Oxford, and one copy to be put into the Bodleian Library; and the expense of printing them shall be paid out of the revenue of the Land or Estates given for establishing the Divinity Lecture Sermons; and the Preacher shall not be paid, nor be entitled to the revenue, before they are printed.

"Also I direct and appoint, that no person shall be qualified to preach the Divinity Lecture Sermons, unless he hath taken the degree of Master of Arts at least, in one of the two Universities of Oxford or Cambridge; and that the same person shall never preach the Divinity Lecture Sermons twice."

PREFACE

I AM aware that all advocacy of Revealed Truth, which does not proceed from the pen of a layman, will in some quarters, at least, be held to be but prejudiced and valueless. I have accordingly made greater use throughout this work of the statements and testimony of adversaries than of friends to the cause of Christianity. To these I have endeavoured to do justice, " setting down nought in malice;" but rather striving to make my own the honest professions of an honoured name in our Church; whose words, and not my own, I desire may linger in the mind of the reader of these pages. "No man may justly blame me for honour-
" ing my spiritual mother, the Church of Eng-
" land, in whose womb I was conceived, at whose
" breasts I was nourished, and in whose bosom I
" hope to die. Bees, by the instinct of nature, do
" love their hives, and birds their nests. But,
" God is my witness, that according to my utter-

"most talent and poor understanding, I have endeavoured to set down the naked Truth impartially, without either favour or prejudice, the two capital enemies of right judgment. The one of which, like a false mirrour, doth represent things fairer and straighter than they are; the other, like the tongue infected with choler, makes the sweetest meats to taste bitter. My desire hath been to have Truth for my chiefest friend, and no enemy but error."—Bramhall (*Works*, II. 21).

I should be ungrateful, were I not here to acknowledge my obligations to the assistance and sympathy of many old and valued friends, more especially to the Rev. William Ince, Sub-Rector and Tutor of Exeter College, Oxford; and to Dr. George Rolleston, Fellow of Merton College, and Linacre Professor of Physiology in the University of Oxford.

CONTENTS

INTRODUCTION xi   PAGE

LECTURE I.

PERMANENCE A TEST OF RELIGIOUS SYSTEMS 1

LECTURE II.

OBJECTIONS TO THE PROGRESS OF CHRISTIANITY CONSIDERED 53

LECTURE III.

OBJECTIONS TO THE PROGRESS OF CHRISTIANITY CONSIDERED 111

LECTURE IV.

OBJECTIONS TO THE PROGRESS OF CHRISTIANITY CONSIDERED 159

LECTURE V.

OBJECTIONS TO THE PROGRESS OF CHRISTIANITY CONSIDERED 205

LECTURE VI.

THE PERMANENCE OF CHRISTIANITY INFERRED FROM THE CHARACTER OF ITS INFLUENCE 251

LECTURE VII.

THE PERMANENCE OF CHRISTIANITY INFERRED FROM THE CHARACTER OF ITS INFLUENCE 295

LECTURE VIII.

THE PERMANENCE OF CHRISTIANITY INFERRED FROM ITS MISSIONARY CHARACTER AND PRESENT STANDING. . . 337

INTRODUCTION

IN the interval between the delivery of these Lectures and their publication a volume has appeared from the pen of the veteran, D. F. Strauss, which has already run through four editions.[1] No work could better illustrate the double line of attack to which Christian belief is at this time exposed. Commencing with the inquiry,—" Are we still Christians?" and taking the Apostles' Creed as his standard of orthodoxy,[2] the writer seeks to show in detail not only the unreality of a belief in the Holy Spirit; not only the unhistorical character of all that is Divine in the Person and Life of Jesus Christ; but further, the needlessness and logical imperfection of the very idea of a Creator of the Universe.[3] That Universe, he holds, is itself both the term of human inquiry and the basis of all reality. In it and in its manifold developments must be sought the ground of all

---

[1] *Der alte und der neue Glaube.* *Vierte Auflage.* Bonn, 1873.
[2] See §§ 5-13.
[3] See more particularly §§ 5, 36, 38. It was a saying of Kant, "Give me Matter; and I will show you how a world might from it arise."

existence,¹ the secret of life, the measure of eternity and of infinity, the limitations of immortality. Duty is resolved into resignation to the invariable Laws of Nature, and into the submission of individual desires to the general good of the race or species.² Religion, if indeed it can be said to exist, is explained to be a sentiment of awe and admiration at the grandeur of that Universe,³ of which the particular soul, if that can be called soul, which is so entirely one with the body, forms a minute fraction.

Such are the results of a criticism of forty years, hitherto supposed to be directed to the examination of the historical documents relating to the Life of Christ. It has closed in landing the critic not in the position of the Unitarian; who denies, indeed, the cardinal doctrine of our Lord's Divinity,

---

[1] " Im Laufe unsrer weiteren Betrachtung bestimmte sich uns dasselbe näher dahin, dass es in's Unendliche bewegter Stoff sei, der durch Scheidung und Mischung sich zu immer höhern Formen und Functionen steigert, während er durch Ausbildung, Rückbildung, und Neubildung einen ewigen Kreis beschreibt."—Strauss, p. 226. See also 228.

[2] " Alles sittliche Handeln des Menschen, möchte ich sagen, ist ein Sichbestimmen des Einzelnen nach der Idee der Gattung."—*Ib.*, pp. 241 and 243. Strauss of course denies free-will, p. 252.

[3] See p. 244. " Das religiöse Gebiet in der menschlichen Seele gleicht dem Gebiete der Rothhäute in Amerika, das, man mag es beklagen oder missbilligen so viel man will, von deren weisshäutigen Nachbarn von Jahr zu Jahr, mehr eingeengt wird;" p. 141. See also 145, 147. Similarly M. Littré on the side of Positivism defines Religion, " La définition de la religion c'est l'ensemble des dogmes et d'institutions qui conforment à la conception du Monde l'éducation et la morale."—*Paroles de la Philosophie Positive*, p. 62. As regards the old theological dogmas he declares himself superior to conviction. *Ib.*, pp. 50, 51.

yet acknowledges "the form," and even, it may be said, "the power of godliness:" but in that of a Pantheistic Materialist,[1] indifferent alike to the existence of God, or of the soul.[2] Professing to write in the interests of a powerful and intellectual minority, Herr Strauss declares his readiness to await the extinction of the popular religion, the doctrines of which, meanwhile, he hardly thinks it necessary to assail.[3]

Now, if such be, indeed, a fair representation of the issues of an union of Biblical Criticism with Natural Philosophy; it will appear that henceforward there may be expected a new line of attack upon Revealed Truth, the result of a junction of the forces which have hitherto been ranged on

[1] "Wenn man hierin den klaren crassen Materialismus ausgesprochen findet, so will ich zunächst gar nichts dagegen sagen," p. 212. Strauss, however, thinks the differences between the Materialist and Idealist of little account. He prefers a system of Monism. This again is the view of the Positivist School. See Littré, *Principes*, pp. 38, 39. Strictly speaking, however, Pantheism supposes a GOD immanent in things; while Positivism sees only Laws.

[2] "Karl Vogt (er ist sonst nicht mein Mann, aber in diesem Felde stimme ich ihm durchaus bei) hat den Schluss gezogen, dass die Annahme einer besondern Seelensubstanz eine reine Hypothese ist: dass keine einzige Thatsache für die Existenz einer solcher Substanz spricht."—*Ib.*, p. 210. Vogt, it is well known, after Cabanis, makes Thought a secretion of the brain. See his *Bilder aus dem Thierleben*.

[3] "Für uns selbst indessen begehren wir von diesen Bewegungen vorerst mehr nicht als Diogenes von dem grossen Alexander. Nämlich nur so viel dass uns der Kirchenschatten fortan nicht mehr im Wege sei."—*Ib.*, p. 296. See also pp. 7, 8, 15, 75. In his *Nachwort als Vorwort*, Strauss quotes a very true observation of Dahlmann: "Wie man eine Kirche auf blos Christlicher Moral bauen könne, das sehe ich vor der Hand nicht ein:" p. 41.

different sides against the cause of Christianity. While, on the one hand, criticism is being directed, legitimately and not unfairly, upon the original documents of our Faith, the trust-deeds of the Gospel; on the other, arguments are advanced, presumably the products of scientific research; which are fatal to the Christian scheme, it is true, but also to the very existence of Religion generally.

Hence the twofold character of the line of proof pursued in these Lectures, involving considerations which may be said to lie at the roots of all faith in GOD and Eternal Life, as well as an examination of facts which concern the history and prospects of Christianity. Both, indeed, are connected by the reflection that the Religion of Christ, if it is to be a permanent gift to mankind, must first be found superior to all objections raised by the free-thinking efforts of the age. It must show itself as ready to assimilate with scientific culture as with the barbarism of ruder times.

The position of the foregoing school of thought, as regards the main tenets of Positivism, is not far to seek. Both equally exclude the Supernatural from History and from the Universe.[1] Both alike

---

[1] " Du moment qu'on ne laisse aucune place aux volontés surnaturelles, ni dans le monde inorganique ni dans le monde organique, ni parmi les phénomènes cosmiques ni parmi ceux de l'histoire, on est nécessairement des nôtres."—Littré, *Paroles de la Phil. Positive*, p. 58. Comp. Strauss, p. 181.

find in the Universe only Matter and Force,[1] neglecting the idea of Form.[2] Both hold that to seek the reason of things in the thought of God is to seek it in a region which is both practically and mentally inaccessible. Thus it is this attempt which has constituted the whole history of Metaphysic and Religion; a history of failure. Both agree in banishing free agency from human life and conduct.[3] Both in the study of things omit the study of man; forgetting the difficulty, if not impossibility, of establishing on *material* grounds alone the ideas of GOD, of immortality, of our own individual personality.[4] Both alike confound the

[1] "Au delà de ces deux termes, Matière et Force, la science positive ne connait rien."—Littré, *Principes*, p. xi. "La force," says M. Janet (*Le Matérialisme Contemporain*, p. 20), " selon Moleschott n'est pas un Dieu donnant l'impulsion à la matière; une force qui plane au dessus de la matière est une idée absurde." Moleschott's ground-principle is, " No force without matter; no matter without force;"= *Allgewalt des Stoffenwechsels.*

[2] " Cette idée de l'espèce qui serait inhérente au germe c'est un principe qui dépasse toutes les données du Matérialisme."—Janet, p. 115.

[3] Thus the old antithesis between Predestination and Free-will is now represented by Naturalism and Religion, Laws of Nature and Human Liberty. We may be content to rest in Dr. Mozley's conclusion (*Augustinian Doctrine of Predestination*, I. 29), " While sufficiently clear for all purposes of practical religion (for we cannot doubt that they are truths so far as and in that mode in which we apprehend them), these are truths upon which we cannot raise definite and absolute systems. All we build upon either must partake of the imperfect nature of the premiss which supports it, and be held under a reserve of consistency with a counter conclusion from the opposite truth."—See also IV., 326.

[4] M. Janet well observes: " Le Positivisme c'est le revanche de l'empirisme contre la phrénésie de la spéculation rationnelle *à priori*."

indestructibility of Matter and the Conservation of Force with its eternity.[1] Both equally ignore the real difficulty of Naturalism; which is to reconcile the consciousness of personal identity with the ceaseless permutations of a material world. How can we prove, or even conceive, a community of consciousness between two particles of matter?[2]

In our own country a school of thought is arising, perhaps more logical and certainly more reverent than that of pure Materialism, which recognizes in the Unknowable the ultimate limit of Science, but also the proper object of Religion. Such a view, amid the turmoil of discussion, is the rather welcome to the Christian believer; as he is himself ready to see and admit Religion to be the Revelation of the Unknowable or Unknown. It has, however, its dangers and its doubts; as to which it is well for the younger student of our time to be on his guard. A system, in which the

---

[1] " Jadis la raison humaine le voyant sujet au changement, alla chercher l'éternel, l'immuable par delà l'horizon et dans les archétypes. Maintenant l'éternel, l'immuable, devenant notion positive, nous apparaît sous la forme des lois immanentes qui gouvernent tout."—Littré, *Principes*, p. 57.

[2] " He, this person, or self, must either be a substance, or the property of some substance. If he, if person, be a substance, then consciousness that he is the same person is consciousness that he is the same substance. If the person, or he, be the property of a substance, still consciousness that he is the same property is as certain a proof that his substance remains the same, as consciousness that he remains the same substance would be: *since the same property cannot be transferred from one substance to another.*"—Bp. Butler, *Dissert.* I. *on Personal Identity*.

Unknowable, *as such*, is made the essential object-matter of Faith, excludes the possibility of the Unknowable becoming known and determined, whether mediately through Revelation, or ultimately in the history of things. In such a view a confusion seems for ever imminent between the physical Unknown in the realm of Nature, and the mentally Unknowable which constitutes the practical principle of Religion. Still more difficult is it to reconcile this doctrine of a Naturalistic Nescience with the aspect under which it is very frequently presented, as " the Power manifested in the Universe."

The argument pursued in Lecture II. (as binding in the sphere of physical philosophy[1]), so far forth as it presumes Motion, as well as Form, to necessitate a First Cause, will be found in Aristotle's *Physics*, Lib. VIII. It must, as it seems to me, hold good till it can be shown that Motion is an original, primary quality of Matter, and so immanent in it. But, as far as appears, Inertia is as much a quality of Matter as Motion, and a body at rest must be acted on externally to be set in movement. The Wolfian supposition of a *tendency* to motion (*in nisu*) was demonstrated by Euler to be both unphilosophical

---

[1] On the necessity or at least desirability of admitting a *physical* element into Philosophy, comp. Janet, *La Crise Philosophique*, p. 106, of whose able train of reasoning I have gladly availed myself in the following remarks.—See *Le Matérialisme Contemporain*, c. iv.

b

and contrary to experience. In point of fact, all movement is now regarded and computed as a resultant; and whereas the rate of velocity might at first sight appear to be in the body, it is found in effect to be otherwise. Attraction and Inertia are equally facts; but if the former be considered to be a relative property of *two* atoms of matter, which singly are indifferent to rest or motion, this is a property which has still to be accounted for. Nor can a universe, however immense,[1] have properties other than those of its integrant parts.

One fact, as it seems to me, must ever remain a stumbling-block in the path of infidel speculation. It is the existence, history, and standing of the Church of Christ.[2] Active, influential, progressive; nurse of the brightest minds that shine in the galaxy of human story, of an Origen, an Augustine, a Dante, a Pascal, a Leibnitz, a Milton, a Newton; handmaid to the spirit of man in his moments of loftiest devotion; mother of modern art; queen of the realm of benevolence and humanity; her doctrines can never be held akin to

---

[1] On the acknowledged immensity of the Universe, M. Littré finely observes: "C'est un océan qui vient battre notre rive; et pour lequel nous n'avons ni barque ni voile; mais dont la claire vision est aussi salutaire que formidable."—*A. Comte et la Phil. Pos.*, p. 529.

[2] Thus it is admitted by Strauss (*Nachwort*, pp. 37, 38), " dass die von Jesus ausgegangene religiöse Bewegung noch mächtig in unsre Zeit hereinwirke, wird Niemand läugnen. . . . . . Christenthum mag in der Menschheit gewirkt haben was es will, und fortwirken wird es in jedem Fall : &c."

Pagan or Oriental superstitions, or be deemed unworthy of modern intelligence: neither can they be explained away, as the unripe fruit of human evolution, or as the outcome of times of unreasoning ignorance. If only we apply to Christianity, as a phenomenon of man's history in the world, the same standard of estimation which we use in other things, and judge of its future by the past, there is small reason either to fear as to its perpetuity, or to predict its fall.

LECTURE I.

PERMANENCE A TEST OF RELIGIOUS SYSTEMS.

Ἀμέραι δ' ἐπίλοιποι μάρτυρες σοφώτατοι.
                                        PINDAR.

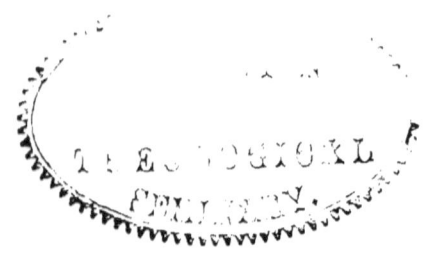

LECTURE I.

"Heaven and earth shall pass away, but My words shall not pass away."—Matt. xxiv. 34.

§ 1. "TRUTH," says S. Augustine, "is the daughter of Time."[1] The weight of prescription in the balance of proof rests rather with the era in which we live than with antiquity, however hoary. For, in comparison with earlier ages, it is of our own days only that it is true that "the world hath lost his youth and the times begin to wax old."[2] The argument from authority has thus been of little avail in the departments of general knowledge either to arrest or to control progress.[3] In the region of religious truth its competence has been more often admitted upon special *Subject stated.*

The argument from prescription now only applicable.

---

[1] So Bacon, *Nov. Org.*, I. Aph. lxxxiv.: "Recte enim Veritas Temporis filia dicitur, non Authoritatis"; and *De Augm.*, I. 458 (ed. Spedding): "Quâ in re Temporis filiae malè patrissant."

[2] 2 Esdras, xiv. 10.

[3] The reason is admirably stated by Pascal: "Les secrets de la nature sont cachés : quoiqu'elle agisse toujours, on ne découvre pas toujours ses effets : le temps les révèle d'âge en âge, et quoique toujours égale en elle-même, elle n'est pas toujours également connue. Les expériences, qui nous en donnent l'intelligence, multiplient continuellement ; et, comme elles sont les seuls principes de la physique, les conséquences multiplient à proportion. C'est de cette façon que l'on peut aujourd'hui prendre d'autres sentiments et de nouvelles opinions sans mépriser les anciens et sans ingratitude ; puisque les premières connaissances qu'ils nous ont données, ont servi de degrés aux nôtres, et que dans ces avantages nous leur sommes redevables de l'ascendant que nous avons sur eux."—*Pensées*, I. 96 (ed. Faugère).

grounds, into which it does not concern me here to enter. It was used at the first, as might be expected, *against* Christianity and not in favour of it.[1] I would rather remind you that, though in the hour of doubt and perplexity we may sigh after that nearness to Apostolic tradition which was the heritage of the first ages of the Church, and cry with Plato, " They of old time dwelt more nigh to God ";[2] yet is there a counter-advantage in our remoteness from the beginning of the faith which it is the purpose of these Lectures to work out. Religions, it must be admitted, are perishable.

> Age to age succeeds,
> Blowing a noise of tongues and deeds,
> A dust of systems and of creeds.

It has been asserted, though no doubt questionably, that there is no country except India which has the same religion now which it had at the birth of Christ.[3] Before the event no one could appeal to experience as an evidence of the power or genius of Christianity. Numberless objections can be imagined which might have been raised to its success. Apparent impossibilities might very

---

[1] " Quanto venerabilius ac melius antistitem veritatis majorum excipere disciplinam? religiones traditas colere?" Minucius F., *Octav.*, cap. v.; and Lactantius, *Div. Inst.*, II. vii.: "Tanta est auctoritas vetustatis ut inquirere in eam scelus esse dicatur."

[2] Οἱ μὲν παλαιοί, κρείττονες ἡμῶν καὶ ἐγγυτέρω Θεῶν οἰκοῦντες. *Philb.*, 16 c.; cf. Cic., *Legg.*, II. xi.: " Antiquitas proxime accedit ad Deos."

[3] See Draper, *History of Intellectual Development in Europe*, i. 63.

easily have been alleged. But eighteen hundred years have passed and the faith of Christ is still a power in the world. "After a revolution," says Gibbon,[1] "of thirteen or fourteen centuries, that religion is still professed by the nations of Europe, the most distinguished portion of human kind in arts and learning as well as in arms." "Its chief home is still in the bosom of enterprise, wealth, science, and civilization, and it is at this moment most powerful amongst the nations that have most of these."[2] If on the wane it is still vigorous.[3] But is it on the wane? And in its collision with the "elements of the world," with political power, national temperament, antecedent tradition, philosophical antagonism, with moral and physical limitations of whatever kind, has it suffered on the way? "The fishermen of Gennesaret," it has

---

[1] Vol. II., p. 151, ed. Milman.

[2] Rogers, *Essays*, ii. 343. In this view Christendom represents what Comte (*Phil. Pos.*, v. 7) calls "*l'élite de l'humanité.*" This fact must be admitted to carry weight in the argument from development. Εἰ μὲν γὰρ τὰ ἀνόητα ὠρέγετο αὐτῶν, ἦν ἄν τι τὸ λεγόμενον, εἰ δὲ καὶ τὰ φρόνιμα, πῶς λέγοιεν ἄν τι; Arist., *N. Eth.*, X. ii. 4. "Christianity," says Dr. Mozley (*Bampton Lectures*, p. 27), "is the religion of the civilized world. . . . This is a great result—the establishment and the continuance of a religion in the world—as the religion too of the intelligent as well as of the simpler portion of society." "Christendom includes the entire civilized world, that is to say, all nations whose agreement on a matter of opinion has any real weight or authority."—Sir G. Cornewall Lewis, *Influence of Authority*, p. 69.

[3] "What the Church has lost in her appeal to the imagination she has gained in philosophical cogency by the evidence of her persistent vitality. She is as vigorous in her age as in her youth, and has upon her *primâ facie* signs of divinity."—Dr. Newman, *Grammar of Assent*, 425, 6.

been picturesquely said, "planted Christianity, and many a winter and many a summer have since rolled over it. More than once it has shed its leaves and seemed to be dying; and when the buds burst again, the colour of the foliage was changed."[1] Something it may, perhaps must, have parted with; something gained: to what extent, and in what directions? Such are some of the thoughts or, it may be said, admissions which crowd upon the mind in approaching the subject of the present Lectures—the steadfastness of Christianity an argument for the truth and ultimate permanence of its doctrines.[2]

This line of proof inductive and appeals to facts.

§ 2. Such an argument, it may be permitted to point out, is drawn from experience and is an appeal to the logic of facts. In this respect it is perhaps suited to the bias of the English mind, and certainly falls in with the intellectual temper of the time. For what is called the spirit of the

---

[1] Froude, *Short Studies*, Series II., p. 32. Thus Pascal, *Pensées*, II. 200 (ed. Faugère): "Il est venu enfin en la consommation des temps, et depuis on a vu naître tant de schismes et d'hérésies, tant renverser d'états, tant de changements en toutes choses; et cette Église qui adore Celui qui a toujours été adoré, a subsisté sans interruption. Et ce qui est admirable, incomparable, et tout à fait divin, est que cette religion qui a toujours duré, a toujours été combattue. Mille fois elle a été à la veille d'une destruction universelle, et toutes les fois qu'elle a été en cet état, Dieu l'a relevée par des coups extraordinaires de sa puissance." Mr. Buckle (*Hist. Civ.*, II. 285) assumes, for he does not go into proofs, that Christianity has been affected by foreign events *contrary to the original scheme*.

[2] "Nulle autre religion n'a la perpétuité; qui est la principale marque de la véritable."—Pascal, *Pensées*, II. 368. "Les trois marques de la religion sont la perpétuité, la bonne vie, les miracles."—*Ib.*

age is unmistakably inductive: and by the inductive spirit is really intended a mental disposition to rest upon observed facts or repetitions of fact, not upon any inherent necessity of sequence or prior proof. There would seem to be three main roads open to mankind for reaching a knowledge of God, of our duties towards Him, and of His will respecting us. These are our own nature and constitution, the testimony of mankind, and the course of the world's history.[1] Of these, the last, as being the most matter of fact, would probably in the present day be held to be the least disputable. The results of a religious system furnish at least an indirect proof of its truth. Taken in connection with prophecy, this proof becomes unanswerable; but it has also a value and importance of its own. Such accordingly, as regards the fortunes of the Roman Empire, an epitome of the history of the world, was the motive of Augustine's masterpiece of Christian Apology, the *Civitas Dei*.[2] There is equal reason

---

[1] See Dr. Newman, *Grammar of Assent*, p. 384.

[2] Dr. Mozley, *Bampton Lectures*, p. 263, points out that Augustine pushes this argument almost to the exclusion of miracles, *e.g. Civ. Dei*, xxii. 5: "hoc nobis unum grande miraculum sufficit, quod eam terrarum orbis sine ullis miraculis credidit." This is no doubt rhetorically expressed. Elsewhere he states the proper relation of miracles to the spread of Christianity. "Ergo Ille afferens medicinam quæ corruptissimos mores sanatura esset, miraculis conciliavit auctoritatem, auctoritate meruit fidem, fide contraxit multitudinem, multitudine obtinuit vetustatem, vetustate roboravit religionem."—*De Util. Cred.*, c. xiv., and cf. *De Ver. Rel.*, c. iii., xxv. Thus he rests his faith on the traditional

for its being the ground of Christian defence now. No analysis of modern civilization can omit to consider the influences of Christianity. A test is thus supplied of its tendencies, its character, and its efficacy.[1]

<small>Possible only after a lapse of centuries.</small>

§ 3. It is with the field of time as with areas of mensurable space. A certain remoteness from the object viewed is necessary to clear and distinct vision. Still more necessary is it for any purpose of determining the relative magnitude and actual proportions of the thing perceived. These can be understood only by the medium of intervening objects. The same holds good in any mental

<small>reception of Christianity. "Nullis me video credidisse nisi populorum atque gentium confirmatæ opinioni ac famæ admodum celeberrimæ: hos autem populos Ecclesiæ Catholicæ mysteria usquequaque occupâsse. . . Credidi, ut dixi, famæ celebritate, consensione, vetustate roboratæ."—*Ib.* Thus antiquity and universality of reception gradually take the place of miracles. Cf. also *De Ver. Rel.*, vii. 13: "Hujus religionis sectandæ caput est historia et prophetia dispensationis temporalis divinæ providentiæ pro salute generis humani in æternam vitam reformandi atque reparandi." The germs of Augustine's argument in the *Civitas Dei* will be found in Tertullian, *Apol.*, cap. xl. At that time the power of the Gods was estimated by the condition of the nations who worshipped them. Cf. Gieseler, *Ch. Hist.*, I. § 16.

[1] "All that we call modern civilization in a sense which deserves the name, is the visible expression of the transforming power of the Gospel."—Froude, *Short Studies*, II. p. 30. "Christianity," writes Mr. Lecky, "the life of morality, the basis of civilization, has regenerated the world." Montesquieu (*Esprit des Lois*, XXIV.) recognizes this argument. "Comme on peut juger parmi les ténèbres celles qui sont les moins épaisses, et parmi les abymes ceux qui sont les moins profonds, ainsi l'on peut chercher entre les religions fausses celles qui sont les plus conformes au bien de la société; celles qui, quoiqu'elles n'aient pas l'effet de mener les hommes aux félicités de l'autre vie, peuvent le plus contribuer à leur bonheur dans celle-ci."</small>

survey of the past, when we take stock, as it were, of the phenomena of history. Only after the lapse of centuries does it become possible to estimate the association and import of facts, the tendency of principles, their falseness or their truth.

> The thoughts of men are widened by the process of the suns.

Christianity is at this time a fact of long standing. Its relative importance among other elements of civilization may now be measured: its effects eliminated from those of other agencies: the laws of its progress determined: its retardations adjusted: its ultimate movements conjectured. But there was a time when these processes could not have been carried on, when any argument grounded on them would have been preposterous: and the more nearly we return in thought to the beginnings of the Faith of Christ, the less room is found for their admission.

The religion of Jesus Christ, we may maintain, has now achieved for itself an actual positive standpoint against the assaults of detractors. Those who impugn its claims have at least to account in some other way for the successes it has gained and the influence which it wields. Men, it may be allowed, may blunder into truth: perhaps even, they must go wrong before they come out right. It is probable that this is the key to much of the

The progress of Truth slow but inevitable.

history of thought, resembling those arithmetical calculations in which error is checked by error to obtain an approximation to the truth.[1] But the mind on looking back can well enough discern its wanderings on the road. It is true that there is much in the career of Christianity to obscure the light of its own progress. The tardiness and partial character of its advance have been often remarked.[2] It has not flashed with meteor brilliancy across the world's story, neither has it shone with steady undimmed effulgence along the track of time; rather, like the sun in heaven, it has struggled through cloud and mist. At the first it wrought irregularly on individual minds, not by an organized system. The Reformation and all returns to its primitive character have

---

[1] Thus "error," as Voltaire remarked, "has its merits." "The history of philosophy," says Sir William Hamilton, "is the history of error." We may say with Virgil,

Pater Ipse colendi
Haud facilem esse viam voluit.

"Encore que les philosophes," says Bossuet, "soient les protecteurs de l'erreur, toutefois ils ont frappé à la porte de la Vérité."

[2] See some good remarks on this subject by the Bishop of Ely in his lecture on *Christ's Influence on History*, p. 28. Thus Neander compares the development of Christianity to a process moving steadily onward, though not in a direct line, but through various windings, yet in the end furthered by whatever has attempted to arrest its course. "Religion," says Mr. Morley, *Crit. Misc.*, p. 95, "must be accepted as a fact in the history of the human mind, . . . and Christianity is undeniably entitled to one of the most important places in it, however we may be disposed to strike the balance between the undoubted injuries and the undoubted advantages which it has been the means of dealing to the civilization of the West."

tended to restore this mode of its operation,[1] and so have ever exhibited degrees of non-conformity. The irony of the lofty author of the 'Variations of Protestantism' may be and has been turned with equal force from the disagreements of opposed sects and rival Churches upon the claims of Christianity at large.[2] The conclusion drawn, it is true, is no more valid in the one case than in the other, and for the same reasons. Indeed, to a fair mind it would rather furnish a presumption against the truth of Christianity, if it did not or had not in its progress exhibited that amount of variation which is alone compatible with the course of human reason on all subjects of thought. The pathology of a religious system assumes the reality of a true core of belief. The existence of controversy is to a certain extent a test of the power and vitality of Christianity. "If any country," says Bacon,[3] "decline into Atheism, then controversies wax dainty; because men do think religion scarce worth the falling out." The co-existence and competition of sects has therefore not unreasonably

Groundless objection drawn from variations of belief.

---

[1] Dean Hook, *Lives of Archbishops*, in his Introduction to the New Series, remarks on "the tendency of the Reformation to *individualize* Christianity."

[2] "Si l'argument de M. de Meaux vaut quelque chose contre la Réformation, il a la même force contre le Christianisme."—Beausobre, *Hist. de Manichée*, I. 526, and see Mr. Buckle's remarks, *H. C. E.*, II. 283. The objection raised disappears when the nature of the subject-matter of Revelation, with its difficulties of application and interpretation, is considered. Compare Hallam, *Literature of Europe*, III. 268.

[3] Bacon's Works (ed. Spedding), VIII. 165.

been held to be the system most in conformity with the nature of society, and most favourable to the solidity and general efficiency of religion.[1] Some, however, may be inclined to attribute to the objection, suggested by the argument of Bossuet, an importance disproportioned to its worth. It certainly entails on the Christian advocate the task of showing that the disagreement among Christians has not been vital, nor its degree such as to neutralize the common effect due to the religion of Christ as a whole. In accomplishing the work whereunto it is sent, the robe of Christ is still " without seam, woven from the top throughout." Moreover, whatever have been its fortunes, its proper tendencies remain; and these undoubtedly act to " draw men together in spite of their worst differences, proving it to be quite as abhorrent of divisions in itself as Nature ever was of a vacuum."[2] Still, if union is strength, persistent differences mean permanent weakness. It is then surely time for the great sections of the Christian world[3] to study unity and not division;

A warning, however, to study the increase of unity.

---

[1] See Guizot's *Meditations*, Pt. II., pp. 5, 165 (E. T.); Paley, *Evid.*, II. c. vii.; and compare Ffoulkes' *Divisions of Christendom*, p. 246. "There is even consolation," &c. It is true, however, as Dr. Westcott has remarked, after Comte, that the tendencies of Protestantism go to obscure the conception of continuity in human progress, reposing too much on logical deduction. "To erect any one age (whether primitive or mediæval) into an idol is to deny implicitly that the Gospel is life."—*Contemp. Review*, VI. 420. See also Dorner, *Hist. Protestant Theology*, Vol. I., p. xviii., E. T.

[2] Ffoulkes, *u. s.*, p. vi. and p. 252.

[3] Compare Guizot, *Meditations*, Pt. I., Pref., pp. ix.–xvii, "Je dis

alliance and not mutual elimination; to give up claims to a several infallibility; to join at least for the defence of the faith " once delivered to the saints"; to exhibit the bases of a common belief; to cherish more strongly than hitherto their underlying points of agreement; to drop dissensions, and go forth to conquer.

§ 4. But it may be asked at the outset—is Permanence of itself a test of truth?[1] Is that which is true always enduring and error never so? Have not unreal systems held sway and made progress in the history of mankind? Is there no such thing as a prescription of ignorance?[2] Is retrogression a thing impossible, and is there no historical proof of it? Are periods of "*denuda-*

<small>*Permanence an actual test of truth.*</small>

---

l'Église Chrétienne: c'est toute l'Église Chrétienne en effet, et non pas telle ou telle des églises chrétiennes qui est maintenant et radicalement attaquée."

[1] It will perhaps be said that truth is strictly an attribute of *propositions* only; and in this sense no one will deny that what is true is true for always, though it may not at all times be recognized. But the term seems not improperly used of whatever answers to the definition of a thing. In the case of institutions, some come up to the idea or notion commonly held of their nature and function; some fall short of it. Christianity is sometimes regarded as a set of dogmas or propositions (such as have been termed *fundamentals*), of which truth is immediately predicable. Sometimes it is identified with the Church, which is the witness and keeper of these truths. In this capacity, as liable to the admixture of error, it may be compared with rival religious systems, and may vary at different periods relatively to itself. Permanence in the form of *persistence in consciousness* seems to lie at the basis of all reality. See Mr. Herbert Spencer, *First Principles*, p. 226.

[2] " Consuetudo sine veritate vetustas erroris est."—Cyprian, Ep. 74. Opp., p. 282.

tion" unknown in the intellectual eras of our race? Does truth always emerge from behind the mists of falsehood and make daylight in the world? Perhaps not; and yet the answer to such doubts may be in no wise doubtful. The day is really past, notwithstanding some pretentious objections, for questioning the tendencies of God's moral government. Exceptions, which constitute only the disorder of Nature, yield no argument against its general laws. "God," says Bishop Butler, "makes use of a variety of means, what we often think tedious ones, in the natural course of Providence for the accomplishment of all His ends."[1] The analogy of reason as against force, which has been employed by the same author to illustrate the tendency of right to prevail in the economy of the world, affords a similar explanation of the victories of error over truth in the working of religious systems.

Liable to apparent exceptions.

Virtute semper prævalet sapientia.

The lesson gained from a criticism of the past is this; that while it is consistent with an overruling Providence to allow the existence of falsehood, extravagance, self-delusion in almost every form, yet there is, on the whole, a constant steady advance towards convictions which are finally recognized

---

[1] *Analogy*, Pt. II. c. iv. Comp. Eurip. *Orestes*, 420:
Μέλλει τὸ Θεῖον· ἐστὶ τοιοῦτον φύσει.

as immutably true. And this progress of truth is not dependent on blind tendencies, but on an intellectual activity which, gradually disposing of error, transforms opinion into knowledge. This which is evident in the experience of the physical sciences holds good equally for the more complex subjects of theology and morals. But the results must naturally be sought not among the least but among the most civilized portions of mankind. Length of time together with reasonable opportunity may be requisite for the extinction of error. Duration and stress of persecution, stamping out conscientious belief, may, in some instances, account for the depression of truth. To some extent they explain and help on its progress.[1] Degradation, partial or temporary, seems to be an historical condition of the general advance of civilization.[2]

[1] "Le besoin perfectionne l'instrument," was a maxim of Turgot. "In times of peace," says Archbishop Leighton, "the Church may dilate more and build as it were into breadth, but in times of trouble it arises more in height. It is then built upwards, as in cities where men are straitened, they build usually higher than in the country."—Op. Coleridge, *Aids to R.*, p. 73.

[2] "Ages of laborious ascent have been followed by a moment of rapid downfall, and the several climates of the globe have felt the vicissitudes of light and darkness. Yet the experience of four thousand years should enlarge our hopes and diminish our apprehensions."—Gibbon, Vol. IV. 400 (ed. Milman). "Humanity accomplishes its necessary destiny but (being composed of free persons) with an element of liberty ; so that error and crime find their place in its course, and we behold centuries which do not advance, but even recede, days of illness, and years of wandering. . . . But mankind never entirely or irremediably errs. The light burns somewhere which is to go to the front of the straying generation and bring it along in its wake. When the Gospel failed in the

But an inversion of the order of the universe, as well as of our inbred convictions, of our experience of things as well as of our inner consciousness, must take place before we can admit indifference or malice, a willingness to deceive or a capacity of deception in the Author and Administrator of the world. And yet this is implied in the assumption that the human race in its most distinguished representatives and on the subjects of the highest moment lies still in darkness.[1] "God owes it to mankind not to lead them into error," is the bold language of Pascal.[2] "Truth," says Milton, "is strong next to the Almighty." As it is ludicrous

grounded on a reasonable conviction.

East it dawned on the races of the North."—Ozanam, *Civilis. Chret.*, I. pp. 18-20, E. T. Mr. Tylor, *Hist. Prim. Cult.*, I. 421, speaking of natural religion, remarks that "the history of religion displays but too plainly the proneness of mankind to relapse, in spite of reformation, into the lower and darker condition of the past."

[1] There is a tendency in the Positivist system to assume not only that in the constitution of things error is employed as a means to truth, but that this theorem covers the whole of religious belief. Thus theology, which in this system of thought is *imaginary*, is allowed to have been an important stage in the advance of the human race, yet only as a sort of "pis-aller." See Comte, *Phil. Pos.*, IV. 693. The language of the Apostle in Acts xvii. 30 (τοὺς μὲν οὖν χρόνους τῆς ἀγνοίας ὑπεριδὼν ὁ Θεός) may in the English version be liable to be mistaken. But his argument on this deeply momentous subject, "the fulness of times," as expanded in Rom. c. i., ii., and Gal. iii., iv., can hardly be misapprehended. See Bunsen, *God in History*, Vol. I. 215, E. T.

[2] "Dieu doit aux hommes de ne pas les induire en erreur."—*Pensées*. "The established order of things in which we find ourselves, if it has a Creator, must surely speak of His will in its broad outlines and main issues."—Newman, *Grammar of Assent*, p. 391. Comp. Farrar's *Witness of History to Christ*, p. 92. See Sir W. Hamilton (*Reid*, 743, 745). Mr. Mill's criticism (*Exam.*, p. 136) is invalid so long as there are truths of consciousness leading up to the recognition of God.

to go about to prove the reality of those perceptions which alone exist to us as the means of discovering facts; so were it futile to suspect the ultimate triumph of truth over falsehood, or to question the tendency of things in the long run to exhibit its progress. The improvement of mankind in successive ages is indisputable, and improvement involves at least approximation to truth. Whatever be the obstacles to their power of self-assertion, the Grand Justiciary of reason and of fact is Time.[1]

§ 5. What, however, is meant by Time in these considerations, and how much may justly be attributed to it? In what respects is it an element of progress in the history of knowledge? It is no mere abstraction or Idol of the Tribe. It is a real condition of all human operation, speculative or practical. Its function may be compared to an analytic yet constructive process; which dividing and disengaging elements before believed to be inseparable, renders re-arrangement and reconstruction possible and simple.[2] Such is the work

Time in what sense an agency.

---

[1] "Le temps, le grand Justicier du passé."—Montaigne. Cicero (*Nat. D.*, II. ii. 5), speaking of the existence of God, says: "Quod nisi cognitum comprehensumque animis haberemus, non tam stabilis opinio permaneret, nec confirmaretur diuturnitate temporis nec una cum sæculis ætatibusque hominum inveterari potuisset. Et enim videmus cæteras opiniones fictas atque vanas diuturnitate extabuisse. . . . Opinionum enim commenta delet dies, naturæ judicia confirmat."

[2] M. Littré (*A. Comte et la Phil. Pos.*, p. 45) well observes: "Le temps, faisant l'office des forts grossissements, montre disjoint ce qui apparaît étroitement conjoint dans l'esprit d'un même penseur."

of continuous generations toiling unconsciously as one man in the quest of Truth, but with this advantage, that they are uninterrupted by individual mortality.[1] Some thinkers use Time too readily and profusely[2] as an agent, whether in physical changes, or in the advance of opinion and the overthrow of superstitions by a sort of natural and spontaneous growth of the human mind—a gradual evolution of conviction, the spirit and tendency of the age, the fruit of time and succession. It should be clearly understood that all such results are, in fact, the work of individual effort, admitting of distinct explanation. The tendencies of an age are the unperceived consequences of foregone argument. They are "changes wrought not *by* Time, but *in* Time." In the work of religious "truth," it has been finely said,[3] "Time means the blood of many martyrs, the toil of many brains, slow steps made good through infinite research." In this manner

---

[1] "De sorte que toute la suite des hommes, pendant le cours de tant de siècles, doit être considérée comme un même homme qui subsiste toujours et qui apprend continuellement."—Pascal (*Pensées*, I. p. 98).

[2] Thus "the prehistoric archæologist," says Mr. Tylor, *Hist. Prim. Cult.*, I. p. 50, "shows even too much disposition to revel in calculations of thousands of years, as a financier does in reckonings of thousands of pounds in a liberal and maybe somewhat reckless way." See, however, Lange, *Gesch. d. Materialismus*, p. 342. In the School of Positive Science, "c'est le temps qui est ici le grand créateur," says M. Janet.—*Le Matérialisme Contemporain*, p. 24.

[3] Greg's *Literary and Social Judgments*, p. 478. Compare Professor Goldwin Smith, *Study of History*, p. 34. Human progress "is a progress of effort, not a necessary development," &c.

it comes about that no great verity once discovered is ever afterwards lost to mankind,[1] but is taken up and carried along by the stream of human effort. In the words of the poet they are

> Truths that wake
> To perish never.

§ 6. The objections which lie against all positive[2] attempts to criticise the plan of a Divine Revelation, do not apply to an inquiry which is relative to a matter of fact. The present argument does not run up into questionable final causes, or depend for its acceptance on dubious interpretations of remote prophecies. It forms no anticipations of the thoughts of Heaven. But rather it humbly seeks to track upwards through

The present argument, a posteriori.

Not dependent on final causes.

---

[1] "No great truth which has once been found has ever afterwards been lost."—Buckle, *Hist. Civ.*, I. 215. "What has once become the common property of humanity, *i. e.* any visible presentation of a principle that has come to be universally recognized and universally operative, cannot perish, but has life in itself. . . . Such ideas form the pathway of God in history—the light of Heaven amid the darkness of the earth."—Bunsen, *God in Hist.*, I. p. 36, 53. Compare Aristotle, *Metaph.*, xi. 7 : Ταύτας τὰς δόξας ἐκείνων, οἷον λείψανα περισεσῶσθαι μέχρι τοῦ νῦν. Bacon's self-contradiction that "Time seemeth to be of the nature of a river or stream which carrieth down to us that which is light and blown up, and sinketh and drowneth that which is weighty and solid," has been very properly exposed by Mr. Mill, *Logic*, II. 428.

[2] Positive, because, though we may see that many parts of Christianity are worthy of God, we are not hastily to conclude that where we do not see this such parts do not come from Him. See Rogers, *Essays*, II. 379. "It is no just consequence that reason is no judge of what is offered to us as being of divine revelation. For this would be to infer that we are unable to judge of anything because we are unable to judge of all things."—Butler, *Analogy*, Pt. II. c. iii.

the past the course of "natural revelation," applying to ascertained matters of fact the lamp of inherited experience. So

> By the light His words disclose,
> Watch Time's full river as it flows:
> Scanning His gracious Providence,
> Where not too deep for mortal sense.

All the irregularity of human affairs arises from our not being able to see the whole at once. But the further we advance along the world's history and in general knowledge, the more we approach an estimate of the reasons of things and of the current of affairs.[1] It is not then the existence of final causes in the formation and working of the world which needs be held unsatisfactory by the

---

[1] "The moral system of the universe," says a powerful but uncertain writer, "is like a document written in alternate ciphers, which change from line to line. We read a sentence, but at the next the key fails us. We see that there is something written there, but if we guess at it we are guessing in the dark." Yet the same author is not long in supplying an antidote to any scepticism which may lurk in such reflections. "If we believe," he adds, "at all that the world is governed by a conscious and intelligent Being, we must believe also, however we can reconcile it with our own ideas, that these anomalies have not arisen by accident, but have been ordered of purpose and design."—Froude on *Calvinism*, p. 5. This, Butler points out, is the necessary result of the government of God considered as a scheme *in progress*, and therefore imperfectly comprehended. See also Shaftesbury, *Characteristics*, II. 363, and the fine passage in Plato, *Legg.*, X. 903. Augustine compares the order of the universe to a tessellated floor, of which we hold the part. "At enim," he adds, "hoc ipsum est plenius quæstionum, quod membra pulicis disposita mire atque distincta sunt, cum interea humana vita innumerabilium perturbationum inconstantiâ versetur et fluctuet."—*De Ordine*, c. i. "La seule question," says M. Renan, *Études*, p. 401, "intéressante pour le philosophe est de savoir de quel côté va le monde."

physical or positive philosophy of our time. Teleology, as such, is not destroyed but rather confirmed by any theory of evolution. For such evolution must either be accidental, a purely fortuitous result, which is hardly credible, and certainly will not satisfy science; or it bears testimony to design; the process, which apparently involves waste, proving ultimately economical.[1] The procedure indicated may be gradual and to appearance precarious, but the result shows an adaptation of means to ends which is all that Paley and other adherents of Natural Theology have maintained. It is the previous assumption of a given design as the basis of argument, to which exception may fairly be taken. The coincidence of facts with the theory of a Divine purpose rests, in the main, on a matter of observation, analogous to the homologies of Natural Science, and open to common apprehension.[2] We

Though coincident with them.

[1] The argument of La Place from chances is well known. Thus, *e.g.* "two properties necessary to the stability of the planetary system are—(1), that the orbital motions must be all in the same direction; (2), that the inclinations of the planes of these orbits must not be considerable. Taking the theory of mere chance, it is 2047 to 1 against the first; 10,000,000 to 1 against the second; more than 20,000,000,000 against the two together," &c. This argument has been much strengthened by more newly discovered planets. The objection sometimes raised to the teleological argument that the Author of Nature, being above Nature, is incapable of analogies drawn from the finite creature, becomes absorbed in a much larger question—the possibility and conditions of a philosophy of the Absolute.

[2] "It has been objected that the doctrine of Final Causes supposes us to be acquainted with the intentions of the Creator, which, it is in-

cannot but see, if we take room enough for observation, which way things have tended in the world. And certainly such a result, gathered from the point of view of comparative history, extending over large areas of countries and times, is of the highest moment to a philosophic survey of affairs. "For what," it has been justly asked, "does it avail to praise and draw forth to view the magnificence and wisdom of creation in the irrational kingdom of nature, if that part in the great stage of the Supreme Wisdom which contains the object of all this mighty display (I mean the history of the human species), is to remain an eternal objection to it, the bare sight of which obliges us to turn away our eyes in displeasure, and, from the despair which it raises of ever discovering in it a perfect and rational purpose, leads

---

sinuated, is a most presumptuous and irrational basis for our reasonings. But there can be nothing presumptuous or irrational in reasoning on that basis, which, if we reject, we cannot reason at all."—Whewell, *Indications*, p. 93. The sense of *order* perceptible in the inorganic world of matter is not identical with *design*, though it may lead up to it. The present relation of physical science to the question of design seems to stand thus: its results point undoubtedly to design, but to design imperfectly comprehended by our natural faculties. The resource lies in Revelation; but it does not follow that Revelation must speak on these points to man. Comp. Lange, *Geschichte v. Materialismus*, pp. 402–404. M. Flourens has well observed: "Il faut aller non pas des causes finales aux faits, mais des faits aux causes finales." It may be doubted whether the human reason can ever truly separate the notions of cause and effect, antecedent and consequent, end and means: all these suggest, and indeed necessitate, a presiding original thought. Whether such thought be regarded as immanent in the universe, or as external to it, must be determined by other considerations.

us finally to look for such only in another world."[1] Hence the perennial faith through successive generations in a God revealed in history, in a Divine government of the world, in human progress based on a moral order accomplishing an Eternal Idea, in a nature not composed of isolated episodes,[2] in an "increasing purpose" running through the ages of the past. Its evidence lies written in the annals of our race, even through periods of stagnancy and devastation, and in no part of it more markedly than in the religious crises of nations.

§ 7. A question may be raised as to the relative character of our ideas of duration and permanence. Christianity is an institution which we believe to be, as to its future, coeval with the world itself. In this way our conception of its continuance is indefinitely extended, and this extension reacts upon its past history. Though its first ages may be bounded by the fact of its historical origin, its "last times" are beyond our grasp, and so, too, all

Objection from the relative character of the notion of duration.

---

[1] Kant, *Idea of a Universal History on a Cosmopolitical Plan*, translated by De Quincey. *Works*, Vol. XIV. 151.

[2] Οὐκ ἔοικε δ' ἡ φύσις ἐπεισοδιώδης οὖσα ἐκ τῶν φαινομένων, ὥσπερ μοχθηρὰ τραγῳδία.—Aristotle, *Metaph.*, XIII. c. iii., ix., x. Compare Bunsen, *God in History*, Vol. I. pp. 6, 13, 20, E. T.: "No one looking back over the past can fail to detect a general advance of humanity, as a whole, in certain definite directions corresponding to what we observe in the fuller development of the man. The progress on a large scale exhibits the harmonious elevation of our whole complex being, even though periods of devastation and fiery trial are needed for the preparation of the fuller growth."—Dr. Westcott, *Contemp. Rev.*, Vol. VIII. 380.

conception of its relative duration. Though already long-lived to all appearance, it may yet not have passed its youth; and the span of its coming years may still far exceed those that are past.[1] "Centuries on centuries," it has been well said, "may be required to discipline fully the human faculties that are to grow into the faith which has been prepared for them."[2] But the standard of dura-

Its answer. bility which we are now applying is external to Christianity itself. We compare it as a mundane institution with all things else that are mundane. In these we find but one and the same law. They tend to decay and subversion.

> Sic omnia fatis
> In pejus ruere ac retro sublapsa referri.

[1] Comp. De Maistre, *Œuvres*, p. 262, ed. Migne: "On parle beaucoup des premiers siècles du Christianisme; en vérité, je ne voudrais pas assurer qu'ils sont passés. Dans un sens l'Église n'a point d'âge.... Elle se relève avec l'homme, l'accompagne, et le perfectionne dans toutes les situations; différente en cela et d'une manière frappante de toutes les institutions et de tous les empires humains qui ont une enfance, une virilité, une vieillesse et une fin."

[2] Hutton's *Essays*, Vol. I. 122: "It is clear that the Divine government of the Jewish race was meant to bring out and did bring out more distinctly the personality of God, while the history of other races brings out more clearly the Divine capacities of man. Hence the co-operation of different nations was requisite for the efficiency of the revelation. Centuries were required for the complete evolution even of that special Jewish history that was selected to testify to the righteous will and defined spiritual character of the Creator. Centuries on centuries will be required to discipline fully the human faculties that are to grow into the faith thus prepared for them." So also M. Guizot: "Civilization is as yet very young: the world has as yet by no means measured the whole of its career; Human thought is at this time very far from being all that it is capable of becoming: we are very far from comprehending the whole future of humanity."—*Civil. in Europe*, p. 18, Ed. Bohn.

It has not been so, however, with the religion of Christ. Its strength is not as its day. Its days are old, if we judge them by man's standard of duration; yet its powers are unenfeebled. Its youth is renewed as the eagle's, and its years do not fail. The revolutions of the heavenly bodies point to an almost infinite succession of ages, through which they have held on their way. Yet science sketches out the trajectory which is followed by our planetary system.[1] So the world may have a long future still before it; and yet it is permitted us to determine the path of Christianity. The progress indicated, whether in nature or in revelation, is not indefinite, but tends to a limit. But if this observation be deemed presumptuous with the long track behind us of geologic time and prehistoric evolution, it is at least not more so than to proclaim the finality of a positive stage of thought, as the "be all and end all" of man's estate. Christianity, while proclaiming the ultimate dissolution of things at the last day, leaves its approach indefinite, though its

[1] "Le cycle du dessin de la Nature semble exiger pour se clore un si long temps que la petite portion que l'humanité en a déjà parcourue ne permet pas d'en déterminer la forme et de conclure la relation des parties au tout, avec plus de sûreté que toutes les observations célestes faites jusqu'à présent ne permettent d'assigner la trajectoire que suit dans le ciel étoilé notre soleil avec toute l'armée de ses satellites. Et cependant remarquons qu'avec le principe général de la constitution systématique de l'univers et avec le peu qu'on a observé, on est autorisé à conclure qu'il existe en effet une telle trajectoire."—Kant, u. s. ap. Littré, *A. Comte et la Phil. Pos.*, p. 63.

arrival be certain.¹ Already it is possible to apply some tests of its persistent vitality. For in what do the organic forces of any religion consist, or at the least exhibit themselves? Surely in their hold upon the consciences, lives, and actions of men; in their tendency to extend themselves by conversion of unbelief; and in their power of assimilating healthfully the altered conditions of advancing civilization. This power, if shown to arise from principles contained in the doctrines of the Gospel, furnishes an argument in favour of the truth of Christianity which has the force of prophecy, for they are long prior to the discovery of the general laws of human progress. But the most ancient as well as the most widely-spread religions of the earth, Brahmanism, Buddhism, the faiths of Confucius, Zoroaster, if not also of Mahomet,² show no tendency to propagate themselves. The duty of conversion is no longer felt; its possibility no longer dreamed. Not so with the Churches of the Christian faith, which acknowledge to the full the obligation of missionary labour, whatever be the measure of success attending their fulfilment of it.

Tests of durability applicable to religions.

Objection from the

§ 8. It is not, of course, denied that ancient

---

¹ See the Bishop of Carlisle's lecture on *the Gradual Development of Revelation*, p. 30.

² M. Littré has justly remarked that the immobility of a religious belief is a proof of a want of genuine belief in its doctrines; citing India and China as proofs to this fact.—*Paroles de la Phil. Pos.*, p. 35.

religions, false and pernicious, have flourished through immense periods. This has been due to the elements of truth¹ which they contained, "a soul of goodness in things evil;" and still more to its adaptation to the order of the development of belief in the history of primitive culture. *Quantum sumus, scimus.* "Men must think," it has been tersely said, "in such terms of thought as they possess."² It is a fact admitting of proof whether Christianity includes elements answering to truths but dimly shadowed forth in heathen systems; in the Triads or Trinities, for example, roughly touched by Brahmanism or Buddhism; or in the Monotheism of the creed of Mahomet. It has been fairly said, "Whatever has been found necessary in the course of 6000 years' experience, we have a right to ask of that which offers itself as the one faith for mankind."³ The question, then, is not one of simple length of date, any more than of the numbers who accept or profess a religion, as if truth were settled by majorities.⁴ The test of any

enormous antiquity of Eastern religions.

Not valid against Christianity, which is comprehensive,

---

¹ "The spiritual self-respect of individuals, the reconcilement of the conscience by means of atonement, the hopes connected with the unseen world, had all once been provided by Paganism: as they must be by every religion which has had a real historical existence."—Mackay, *Rise and Progress of Christianity.* A remark true, but only partially so: for had Paganism actually fulfilled this work, it had never passed away.

² Herbert Spencer, *First Principles,* p. 116.

³ Maurice's *Kingdoms of the World,* p. 162. A profound view of the religious history of mankind will regard these religions rather as testimonies than as rivals to the truth of Christianity.

⁴ Ὥσπερ ἐν ταῖς χειροτονίαις.—Lucian, *Hermotimus,* c. xvi. Compare

progressive, system will lie in the character of its doctrines, combined with its permanence as exhibited in their progressive capacity. If Christianity be an imperfect theory of our relations to God and the universe, it must needs prove transitory. Mere antiquity in a fixed locality decides little; though even in this aspect it must be remembered that the faith of Christ must be measured by the age of Judaism.[1] But where still extant, these world-old theologies lack the criteria of permanence. The wild erratic doctrines of Oriental religions have

Max Müller, *Chips*, I. p. 215. On this point the Reformers *protested* at Spires in 1529. " The number of persons holding an idea is no warrant for its objective character, else the many never could be wrong; for uniformity of education, or the sympathy kindled by enthusiasm, may carry many minds into one state in which belief in certain ideas and the mistake of formulæ or usages for external truths will be natural or necessary."—Newman, *Essay on Development*, p. 31.

[1] "Que l'on considère la perpétuité de la religion Chrétienne, qui a toujours subsisté depuis le commencement du monde, soit dans les saints de l'ancien Testament," &c.—Pascal, *Pensées*, II. p. 367. This is flippantly stated by Salvador (*Paris, Rome et Jérusalem*, I. 243): "Avance, dit-on au Juif, et déclare-nous quel est ton nom . . . . ton âge. Mon âge? Deux mille ans de plus que Jésus-Christ." " If it be said " (writes Dr. Newman, *Gramm. of Assent*) " the Oriental religions are older than Christianity by some centuries, it must be recollected that Christianity is only the continuation and conclusion of what professes to be an earlier revelation, which may be traced back into prehistoric times." " Die Geschichte dieses alten Volkes (Israel) ist im Grunde die Geschichte der durch alle Stufen bis zur Vollendung sich ausbildenden wahren Religion, welche auf diesem engen Volksgebiete durch alle Kämpfe hindurch sich bis zum höchsten Siege erhebt und endlich in aller Herrlichkeit und Macht sich offenbart; um dann von da aus durch ihre eigene Kraft sich unwiderstehlich verbreitend nie wieder verloren zu gehen, sondern ewiger Besitz und Segen aller Völker zu werden."—Ewald, *Gesch. d. V. Israel*, I. 9, whose testimony to the eternity of Christianity I could not willingly omit.

produced neither in respect of moral or spiritual truth results suitable to the facts of human nature, its dignity and its capacities. They have wandered into Polytheism. "Insufficient for time, and rejecting eternity, their utmost triumph is to live without fear and to die without hope."[1] Their power has steadily declined; and, however Buddhism may with truth boast of its ancient missionary zeal,[2] they have long since ceased to extend the area of their beliefs. They have never yet borne the brunt of advancing civilization. These are the questions of fact with Christianity. The religion of Europe has passed through storms of barbarism, persecution, and doubt; while over Asia has brooded an immemorial calm, broken only by tides of military conquest.[3] Nor is it any way surprising that the

and has survived the advance of knowledge.

---

[1] Sir J. E. Tennant, *Christianity in Ceylon*, p. 227. On this subject see Hardwick, *Christ and other Masters*, II. 69; Tylor *On Primitive Culture*, II. 89, 96; B. St. Hilaire, *Le Bouddha*. " Unquestionably," writes Mr. Farrar, *Witness of History to Christ*, p. 145, "Confucianism and Buddhism are in their social influence gigantic failures; and in these cases M. Renan says, 'Success is a decisive criterion.'" Mr. Picton, *New Theories and Old Faith*, answering a remark of Mr. Armstrong that "the cohesion and endurance of Buddhism mocks and shames Christianity with her many convulsions and her reiterated revolutions," ably replies, "that one might as well say that the cohesion and endurance of China mocks and shames Europe with its convulsions and its reiterated revolutions. The higher the life the more violent often are the crises of growth, and certainly the more extreme is the differentiation of parts."

[2] Max Müller, *Chips*, I. 269.

[3] "The popular religions of antiquity answered only for a *certain stage* of culture. When the nations in the course of their progress had passed beyond this, the necessary consequence was a dissevering of the

faiths of Brahma or of Buddha should linger in the world. "The extinction of a religion," it has been said with truth, "is not the abrupt movement of a day; it is a secular progress of many well-marked stages."[1] The success of Buddhism rested on the assertion of the dogma of the absolute equality of all men; and this in a country which *Symptoms of decline in the religions of the East.* for ages had been oppressed with caste.[2] But its continuance, as well as that of Brahmanism, philosophically considered, is involved in its representation of an inherent polar opposition to the theology of Christian belief. The doctrine of a transmigration of souls, of a simple "continuance-theory" as to a future state, confronts the teaching of the independent existence of a personal spirit, of a permanent "retribution-theory" of after-being. Materialism, as opposed to Theism, must ever present two alternatives; a doctrine of absorption, ultimately equivalent to Pantheism; or of extinc-

spirit from the religious traditions. In the case of the more quiet and equable development of the Oriental mind—so tenacious of the old—the opposition between the mythic religion of the people and the secret *theosophic* doctrines of a priestly caste, who gave direction to the popular conscience, might exist for centuries without change. But among the more excitable nations of the West, intellectual culture, as soon as it attained to a certain degree of independence, must necessarily fall into collision with the mythic religion handed down from the infancy of the people."—Neander, *Church Hist.*, I. 6, E. T. "Le repos est le supplice de l'Européen, et ce caractère contraste merveilleusement avec l'immobilité Orientale."—De Maistre, *Œuvres*, p. 494. "Better," says Tennyson, "fifty years of Europe than a cycle of Cathay."

[1] Draper, *Hist. of Intellectual Development in Europe*, I. 37.
[2] *Ib.*, I. 62. Max Müller, *Chips*, I. 220, 246.

tion, practically undistinguishable from a declared Atheism.[1]

§ 9. In commencing the argument of these Lectures (which, it will be remembered, is the proof of the truth of Christianity arising from its past continuity and tenacity, and from its indications of ultimate permanence), I assume the existence, from the earliest days of the Church, of a nucleus of belief sufficient to produce practical effects. On the other hand, no *consensus* or standing uniformity of doctrinal opinion is demanded, such as would be in small accordance with the laws of mental progress in other subjects under the varying stages of early and advanced civilization, and national differences of climate and race. While the original of Christianity can only be accepted as divine, it is no part of Christian philosophy to except the historical development of the faith from such movements of the human mind as are natural to its exercise on any subject-matter whatsoever. Believers in the truths of the Christian religion have sometimes been described in terms of disparage-

A practical standard of belief assumed in this argument.

How far guaranteed in the existence of the Holy Scriptures,

---

[1] See Tylor, *Prim. Culture*, II. 69, and compare Dr. Mozley, *Bampton Lect.*, pp. 187, 368: "The Brahman doctrine of the final state professes some difference from the Buddhist; but both schools maintain in common the characteristic of impersonality as attaching to the final state." See also Fairbairn on *Belief in Immortality*, pp. 50, 51, 53. Sir H. Maine, *Ancient Law*, p. 17, observes that "the physical conformation of Asiatic countries had the effect of making individual communities larger and more numerous than in the West; and it is a known social law that the larger the space over which a particular set of institutions is diffused, the greater is its tenacity and vitality."

ment as Bibliolaters,[1] the worshippers of a book and of a stereotyped revelation. It is not necessary to consider to what portions of the Church, or to what theory of Christian belief this criticism is most applicable. But it is by no means true that the religion of Christ is contained in the New Testament, only in the same manner as the Mosaic system depended on the Pentateuch, or as Mahommedanism is found in the Koran, or the faith of Vishnu or Buddha in the Vedas or the Sûtras. The very power of Christianity lies in this: that preaching the purest morality under the highest sanctions, with the force of a Divine Exemplar, and on the foundation of historic facts, it never sacrifices it to ceremonialism, and is thus superior to the decline of positive forms.[2] In written codes

---

[1] "Bibliolatry has been, and is long likely to be, the bane of Protestant Christianity."—Hutton, *Essays*, I. 142. As with all exaggerations, this contains an element of truth. That "the Bible only is the religion of Protestants," was the dictum of Chillingworth.—(C. iv.) "Protestantism," writes Dr. Dorner (*Hist. Prot. Theol.*, I. 2), "seeks, indeed, its ultimate foundation in the nature of Christianity, as it is handed down to us in a documentary form in the Holy Scriptures." See some good remarks on this subject in Rogers' *Essays*, II. 334, and Dean Merivale's *Lectures on Conversion of the Empire*, pp. 140, 141. Christians are known to Mahometans as "the people of the Book." But the vivid language of Napoleon at St. Helena (*Bertrand's Memoirs ap. Luthardt Apol.*, p. 355, E. T.) is here applicable, "The Gospel is no mere book, but a living creature with an agency; a power that conquers all that opposes it."

[2] This is the real answer to objections such as those of Mr. Buckle, *Hist. Civil.*, II. 51: "The actions of men are governed not by dogmas, and text-books, and rubrics, but by the opinions and habits of their contemporaries, by the general spirit of their age, and by the character of those classes who are in the ascendant. This seems to be the origin

of ceremonial worship and practice, it is difficult to distinguish between principles and details, so overlaid is the spirit by the letter of the particular ordinance. There is a constant tendency to crystallize into formalism. In these it is almost impossible to see how tradition could long supply the place of an authorized formula. But the faith of Jesus Christ makes, as it requires, no such claim. "The Gospel," it has been truly said,[1] "is not a system of theology, nor a *syntagma* of theoretical propositions and conclusions for the enlargement of speculative knowledge, ethical or metaphysical, but it is a history, a series of facts or events related or announced. These do indeed involve, or rather they at the same time are, most important doctrinal truths, but still facts and declarations of facts."

of that difference between religious theory and religious practice of which theologians greatly complain as a stumbling-block and an evil."—See Tylor, *Hist. Prim. Cult.*, II. 337. Mr. Mackay, *Progress of Intellect*, I. 17, remarks: " Forms (*i.e.* creeds and ceremonies) are in their nature transitory; for, being destitute of flexibility and power of self-accommodation to altered circumstances, they become in time unconformable to realities, and stand only as idle landmarks of the past, or like deserted channels requiring to be filled up." On the growth of sacerdotalism in the Vedic religion and in Buddhism, see Mr. Fairbairn's able and learned essay, *Cont. Rev.*, XX. pp. 36–55.

[1] S. T. Coleridge, *Aids to Reflection*, p. 153. " Religions," says Prof. Max Müller, " have sometimes been divided into *national* or *traditional*, as distinguished from *individual* or *statutable* religions. The former are like languages, home-grown, autochthonic, without an historical beginning, generally without any recognized founder, or even an authorized code: the latter have been founded by historical persons, generally in antagonism to traditional systems, and they always rest on the authority of a written code." This division Professor Müller with justice thinks too sharply drawn.—*C. R.*, XIX. 102.

and in their special characteristics.

The New Testament (if with one exception) may be regarded as a compilation of strictly historical documents, connected together by what might, at first sight, seem a wholly fortuitous conjunction. Not so, however. The narrative and historical mould in which the Gospels, Acts, and Epistles are cast, can only be regarded as a providential feature,[1] differencing at once the authoritative instruments of the religion of Christ from those of all other systems. Whatever theory of biblical inspiration be adopted, mechanical or dynamical, it will hardly be maintained that the writings of the New Testament proceeded like the syllables of Mahomet from the pen of an archangel.[2] It may be held, for example, without irreverence, that the letters of St. Paul would have been worth much less to us if they had not been called forth by the particular occasions which are evident in each. In them we

---

[1] "Let us look to the great characteristic of our holy faith; that unlike all other assumed religions it is not a collection of mystic writings presenting to the view of man the scenes and the events of the invisible world in minute description, such as admits no test from experience and the course of the world; but consists in those very events which it narrates, and out of which it is evolved, and may be tracked continuously through more than three thousand years in the successive periods of its delivery to mankind; thus occupying a large field in the history of God's providence; and that we have just the same ground for believing its truth as we have for believing any other matter of history equally authenticated by events."—Bp. Hampden, *Memorials*, p. 221.

[2] Μὴ οὖν says Africanus finely (ap. Routh, *Rell. Sacr.*, II. 229) κατίωμεν εἰς τοσαύτην Θεοσεβείας σμικρολογίαν, ἵνα τῇ ἐναλλαγῇ τῶν ὀνομάτων τὴν Χρίστου Βασιλείαν καὶ ἱερωσύνην συνιστῶμεν.

see the man himself dealing with men whom we can see likewise. It is the difference between a portrait that we recognize and a face which we have never seen, or, as a map of places familiar to us by the side of a chart of countries yet unknown. Such is our gain in holding in our hands the letters of the living man, and not cold abstract articles of religious profession. And if this be so with the Epistles, how much more with the life of Him, "Who spake as never man spake;" in whose acts and words is centred still the faith of Christendom.[1] Those words, "the primal, indefeasible truths of Christianity," we have the promise, "shall never pass away." In the imitation of His life[2] and spirit lie perennial springs of endless improvement and advance. "All true moral progress," it has been well said,[3] "is made through admiration, and it is characteristic of our religion that it makes a greater use of example than any other system." "It cannot be too steadily borne in memory," says

Nature of influence of the example of Christ and His Apostles.

[1] It is strange that M. Comte, constantly ignoring Jesus Christ, recognizes Paul as the meeting-point of Jew, Greek, and Roman. See *Pol. Pos.*, III. 409. For some good remarks on the office of the Bible in prolonging the solidarity of the life of Christ, see Mr. Picton, *New Theories, &c.*, pp. 161-5.

[2] See Milman, *Latin Christianity*, VI. 447. Hence perhaps (with all its shortcomings) the boundless popularity and influence of the 'Imitatio Christi.' No book has been so often reprinted, so often translated, or into so many languages.—*Ib.*, VI. 303. It is a remarkable fact that this volume was a favourite one with A. Comte towards the close of his life.—*Littré*, p. 586.

[3] By Professor Seeley, *Lectures and Essays*, p. 262. See also Hutton's *Essays*, I. 140.

another living writer,[1] "that *Christianity is Christ*. So He taught; so His disciples after Him; not a law, not a theory, not a code of morals, not a system of casuistry, not even an elaborate theology. But they ceased not to teach and to preach Jesus Christ." "Jesus," writes Dr. Newman,[2] "through His preachers imprinted the image or idea of Himself in the minds of His subjects; it became a principle of association and their moral life. It was the instrument of their conversion." Thus (to quote yet one other author) "the Platonist exhorted men to imitate God; the Stoic to follow reason. It was reserved for Christianity to present to the world an ideal character which, through all the changes of eighteen centuries, has inspired the hearts of men with an impassioned love, has shown itself capable of acting on all ages, nations, temperaments and conditions, which has been not only the highest pattern of virtue, but the strongest incentive to its practice, and has exercised so deep an

---

[1] The Bishop of Ely, Lect. on *Christ's Influence on History*, p. 17. So also Canon Liddon (*Bampton Lect.*, p. 308). "Christianity, as a creed and as a life, depends absolutely upon the personal character of its founder." Coleridge, *Aids to Reflection*, p. 288, writes: "In the strictest sense of essential, this alone is the essential in Christianity, that the same spirit should be growing in us, which was in the fulness of all perfection in Christ Jesus." See also an eloquent passage in Farrar's *Witness of History to Christ*, p. 79.

[2] *Grammar of Assent*, p. 460. An illustration of this sentiment may be found in the early use of the word κυριακός; e. g. κυριακὸν δεῖπνον, κυριακὴ ἁγία ἡμέρα, κυριακαὶ γραφαί, τὸ κυριακὸν, dominica solennia. μηκέτι σαββατίζοντες, ἀλλὰ κατὰ κυριακὴν ζωὴν ζῶντες, says Ignatius, *ad Magnes.*, c. ix.

influence, that it may be truly said that the simple record of three short years of active life has done more to regenerate and soften mankind than all the disquisitions of philosophers and all the exhortations of moralists. This has, indeed, been the wellspring of whatever is best and purest in the Christian life. In the character and example of its Founder, Christianity has an enduring principle of regeneration."[1]

§ 10. The form and character of the New Testament records involve, indeed, the consideration of their relation to the earliest standards of doctrine.[2]

Relation of Scripture to the Creeds.

---

[1] Lecky, *Hist. Eur. Mor.*, II. 9, and see *Hist. Rat.*, I. 337. Thus also Mr. Carlyle, *Sartor Resartus*, p. 155. "If thou ask to what height man has carried it in this manner, look on our Divinest Symbol—on Jesus of Nazareth and his life and his biography, and what followed therefrom. Higher has the human thought not yet reached: this is Christianity and Christendom: a symbol of quite perennial, infinite character; whose significance will ever demand to be anew inquired into and anew made manifest." We need hardly point out the fallacy and evasion which is met with in some quarters, of admitting to the full the perfectness of Christ's moral character while suppressing its supernatural element.

[2] On Creeds as a peculiarity of Christianity, see Leibnitz, *Théodicée*, Pref. sub init.: on their employment in practice, Neander, *C. H.*, I. 420, who connects them with oral traditions. Dorner, *Hist. Prot. Th.*, I. 12, remarks on the *tacit* growth of dogma. "In order to a development of the system of doctrine, there is no necessity for Councils nor for the formal fixing of the dogma by a positive Canon. The opposite is proved by the three first centuries of the Christian Church, in which, without œcumenical synods, the progress of dogma was as rapid as it was sure and constant. Never, however, was dogma created or constituted truth by the sanction of the Church in a juridical, canonical form: but on the contrary, because it had in its substance established itself in the common faith, there followed the declarative sanction." See also Dr. Newman's profound and just observations, *Arians*, c. I. § ii., and c. II. § i.; Waterland, *Works*, III. 254; and Dr. Pusey's note in *Library of Fathers*, Tertullian, p. 490.

They nowhere claim for themselves to be regarded as precise authoritative statements of articles of belief. That such existed in very early times, probably in the sub-apostolic age, seems now sufficiently established. The want of creeds must have been hardly felt in the lifetime of the Apostles, whether they be viewed as a sacred deposit, or tradition of Apostolic teaching, or as agglomerations of doctrinal expressions, the products of the earliest controversies. But the ultimate and co-ordinate authority of the written word remains beyond question; being proved by the custom of Scriptural citation found even in the Apostolical Fathers, though at first, as was natural, employed much more largely on the Old than upon the New Testament.[1] From the first there would seem to have existed a body of traditional Apostolic doctrine, according with the tenor of Holy Scripture and forming the nucleus of later and more elaborate Creeds. We are concerned, however, only with the recognition by believers from Apostolic times of certain revealed truths, and of historical

[1] Thus Clemens Romanus quotes profusely from the Old Testament, but rarely from the New (*i.e.* from the words of Christ). See c. xiii. In the Second Epistle, however, the New Testament quotations are frequent, and apparently from Apocryphal Gospels. One reason for this practice may be found in the fact that the Gentile converts would commonly be ignorant of the Sacred writings, while, at the same time, their antiquity, authority, and testifying power would be strongly felt. Thus the Apostles proved both for Gentile and Jew out of the Old Testament, applying the evidence of prophecy by the side of direct testimony.

events embodying these truths which contained implicit obligations of a practical kind. In this way a fixed character was impressed on the religion itself, and on its followers, sufficient in the aggregate to produce distinct effects. "The growth of Christian faith became a permanent and hereditary belief by a natural law of transmission."[1] Thus we might argue either from the contents of the New Testament, together with the Creeds, to the lives of believers, as exemplifying and verifying the nature of the doctrines believed; or inversely from the life and character of believers, we may argue up to the character of the truths believed. In either case it must be admitted that the first ages of a faith are those in which its tenets are most enthusiastically received and vigorously acted on, and which therefore exhibit most plainly the tendencies and characteristics of the system.[2] The emotions are stirred rather than the intellect; and it is with these that religion, as a motive power among men, is principally concerned. But further, by the aid of the Canon of Holy Scripture, cautiously framed, gradually accepted and transmitted to after-times,[3] the *personal* influence, which marked

Belief effective on practice.

---

[1] Dr. Mozley, *Bampton Lect.*, p. 140.

[2] "The life of intense hope," says Mr. Goldwin Smith, with his accustomed beauty and strength of expression, "that is lived in the morning of all great revolutions, may partly make up for the danger, the distress, the disappointment of their later hour."—*Lect.*, p. 59.

[3] Pascal, speaking of the Old Testament, says: "C'est le plus ancien

the primary records of Christian truth, was indefinitely extended and conveyed with individual force to succeeding generations. And here the importance of the form in which the New Testament was composed, becomes still more apparent. For it is such as to guarantee permanence. The influences of the Gospel in the example and oral teachings of Christ and His Apostles are brought to bear continuously on successive ages in a degree much greater than could have been achieved by the bare institutions of ceremonies, however significant, or the enunciation of abstract doctrines, however pregnant with principles of action. The flexibility and power of self-accommodation essential to a religion destined for perpetuity are thus secured. In this manner, also, fundamental departures from the pure spirit of pristine Christianity have ever retained their antidote with them. For they have all along held firm to the Canon of Scripture, by which accordingly they may be tested and purged. In this fact, and not in any single doctrine of "justification by faith only" lay the true value of the Reformation as an ecclesiastical movement.[1] Print-

Permanent influence consequent on the form of the New Testament.

---

livre du monde, et le plus authentique; et au lieu que Mahomet, pour faire subsister le sien, a défendu de le lire; Moïse, pour faire subsister le sien, a ordonné à tout le monde de le lire."—*Pensées*, II. 186.

[1] It has hence been called "the resurrection of the Bible."—Compare Hallam, *Literature of E.*, I. iv. § 58; Lecky, *H. Rat.*, II. 227; Milman, *Hist. Latin Chr.*, VI. 438. Mr. Hutton, *Essays*, I. 400, takes a different view; but see also p. 415. Erasmus, *De Ratione Veræ Theologiæ*, p. 67, says: "Non paucos vidimus olim Lutetiæ, quibus si quid depro-

ing restored the authority and efficacy of the Bible, which in dark ages inevitably succumbed to tradition. Is there any other example, we may ask, of a religion surviving and drawing fresh strength from the resurrection of its original records? I do not desire to deny that some periods or conditions of society may be more receptive of one sort of teaching than another. And the same law may hold good in respect of individual temperament. Thus the medieval ages of Christianity were bound together by ceremonial uniformity and a ceremonial faith, perhaps essential to a system of centralization such as alone could evict and control the evils of surrounding barbarism. But with the Reformation the Church returned at least in part to its early appreciation of moral and spiritual truths, and to a Scriptural Christianity as their best and most permanent expression.

§ 11. It should perhaps be considered how far a theory of development tends to undermine an argument resting on the persistence of Christian doctrine. It could not, indeed, be viewed as fatal to it, except the identity of the religion itself were *Objection to the permanent influence of Christianity drawn from the theory of doctrinal development.*

mendum fuisset ex Paulo, videbantur sibi prorsus in alium mundum translati;" and Robert Stephens (*ap. Gieseler*, V. 57, E. T.) wrote in his own defence, "Ante paucos annos quidam ex Sorbonâ sic loquebatur: miror quid isti juvenes nobis semper allegent novum testamentum. Per Deum ego plus habebam quam quinquaginta annos quod nesciebam, quod esset novum testamentum." The doctrine of a "depositum fidei" is not necessarily opposed to all attempts to seek out the truth. This, no doubt, may become incrusted, and need to be reburnished.

compromised; and this would be contended for but by few. In the case supposed it would not be one Gospel, but many, which has been preached throughout the world. The introduction of particular doctrines unknown to the first ages of the Church has certainly exercised an important practical influence on the history of Christianity. But if it should appear that the simplicity of the faith has outlived these and similar importations, and through its native purity still works its own work upon mankind, then the line of proof survives, and an additional evidence is secured for its inherent sanctity, its Divine origin, and its imperishable permanence. It would, no doubt, be possible to maintain upon a theory of doctrinal evolution the progressive unity of Christian truth, together with the continuity of its ideas, and so to lay claim to the effects of the system as flowing from a single source. The difficulty lies in reconciling the theory with the facts. The coldness with which it has been received in the house of its friends throws a just suspicion upon its demands.[1] A system of development, however, necessarily

Insufficiency of this theory.

---

[1] "Rome founds herself upon the idea that to *her* by tradition and exclusive privilege was communicated once for all the whole truth from the beginning. Mr. Newman lays his corner-stone in the very opposite idea of a gradual development given to Christianity by the motion of time, by experience, by expanding occasions, and by the progress of civilization."—De Quincey, *Essay on Protestantism*. On this subject see Dr. Mill's *Five Sermons*, Serm. I., and for the view of the Eastern Church, compare Dean Stanley, pp. 42, 173.

renounces the appeal to antiquity or uniform tradition. This is replaced by a different principle, *viz.* of authority. It assumes the variation of doctrine for which it would account. It renounces, therefore (a fact of especial importance in the present argument) that element of permanence which, we contend, is a marked characteristic of Christianity. It cannot then lay any claim on behalf of the religion of Christ to effects as the results of its character and doctrines. In other words, the sort of permanence which it affects is fictitious and of an arbitrary kind. But there is further as little limit in this view of the subject as respects steadfastness of doctrine on the side of the future as in the past. The Christianity of the future might require another name. Nor can the ultimate aspect or effects of our religion be predicted with any attempt at precision under such a system. Its incompatibility with fixedness of doctrine.

§ 12. But it may be said, while rejecting the theory of development as an adequate explanation of facts, it must still be admitted that the facts remain; and it is these which may be held to break off the continuity, as they undoubtedly do, the "simplicity of the faith which is in Christ Jesus." In this matter a distinction has been introduced between identity of *principle* and identity of *doctrine*.[1] It confounds historical corruptions with authoritative beliefs.

---

[1] Newman, *Essay on Development*, I. iii. § 4, p. 70: "Principles are abstract and general, doctrines relate to facts; doctrines develope, and

With this, indeed, we are not now concerned, the former being sufficient for our purpose. But the historical development of Christianity is one thing, its doctrinal unity another. This development may be presumed to be subordinate to a system of law and general evolution, similar to the progress of all philosophical thought. It is the idea of such a development as this, subject, indeed, to a secondary process of degradation, due to the mingled presence of lower and higher elements in man's nature, of corruption and perfectibility, which, as has been truly said,[1] "gives a continuity to any distinct account of the progress of Christendom, a life to any intelligent analysis

principles do not; doctrines grow, and are enlarged, principles are illustrated; doctrines are intellectual, and principles are more immediately ethical and practical. Systems live in principles and represent doctrines." See some excellent remarks on this subject in Canon Robertson's *Hist. of Chr. Ch.*, I. pp. 82, 91. Döllinger, *First Age of the Church*, I. 228–233, leans too far to the side of development, confounding an original tradition of doctrine (which seems necessary and reasonable) with a continuous one, which it was the object of Creeds and of the Canon of Scripture to obviate. Thus Augustine's rule is a positive one: "Nec ego Nicænum nec tu debes Ariminense tanquam præjudicaturus proferre concilium: nec ego hujus auctoritate, nec tu illius detineris: Scripturarum auctoritatibus, non quorumque propriis, sed utriusque communibus testibus, res cum re, causa cum causâ, ratio cum ratione concertet."—*c. Maximin. Ar.*, II. xiv. 3.

[1] Dean Stanley, *Essays*, pp. 465, 470. So Ozanam, *Civilis. Chret.*, I. 22, E. T.: "Every great era of history takes its departure from ruin and ends in a conquest." On the fact that αἵρεσις αἵρεσιν φυτεύει, "posthumi hæresium filii," see Bacon, *Works*, ed. Spedding, VIII. 83. De Quincey, *Ess. on Protest.*, admits three kinds of development in doctrine—(1), philological; (2), philosophical, from advance in knowledge; (3), moral and historical; Christianity awaking new powers in man, and being itself modified by times and climes.

of Creeds and articles. In this manner the theology, like the architecture of each age, has always built itself upon the ruins of its predecessors." It is like a tree drawing its growth from its own dead leaves. It is this, in fact, which constitutes the solidarity of human history, and of the laws which compose it, which enables it to be treated philosophically, if not scientifically. It has plainly been the will of God that in the examination and handling of Divine truth the human element should not remain free from controversial doubt and absolute error. The hand of God is manifest here, as in other examples of His superintending providence. It has been finely said, "He never yet sent a gift into the world, which man did not deteriorate in the using."[1] Whatever be the extent of His promise to His Church at large, as regards indemnity from error; whether this apply to all degrees of it, both in principle and practice; yet for each individual Church no such immunity can be pleaded, any more than from corruptions in manner of living.[2] But unless it can be shown that, of the larger and dominant divisions of the Christian Church any have cut themselves off from the essentials of primitive teaching, from all that is vital to the unity of the faith; the

Immunity from error nowhere promised to the Church.

---

[1] Archer Butler, *Lectures on Romanism*, p. 61. See also pp. 288–9, 316–18.
[2] See Field, *Of the Church*, Book IV. c. v.

active power of Christ's religion may, though various, be still regarded as uniform in its operation, and definite in its effects.

<small>A rationalistic development likewise fatal to the permanence of Christian belief.</small>

§ 13. But there is another side to a theory of development which demands consideration. It is that which, looking at Christianity on the whole as merely a stage of progress in the human mind, and regarding all religious truth as necessarily progressive,[1] because man's powers are so, while accounting for its rise, prognosticates its fall. This system of thought strikes, indeed, at the very root of any defence of our holy religion which rests upon the permanent character of its teaching. An eclectic Christianity, making up a cento of doctrines and precepts, would undertake to distinguish between the permanent and the temporary, the universal and the partial elements of the teaching of Christ. Thus particular doctrines are rejected as forming no part of the Christian consciousness, and are yielded, as a sacrifice, to the speculative difficulties of the time.[2] We cannot, however, accept, we can only repudiate and challenge all asserted improvements whether by substitution or omission, *in the subject-matter of*

---

[1] Mr. Buckle, *H. Civ.*, II. 21, fathers this view on Charron. It was carried on by Hume in his *Natural History of Religion*, but has reached its climax in the system of M. Comte.

[2] See Dean Mansel's *Bampton Lect.*, pp. 250, 258; Palmer *On the Doctrine of Development*, pp. 91-100; Dewar on *German Protest*, p. 196; Blanco White, *Life*, III. 77.

Christianity itself, effected by alleged advances in knowledge and civilization. The progress of science, so far as it extends to religion, touches it on its natural or moral side: not as it is a revelation of spiritual truths. These, simple in their character, are also final, and admit of no rationalizing process of accommodation to a fancied advance in knowledge. Obviously, there can be no progress of this character in regard of truths which human reason is incapable of discovering for itself. In this respect the religion of Christ is really stationary. Civilization and knowledge may be regarded as witnesses to the permanent character of Christian truth, which absorbs, appropriates, and assimilates them without detriment to its own announcements. In a certain sense they form part of that *natural* revelation of Himself and His dealings with mankind which is a necessary consequence of a Divine government of the world, and which supplements His more special manifestations. Those improvements, however, in the condition and destinies of man which are due to the particular operation of Christianity, form part of the proper subject-matter of these Lectures, and will be adverted to in the course of them. This will be further treated.

§ 14. It may perhaps be thought that as he who excuses himself and his own cause, in effect becomes the accuser; so there is a certain want of confidence in the credentials of Christianity, Reasons for entering on the present argument.

when it is consented to weigh the probabilities of its duration. It is enough to reply that the form assumed, and the direction taken by the controversies of an age depend, doubtless, upon laws of thought beyond our volition or control. The course of Christian defence must ever follow that of attack; and arguments which in one age are satisfactory enough, in another fall pointless and beside the mark. There is, then, a duty which belongs to the Church of God in every age and to his " watchmen " in every generation, which may be described as the discerning of the signs of the times. Much of the influence, much of the usefulness of individual ministers of religion, will always depend on their appreciation of the needs and tendencies of the day.[1] Much of the narrowness of thought and want of practical knowledge which has been falsely, because extravagantly, attributed to the clerical mind, has been due to this;—an absence of clear-sightedness in apprehending the intellectual posture of the age, its information and particular bent of thought. " Watchman, what of the night? Watchman, what of the night?" must still be our question, when the clouds of doubt are hanging low, and the darkness of unbelief seems settling on the horizon of faith. It is not always sunshine in the courts of the Lord's house at Jerusalem. Rather

marginal note: Duty of teachers of Christianity.

[1] See some interesting remarks of Mr. Lecky, *Hist. Rat.*, I. 123.

the answer is re-echoed from the towers of observation and the ramparts of defence. "The morning cometh, but also the night. If ye will inquire, inquire ye; return, come."[1] It cannot be the part of Christian wisdom to refuse the labour of accommodating its teaching to the requirements of existing knowledge, and of anticipating, so far as it may, the difficulties of present thinkers. It needs but little insight into the course of speculation at this time to estimate the direction of the conflict which must henceforward be considered inevitable, between Science and Faith. The opposition and repugnancy which in former days were more speculative than practical, now show themselves immediate and direct, and are pushed into minute details. The question is fast becoming one of mutual compatibility. But there is comfort in the manliness with which the challenge has been accepted on the side of Christian belief. Unworthy suspicions of the candour of opponents, unwarrantable confusion of intellectual with moral error; illogical estimates of the consequences of unsound opinions,[2] are fast being laid aside. The supreme obligation due to truth is everywhere acknowledged. It is seen that the

Importance of the present crisis.

Grounds of hopefulness.

---

[1] Isaiah xxi. 11, 12.

[2] In the treatment of Holy Scripture (it has been well observed), "there is an abatement of that most wild and pernicious line of defence which may be called the 'all-or-nothing principle': because it poises the vast and glorious edifice of Revealed truth upon the point of a single

cause at stake is the cause of all, and not of a class; and those who make or rather find the difficulties which threaten to divorce Faith from Science, are now credited with a willingness to join in the work of subduing them. On the other hand, there is in many respects a kindlier feeling stirring in the antagonists of dogmatic belief towards their opponents. The services and benefits of Christian teaching in the history of mankind are more largely understood. It is acknowledged that there is something, at least, to be said for the claims of Christianity; nor are its professors merely the ready instruments of credulity and imposture. There is comfort, too, when confronted by an intellectual revolution in the scientific temper of the age, in the retrospect of past dangers and past escapes. "The centre of gravity of religious questions," it has been eloquently said from this place, "may have become altogether shifted and displaced. Anchors are lifting everywhere, and men committing themselves to what they may meet with on the sea. But Christians have had bad days before."[1] "Passi graviora" may then well be for the time to come the watchword of the Church of Christ. We are not enter-

incidental statement of some fact either of history or science, and then declares, with an audacity which makes one shudder, that if that single statement can be disproved, the whole structure must fall to the ground."—*Christian Remembrancer*, Vol. LIV. p. 132.

[1] Dean Church, *Univ. Sermons*, Serm. IV.

ing for the first time on the encounter with Materialism or with secular modes of thought. At present, certainly, the tone and feeling of society is not anti-Christian: it only needs to be reassured. We are not entering on a conflict unexpected, unforeseen. He who came "not to send peace upon the earth but a sword," has with that sword, "even the Word of God," armed His warriors for the fight of Christian truth with human imperfection.[1] We are contending for a faith which from the first has been the religion of progress:[2] whose cardinal doctrine is the love of our kind, the source of all just and enduring liberty:[3] which has been ever the enemy of social injustice: which in nowise denies the unity of the human race and is confined to no one clime, to no one tribal division of mankind, Aryan or Semitic, to no one form of political constitution:[4] and which in its deep sense of human

Elements of permanence inherent in the religion of Christ.

---

[1] See M. Guizot, *Meditations*, Vol. I. p. xx.

[2] This is admitted by M. Comte, *Phil. Pos.*, IV. 231, and comp. Dean Merivale, *Lect. on Conversion of the Empire*, p. 210; also Guizot, *Civ. in Europe*, I. 94, ed. Bohn; Ozanam, *Civil. in Fifth Cent.*, I. 4, E. T.; Lecky, *Hist. Rat.*, II. 234–5.

[3] Professor Goldwin Smith, *Study of History*, Pref.

[4] Thus Cardinal Wiseman, *Lect. on Science and Religion*; Ffoulkes, *Div. Christendom*, p. 247. "Christianity alone has a definite message addressed to all mankind. The character of the teaching of Mahomet is too exact a reflection of the race, time, place, and climate in which it arose to admit of its being universal. The same objection applies to the religions of the far East," &c.—Dr. Newman, *Gram. of Assent*, p. 425. "Christianity is a living truth which never can grow old," &c. —*Ib.*, p. 480.

responsibility has been the handmaid of man's perfectibility, leading him up to "the fulness of the stature of Christ." We are contending for a faith which claims to be coeval with the powers, the wants, the destinies of human nature: which alone is potent in virtue of Christ's Mediation to heal the wounds of conscience and dry the tears of sin: which has extended our very conceptions of purity and holiness, as possible to man: and which alone satisfies the boundless yearnings of his spirit by filling it with the promise of the likeness of its God. Why should we not assert for such a religion as this, the living germs of permanence and truth, a vitality surviving modification, a vigour which can never decay, a life immortal as the soul for which it lives and works?[1]

Μέγας ἐν ταύτῃ Θεός, οὐδὲ γηράσκει.

---

[1] "Nemo dubitat cum qui veram religionem requirit, aut jam credere immortalem esse animam, cui prosit illa religio, aut etiam id ipsum in eâdem religione velle invenire. Animæ igitur causâ omnis religio. . . . Animæ causâ vel solius vel maximè vera, si qua est religio, constituta est."—Augustin. *de Utilit. Cred.*, c. vii.

LECTURE II.

OBJECTIONS TO THE PROGRESS OF CHRISTIANITY CONSIDERED.

C'est un vieux bâtiment : si on y touche, il croulera.

"Je suis donc très-disposé à croire que chez des hommes que ceux qui m'entendent l'instinct secret devinera juste assez souvent même dans les sciences naturelles. Mais je suis porté à le croire à peu près infaillible lorsqu'il s'agit de philosophie rationnelle, de morale, de métaphysique et de théologie naturelle."

DE MAISTRE, *Soirées*, 1er *Entret.*

LECTURE II.

"*If thou sayest, Behold we knew it not: doth not He that pondereth the heart, consider it? and He that keepeth thy soul, doth not He know it? and shall not He render to every man according to his works.*"—Prov. xxiv. 12.

§ 1. WE have been hitherto occupied with the consideration of permanence as a criterion of truth, and the conditions of its applicability to the Gospel of Jesus Christ. Christianity, we contend, is the only religion which has stood its ground, which has taken part in the general advance of modern civilization as represented by the nations of Europe, the foremost portion of mankind. There is, then, good reason to believe that it must be true, and will prove to be an accompaniment of human progress to the end. The argument thus afforded to its claims to reception is laid on grounds which are common to any religious system. It does not, then, rest principally, or in the first instance, on the contents of the religion as revealed. These, however cogent to the mind of the believer, can have no binding force in relation to an objector. To all who accept the faith of Christ it must be plain enough, that our holy religion can be no passing phase of thought or sentiment in the

The past history of Christianity a ground for believing in its permanence.

This argument, independent of the particular

contents of the religion, history of the human race, to be succeeded by others equally ephemeral. If true, it is true for eternity. It has closed the roll and completed the career of the religions of mankind.[1] Christ, if He be Christ, is "with His Church always, even unto "the end of the world."[2] Incarnation, Redemption, Regeneration, Sanctification, are no catchwords of sect or school. They connote facts touching the destinies of the whole race of man. Nor can Christianity be regarded only as a revelation of doctrine.[3] It is far more a Divine work of restoration: in this lies its proper characteristic. "There is one Mediator" (and but one) "between God and man, the Man Christ Jesus."[4] "This faith was once" (and once for all) "delivered to the Saints."[5] "No man may deliver his brother, nor make agreement unto God for him. For it

---

[1] "Le Christianisme a fermé la carrière des religions .... parce qu'elle est la seule parfaitement digne de l'homme, d'où il suit par une conséquence nécessaire qu'elle est la plus parfaite et la dernière des religions."—Saisset, *Essais*, p. 300.

[2] Matt. xxviii. 20.

[3] See some excellent remarks in Dorner, *Hist. Prot. Theol.*, I. 19, E. T.: "To this intellectual tendency towards objective truth, and the delusion it nourished concerning the magical power of pure doctrine as a means for the protection and blessing of the whole man, there was united a moral security and religious torpidity which were maintained by the kindred delusion that the knowledge of the truth—even its mere reception as a matter of memory—brings with it the Christian salvation—that sin is essentially only a want of knowledge, or error. *Christ is thus reduced to a mere revealer of the true doctrine concerning God and concerning the past and future.*"

[4] 1 Tim. ii. 5.

[5] Jude 3: Τῇ ἅπαξ παραδοθείσῃ τοῖς ἁγίοις πίστει.

cost more to redeem their souls : so that he must let that alone for ever."[1] As we have seen, there can be no improvements upon the *subject-matter* of Christianity, no additions to it, no derogations from it. Christianity, whether true or false, speaks for itself: it lays its own claim to be received as the final announcement on the part of God to His creatures. But in regard to those "who are without," we may still seek to prove that the elements in which the vital forces of all religions consist, are to be found unimpaired and vigorous in the constitution of the faith of Christ.

calculated to satisfy objectors.

§ 2. For in some quarters undoubtedly an impression prevails, or at the least is very industriously circulated, that Christianity has been tried and has failed. We live in times when all institutions, political, social, religious, the cherished heritage of many generations, are seen to be on their trial. Nor is the religion of Christ, the sacred deposit of the whole history of the Church, in its turn exempt. Sometimes its failure is spoken of as evident in practice, sometimes on speculative grounds. The world, it is hinted, sits loose to faith in Christianity, and is beginning to disregard

A prevalent assumption of the failure of Christianity.

---

[1] Ps. xlix. 7, 8, with the comment of Delitzsch. On the perpetuity of the Church, as a doctrinal tenet, see Field, *Of the Church,* l. c. x., Palmer, *Treatise on the Church of Christ,* I. i. § 2. It was received alike by the Romish and Protestant divines, and is maintained equally by the Confession of Augsburg, the Helvetic Confession, and the Institutes of Calvin.

it. "Only a fourth part of mankind," it is said, with whatever truth, "are born Christians. The remainder never hear the name of Christ except as a reproach . . . These are facts which no casuistry can explain away."[1] Again, "Christianity, according to a well-known saying, has been tried and failed. The *religion* of Christ remains to be tried . . . To-day that failure is too patent."[2] Proudhon hardily proclaimed that Christianity will certainly die out in about three hundred years.[3] M. Comte, it is well known, argues speculatively that all Theology, as well as Metaphysic, is unreal; for they deal with the origin and the end of things; and of these, he thinks, we can know nothing. They serve, indeed, a preparatory function in affording a temporary stimulus, an artificial basis to intellectual effort. But it is only by laying them aside, and ignoring them, that knowledge has made real progress. Thus Catholicism, *i. e.* Christianity, the highest, yet the last type of Mono-

Of its temporary character.

---

[1] Froude *on Calvinism*, p. 4. He adds, "The Chinese and Japanese, we may almost say every weaker race with whom we have come in contact, connect it only with the forced intrusion of strangers whose behaviour among them has served ill to recommend their creed." Again, *Short Studies*, Ser. II. p. 98, "We wonder at the failure of Christianity; at the small progress which it has made in comparison with the brilliancy of its rise," &c. This part of the subject will be considered in Lecture VIII. On the numerical division of the human race according to religions, see Prof. Max Müller, *Chips*, I. 216. Christianity should probably rank highest in the scale.

[2] Morley's *Critical Miscellanies*, pp. 190, 191.

[3] See Rogers' *Essays*, II. 342.

theism, has now done its work. It has prepared the way for Positivism, that is, for the belief in Laws; and soon the present stage of mental and moral anarchy must draw to a close.[1] It cannot, *This view due to the circumstances of the age,* I fear, be denied that there are many solvents of customary belief at work among us. The advance through improved means of locomotion and mechanical appliances of our knowledge of mankind, of nature, and the earth which we inhabit; the tendencies of physical inventions, of political and social concentration, of scientific discovery, and of philosophical criticism, are all acting in one direction. They will strip off, no doubt, the unessential garb of Christianity. It remains to be seen whether its inward frame can be shaken. I make no excuse for putting the matter thus bluntly before you. It is well even for the youngest of my hearers, who are, thank God, least, if at all, familiar with the philosophy of unbelief, to know something of its language and mode of assault. Let them not be startled. When has the religion

---

[1] See *Phil. Pos.*, III. 418, V. 299. He holds l'état théologique to be l'état fictif. The Church is with Comte a speculative corporate body, destined to give way when the interests of speculation and practice are combined in the advance of knowledge. " La théologie et la physique sont profondément incompatibles."—*Lec.* I. No doubt, it is the function of Religion and of Philosophy to offer a general theory of the universe. This theory is slowly verified or improved on by the progress of knowledge contained in particular sciences. In this manner religion is always on its trial; but it has not failed yet, nor is there any reason to believe it will. For an eloquent description of the joint aims of Philosophy and Religion, see Saisset, *Essais*, pp. xxxiv.-vii.

but must be without delay encountered.

of Jesus Christ not been upon its trial; or when has it shrunk back from the test? But the charge of failure whether meant as a gibe,[1] or as a serious objection, as a ready weapon of attack, or as an honest stumbling-block, cannot be overlooked; it must not be postponed. To ignore a doubt, is not only open to the imputation of cowardice: it is unwise. For it cannot but operate to the prejudice of the truth: and when at last it comes up, as come it will, for answer, the fault bears its own punishment.

Nature of the current attacks on the success of Christianity.

§ 3. It cannot indeed be denied that the imputations to which I have alluded, are current in the literature of the day. "The popular religion," it is said, "has entered on its last phase;"[2] "Christianity has dwindled down to a drivelling, feeble, desultory thing." "It is now obvious that the theology of former ages cannot be maintained. . . . A change in religious thought has gradually forced its way through the cultivated classes of the community. The educated man no longer believes what the Evangelist believed and affirmed."[3] "The

---

[1] Bishop Fraser is reported to have said: "It is a common gibe that Christianity is losing power; and to a certain extent, I think, we cannot deny that the gibe is true and deserved."—*Guardian*, August 16, 1871.

[2] No new view. See ap. II. J. Rose, *Protestantism in Germany*, p. 163, 2nd ed. Schmidt and other Rationalists held that Christianity is a mere temporary dispensation, and that the world should return to Natural Religion.

[3] *Christian Theology and Modern Scepticism*, by the Duke of Somerset, *passim*. Fabri (*Briefe gegen Materialismus*) complains that

theological spirit is too much decayed and too far neutralized to be any longer really formidable in any part of Western Europe."[1] Such are some of the statements not unfrequently made. It is of moment, therefore, to estimate the grounds on which they rest, and the amount of truth they may contain. Nothing is easier than to repeat a charge when once it is made. Repeated, it soon begins to be believed, and held more largely on a tacit principle of authority; and then a fresh start is made from the assertion as if it were a fact both proved and acknowledged.[2] On what grounds, then, we ask, is the career of Christianity believed to have closed? Is there any present pressing proof of it? Is it truer now than at any former time? Is it plainer now

Reasons of their importance.

---

the majority of Christians now-a-days are pagans as to head; though accepting the faith with their hearts.

[1] "L'esprit théologique est trop déchu ou trop neutralisé pour être encore vraiment dangereux dans aucune partie de notre Occident Européen. C'est partout l'esprit métaphysique qui constitue désormais le seul antagoniste que le Positivisme doive avoir sérieusement en vue : lui seul prolonge désormais l'influence; impuissante pour rien fonder, mais trop efficace pour entraver du génie religieux qui s'éteindrait spontanément sans un tel remaniement." Comte to J. S. Mill, ap. Littré, *A. Comte et le Posit.*, p. 448, written 1843. See also *Paroles de Phil. Pos.*, p. 24.

[2] "Ideas obtain authority and dominion, not altogether from their intrinsic truth, but rather from their constant asseveration, especially when they fall in with the common hopes and fears, the wants and necessities, of human nature. The mass of mankind have neither leisure nor ability to examine them: they fatigue, and so compel the world into acceptance."—Milman, *Latin Christianity*, III. 437. "Les fausses opinions ressemblent à la fausse monnaie, qui est frappée d'abord par de grands coupables et dépensée ensuite par d'honnêtes gens qui perpétuent le crime sans savoir ce qu'ils font."—De Maistre, *Soiré s*, p. 26.

than it has ever been before? Are there no special reasons to indicate that the wish may be father to the thought? Is Christianity less an object of dislike and suspicion than it has ever been with some prevalent systems of philosophy? Is it less of an obstacle to their reception? Is there any less impatience in the heart and mind of man than of old to anticipate the designs of Providence or to foredate the beginning of the end? Something may not unreasonably be attributed to the expectation on the part of its detractors that Christianity may be killed or scotched by a policy of indifference. To pass it by as already foredoomed, to deal with it as a thing of the past, much may perhaps be looked for from this course of treatment. Dogmas ere now have perished of pretermission, if not of controversy, have given way to a modification of opinion, if not to argument, have yielded to insensible decay. Such has been the fate of many an extinct superstition. This in the eyes of some critics is "the great turning-point in the history of civilized nations."[1] Why, then, should it be otherwise with the time-worn, cum-

and of their being at present brought forward.

---

[1] "When in the progress of society its theological element begins to decay, the ardour with which religious disputes were once conducted becomes sensibly weakened. The most advanced intellects are the first to feel the growing indifference, and therefore they are also the first to scrutinize real events with that inquisitive eye which their predecessors had reserved for religious speculations. This is a great turning-point in the history of every civilized nation."—Buckle, *Hist. Civil.*, II. 263. Compare Mr. Lecky, *Hist. Rat.*, I. 101.

brous fabric of Christian tradition? The increasing secularization of politics, the loss of temporal influence by the Church,[1] mark, it is urged, the decline of dogmatic theology as a practical power. Moreover, something of a just retribution clings about such a change of fortune, which must render it not wholly displeasing to the taste of the physical philosopher. In past days Theology began by monopolizing science, metaphysic, even history itself. In the hands of the Fathers of the Church she early invaded the realm of Natural knowledge,[2] quickly subordinating it to Revelation, and thereby rendering its progress impossible. In this manner Lactantius denied the sphericity of the earth, and Augustine antipodes. "From the fifth to the twelfth centuries," writes Guizot, "it is Theology that possessed and directed the human spirit. All opinions are impressed by Theology: philosophical, political, and historical questions are all considered under a theological point of view. So all-powerful is the Church in the intellectual order that even the mathematical and physical sciences are held in submission to its doctrines. The theological spirit is in a manner the blood which ran in the veins of the European world

Grounds for prepossessions on the part of Natural philosophers.

Former relations of Theology to physical science.

---

[1] This view, of course, loses sight of the possibility that such a severance may even advance the ultimate influence of religion. Otherwise Dissent must equally decline with Established religions.

[2] Compare Bacon, *Nov. Org.*, Aph. lxxxix.

<small>Haureau.</small> down to Bacon and Descartes."[1] Everywhere and on all subjects the maxim was in force, 'Philosophia ancillans theologiæ.' Few cared to perceive that the true sphere of science lies altogether outside of theological study. The Christian is but implicitly and in a secondary degree called on to inquire into the nature and constitution of things and of God. On this side the true defence of his system of belief is to isolate its claims, repelling attack and implied or asserted contradictions.[2] History is the proper mode of exhibiting the general character of the faith of Christ, as it is of orthodoxy in detail; showing the particular dogma to be either a just or false outcome of Scriptural Revelation. Now, however, the tables are turned: and the human intellect, "waxing," it is said, "in strength, learns to rely upon its own resources, and to throw off incumbrances by which the freedom of its movements has been long impaired."[3] So also the

---

[1] *Civilization in Europe*, E. Tr., I. 114, ed. Bohn. See also Comte, *Phil. Pos.*, V. 478. Kepler's bold and plain words (Introd. ad Stell. Martis) are well known. "In Theology we balance authorities, in Philosophy we weigh reasons. A holy man was Lactantius, who denied that the earth was round: a holy man was Augustine who granting the rotundity, denied the antipodes: a holy thing to me is the Inquisition, which allows the smallness of the earth, but denies its motion. But more holy to me is Truth," &c. See ap. Whewell, *Indications of the Creator*, p. 143, and at length, *Hist. Induct. Sc.*, IV. i. 6, 7.

[2] "Tout ce qui nous reste donc après avoir ajouté foi aux mystères sur les preuves de la vérité de la religion (qu'on appelle motifs de crédibilité) c'est de les pouvoir soutenir contre les objections," &c.—Leibnitz, *Théodicée*, § 5.

[3] Buckle, *Hist. Civ.*, II. 263.

founder of Positivism looks forward to a Church, Catholic, but not Christian, which shall preside over the regeneration of society, and "the irresistible emancipation of human reason."[1]

§ 4. Certainly, we have no right to complain that false assumptions should have borne their natural fruit and have yielded to fair attack. "Men," wrote Jeremy Taylor,[2] "will call all opinions by the name of religion, and superstructures by the name of fundamental articles, and fancies by the glorious appellative of faith." Those, then, who made Theology the essence of the faith, and next installed her in the throne of all knowledge, divine and human, natural and supernatural, poising on some solitary statement as to a fact of history or science the whole truth of Holy Scripture itself: such men were perforce sowing to the wind, and were the unwitting pioneers of a whole revolution of belief. "Science," wrote De Maistre[3] (and his sentiment is far from exploded), *Inversion of this relation.*

---

[1] *Phil. Pos.*, V. 490. It is a melancholy satire on the tendencies of Comtism that, forsaking the Materialism which is its proper base, its author should have returned, as M. Littré reluctantly admits, to a Theology, a Fetichism (*sic*), a worship of Humanity, "le Grand Être." Prof. Huxley's strictures on this subject are as just as they are able.

[2] *Works*, V. 348, ed. Eden.

[3] See *Examen de Bacon*, vol. ii. 46; *Soirées de Saint-Pétersbourg*, V. Entret. *Works*, I. 198. See, however, also, p. 172, where the metaphor is borrowed. Leibnitz, *Théodicée*, § 17, speaks of those who held as to philosophy, "qu'elle devoit être traitée en servante et non pas en maîtresse par rapport à la Théologie. Enfin que c'étoit une Hagar auprès de Sara, qu'il falloit chasser de la maison avec son Ismael, quand elle faisoit la mutine." It must not be forgotten that Metaphysic, under

"must be kept in its place; for it resembles fire which, when confined in the grates prepared for it, is the most useful and powerful of men's servants; scattered about anyhow, it is the most terrible of scourges." For this reason he argues that physical science was not given to men until Christianity was dominant in the earth. What wonder if we now hear the opinion loudly proclaimed that physical knowledge is the proper supplement to theological conceptions; that "the gradual destruction of the old theology is everywhere preceded by the growth and diffusion of physical truths."[1]

Science now tends to the adoption of a sensuous philosophy.

§ 5. The reverse excess is now more to be feared. The spirit of the age proves, indeed, that mankind is still governed by its prejudices rather than by reason. As the medieval temper was theologically led to an excessive credulity, so the sceptical tendency of the present day leads men to limit their vision to objects of sense. Now it is asserted that there is no knowledge but of things visible: no truth which is not *real*: no philosophy which is not "positive."[2]

       We have but faith: we cannot know;
       For knowledge is of things we see;

sings the greatest of our metaphysical poets, con-

the name of Θεολογική, had of old assumed the highest rank in the scale of sciences. See Arist., *Metaph.*, Bk. V.

[1] Buckle, *Hist. Civ.*, III. 478.

[2] Positivism, by Comte identified with Natural Philosophy in its largest sense including *Social Physics*, through a huge fundamental assumption, has come to be purely negative. The term "positive" was by the grammarians opposed to "natural," and hence transferred to the

descending to the language of his time.[1] Thus the most popular Professor of the day asserts, "there is but one kind of knowledge and but one method of acquiring it. . . . What is the history of every science but the history of the elimination of the notion of creative or other interferences? . . . Harmonious order governing eternally continuous progress, the web and woof of Matter and Force interweaving by slow degrees, without a broken thread, that veil which lies between us and the Infinite, *that universe which alone we know or can know.*"[2] Here is something very different from

Excluding a belief in the Unseen.

---

distinction between legal and moral obligations. "In laws," says Hooker, "that which is natural bindeth universally; that which is positive not so."—*E. P.*, l. x. 7. Thus also Bishop Butler contrasts *moral* and *positive* duties. *Analogy*, Pt. II. c. i. Its present use seems derived from its logical sense, denoting "rem quasi præsentem." The intermediate notion, however, by which laws of nature are regarded as positive, is thus stated by Leibnitz:—"Il y en a d'autres vérités qu'on peut appeler *positives*, parce qu'elles sont les lois qu'il a plu à Dieu de donner à la Nature, ou parce qu'elles en dépendent."

[1] And truly enough: only it must not be forgotten that faith is to man the very "evidence of things not seen," the fundamental condition of all true human knowledge, intellectual or moral. We may justly ask whether the materialism of the day, resting on physical philosophy, has any *new* proof or necessity to offer, not open to earlier speculation.

[2] Huxley, *Lay Sermons*, p. 310. "Notre âme," says Pascal, "est jetée dans le corps où elle trouve nombre, temps, dimension. Elle raisonne là-dessus et appelle cela Nature, nécessité, et *ne peut croire autre chose.*" Yet he acknowledges fully the modest limits of human apprehension. "Les sciences ont deux extrémités qui se touchent: la première est la pure ignorance naturelle où se trouvent tous les hommes en naissant: l'autre extrémité est celle où arrivent les grandes âmes, qui ayant parcouru tout ce que les hommes peuvent savoir, trouvent qu'ils ne savent rien, et se rencontrent en cette même ignorance d'où ils étaient partis. Mais c'est une ignorance savante qui se connaît." (*Pensées*, II. 163; I. 180.)

the doctrine of the relativity of human knowledge. No alternative is presented between materialism[1] and sheer ignorance; either alike incompetent to satisfy the demand of man's intelligence or spirit. So extremes meet. The ultimate analysis of science, the rudimentary ignorance of barbarism, have kissed each other. Both refuse to travel beyond the avouchments of the senses. Mr. Bailey, long a resident among the Veddahs of Ceylon, says:—"They have no knowledge of a Supreme Being. 'Is He on a rock—on a white ant-hill—on a tree? I never *saw* a God,' was the only reply I received to repeated questions."[2]

---

[1] How dangerously near such teaching approaches to materialism may be seen from the language of Feuerbach. "Personality, individuality, consciousness, without Nature is nothing; or, which is the same thing, an empty, unsubstantial abstraction. But Nature is nothing without corporeality. . . . Real sensational existence is that which is not dependent on my own mental spontaneity or activity, but by which I am involuntarily affected: which is when I cannot, do not think of it or feel it. The existence of God must therefore be in space: in general a qualitative, sensational existence. But God is not seen, not heard, not perceived by the senses. He does not exist for me, if I do not exist for Him."—*Essence of Christianity*, E. T., pp. 90, 199. Augustine thus characterizes the Positivism of his day:—"Sed res est longè remota a vanorum hominum mentibus qui nimis in haec corporalia progressi atque lapsi nihil aliud putant esse quàm quod istis quinque notissimis nuntiis corporis sentiunt: et quas ab his plagas atque imagines acceperunt eas secum volvunt etiam cum conantur recedere a sensibus et ex earum mortiferâ et fallacissimâ regulâ ineffabilia penetralia veritatis rectissimè se metiri putant."—*Util. Cred.*, c. i.

[2] Quoted by Mr. Farrar on the *Universality of a Belief in God*. (*Anthropological Review*, August, 1864.) As to the Veddahs, however, see Tylor, *Prim. Cult.*, I. 45; and on the whole question of savage races being destitute of the elements of religion, id. l. c. xi., pp. 377-83. Also Luthardt, *Apolog.*, E. T., p. 42.

Thus religion, the science of spiritual things, whose subject-matter, passing the sphere of experience, is the soul and spirit of man, and his relations to the Maker of the universe, "dwelling in the light which no man can approach unto; Whom no man hath seen, nor can see,"[1] is in this school of thought dethroned, discrowned, nay, thrust out for final extinction: her occupation gone, the reason of her being disallowed.[2]

§ 6. The inquiry remains, Why must we believe that Christianity has failed? If the charge be true, it must be capable of proof, either from the exhibition of a fixed tendency to decline—the religion of Christ must be shown to have already passed its meridian, and to have yielded only disappointing results—or from a present feebleness and prostration, so utter and unquestionable, so chronic and inherent, as to defy dispute; or, lastly, from the discovery that the tenets of Christianity

Assumptions necessary to a belief in the failure of Christianity,

---

[1] 1 Tim. vi. 16. Comp. Tertullian, *Apol.*, c. xviii. Invisibilis est etsi videatur: incomprehensibilis, etsi per gratiam repræsentetur; inæstimabilis, etsi humanis sensibus æstimetur. It is in this sense that Augustine writes: "Summus ille Deus qui scitur melius nesciendo." *De Ord.*, II. xvi.

[2] Lange, *Geschichte des Materialismus*, p. 60, has some good remarks on the insensible stages by which the physical philosophy of the day passes into dogmatism. "Unsere Materialisten vergessen nur zu häufig, dass sie ganz einerlei, ob sie von Beruf etwa Professoren der Physiologie sind oder nicht,—sich alsbald auf dem Boden der Philosophie und nicht der Natur Wissenschaft befinden, wenn sie sich zu einer Gesammtanschauung des Weltganzen zu erheben versuchen, und dass sie dogmatische Philosophen sind, wenn sie die Resultate ihrer Anschauungen kategorisch als Thatsachen vortragen."

are incompatible with truths now very generally acknowledged, and with that marked progress in intellectual effort which is a main ingredient in the present condition of affairs. It is with the last of these alternatives that we shall first, and for some time, be occupied; for the particular objections which it covers are fatal not only to the continuance of Christianity, but to all systems of religion acknowledging or implying Theism.[1] These, then, require to be met before entering on the direct historical proofs which guarantee the prospects of our common faith. With one of these, indeed, the refutation of such objections is immediately connected, and practically identical. For the power, which they impugn, of assimilating healthfully the varying conditions, the attendant conceptions of progressive civilization, must ever be a most important ingredient in a religion destined for permanence. It is this element which is mainly neutralized or denied in the observations which will now be considered.

<small>constituting a denial of its power to co-exist with advancing civilization.</small>

<small>Particular objections</small>

§ 7. The difficulties still urged against the re-

---

[1] It is evident that, though a man may be a Theist and not a Christian, a fact which has recently been somewhat ostentatiously proclaimed (*Christianity and Modern Scepticism*, sub fin.), it is impossible for him to be a Christian and not a Theist. Thus, Shaftesbury, *Works*, II. 209, writes: "Averse as I am to the cause of Theism, or name of Deist, when taken in a sense exclusive of Revelation, I consider still that in strictness the root of all is Theism; and that to be a settled Christian, it is necessary to be first of all a good Theist."

ception of Christianity are partly very ancient, though now advanced upon new grounds: some are essentially modern in their character and bearings, and, as such, are at present most frequently encountered. Though general in their scope, they are brought to bear particularly on the dominant, that is, upon the Christian faith. All 'progress, it is asserted, in human affairs, of whatever kind, is intellectual. Moral subjects form no exception.¹ The progress of Nature is towards intellectual, not moral development. Moral dogmas, if they advance at all, which is very questionable, advance only through intellectual processes. The same is true no less of theological and religious beliefs, which owe their virtue to their moral element. Religion has never been a true source of culture, which is really derived from knowledge and not from belief.²

on which this assumption is founded,

---

¹ Pascal long ago noted the source of this confusion. " Les inventions des hommes vont en avançant de siècle en siècle. La bonté et la malice du monde en général en est de même."—*Pensées*, I. 205. The notions of Mr. Buckle and kindred thinkers on these subjects are traceable to Condorcet and Turgot. " Progress," says Mr. Morley, *Crit. Misc.*, p. 91, " in Condorcet's mind is exclusively produced by improvement in intelligence. It is the necessary result of man's activity in the face of that disproportion ever existing between what he knows and what he desires and feels the necessity to know. Hence the most fatal errors of his sketch. He measures only the contributions made by nations and eras to what we *know*; leaving out of sight their failures and successes in the elevation of moral standards and ideals, and in the purification of the passions."

² See Buckle, *Hist. Civ.*, I. 254. " When religious opinions are deeply rooted, they do, no doubt, influence the conduct of men; but before they can be deeply rooted, some intellectual change must first have taken place," &c.

Civilization explains religion, and not religion civilization. "The history of the civilization of the earth," it has been quaintly said, "is the history of the civilization of Olympus also."[1] Thus Christianity has been no cause of civilization, but its effect. The consequences very commonly attributed to Christianity in the history of mankind are really due to an advance in civilization. The Church of Christ may seem to have done some good in things where her interest did not happen to clash with the interests of Europe, as in helping to abolish slavery; but, after all, circumstances and manners would have produced the result necessarily and of themselves.[2] The essence of all religions is in a moral code, and this is found to be nearly everywhere identical. So in the moral part of Christianity there is nothing new. All providential interposition, speculatively or historically considered, is inadmissible, and therefore, also, every religion resting upon such interposition. Such notions belong altogether to the

current in the literature of the day,

---

[1] Morley, *Crit. Misc.*, p. 153.
[2] See Condorcet ap. Morley, *Crit. Misc.*, p. 94, and M. Comte, *Phil. Pos.*, V. 397. The case is temperately and honestly stated by Guizot, *Civ. in E.*, I. 110, ed. Bohn. "It has often been repeated that the abolition of slavery among modern people is due entirely to Christians. That, I think, is saying too much: slavery existed for a long period in the heart of Christian society, without its being particularly astonished or irritated. A multitude of causes and a great development in other ideas and principles of civilization were necessary for the abolition of this iniquity of all iniquities. It cannot be doubted, however, that the Church exerted its influence to restrain it."

infancy of knowledge; its progress is marked by their decay and extinction. Since the discovery of the great laws and agencies of Nature all miraculous tales have been given up. Every advance of science is an extension of the idea of Law, and that into regions of thought and phenomena hitherto held exempt.[1] But the theory of universal invariable law is abhorrent from Christian doctrine, and, indeed, from all systems which are not of a pantheistic character, or, at least, go beyond pure theism. Religion itself, and so-called revelation, are parts of the order of Nature, and may be explained out of phenomena which leave no room for supernatural considerations. Religion is a natural infirmity of the human mind in its immature stages, just as there are specific disorders in childhood incident to the human body. Thus Christianity is a partial and evanescent form of anthropomorphism, necessary perhaps to a transitional mode of thought. It is the tendency of knowledge, and so of civilization, to extinguish religion. Advancing culture removes the feelings, or more strictly the occasions of the feelings, which are the elements of religious sentiment. By eliminating fear and wonder from the mind, in its gradually increased acquaintance with the

fatal to the permanence and power of Christianity and of all genuine religion.

---

[1] Such as the special Providence of God, the foundation of all religion: the freedom and personality of man: with its consequences on social law and morality. See some good remarks in *Christian Remembrancer*, No. CXXXI., p. 240.

facts of the external world, the ingredients of veneration are dissolved, and religion itself disappears in the analysis. And, lastly, the sense of free agency is more than suspected to be only a trick of consciousness, a product of organic evolution, and to be incompatible alike with just theories of a natural causation, and with statistical results. But if moral responsibility be removed, most, it must be admitted, of the groundwork of religious truth, under whatever system, will fall away with it. Prayer, for example, can no longer be regarded as "man's rational prerogative," but rather as "a transient bewilderment of the social instinct," the "misapplication of a social habit," or "the delusive self-confidence of human feeling."[1]

They are for this reason answered in detail.

I proceed to enter more or less fully on the topics indicated. All are more or less directly connected with the permanence of the faith of Christ. The world at large is always ready to mistake difficulties which really underlie all human thought for difficulties in the way of Christian

---

[1] See Coleridge's remarks on this subject in *Aids to Reflection*, p. 55, and on the other side Comte, *Phil. Pos.*, IV. pp. 671–3. I cannot refrain from quoting a noble passage from Mr. Hutton, *Essays*, I. 308:—
"Prayer is and can only be possible on the assumption that it is a real influence with God: that, whether granted or denied, it is efficient as an expression of our spiritual want and resolution: that the breath of power which answers it is a living response, and like all living responses the free utterance of the moment, not the pre-ordained consequent waiting for a pre-ordained antecedent: that there is a sphere beyond all necessary law, in which both the Divine and human life are not constrained by immutable arrangements, but free."

belief. So far forth, however, as they affect the *permanence* of Christianity, being themselves involved in the current philosophy of the age, and representing the spirit of its thought, they will be properly considered here. For certainly of most of them it may be said that, if these views must be accepted, the days of the reception of the faith of Christ by mankind, or at least by its most civilized portion, are undoubtedly numbered, and perhaps quickly told. Whatever may have been the benefits it has conferred upon past generations, whatever its connections with foregone civilization, its part, if these things be so, has been indeed played out, its work is done, its glory departed, and "the ark of our God is taken."

§ 8. The limits assigned me in these Lectures will be best observed by grouping the objections specified under three general heads. They will be found to involve the relations either (I.), of causation to free agency; or (II.), of universal law to providential agency; or (III.), of intellectual to moral and religious action. "Every religion," says a distinguished living philosopher,[1] "may be defined as an *a priori* theory of the universe." "Every perfect religion," writes another careful and precise thinker,[2] "must give account of three

Classification of such objections.

---

[1] Mr. Herbert Spencer, *First Principles*, p. 43.
[2] Dr. Westcott, Comte on *Christianity*, *Cont. Rev.* VIII. 373.

elements—the individual, the world, and God." Our immediate task is to examine whether the principles on these subjects, necessary to the existence of Christianity, are irreconcilable with the conclusions of existing science.[1] No fact is more suggestive of the intellectual temper of our time than the manner in which the question of man's liberty of action is now discussed, and the grounds on which it is not uncommonly set aside. Relegated on its metaphysical side[2] to the limbo of unfruitful disputations, it is approached and decided by physical considerations, as a material rather than a mental fact, or as a mental fact capable of material explanation. Minds occupied only or mainly with physical inquiries readily apply the notion of material causation, the *nexus* between antecedent and consequent, with which they are familiar, to the phenomena of thought and action.[3] Uniformity of result, statistically obtained, is taken to prove identity of origin; and moral operations

Those relating to the existence of free agency in man first considered.

The present aspect of science materialistic.

---

[1] "The questions which belong to natural theology are in substance the same from age to age; but they change their aspect with every advance or supposed advance in the inductive sciences."—Whewell, *Indic. of the Creator*, p. ix.

[2] Sir H. Maine, *Ancient Law*, p. 354, has pointed out that the problem of free-will arises when we contemplate a metaphysical conception under a legal aspect. Dean Merivale has traced the theological history of the controversy to the expressions of Roman law.

[3] Compare Augustine, *Ver. Relig.*, c. xxxvi. "Quoniam opera magis Artificem atque ipsam artem dilexerunt hoc errore puniuntur ut in operibus artificem artemque conquirant: et cum invenire nequiverint (Deus enim non corporalibus sensibus subjacet sed ipsi menti supereminet) ipsa opera existiment esse et artem et artificem."

are confounded with material processes.¹ Thus it is asked, as an inquiry decisive of the matter in hand, whether the actions of men, and therefore of societies, are not governed by fixed laws; or whether they are to be regarded as the result of chance or of supernatural interference.² For on this issue depends the *desideratum* of the Positive School, the possibility of an exact science of man and history. Now chance, it may at once be admitted, is but another name for ignorance of causation.³ We know nothing in Nature, or, if it may be so said, out of Nature, which is not under the

---

¹ This is, no doubt, the first effect of the enthusiasm and instinct of symmetry which are the just results of the surprising triumphs of physical discovery. Mr. Lecky well remarks, *Hist. Rat.*, I. 322, " In the present day, when the study of the laws of matter has assumed an extraordinary development, and when the relations between mind and body are chiefly investigated with a primary view to the functions of the latter, it is neither surprising nor alarming that a strong movement towards materialism should be the consequence." Leibnitz finely observes: " Il paroit d'abord que tout ce que nous faisons n'est qu'impulsion d'autrui: et que tout ce que nous concevons vient de dehors par les sens, et se trace dans le vuide de notre esprit, *tanquam in tabulâ rasâ*. Mais une méditation plus profonde nous apprend que tout (même les perceptions et les passions) nous vient de notre propre fonds avec une pleine spontanéité."—*Théod.*, Pt. III. § 296.

² See Buckle, *Hist Civil.*, I. p. 8 ff.

³ " Ne parlons plus de hasard ni de fortune, ou parlons-en seulement comme d'un nom dont nous couvrons notre ignorance."—Bossuet, *Disc. sur l'Hist. Univ.*, III. viii. " Tous les sages," says Leibnitz, " conviennent que le hasard n'est qu'une chose apparente: c'est l'ignorance des causes qui le fait." Δοκεῖ μὲν αἰτία ἡ τύχη, ἄδηλος δὲ ἀνθρωπίνῃ διανοίᾳ.—Arist., *Phys.*, II. iv. Mr. Tylor, *Hist. Prim. Cult.*, I. 17, furnishes an admirable illustration. " The Great Spirit," say the Sioux Indians, " made all things except the wild rice; but the wild rice came by chance." Here the ambiguity is apparent, which opposes chance not to causation, but to design.

and tending to bring man's liberty of action under the uniformity of laws of Nature.

direction of fixed principles and ascertainable elementary causes.[1] But when, this correction made, the question is again stated, does it present a real dilemma? The will of man, it may be reasonably contended, is itself a cause, subject to conditioned action,[2] governed therefore by fixed laws of choice as well as of subsequent operation, yet in its nature *motive*, and analogous, so far considered, to any simple elementary force or form of force in physics. There is no greater antecedent difficulty in conceiving the agency of the one than of the other.[3] But then the action of man's will, it may be said, is in this view hypothetically different from that of all natural forces. For while the cause of motion to things external to itself, its own movements are

---

[1] "The *nature of a thing* is the answer both of the ignorant and of the philosopher. Search for *laws*."—Faraday, *Life*, II. 86. Law may be said to be the first announcement of Holy Scripture; when God spake, "Let there be light;" and there was light.

[2] Rom. viii. 20. "For the creature was made subject to vanity, not willingly, but by reason of him who hath subjected the same in hope."

[3] The embarrassments attending the notion of Force as a *property of Matter* are now understood. Thus the terms *energy*, *behaviour*, and the like have been transferred by modern physicists from moral phenomena as the best exponents of natural force. See Prof. Tyndall, *Fragments of Science*, p. 22. Whewell's *Indications of the Creator*, p. 90. Lange, *Geschichte des Materialismus*, pp. 376-7, has some good remarks on the bearing of this fact upon a doctrine of materialism. While recognizing to the full the charm of style and language possessed by a Tyndall and a Huxley, I cannot forbear to point out the responsibility attaching to their vast powers in this respect. This has been ably touched by a writer in the 'Quarterly Review,' No. CCXX. p. 370. Leibnitz has well said, "Souvent les expressions outrées et pour ainsi dire poétiques, ont plus de force pour toucher et pour persuader que ce qui se dit avec régularité."

assumed to be ultimately free, that is, uncaused, however biassed by the conditions and circumstances of acting. Now, the bowl will roll indeed according to its bias, but it must first find elsewhere an origin of movement. This supposition, then, it is urged, is inconsistent with the whole analogy of Nature, and is unsupported by the evidence of facts.

§ 9. The question thus stated will be perceived to have no immediate connection with the theological tenet of free-will.[1] By this is properly covered the relation of man's will to supernatural or Divine interference, the measure, so to speak, of its subservience, the will being assumed, as to itself, to be an instance of causation in Nature. At present we are concerned only with the scientific fact of the existence of will in man, as being a fundamental condition of the permanence of our religion. To the mode of its operation the old physical axiom may with reason be applied—" Corpora non agunt nisi soluta." For it needs hardly to remark that to speak of free-will is no better than a tautology, not to rank it among the "question-begging appellatives" of Bentham, a will not free being a contradiction in terms, a conception which excludes itself.[2] There is, indeed, an aspect in which the

The theological tenet of free-will to be distinguished from the ethical or metaphysical question.

---

[1] Mr. Buckle, *Hist. Civ.*, I. pp. 9, 20, has indeed exhibited this subject very differently; yet, as it seems to me, with some confusion.

[2] This, it is found, was the view of Spinoza (Ed. Auerbach). Coleridge justly remarks:—" A will, the state of which does in no sense

The theological dogma not necessarily incompatible with the view of natural science.

theological dogma is not unconcerned with the scientific question. Thus, if the assumption of universal law as a principle of science, or of natural selection and gradual evolution as applications of it, require in regard of human action the reception of a system of fatalism, whether pure or modified, it would not be difficult, by means of a doctrine of predestination, determinism, or even of eternal reprobation, to institute an apparent alliance between some aspects of Christianity and science.[1] This subject it is not within our limits to pursue further, though it has been stirred by some leading writers of the time.[2] I would remark only that among defensive arguments such reasoning is at least not inadmissible.

The argument from

§ 10. Are, then, the grounds on which the human

---

originate in its own act, is an absolute contradiction. It might be an instinct, an impulse, a plastic power, and if accompanied with consciousness, a desire; but a will it could not be."—*A. R.*, p. 104. Scientific and theological determinism may thus practically coincide. A will, which is absorbed in the conditions of its operation, is no will; and if the actions of men "are merely the product of a collision between internal and external phenomena," responsibility of conduct is evaded. "Voluntas," said even Luther, "quæ potest cogi et cogitur, non est voluntas sed noluntas."

[1] Thus the Leibnitian doctrine of Monads and a Pre-established Harmony, when assailed as involving Fatalism, was defended by its author as not incompatible with the Christian doctrine of Grace.

[2] It is suggested by Mr. Buckle in his highly interesting comparison of Calvinism with Arminianism, *H. Civ.*, II. 342; and by Mr. Froude in his most eloquent, though somewhat vague, lecture on Calvinism. See also Mr. J. S. Mill, *Exam. of Sir W. Hamilton*, p. 492. Sir William (*Appendix to Reid*, p. 977) is careful to point out that the Calvinist theologian holds to the liberty of man by the side of a doctrine of predestination and foreknowledge of God.

race has ever attributed to itself the possession of will, of an independent power of acting, and an ultimate freedom of choice, are these indeed real, or to be accounted imaginary? Is there anything in the present state of our knowledge which renders such a belief incredible through a diverse, yet adequate, explanation of admitted facts? Are the sentiments and volitions which have hitherto been presumed to be the properties of our personal activity, to be henceforward referred to general laws? Do our "thoughts, wills, and actions accord with laws as definite as those which govern the motion of waves, the combination of acids and bases, and the growth of plants and animals?"[1] The observation of religious instincts, of ideals unrealized,

natural instincts in favour of free-will.

> That type of perfect in his mind
> In Nature can he nowhere find;

of moral intuitions and indestructible beliefs, the very capacity of self-reproach, "the implicit creed of the guilty;" these facts in our mental constitution have ever been held to presume the existence of will in man as a precedent condition of their reality.[2] Nor is the existence of such instinctive

Testimony of positive thinkers to their validity.

---

[1] Tylor, *Hist. Prim. Cult.*, I. p. 2.

[2] It has indeed been urged (chiefly by writers of the school of Kant), that "presentiments cannot be regarded as proofs of external existence." Compare Mr. Hutton, *Essays*, I. 26. But such an objection is in truth suicidal, striking at the roots of all knowledge. Spinoza said the stone, if it could think, would account its gravitation a voluntary

beliefs, showing an uniform but independent genesis in different places and times, altogether denied in the school of thought which I have now in view. Mr. Mill, indeed, says with some causticity, "The universal voice of mankind, so often appealed to, is universal only in its discordance."[1] Yet M. Comte recognizes "essential inclinations of the intellect," "primordial tendencies," an "inherent need of ideality," and the like. "The universality of religious ideas," writes[2] Mr. Herbert Spencer, "their independent evolution among different primitive races, and their great vitality, unite in showing that their source must be

---

movement; and Leibnitz (probably with the dictum of Thales (Arist. de Anim., I. 2) in his mind) made the same remark of the magnet. But Hegel replies that with thought would come the perception of an infinite variety of motion, which, if limited, would be felt as compulsion. See Weisse, *Vorlesungen*, p. 126.

[1] *Dissert.*, II. 498. See Comte, *Phil. Pos.*, VI. 642, &c.

[2] *First Principles*, pp. 10, 14. And again (p. 4), "Admitting, as we must, that life is impossible unless through a certain agreement between internal convictions and external circumstances; admitting, therefore, that the probabilities are always in favour of the truth, or at least the partial truth of a conviction; we must admit that the convictions entertained by many minds in common are the most likely to have some foundation." Cicero, *Nat. D.*, I. xvii., says indeed the same thing. De quo omnium natura consentit, id verum esse necesse est. "No pre-assurance common to a whole species does in any instance prove delusive. All other prophecies of nature have their exact fulfilment in every other *ingrafted word* of promise. Nature is found true to her word; and is it in her noblest creature that she tells her first lie?" —Coleridge, *A. R.*, p. 277. Mr. Mill, *Logic*, II. 466, sees a fallacy of reasoning in a circle in this assertion of natural or instinctive sentiments among mankind. But he has no right to demand these generalizations, any more than others in nature, to be unexceptionable and not approximate.

deep-seated instead of superficial." "A postulate which is not consciously asserted, but unconsciously involved, and which is unconsciously involved not by one man or body of men, but by numerous bodies of men, who diverge in countless ways and degrees in the rest of their beliefs, has a warrant far transcending any that can be usually shown." "That religious instincts," says Mr. Lecky, "are as truly a part of our nature as are our appetites and our nerves, is a fact which all history establishes, and which forms one of the strongest proofs of the reality of that unseen world to which the soul of man continually tends."[1] Is their testimony, then, negatived or overthrown, is the light that is in them darkened by our increasing acquaintance with the regularity of events in nature, with the evolution of animal life, or with the automatic development of faculties? Of this class of notions, it may suffice to remark that even if instincts be, as Mr. Darwin believes, "inherited habits," this does not

They are not inconsistent with a theory of evolution,

[1] *Hist. European Morals*, I. 340. Mr. Mill, *Examination*, p. 503, ff., contends that we are not conscious of free-will, but of responsibility implying free-will. We are, he admits, conscious of a *feeling* that we might have chosen differently had we *preferred* to do so. By responsibility is meant not the fact of future punishment, but the sense that it is right we should be punished. This, argues Mr. Mill, is a natural deterrent, and it enables a man to help acting as he does. If so, it renders him justly liable to punishment. I cannot see how it does on the theory of Necessity, which admits, as Mr. Mill (p. 511) half seems to perceive, no such saving clause. It is of course always open to analyze Conscience into association; viz. a gradually formed conviction that as we are accountable to man, so we are to the Deity. But such an explanation really decides nothing.

necessarily mar their cogency or plausibility of proof.

> Reason is often pressed,
> But honest Instinct comes a volunteer.[1]

The standard of nature is the perfect and, therefore, the mature instance.[2] The highest stage of civilization is, in the truest sense, a state of nature; nor are instincts confined or necessarily correspondent to the primeval beliefs of savages. There may be a rudimentary belief, natural and instinctive to human tribes, which, at any given stage, may not have yet emerged into a condition which can be pronounced as definitely apprehended.[3] It must be remembered that results obtained through evolution, being strictly natural, may, in themselves, be regarded as instinctive. And, certainly, the belief in spiritual beings, the conviction of the existence of an all-seeing Deity, controlling the course of

---

[1] "Les principes se sentent: les propositions se concluent."—Pascal, *Pensées*, II. 108. Instinct, says De Maistre, is like an Asymptote to Reason, ever approaching but never invading its domain.

[2] "Num dubitas quin specimen naturæ capi debeat ex optimâ quâque naturâ?"—Cic., *Tusc. Disp.*, I. xiv. Δεῖ σκοπεῖν ἐν τοῖς κατὰ φύσιν ἔχουσι μᾶλλον τὸ φύσει καὶ μὴ ἐν τοῖς διεφθαρμένοις.—Arist., *Pol.*, I. v. 5, and *N. Eth.*, IX. ix. 8. That which is the consummation in order of time or development is the original or end respectively in the order of Nature.

[3] Mr. Herbert Spencer indeed holds that "fundamental moral intuitions have been and still are developing in our race." The abortion of this truth is to hold with Feuerbach that the Deity Himself is a creation of the human conscience; that man has made God in the likeness of man. Any way these intuitions must be regarded as facts; and, being parts of an organization, imply design. They are the "practical proofs" of Bishop Butler. On the whole question, see Comte, *Phil. Pos.*, IV. 624. Waitz, *Anthrop.*, I. 322; Tylor, *H. Pr. Cult.*, I. 384.

events, of a possible communion with Him as the aim and end of being, of a sense of duty and responsibility, of the existence, present and future, of the soul, and other similarly connected fundamental truths, are some of these. Even if originally traceable to social tendencies and social sympathies, or, which we cannot admit, to inherited experiences of *utility*,[1] accumulated and transmitted, and thus not innate but acquired, they are not for that reason less natural. Such instincts may be termed derivative;[2] but they still speak with the voice of Nature and of Nature's God, and their utterance is this. They prove that community of feeling and nature with the Divine which is denied or ignored in the philosophy of Nescience, but is of the essence of the faith of Christ ($\tau o\hat{v}\ \gamma \grave{a} \rho\ \kappa a\grave{i}\ \gamma \acute{e} \nu o\varsigma\ \dot{\epsilon} \sigma \mu \acute{\epsilon} \nu$). For Christianity, it must ever be remembered, is no mere Monotheism;[3] it is rather, as

and have the character of positive facts.

Nature of their testimony.

---

[1] Mr. Spencer says, "Moral intuitions are the results of accumulated experiences of utility. Gradually organized and inherited, they have come to be quite independent of conscious experience." See Bain, *Mental and M. S.*, p. 722.

[2] See Darwin, *Descent*, II. 395, and J. S. Mill, *Utilitarianism*, p. 45. *Exam. of Sir W. Hamilton*, p. 167. The question whether we have, given in consciousness, an *immediate* intuition of God, is not essential; we are at least conscious of truths which render the existence of God matter of inference.

[3] As a form of Monotheism, Christianity might be nothing more than the outcome of the development of our race. Thus Mr. Tylor, *Hist. Pr. C.*, II. 302, regards the religion of savages as a polytheism which culminates in the worship of one God. Humboldt in a fine passage shows that Monotheism alone is consistent with a view of the unities of Nature, of the order of the universe. "Es ist ein charakterisches Kennzeichen der Naturpoesie der Hebräer, dass als Reflex des Monothe-

it has been called, Theanthropism, the taking of the manhood into God.

Objection raised by the Evolutionists answered.

§ 11. It is a difficulty more apparent than real, that a being apprehensive and recipient of will should, if indeed it be so, be descended from progenitors without it. It is evident when we take into account the expansive force of mind and the vast differences which sever civilized from barbarous tribes, that, whatever his origin, man's capacity for improvement, or, as we should prefer to term it, renovation, is practically infinite. Nor is it easy to say where a difference of degree in respect of faculties may merge into one of kind. An illustration of this truth may be found in the long-delayed maturity of the more complex and highly endowed embryos, which yet recall, in various stages of growth and infancy, the rudimentary phases of specific evolution. If the sense of personality, of responsibility and moral consciousness be our guarantee of the soul's reality, it may afford some clue to the point of transition from animal to human existence in the higher and truer sense. Doubtless "there is a natural body, and there is a spiritual." Howbeit "that was not first which is

ismus, sie stets das Ganze des Weltalls in seiner Einheit umfasst sowohl das Erdenleben, als die leuchtenden Himmelsräume. Sie weilt seltener bei dem Einzelnen der Erscheinung, sondern erfreut sich der Anschauung grosser Massen. Man möchte sagen, dass in dem einzigen 104. Psalm das Bild des ganzen Kosmos dargelegt ist," &c. On Christianity as wholly depending on the doctrine of the Incarnation, see Dorner, *Doct. of Person of Christ*, l. 2, sub init., and Dr. Westcott in his able critique of *Comte on Christianity, Cont. Rev.*, VI. 418.

spiritual." We may have "borne the image of the heavenly." It is probably through the medium of sensation that we learn to distinguish our separate personality. Yet it is a knowledge too wonderful and excellent for the mere brute: he cannot attain to it. The moral qualities which he displays[1] are probably derived from his intercourse with man, and admit of very limited culture. So with the sense of immortality, of freedom, and responsible activity. Part of the native generic consciousness of our race, this may yet be developed slowly, partially, precariously.[2] Still the fact of such development remains with its attendant consequences; for which the same evidence exists as determines the reality of all our knowledge.

Relation of man to the animal world.

§ 12. The old familiar generalization that there is no effect without a cause[3] has been so far ex-

Admitted uniformity of the course of Nature.

---

[1] "Take an example of a dog, and mark what a generosity and courage he will put on when he finds himself maintained by a man, who to him is instead of a God or *melior natura*; which courage is manifestly such as that creature without that confidence of a better nature than his own, could never attain."—Bacon, *Essay on Atheism*. Augustine, *Civ. Dei*, XI. xxvii., remarks, "Verumtamen inest sensibus irrationalium animantium etsi scientia nullo modo, at certe quaedam scientiae similitudo."

[2] See Mr. Picton's able speculations in *New Theories and Old Faith*, Lect. II., &c. The "survival of the *fittest*," in spite of Mr. Spencer's answer to Mr. Martineau (*Cont. Rev.*, XX. 147), implies to my mind pre-arrangement and a directive Will. The benevolence of the originating Mind requires a distinct proof.

[3] Of this Leibnitz, *Théod.*, I. § 44, remarks: "Sans ce grand principe nous ne pourrions jamais prouver l'existence de Dieu." An illustration of his method will be found in his *Confessio Naturæ contra Atheistas* (*Works*, pp. 45, 46, ed. Erdmann), and *Théodicée*, I. § 7. Dieu est la première raison des choses, &c.

tended in experience as to receive the addition, and one which is itself uniform. Thus if Physical Science should ever ultimately resolve the bulk of natural facts into forces, compounds into substances, organic structures into inorganic, or inorganic into organic, vital into material, or material into vital; these forces, we may presume, will be found to be *qualified;* for else they would be incapable of differentiation. Or if ultimately resoluble into a single force, this must, so far as we can conceive, be itself *qualified,* to be what it is.[1]

> Eternal form must still divide
> The eternal soul from all beside.

Leads to the acknowledgment of a First Cause.

But as that which is itself the origin of movement to all other things, must be either self-caused, that is, can in no manner be itself an effect;[2] or must be in its operation eternal *a parte ante;* it is necessary to determine the alternative. It is not enough to say with one of its most distinguished teachers[3] that "the positive philosophy does not busy itself with the beginnings of the universe, if the universe had a beginning." Or, again, with

---

[1] "Cette idée de l'espèce qui serait inhérente au germe, c'est un principe qui dépasse toutes les données du matérialisme."—Janet, *Le Mat. Contemporain,* p. 115.

[2] Comp. Arist., *Metaph.,* XI. vi. vii.; *Phys.,* VIII.; Plato, *Phædrus* p. 245. Compare Sir W. Hamilton's argument, *Lect.* I. 60, to show that philosophy, as the knowledge of effects in their causes, tends not to a plurality of ultimate causes, but towards one. Comte views the resolution of laws or forces into unity as chimerical.

[3] Littré, *Paroles de Phil. Pos.,* p. 53.

Lect. II.] *PROGRESS OF CHRISTIANITY.* 89

one of its most distinguished critics,[1] that "the positive mode of thought is not necessarily a denial of the supernatural, since it merely throws back the question to the origin of all things. If the universe had a beginning, its beginning by the very conditions of the case was supernatural; the laws of Nature cannot account for their own origin." This, we reply, is to renounce a legitimate function of man's intelligence,[2] the "obstinate questionings of sense and outward things"; and to quench within him an ever-rising instinct of inquiry into the origin of the world of nature. His understanding and reason, no less than his moral faculties, direct him to its solution. Of the

---

[1] J. S. Mill, *A. Comte and Positivism*, p. 15.
[2]   Tentat enim dubiam mentem rationis egestas,
      Ecquaenam fuerit mundi genitalis origo.—Lucret., v. 1210.
See De Maistre, *Soirées*, Vme Entret. "Il ne dépend nullement de nous de n'y pas regarder. Il est là devant nous," &c. M. Comte, *Phil. Pos.*, IV. 669, calls it "an infantine curiosity which pretends to know the origin and end of all things." Not so Leibnitz. "Rien ne marque mieux l'imperfection d'une philosophie que la nécessité où le philosophe se trouve d'avouer qu'il se passe quelque chose suivant son système dont il n'y a aucune raison."—*Théod.*, II. § 340. "Moi, je crois qu'il y faut reconnoître des marques de la force de l'esprit humain qui le fait pénétrer dans l'intérieur des choses. Ce sont des ouvertures nouvelles et pour ainsi dire des rayons de l'aube du jour qui nous promet une lumière plus grande."—*Ib., Disc.*, § 81. Kant, though holding that no theological beliefs can be based on cosmological notions, *Prolegg.* § 44, yet finds a firm foundation in the ideas which are the offspring of Reason, such as the soul, the world, and God. Whewell, *Bridgewater Tr.*, p. 159, ed. Bohn, observes that "the same reasoning faculty which seeks for the origin of the present state of things, and is capable of assenting to, or dissenting from, the hypothesis propounded, is necessarily led to seek in the same manner for the origin of any previous state of things," &c. See also *Indications of the Creator*, p. 153.

alternatives before him, the eternity of matter is liable to many objections,[1] one only of which needs here to be noticed. While science nowhere contradicts the fact of a beginning, its absence is inconsistent and in the judgment of the highest authorities in physical philosophy incompatible with the state of our knowledge of Nature (*Werden*) as a continuous effect, and of natural agents and their mode of operation as causes. Thus astronomy, in the opinion of Professor Huxley[2] "leads us to contemplate phenomena, the very nature of which demonstrates that they must have had a beginning, and that they must have an end." "The principle of the dissipation of energy," according to another distinguished professor,[3] "as it alone is able to lead us by sure steps

The alternative of an eternity of matter

rejected by natural philosophers.

---

[1] As, for example, that it really explains nothing: æternitas quippe nullius rei causa intelligi potest.

[2] *Lay Sermons*, p. 17, probably referring to the fact of the earth's retardation in a resisting medium. Comp. Whewell, *Bridg. Tr.*, Bk. II. c. viii. Sir John Herschel, *Disc. Nat. Phil.*, § 28, says: "If we mistake not, then, the discoveries alluded to effectually destroy the idea of an *eternal, self-existent matter*, by giving to each of its atoms the essential characters at once of a manufactured article and a subordinate agent."

[3] Professor Tait, *Report of British Assoc.*, 1871. He adds, "Sir William Thomson's splendid suggestion of Vortex Atoms implies the absolute necessity of an intervention of creative power to form or to destroy one atom even of dead matter." Dr. Whewell, *Indications*, pp. 14, 17, 115, remarks, "A perpetual motion is impossible in chemistry as it is in mechanics; and a theory of constant change continued throughout infinite time is untenable when asserted upon chemical no less than upon mechanical principles." Liebig, 23 *Brief* ap. Lange, *Gesch. des Mat.*, p. 342, considers the same to be proved by physiology. Die exakte Naturforschung hat bewiesen, dass das organische Leben auf Erden einen Anfang hatte.

of deductive reasoning to the necessary future of the universe (necessary, that is, if physical laws for ever remain unchanged); so it enables us to say that the present order of things has not been evolved through infinite past time by the agency of laws now at work; but must have had a distinctive beginning, a state beyond which we are totally unable to penetrate; a state, in fact, which must have been produced by other than the now acting causes." We may dismiss, then, the theory of the eternity of matter, and with it some ancient fancies which, while admitting a creation, supposed it to be coeval with the Creator as being of His essence.[1] But if self-caused or altogether motive and yet *material*, the ultimate force in natural phenomena turns out to be wholly and inherently different from the effects for which it is required to account. It is contrary to all experience, and all our knowledge of matter, such as it is, is gained from experience.[2] Its *raison d'être*, therefore, dis-

<small>The First Cause creative</small>

---

[1] See Milman, *Lat. Christ.*, VI. 279. "Nature and Time were created together," is the truer thought of Scotus Erigena (ap. Guizot, *Civil. en France*, Lec. 28). See, however, Milman (*Ib.*, III. 244), after Haureau. Saisset indeed (*Essais*), while quoting Augustine and Leibnitz as inclining to the opinion of the eternity and infinity of the universe, remarks, "Dieu a toujours été avant les créatures sans jamais exister sans elles; parce qu'il ne les précède point par un intervalle de temps, mais par une éternité fixe."

[2] "Laws of Matter" imply a distinction between matter and form, and by consequence an original conception of matter which is metaphysical rather than physical, and involves a whole theory. With the admission that we know nothing of *physical causes* materialism properly disappears.

appears. It is opposed to that great generalization of modern science, known as the conservation of energy or persistence of force. "*A creation of power*," says Faraday,[1] "is like no other force in nature.... In no case, not even in those of the *gymnotus* or *torpedo*, is there a pure creation or a production of power without a corresponding exhaustion of something to supply it." It must then, this ultimate force or centre, or more strictly this origin of force, be other than material in character and essence. No theory of tension or pressure, or of their co-existence, is adequate to the case supposed. All motion with which we are acquainted has its commencement in some pre-existing source of power. If physical, it is itself an effect. For all experience and observation, not to rest upon principles of reason, lead us to conclude that there is no phenomenon in nature which is uncaused. But if itself a cause and immaterial, a new mode of agency is introduced into the universe. True; and it is this consideration which answers the objection that if there can be something uncaused, there is no reason to assume a cause for anything. It is one, moreover, the mode of whose operation must always remain inacces-

and immaterial,

[1] *Life*, II. p. 108. "Perpetual motion is deemed impossible, because it demands the creation of force, whereas the principle of conservation is no creation but infinite conversion." — Prof. Tyndall, *Fragments*, p. 35. Sir Isaac Newton in his *Letters to Bentley* leaves it to his readers to determine whether the agent which produces gravitation is material or immaterial.

sible to our present living powers, one which may be fitly termed *super-essential*. It answers, there-fore, the criterion laid down by modern thinkers, of "an omnipresence of something which passes comprehension."[1] The action of mind or spirit upon matter (whether properly to be considered supernatural or not) seems incapable of determination, if for no other reason, that it cannot even by reflection see itself.[2] This cannot therefore

answering to our notions of spiritual action,

> Come
> Into the eye and prospect of the soul.

One thing only can we infer respecting it in the case of the Primal Mind or Eternal Spirit. This cannot be subject to laws in the same sense as the phenomena of Nature. It must be, as the type of pure action, free in operation; and, if not indifferent but capable of motive (for motives are not necessarily "symptoms of weakness"), it must be self-determined, "a law unto itself." It seems, then, impossible to assert that there can be

prior to law and free in operation.

---

[1] Herbert Spencer, *First Princ.*, p. 45.

[2] "Modus quo corporibus adhæret spiritus comprehendi ab hominibus non potest: et hoc tamen homo est."—Augustin. *de Spir. et Anim.* "Ubi igitur aut qualis est ista mens? Ubi tua aut qualis? Potesne dicere? . . . Non valet tantum animus ut sese ipse videat. At, ut oculus, sic animus, se non videns, alia cernit."—Cic., *Tusc. Disp.*, l. xxvii. "En un mot," says Leibnitz, "que l'âme change la quantité de la force, et qu'elle change la ligne de la direction, ce sont deux choses également inexplicables." Hence his supposition of a *parallelismus inter corpus et animam*, and the several theories of a physical influx, of a Divine assistance, of occasional causes, due respectively to Thomas Aquinas, Descartes, and Malebranche.

Analogy of the human will.

nothing homologous or at the least analogous to such a mode of agency[1] in the case of human volition and moral causation. Why should it be thought a thing incredible that man should exist in the image and likeness of God, who made him?[2]

This line of proof, being from phenomena, suitable to the demands of Positivism.

§ 13. In this argument it has been sufficient to view the Divine Being as only a logical postulate in the scale of causation. I have done so, not, of course willingly, (for who, after all, can love or reverence a *probable* or even a *demonstrated* God?)

---

[1] "Sicut ab exemplari, non secundum æqualitatem."—Thom. Aq., *Sum.*, I. i., p. 93, Art. I., and see Origen, *c. Cels.*, VI. lxiii. "Il est vrai que Dieu est le seul dont l'action est pure et sans mélange de ce qu'on appelle *pâtir*: mais cela n'empêche pas que la créature n'ait part aux actions aussi, puisque l'action de la créature est une modification de la substance qui en coule naturellement, et qui renferme une variation non-seulement dans les perfections que Dieu a communiquées à la créature, mais encore dans les limitations qu'elle y apporte d'elle-même pour être ce qu'elle est."—Leibnitz, *Théod.*, Pt. I., § 32. "Causa itaque rerum quæ facit nec fit, Deus est. Aliæ vero causæ et faciunt et fiunt; sicut sunt omnes creati spiritus et maximè rationales. Corporales autem causæ, quæ magis fiunt quàm faciunt, non sunt inter causas efficientes annumerandæ: quoniam hoc possunt quod ex ipsis faciunt spirituum voluntates."—August., *Civ. D.*, V. ix.

[2] Thus is it literally true, *ubi spiritus Domini, ibi libertas* (τὸ νοερὸν καὶ αὐτεξούσιον). Cf. Delitzsch, *Biblical Psych.*, p. 84, E. T. "Man in perfection of nature being made according to the likeness of his Maker, resembleth Him also in the manner of His working: so that whatsoever we work as men, the same we do wittingly work and freely: neither are we according to the manner of natural agents so tied, but that it is in our power to leave the things we do undone."—Hooker, *Eccl. Pol.*, I. vii. 2. "God created man in His own image: to be the image of His own eternity created He man! Of eternity and self-existence what other likeness is possible, but immortality and moral self-determination?"—Coleridge, *Friend*, I. 146. See the whole passage. Comp. Hazard on *The Will*, Pt. I. "Well said Saint Chrysostom with his lips of gold, 'The true Shekinah is man.'"—Carlyle, *S. R.*, p. 44.

but because of some prevailing modes of thought which should, where possible, be encountered on common ground.[1] The original sin of Positivism is the refusal to acknowledge the idea of a true efficient cause (also a final one) to the universe, which thus emerges from nothing, and ends in nothing.[2] Though philosophy properly denies to the human mind the knowledge of an efficient or physical cause to phenomena, it cannot, as it seems to me, ignore the necessity of a First Cause; or, as a fact in nature, of the common sense of a Divine original. A double error is committed. Engrossed with the material world, the subjective portion of the universe, with its necessities and claims, is

[1] See Janet's remarks, *La Crise Philosophique*, p. 106. "No generalisation," it has been truly said, "of the phenomena of space, of time, of matter, or of force, can become a *religious* conception."—H. Spencer, *First Princ.*, p. 23. Thus Pascal argued that from number we know there is an Infinite, but *not its nature*—only it must be different from any aggregation of number. But while admitting with Dean Mansel, *Aids to Faith*, p. 25, that "mind and not matter is the truer image of God," following Kant, *Kritik*, *Werke*, II. 478-81, I cannot but think Sir W. Hamilton goes too far in his assertion that "the phenomena of matter, taken by themselves, do not warrant any inference to the existence of a God."—*Lect. on Metaph.*, I. p. 26. See some good remarks of Mr. Mill, *Exam.*, p. 491, on the danger of sacrificing successively one kind of evidence to another.

[2] See Comte, *Phil. Pos.*, IV. 388. I have already remarked (p. 65) on the inconsistency of Comtism, in that, forsaking its fundamental Materialism, it reverts to a *worship* of humanity, "le Grand Être." Comte's own words were in a manner prophetic. Speaking of those who give up Positivism after holding it, and that they pass temporarily into Pantheism, "l'esprit," he says, "retombe involontairement dans la théologie ordinaire, *la seule solide et conséquente*, parce qu'elle a été construite par des esprits d'une toute autre trempe."—Littré, p. 174.

neglected; while further in the analysis of the object itself one antecedent in causation is omitted. The connection of such a frame of thought with Pantheism is a very close one. For the essence of Pantheism lies in insisting on a *necessary coalition* of the Infinite with the finite.[1] Its precursor is the absorption of the individual in the general, of the personal in nature. Its antidote is the dogma of a creation, not, indeed, from eternity, but in time; for eternity is no attribute of the finite. In this sense only is it true to say with Carlyle, (though the expression is not altogether free from objection), that "Nature, which is the time-vesture of God, and reveals Him to the wise, hides Him from the foolish."[2] Nor can the view be admitted which is held by some leading physicists of our time, who, while rejecting materialism from their creed,[3] look upon matter (after Goethe) as

The doctrine of a creation the remedy to Pantheism.

---

[1] Hence the theories of an "Anima Mundi"—as though the world could be considered as an animal or a substance. See Leibnitz, *Works*, p. 564, ed. Erdmann. "Personality," says Feuerbach with truth, "is the antidote to Pantheism."—*Ess. of Christianity*, p. 220.

[2] *Sartor Resartus*, p. 183. What Bossuet said of Polytheism, is true of Pantheism, "Tout est Dieu: excepté Dieu même."

[3] Thus Prof. Huxley (on Yeast, *Cont. Rev.*, XIX. 36) states that "one great object of 'Protoplasm' is to show that what is called 'materialism' has no sound philosophical basis." Lange (*Gesch. des Materialismus*, p. 238) most truly remarks, "Dies ist in der That die Stellung unserer meisten heutigen 'Materialisten.' Sie sind wesentlich Skeptiker: sie glauben nicht mehr dass die Materie, wie sie unseren Sinnen erscheint, die letzte Lösung aller Räthsel der Natur enthalte: allein sie verfahren grundsatzlich als ob es so sei, und warten, bis ihnen aus den positiven Wissenschaften selbst eine Nöthigung zu anderen Annahmen entgegentritt."

an omnipresent form in which the unknown cause is manifested to us. They seem to regard it as noble only because, after all, it is incomprehensible; and are at least as ready to formulate all phenomena even of life, mind, and society, in terms of matter, motion, and force, as in any other terms.[1] A latent assumption here lurks under a professed nescience.

Faulty identification of matter with the Divine mind by present thinkers.

§ 14. It is not enough to urge that Positivism does not in its principles negate Deity or render God impossible. It seeks not to require Him. As a system it leaves no mysteries; it resolves all into laws of physical agents; it has no Heaven;[2] it professedly renounces all concern with what happens to living things after their death; or, as it is said, " at the consummation of the ages, if the ages have a consummation." It makes the attempt to divide the area of knowledge[3] into Sciences

Defects of Positivism as an explanation of phenomena,

---

[1] See Prof. Huxley, *Lay S., Lecture on Descartes.* Tyndall, *Fragm. of Thought*, p. 87. H. Spencer, *Princ. of Psych.*, I. § 63, 272. *First Princ.*, pp. 222, 280, 502. It would seem evident that if the notion of an intelligent First Cause is in abeyance, all progress and morality become at most *facts*, and are no longer *laws* of the universe.

[2] Mr. Morley, *Crit. Misc.*, p. 257, speaks of Goethe as the poet of that "new faith which is as yet without any universally recognized label; but whose Heaven is an ever closer harmony between the consciousness of man and all the natural forces of the universe, whose liturgy is culture, and whose Deity is a certain high composure of the human heart." The tendency of Positivism in declining to investigate causes, is to omit the notion of cause altogether. This reduces all forms of existence to modifications of a substance, *i.e.* to Spinozism.

[3] *Phil. Pos.*, Leçon II. and V., pp. 13, 14. G. H. Lewes, *Comte's Phil. of Sciences*, p. 41. Littré, *Paroles*, p. 33. "La philosophie Positive ne nie rien, n'affirme rien : car nier ou affirmer ce serait déclarer que l'on a

Concrete, those relative to beings or objects, and Sciences Abstract, those relative to events; that is, to the general laws and possibilities of operation. But this encyclopædic purview of the realm of knowledge will be found defective. A fact in nature, the elementary atom of a positive system, is not simply explained[1] by an enumeration of physical agents working uniformly or under fixed laws. The collocation or co-presence of those agents is a necessary condition of the result, and should form part of the definition of causation. But of this co-existence and combination of phenomena, or of the part-causes of phenomena, of the organism with its environment, no scientific account can be rendered. It is a fact unique, *sui generis*, yet undoubtedly a fact; and it is incumbent on a positive philosophy to estimate and include it. Neither atomic particles nor elemental forces can be "the joint artists of their own combinations."

[margin: and in its definition of causation,]

une connaissance quelconque de l'origine des êtres et de leur fin." "Au delà de ces deux termes, Matière et Force, la Science Positive ne connaît rien."—*Principes*, Pref., II.

[1] This is recognized by Mr. Mill, *Logic*, I. 417, 549, II. 44. "The element which is not a law of causation but a collocation of causes, cannot itself be reduced to any law . . . . . The utmost disorder is apparent in the combination of the causes, which is consistent with the most perfect order in their effects. For when each agent carries on its own operations according to an uniform law, even the most capricious combination of agencies will generate a regularity of some sort, as we see in the kaleidoscope, where any casual arrangement of coloured bits of glass produces, by the laws of reflection, a beautiful regularity in the effect." This remark, it will be observed, *assumes the uniformity* of the operation of the agencies in accounting for the order resulting in their effects.

In any co-arrangement the principle or operating cause of the combination must be taken into account.[1] The unity evident in the universe cannot be explained out of its mere component parts. So, in the sequence of events, a commencement must be sought exterior to the phenomena themselves, sufficient to account, not only for their origination, but for their order of existence. Of such a kind is our notion of Divine agency determining in whatever manner, mediately or immediately, the arrangement of physical events. But in the infinite play of consequences dependent on the variation of antecedents in time or space and admitting of endless modification, the consent of the human will may find a place.[2] Homogeneous in its ultimate independence with the operation of Divine purpose, it is yet essentially distinct in being conditioned in its exercise, subordinate,

which should include an account of the collocation of phenomena.

Its relation to Divine and human agency.

---

[1] Coleridge, *A. R.*, pp. 44, 313.

[2] "Conceive," says M. Guizot, *Civ. in Europe*, I. 197, ed. Bohn, "a great machine of which the idea resides in a single mind, and of which the different pieces are confided to different workmen who are scattered and are strangers to one another; none of them knowing the work as a whole, or the definitive and general result to which it concurs, yet each executing with intelligence and liberty by rational and voluntary acts, that of which he has the charge. So is the plan of Providence upon the world executed by the hand of mankind," &c. "Dieu fait présent à l'homme d'une image de la Divinité en lui donnant l'intelligence. Il le laisse faire en quelque façon dans son petit département; c'est là où le franc arbitre joue son jeu; l'homme y est comme un petit Dieu dans son propre monde."—Leibnitz, *Works*, p. 548. Hence the scholastic distinctions of the antecedent and consequent Will of God, of Secondary Councils, and of the First and Second Law Eternal. See Hooker, *Eccl. Pol.*, I. iii.

permissive.[1] For, under whatever theory of the freedom of the will, the original grant of such freedom must be assumed in the same manner as the primary underived properties of matter.[2]

The action of the will conditioned,

§ 15. But if such be the testimony of reason to the existence of will in man, what is the stumbling-block on the side of experience to its reception? Not the assumption that its choice is unconditioned, for no such assumption is made. The will may act under fixed laws of choice, or, as it has been happily expressed, " by confluence with the laws of nature " determining in ordinary cases an uniform result, and yet may be free to choose.[3] The part ultimately adopted in action, without being an instance of causeless or indifferent spontaneity, may be contrary to all expectation, and yet there may have been ground for expectation. The possession

---

[1] " Nec tamen ita liberum arbitrium animæ datum est, ut quodlibet eo moliens, ullam partem Divini ordinis legisque perturbet."—Augustine, *De Quant. Anim.*, c. xxxvi.

[2] " L'âme a en elle le principe de toutes ses actions et même de toutes ses passions: le même est vrai dans toutes les substances simples répandues par toute la nature."—Leibnitz, *Works*, p. 526.

[3] This is the *erreur-mère* of the paradox of Hobbes, that deliberation does not exclude necessity, for the choice itself is a necessary one. " A finite will constitutes a true beginning; but with regard to the series of motives and changes by which the free act is manifested and made effectual, the finite will gives a beginning only by coincidence with that absolute will which is at the same time Infinite Power."—Coleridge, *A. R.*, p. 204. See also Dean Mansel, *Aids to Faith*, pp. 19, 20. Sir W. Hamilton writes, " A motiveless volition is only casualism; and the free acts of an indifferent are morally and rationally as worthless as the pre-ordered passions of a determined will."

of will does not necessitate irregularity of conduct, even if considered absolutely free. A die often comes up several times running, though this does not leave the chances of the next throw other than even. Still less, if it be considered to any extent limited by laws. Yet, in most men, we find "occasional revolutionary moments," "a turn of the tide in mind and character," a power of breaking loose from the continuity of habit, which in theology has received the name of an Effectual Call.[1] The profligate man (ἑκὼν ἀέκοντί γε θυμῷ) may, all at once, cast his slough of immorality; the irresolute renounce his hesitancy, the virtuous all his old propriety of choice. Such conduct, and it is by no means unfrequent, may admit, when examined, of a so-called natural explanation. Men are always guided, it is said, by the strongest motive. Well, but what is strength when we apply the laws, or even the analogies, of matter to that which is, in its nature, spiritual?[2] It may be thus

yet exhibiting an ultimate independence.

Our ignorance of the nature of motives.

---

[1] Coleridge, *u. s.*, p. 40. It cannot be denied that we have the power of contributing indirectly at least to frame our will at any future time. "On se peut chercher de nouvelles raisons et se donner avec le temps de nouvelles dispositions; et par ce moyen on se peut encore procurer une volonté qu'on n'avoit pas, et qu'on ne pouvoit pas se donner sur-le-champ."—Leibnitz, p. 631. This fact is also relied on by Kant in his Metaphysics of Ethics.

[2] What right have we to presume that motives act on the mind, as bodies upon bodies? "Every system," says Mr. Hutton, *Essays*, I. 87, "but distorts and caricatures the moral nature of man which takes the analogies of material science into the region of the spiritual life." See the whole question as discussed by Dean Mansel, *Prolegg.*, p. 302; and Mr. Mill, *Exam.*, p. 518, who explains it as the motive strongest in

liable to explanation, or *it may not*. If it be, it will be found to involve the same assumption of moral consciousness which, whether original or derived, the result of organism, inheritance, custom, or association, makes part of the furniture of our being. Nor is it possible to believe the whole human race to be, and to have always been, in error upon such a matter. Our senses, it is true, sometimes deceive us,[1] and there may be such a thing as colour-blindness in moral perceptions. Yet we habitually follow their impressions. Fatalism, the antithesis of voluntariness, has ever been the offspring of dogma, whether in philosophy or religion. It is the resort of dialectical difficulties, not of hearty natural suggestion. It has never yet proved itself the outcome of unmixed human consciousness.

<small>Fatalism opposite to consciousness.</small>

<small>Objection to man's freedom of action drawn from the universality of laws of Nature.</small>

§ 16. There is, however, undoubtedly, a growing tendency to confound law with causation; and, by consequence, physical laws with moral causation. A law, considered as an agent, is "like an idol, nothing in the world."[2] Yet, while admitted to be

relation to pain or pleasure. But, though these be, as Locke calls them, "the hinges on which our actions turn," we know nothing as to their acting directly on the will.

[1] A topic which has accordingly formed the constant stock-in-trade of scepticism. Cf. Montaigne, *Essais*, II. c. xii.; Pascal, *Pensées*, II. 47. But in the end it is sufficiently apparent that we have ourselves to blame, having through haste and inconsideration misread the testimony of the senses. Compare Bacon, *Works*, III. 388, ed. Spedding.

[2] See some good remarks on this subject by Dr. Rigg in his Lecture on Pantheism, pp. 14, 31; and by the Duke of Argyll, *Reign of Law*,

only a mental creation, a metaphysical entity abhorred of Positivism, a generalization of relations among phenomena, it is too often made into a *theory* to explain their mode of existence. An argument is raised from the universality of laws of causation in Nature to the case of human action. But the major premiss rests upon a simple enumeration, which is incomplete till the will of man can be shown to be reducible to the general formula. Again, the generality of laws, it is acknowledged, does not imply their necessity. But the fact of such generality existing is held to be enough.[1] Hence, if statistics prove the uniformity of human action, the question of a will in man is thought practically to be given up. But the law here stands not only for what is; it becomes a synonyme for what must be. It is no longer a mode only of expressing facts; it assumes a necessity of operation.

<small>In what respects defective.</small>

p. 230. "Ainsi," writes De Maistre with much passion and fire, "nous laisserons dire les sophistes avec leurs *Lois éternelles et immuables* qui n'existent que dans leur imagination et qui ne tendent à rien moins qu'à l'extinction de toute moralité et à l'abrutissement absolu de l'espèce humain."—*Soirées*, p. 175. Leibnitz (*Works*, pp. 542, 614, &c.) constantly distinguishes between what follows *naturally* and what follows *necessarily*. Present physicists profess themselves satisfied with the former, and thus do away with the office of metaphysics. It may some day appear as unreasonable to deny human liberty on physical grounds, as it would now seem to found, like Epicurus, man's freedom in acting on the original declination of atoms. Cf. Lucret., II. 251.

[1] See Mill, *Examination*, p. 150. "A volition is a moral effect which follows the corresponding moral causes as certainly and invariably as physical effects follow their physical causes. Whether it *must* do so, I acknowledge myself to be entirely ignorant; . . . all I know is that it always *does*."

Man becomes lost in the race; the individual in the species.¹

> Tho' thou wert scattered to the wind,
> Yet is there plenty of the kind.

Thus, Law is made a Juggernaut riding forth and demanding victims on his way. But it may be said,—*Does it not always find them?* Granted: I mean the uniformity of the facts which it regulates. *[Confusion of uniformity with necessity of operation.]* But is it thus explained why this one or that should be the victims? This depends, it is replied, on *special* laws as distinct from general, with which we are not at present acquainted.² But why, we answer, should necessity of action

---

¹ Justin Martyr, *Dial. c. Tryph.*, c. i., notices this view as current in the philosophy of the time, ἀλλὰ καὶ ἡμᾶς ἐπιχειροῦσι πείθειν ὡς τοῦ μὲν σύμπαντος καὶ αὐτῶν τῶν γενῶν καὶ εἰδῶν ἐπιμελεῖται Θεός, ἐμοῦ δὲ καὶ σοῦ οὐκ ἔτι καὶ τοῦ καθ' ἕκαστα.

> So careful of the type she seems,
> So careless of the single life.

Feuerbach, *Essence of Christianity*, p. 150, E. T., catches this vital difference in Christian teaching. "Christianity cared nothing for the species, and had only the individual in its eye and mind." Compare Prof. Huxley, *Lay Sermons*, p. 158. Epicurus himself struggled hard against the doctrine of a physical necessity. Cf. ap. Diog. Laert. x. 133, 134, ἐπεὶ κρεῖττον ἦν τῷ περὶ Θεῶν μύθῳ κατακολουθεῖν ἢ τῇ τῶν φυσικῶν εἱμαρμένῃ δουλεύειν ὁ μὲν γὰρ ἐλπίδα παραιτήσεως ὑπογράφει Θεῶν διὰ τιμῆς, ἡ δὲ ἀπαραίτητον ἔχει τὴν ἀνάγκην.

² "In a given state of society, a certain number of persons must put an end to their own life. This is the general law; and the special question as to who shall commit the crime depends of course upon special laws: which, however, in their total action, must obey the large social law to which they are all subordinate."—Buckle, *H. C.*, I. 28. Mansel well points out that the uniformity represented by statistical averages is one which is observed in masses only, and not in individuals; and hence the law, if law it be, indicated is one which offers no bar to the existence of individual freedom exercised, like all human power, within limits.

(and a latent necessity is certainly assumed) be any more admissible in respect of special than of general laws? No man when he has apprehended the conditions of his being thinks of contravening them. He feels that laws, as Butler long ago pointed out, imply penalties appointed by the Author of Nature for the well-being of mankind. He turns them, then, to His own purposes through the very circumstance of their fixedness without, however, losing the conviction that he is himself responsible for what he does. But responsibility is incompatible with constraint. The facts, then, seem to be these. A large proportion of mankind, submitted to certain tests, will act in a given way and in the same way. But all do not.[1] And, what is more, in acting they are conscious that they might, and in particular cases ought, to act differently. This consciousness is itself a fact as patent as the uniformities of statistical averages, and points to something further, *i. e.* to freedom in acting. These, as facts, must first be admitted on positive grounds and then be scientifically ex-

Apparent design of natural uniformity.

---

[1] 'Tis one thing to be tempted, Escalus;
Another thing to fall.—*Measure for Measure*, act ii. sc. 1.

Inclination, that is, is not constraint: it rather implies freedom. See Harless, *System of Christian Ethics*, pp. 20, 85, E. T.; Delitzsch, *Bib. Psych.*, p. 194. "Man," said Luther (*Comm. on Gal.*), "is not two beings opposed to each other, but is like the dawn of the morning, which is neither night nor day." This is the answer to the dilemma, that motives must either determine a man to act, or influence him to determine himself to act. See Hamilton's *Reid*, p. 608.

plained.¹ If subordinated to physical laws and method, they are not thereby rendered inconsistent with every form of Christian theology.² But it is no such explanation to reply that consciousness is no faculty, only a state or condition of mind, liable to occasional error;³ occasional, indeed, for if it be held a permanent delusion, the whole human race must needs have lain in darkness until now. Yet why, it has been justly asked,⁴ are we now to unclothe our minds of that large outfit of existing thoughts, desires, hopes, and fears, which make us (and have made us) what we are? Neither, again, can we admit the fact of this inward testimony of a soul, naturally Christian, without acknowledging further its cogency and truth. It would be as easy else to disprove on the same grounds the existence of an external world, of the whole fabric of Nature, and of those very laws the extent of which is the real and sole object of contention. Even if an act of consciousness involve an operation of inference, it is one of the same

Objection based on the nature of consciousness.

Consciousness analogous to perception.

---

[1] There are some good remarks on Buckle's interpretation (I. 38) of the views of Kant upon Free Will, in Lange, *Gesch. des Materialismus*, pp. 478–81.

[2] Compare Huxley in his essay on Descartes, *Lay S.*, pp. 374, 375.

[3] Buckle (*u. s.*, I. 15), who is really following the guidance of Bayle in his strictures on the Cartesian doctrine. Leibnitz, though unwilling to rest man's independence on a sentiment, justly claims it as the result of a minute investigation of the elements of consciousness. Non enim et sentire intelligere est, et intelligere sentire est? asks Tertullian (*Anim.*, c. xviii.).

[4] J. H. Newman, *Grammar of Assent*, p. 419.

kind with perception, and no further liable than it to disproof or mistrust.

§ 17. Nor, lastly, is this view of free agency, that in the practical exercise of it we are always guided by motives, consciously or unconsciously, which yet do not necessitate conduct, "a barren proposition," incapable of translation into action.[1] To regulate the conditions of society in the most favourable manner; to teach that the individual is no mere slave of circumstances; that the knowledge of the risks of temptation entails the duty of keeping clear of unwholesome tendencies to action and of bearing ourselves firmly and manfully when submitted to them, thus "redeeming the time because the days are evil," this is a task worthy alike of the statesman and the philanthropist, and is the proper duty of the clergyman, the tutor, and the schoolmaster. A barren proposition! Then let Religion indeed cease her office and the faith of Christ its professions. What need of exhortation where there is no choice?[2] Or of atonement where there can be no sin? Or of promises which have

A conditioned will no barren proposition.

Its resulting responsibilities.

Moral results of the Materialistic or Positivist view.

---

[1] "If any one says that we have this power of acting without motives, but that in the practical exercise of the power we are always guided by motives, either conscious or unconscious — if any one says this, he asserts a barren proposition."—Buckle, I. 18, *n*. Holy Scripture, while it nowhere speaks of man as free, says everywhere that he can choose (Cf. Is. vii. 15); thus making self-determination the property of human nature. See Delitzsch, *Bibl. Psych.*, p. 192.

[2] It may, perhaps, be contended that in practice the morality of necessity does not enfeeble the claims of duty, because the Predestinarian schools have always been rigorists. This may be explained to some

no real hold in the heart or soul of man? What need to discuss the permanence of a belief which can be the fruit but of hypocrisy or ignorance? But what, on the other hand, is to be thought of a philosophy, the boasted result of science, which, extinguishing motive,[1] abolishes the reasons of action, and filches together with these the very savour of human existence; which annihilates duty, makes benevolence impossible, the enthusiasm of humanity absurd; which degrades the immortal spirit, the "blessed part" of man, to the level of Protean matter and the dominion of brute forces;[2]

extent by prudential considerations; but hardly by any logical connection. This is discussed in Merivale's *Conv. of N. Nations*, pp. 167-171.

[1] The philosophical error of Positivism is to ignore the free play of individual action as beneficial to human progress. Hence, perhaps, Comte's well-known aversion to Protestantism. This is, indeed, but one form of his disinclination to recognize Causation as open to the reach of man's faculties. The result is undoubtedly to measure all knowledge by the Laws of Phenomena. On this subject the reader is referred to Mill's *Logic*, Book III., v. § 9, and on the materialistic tendencies of Positivism to Mr. Lecky, *Hist. Rationalism*, II. p. 408, together with Mill, *A. Comte and Positiv.*, p. 15, &c. It is, indeed, denied by M. Littré, *Principes*, pp. 38, 39.

[2] "Positivism, allowing spirit no place in its system, denies immortality to man, but confers it on humanity."—Mr. A. Fairbairn on *Belief in Immortality* (*Cont. Rev.*, XX. 28). Compare Mill, *Comte and Pos.*, pp. 135, 152. Prof. Huxley, *Lay S.*, p. 191, quotes a beautiful but melancholy passage from M. Comte, attesting the unsatisfactory results of so baseless a fabric of belief as that of Positivism. "La philosophie est une tentative incessante de l'esprit humain pour arriver au repos. Mais elle se trouve incessamment aussi dérangée par les progrès continus de la science. De là vient pour le philosophe l'obligation de refaire chaque soir la synthèse de ses conceptions; et un jour viendra où l'homme raisonnable ne fera plus d'autre prière du soir."

which consecrates selfishness by enthroning it in the struggle for existence above wisdom and virtue; and which views, alike unmoved and powerless of consolation, the agonies of remorse, the isolation of bereavement, and the yearnings of the saint after communion with Divine holiness? Only if free to choose, is man capable of duty in any sense of the word which is not simply nominal but worth retaining. But, if capable of duty, he is capable of religion. He is still, though conscious of sin, nobler than the tame creatures of a dull uniformity, the ready vassals of a law they can never break. In those unreasoning creatures, devoid of abstraction, idealization, reflection, yet from which it is now the fashion to derive all the properties of man, the will is absorbed in the law.¹ "The law is their nature." In the original purity of a rational being, the uncorrupted will is one with the law of his nature. And so it will be hereafter. *Freedom of choice necessary to all practical religion.*

> Mind and soul according well,
> Shall make one music as before,
> But vaster.

If man, it has been finely said, "be no higher in his destinies than the beast or the blade of grass, it might be better to be a beast or a blade of grass *Man superior to the animals in his capability and consciousness of sin.*

---

¹ See Coleridge, *A. R.*, p. 233. The fine lines of Juvenal will be readily remembered:—

> Principio indulsit communis Conditor illis
> Tantum animas, nobis animum quoque, &c.

than a man."[1] But it is not so, brethren. The stork in the heavens may know her appointed times; the turtle, the crane, and the swallow may observe the time of their coming; and when they wing their flight may leave without remorse their unfledged young to die.[2] They run their allotted course. But man, even though he perish, though sin becomes the law of his nature, and evil clings about him like a robe, is great in the ruin of his fall. He knows why he perishes,[3] and worships, in the bitterness of his soul, the purity, the nobleness, the love which he has forfeited for himself for ever.

---

[1] Prof. Goldwin Smith, *Lectures on the Study of History*, p. 12.
[2] See Mr. Darwin, *Descent of Man*.
[3] "Quando autem melior homo et pecoribus præponendus? Quando novit quod facit."—August. *de Ord.*, II. xix.; and again, *Civ. D.*, xxii.: "Sicut cæcitas oculi vitium est, et idem ipsum indicat ad lumen videndum oculum esse creatum, ac per hoc etiam ipso vitio suo excellentius ostendit ut cæteris membris membrum capax luminis (non enim alia causa esset vitium ejus carere lumine): ita natura quæ fruebatur Deo, optimam se institutam docet etiam ipso vitio, quo ideo misera est, quia non fruitur Deo." Compare Chateaubriand, *Génie du Christ.*, I. 208. "Pourquoi le bœuf ne fait-il pas," &c. Strauss, *Leben Jesu*, II. 697, admits that while animals are but races, men have the knowledge that they are a race. Hence arises the possibility of history with all its consequences. Cf. Dorner, *Hist. Prot. Th.*, II. 370.

LECTURE III.

OBJECTIONS TO THE PROGRESS OF CHRISTIANITY CONSIDERED.

Καθόλου, ὥς φημὶ, δύο πάσης γενέσεως αἰτίας ἐχούσης, οἱ μὲν σφόδρα παλαιοὶ θεολόγοι καὶ ποιηταὶ τῇ κρείττονι μόνῃ τὸν νοῦν προσέχειν εἵλοντο, τοῦτο δὴ τὸ κοινὸν ἐπιφθεγγόμενοι πᾶσι πράγμασι.

Ζεὺς ἀρχή, Ζεὺς μέσσα, Διὸς δ' ἐκ πάντα πέλονται.

Ταῖς δ' ἀναγκαίαις καὶ φυσικαῖς οὐκ ἔτι προσῇεσαν αἰτίαις. Οἱ δὲ νεώτεροι τούτων καὶ φυσικοὶ προσαγορευόμενοι τοὐναντίον ἐκείνοις τῆς καλῆς καὶ θείας ἀποπλανηθέντες ἀρχῆς, ἐν σώμασι καὶ πάθεσι σωμάτων, πληγαῖς τε καὶ μεταβολαῖς καὶ κράσεσι τίθενται τὸ σύμπαν.—PLUTARCH, *Defect. Orac.*, c. xlviii.

LECTURE III.

"Wherefore should they say among the people,—Where is their God?"—
Joel ii. 17.

§ 1. IT would be but futile to build any argument upon the past or the future of the Faith of Christ, were the fundamental truth denied of the controlling Providence of God. As religion itself is a thing not worth contending for, when free-will in man is given up, so Christianity, devoid of a special and personal relation to the Almighty in His work of grace (which may be said to be in respect of all Pagan religions its cardinal and characteristic doctrine), is a shadow without substance.[1] It becomes, then, of the first importance to inquire on what grounds the belief in a special Providence is held to be in course of being sur-

The truth of a Divine Providence essential to the being and permanence of religion.

---

[1] "Si Dei Providentia non præsidet rebus humanis, nihil est de religione satagendum."—August., *Util. Cred.*, cxvi. "Deum nisi et esse et humanis mentibus opitulari credimus, nec quærere quidem ipsam veram religionem debemus."—*Ib.*, c. xiii. Comp. Lactant., *Instit. Div.*, VII. c. vi. See Waterland, *Discourse of Fundamentals* (*Works*, V. 80). "The theory of Providence," writes Mr. Hutton, *Essays*, I. 88, " is one which, unless harmonized with general moral and physical laws, can assuredly stand no longer; and yet it is one which has exerted so profound an influence over every Christian mind from the earliest Christian ages to our own, that to part with it would be to give up the very life of religion." " 'Point de religion sans prière' a dit ce même Voltaire. Rien de plus évident; et par une conséquence nécessaire, point de prière, point de religion."—De Maistre, *Soirées*, p. 158.

rendered; how this incredulity has arisen, whether it is a necessary consequence of the existing state of knowledge, a permanent menace to the progress of Christ's religion. That rude assaults are being made on this cardinal tenet of the faith can no longer be doubted. M. Comte[1] treats the doctrine of even a general Providence as an antique destiny under a new dress, as a metaphysical artifice, a provisional conception, a concession or compromise made to the theological spirit. "The future of the world," writes a living Positivist,[2] " will justify the faith that man can be a providence to himself in a more practical and beneficial sense than any of the various providences he created in his earlier existence." "Science," says another, " is the true providence of man. We lay no faith on a personal God, we use our own faculties." Such *dicta*, at least, suffice to mark the present stand-point of opinion and feeling in certain quarters in regard to this fundamental postulate of all practical religion.

Present assaults on this belief.

[1] "La Providence des Monothéistes n'est réellement autre chose que le destin des Polythéistes."—*Phil. Pos.*, V. 280. Elsewhere he argues that were the conceptions of theology true, prayer would be the proper means of human progress. *Ib.*, IV. 695, 700. On the views of the so-called "Secularists," cf. Dr. Farrar, *Bamp. Lect.*, p. 441.

[2] Dr. Congreve, *Prop. of New Religion*, ad fin. "Quisquis sibi Deus" is a maxim in the philosophy of Stirner. "Du moment qu'on ne laisse aucune place aux volontés surnaturelles, ni dans le monde inorganique, ni dans le monde organique, ni parmi les phénomènes cosmiques, ni parmi ceux de l'histoire, on est nécessairement des nôtres." —Littré, *Paroles de Philosophie Positive*, p. 58.

§ 2. The Epicureanism of the age, not speculative, not anticipatory, but positive and evidential, is the product, doubtless, of a vast and rapid advance in physical knowledge, which, commencing with the sixteenth century, has culminated in our own.[1] It has, in a manner, carried all before it. It has reacted on the older metaphysical modes of thought. It has produced a twofold effect. First, the conviction of the *invariability* of laws of nature has been indefinitely strengthened by each freshly-observed uniformity, and explanation of related phenomena. Next, the suspicion of the *universality* of the reign of law is heightened by each new discovery in distinct departments of science, and a method of Comparative Physics, now first rendered possible, is continually furthering this impression. It is thus deemed the central element of intellectual progress. The relation of laws of nature to general laws soon comes into question.[2] Now, though law can never be justly held, in any true sense, a medium between God and His works, yet it may, and constantly does, arrest the attention of the creature. This stopping

Rise of these opinions in the conviction of the invariability and universality of laws of nature.

Joined with an imperfect explanation of them.

[1] "Jadis la raison humaine le voyant sujet au changement alla chercher l'éternel, l'immuable par delà l'horizon et dans les archétypes. Maintenant l'éternel, l'immuable devenant notion positive, nous apparaît sous la forme des lois immanentes qui gouvernent tout."—Littré, *Principes de l'Phil. Pos.*, p. 57.

[2] See Mozley, *Bamp. Lect.*, p. 176: "The only intelligible meaning which we can assign to *general laws* is, that they are the *laws of nature*, with the addition of a particular theory of the Divine mode of conducting them; the theory, *viz.* of secondary causes."

short in the process of analyzing nature may eventuate in different directions, in Naturalism, in Materialism, in Pantheism, in virtual Atheism.[1] For, if the present control of Divine agency be disallowed, what remains but a practical negation of belief, or total incredulity?

Physical studies not irreligious. § 3. It is not, of course, intended to imply that physical studies are in themselves atheistic or irreligious. The reverse would be nearer the truth. *Religio ascensio mentis in Deum per scalas creatarum rerum* should still be the proud motto of Natural Science.[2] There is no proper reason why supernaturalism should not do full justice to nature; none why nature should not do justice to supernaturalism.[3] Too much, indeed, of what has

---

[1] On the history of the term Naturalism, and its relation to a system of Rationalism, see H. J. Rose, on *State of Protestantism in Germany*, pp. 19-23. Wegscheider (*Inst. Theol.*, p. 32) holds it to consist in deriving all effects in nature from a necessity, as it were, of nature alone without regard to Divine Providence, rejecting, therefore, all efficacy of God in imparting religious knowledge to men, together with Revelation of all kinds. Dr. Farrar, in his truly learned lectures on the *Critical Hist. of Free Thought*, pp. 478, 587, notices the twofold employment of the term, and remarks that Positivism only differs from Naturalism in expressing a particular theory concerning the limits and method of science, as well as a disbelief in the supernatural.

[2] Compare Bacon, *Works*, III. 357, ed. Spedding. The dangers of *exclusive* physical study are pointed out by Sir W. Hamilton in his *Lectures*, I. p. 35 ff.

[3] Nature, the world of phenomena, being itself a totality of effects, can determine nothing as to ulterior causes. Yet, as Mr. Hutton has finely observed, "Men are haunted with the phantom of a power they dare not challenge, which is rumoured to have superseded and exposed natural theology, and to be gradually withdrawing every fold of mystery from the universe without disclosing any trace of God."—*Essays*, I. 45.

been termed Agnosticism or Nescience, and by its detractors Antitheism, has been developed among leading physicists of the day.[1] A know-nothing system of philosophy is cheap ware, and easily offered for acceptance. It can hardly, however, be held to amount to a denial of preternatural facts, and by inference of truths of Revelation. The sphere of our belief may well be more extensive than the sphere of our knowledge. An honest effort is, doubtless, being made by many minds to couple with the operation of general laws a religious sense of the Divine agency. Passages in older and unsuspected writers are eagerly seized which seem to reconcile remote causation with the Being and Providence of God.[2] This is not, of course, the whole, or strictly the real question. Doubtless there is nothing essentially contradictory or mutually exclusive in the notions of Natural law and Divine superintendence. So Spinoza argued that Providence is best elicited, from the

Temptations to a system of nescience.

Providence not incompatible with fatalism.

---

[1] Compare Mr. Hutton, *u. s.*, p. 27; and Prof. Tyndall, *Fragments of Thought*, pp. 93, 105, 442; Huxley, *L. S.*, p. 20: "If the religion of the present differs from that of the past, it is because the theology of the present has become more scientific than that of the past, because it has renounced idols of wood and idols of stone; but begins to see the necessity of breaking in pieces the idols built up of books and traditions and fine-spun ecclesiastical cobwebs, and of cherishing the noblest and most human of man's emotions by worship, 'for the most part of the silent sort,' at the altar of the Unknown and Unknowable."

[2] See Mr. Lecky's remarks, *H. Rat.*, 1. 195, on the advancing *rapprochement* between writers of the evidential school and the supporters of the inviolability of natural laws. Compare Whewell, *B. Tr.*, p. 312, &c.

fact of an eternal and changeless order of Nature.[1] So, if the ideas of individual freedom of action in man, or of casual irregularity in physical events, be gradually thrust out from the cycle of tenable theorems and accepted beliefs, the result, however much to be regretted, might not be inconsistent with the truth of a Divine Creator, and, in a modified sense, of a Divine Providence.[2] It might, indeed, seem strange that the world should turn out to be a puppet-show, devoid of real life or originality. But it will be answered that we are concerned only to ascertain the truth of things, and not with the issues involved in them. We are recalled, then, to the prior question, whether it be a fact that the realm of Law is co-extensive, as far as appears, with the universe of matter and of mind.

A prior question arises as to the real nature of physical laws, whether objective or subjective only.

Is Law a necessity, or, at least, an invariable accompaniment of the Divine agency, so far as it is known to us? Is it, indeed, a constant course of procedure, a necessary stage in an unknown order

[1] Præterea cœli rationes ordine certo
Et varia annorum cernebant tempora verti :
Nec poterant quibus id fieret cognoscere causis.
Ergo perfugium sibi habebant, omnia Divis
Tradere et illorum nutu facere omnia flecti.
                                    Lucret., V. 1182.

[2] "The natural generation and process of all things receiveth order of proceeding from the settled stability of Divine understanding. This appointeth unto them their kinds of working; the disposition, whereof in the purity of God's own knowledge and will, is rightly termed by the name of Providence. The same being referred unto the things themselves here disposed by it, was wont by the ancient to be called natural destiny."—Hooker, *E. P.*, I. iii. 4.

of the universe? Or is it, on the other hand, anything more than a mode of human thought,[1] (for this also has been held respecting it), analogous to Time and Space, conditions regulative of all perception of phenomena, yet in a manner unessential, relative, not absolute, the elimination of which is not beyond conception? Is law more than an act of the mind,[2] a description of its state of expectation in respect of any event? Is it capable of manifestation to aught but the spirit and intelligence of man? Can the order of the material universe be shown to be other than the complement of the human understanding? Does not the

---

[1] "Long, indeed, will man strive to satisfy the inward querist with the phrase, Laws of Nature. But though the individual may rest content with the seemly metaphor, the race cannot."—Coleridge, *Friend*, III. 199. "Thought, involving simply the establishment of *relations*, may be readily conceived to go on, while yet these relations have not been organized into the abstracts we call Space and Time; and so there is a conceivable kind of consciousness which does not contain the truths commonly called *a priori*, involved in the organization of these forms of relations."—H. Spencer, *First Pr.*, p. 258.

[2] The forms in nature which we denominate laws, how do they become ideas in the mind? Only it would seem by a faculty of generalization due to the higher Reason. See Arist., *Anal. Post.*, II. xiv. The facts are objective: "Toute réalité," says Leibnitz, "doit être fondée dans quelque chose d'existant;" but it is the mind which invests them with generality. "What we call a general law is, in truth, a form of expression including a number of facts of like kind. The facts are separate; the unity of view by which we associate them, the character of generality and of law, resides in those relations which are the object of the intellect."—Whewell, *B. T.*, p. 259. See Sir W. Hamilton, *Lect.*, III. 78, and Ueberweg's *Logic*, §§ 38–44, who, however, does not escape from the circle of employing mathematical, *i.e.* objective, conceptions, which are themselves only guaranteed by our *inner experience*.

course of the revelation of law to the mind of man follow the very law or constitution of his mind? Again, the impossibility of all creation might be argued from the eternity of God, if this attribute were indeed other than the negation of the conditions of Time in the case of an Infinite Being.[1] Is the case different in respect of Law as a mode of Divine operation? When it gives rise to similar perplexities, is it to be held incompatible with the notion of Providential action?

In what sense is law a mode of Divine operation.

§ 4. Neither can it be assumed, unless rhetorically,[2] that at present the reign of Law is as wide as the world in which we live. Many an ample demesne of thought and feeling, of social action, nay, of physical processes, is as yet but partially explored, and remains debateable land. M. Comte, in fact, holds that many phenomena will never be brought within the range of definite laws, because each science, as it increases in complexity, admits also of greater variations.[3] This is, in effect, to repeat the axiom of Bacon, that "the subtilty of

The universality of law not yet established.

---

[1] ταῦτα δὲ πάντα μέρη χρόνου, καὶ τό τ' ἦν τό τ' ἔσται, χρόνου γεγονότα εἴδη, ἃ δὴ φέροντες λανθάνομεν ἐπὶ τὴν ἀΐδιον οὐσίαν οὐκ ὀρθῶς.—Plato, *Timæus*, 37, E. Cf. August., *Serm. ad Catech.*, c. viii.: "Natus est ante omnia tempora; natus ante omnia sæcula. Natus ante; ante quid, ubi non est ante?" &c. There was an old view (Id., *Civ. D.*, XI. iv.) that the world was eternal not *in time*, but in respect of *its creation*. This savoured too much of a saving clause.

[2] "Nothing is that errs from law."—Tennyson. See on this subject the Duke of Argyll, *Reign of Law*, p. 53, and Mozley, *B. L.*, p. 325, and some fine remarks of Dr. Chalmers, *Works*, VII. 204.

[3] See also Littré, *Paroles de la Phil. Pos.*, p. 17.

nature far surpasses the subtilty of the mind of man." Let it, however, be conceded that there is good prospect of their yielding sooner or later to the advance of scientific uniformity. Certainly many effects in nature which have seemed irregular, precarious, lawless, have bowed to the force of inductive analysis and suggestive analogies, until generalization has prevailed in these also, and they have taken their place beside the earlier triumphs of scientific inference. Thus has arisen yet is very generally that habitual recognition of the notion of Law assumed, which, as has been truly said, is a distinguishing characteristic of modern from ancient thought.[1] It may also be conceded that the Divine Mind, if conceived as projecting its fiat upon natural agents in the form of universal laws, must likewise be apprehended as adequate to sustain them through any limits of time and space. The hand which has so moulded can, and, indeed, must equally uphold them, and enforce their operation.[2] Let us, then, strive to estimate the result of the

[1] Herbert Spencer, *First Principles*, p. 142. Yet an apprehension of laws of nature is undoubtedly very ancient—lying at the foundations of Greek philosophy and poetry. Comp. Soph., *Œd. T.*, 865. *Antig.*, 455. It had also sunk deep into the Hebrew mind and heart. Cf. Ps. 148, 6. Jer. v. 22; xiii. 23. Eccles. i. 4–7.

[2] "La conservation de Dieu consiste dans cette influence immédiate, perpétuelle, que la dépendance des créatures demande. Cette dépendance a lieu à l'égard non-seulement de la substance, mais encore de l'action ; et on ne saurait peut-être l'expliquer mieux qu'en disant avec le commun des théologiens et des philosophes, que c'est une création continuée."—Leibnitz, *Works*, p. 512.

state of things supposed. When the physical antecedents of all events shall have been assigned, the tendencies of human nature mapped out and ascertained, will the sum of man's knowledge have been reached, and with it the limits of his belief? Shall we then "know even as we are known"?

and viewed as the term of knowledge.

§ 5. The attainment of a clear conception of law is by some [1] regarded as the highest point attainable by the human understanding. "The sum of all education," says Professor Huxley,[2] "is the instruction of the intellect in the laws of nature." I do not stay to remark upon the narrowness of such a view of human nature, when we take into account its moral and spiritual capacities; nor again, on its logical insufficiency without some postulate as to the origin and nature of things. But does it correspond, so far as it reaches, with the teaching conveyed by the facts of the external world? Is there no region suggested to us in experience above the level of material causes?

Facts, however, suggest a further analysis.

—no law higher than the subsidiary laws which bind particular forces? Is there no element, no

---

[1] Buckle, *Hist. Civ.*, II. 343. "La méthode objective ou expérience ne parvient qu'à des lois, c'est son suprême effet, rendant de plus en plus impersonnelle l'idée de Providence il va se perdre d'une façon plus ou moins confuse dans l'immanence des lois qui régissent les choses."— Littré, *Paroles*, p. 18.

[2] *Lay Sermons*, p. 36. See also the magnificent passage commencing, "That man, I think, has had a liberal education," &c. It altogether omits any *spiritual* element in man. Compare Dr. Westcott's remarks in *Cont. Review*, VIII. 378.

"law within the law," required to account for the co-adjustment of phenomena? It is such an element, if any, which, satisfying this unknown yet necessary coefficient, answers to the notion of Providence, to the movement of a Supreme Free Agent,[1] of One who is not content to reign and not to govern. The distinction very commonly made between a general and a special Providence may prove in some respects misleading. If general without being special, it is to the individual soul no Providence at all. While from a scientific point of view,[2] the intercalation of an adjustment of relations between agent and effect, is as necessary for each single event as for any general law of uniform results arising out of the repetition of

A distinction made between general and special Providence.

---

[1] "Is there above the level of material causes a region of Providence? If there is, Nature there is moved by the Supreme Free Agent, and of such a realm a miracle is the natural production."—Mozley, *Bamp. Lect.*, p. 164. Compare also Prof. Goldwin Smith (*Lect.*, II. 47): "This God, Who is to reign over His own world on condition that He does not govern it, what is He—the Supreme Law of Nature?" &c. In his *Address at Liverpool*, p. 22, Mr. Gladstone writes: "On the ground of what is termed evolution, God is relieved of the labour of creation; in the name of unchangeable laws, He is discharged from governing the world."

[2] Leibnitz very justly warns that "il faut considérer aussi que l'action de Dieu conservant doit avoir du rapport à ce qui est conservé, tel qu'il est, et selon l'état où il est : ainsi elle ne sauroit être générale ou indéterminée. Ces généralités sont des abstractions qui ne se trouvent point dans la vérité des choses singulières."—*Works*, p. 511. "The Laws of Nature are the laws which the Divine Being in His wisdom prescribes to His own acts. His universal presence is the necessary condition of any course of events; His universal agency the only origin of any efficient force."—Whewell, *B. T.*, p. 311. "Je ne demande ni les aïeules, ni les trisaïeules du phénomène; je me contente de sa mère."—De Maistre, *Soirées*, p. 190.

Insufficient. individual instances. That is to say, the notion of general laws does not supersede a particular Providence. Ridicule has, indeed, been sometimes cast upon what has been contemptuously called "a carpenter theory" of creation, upon the notion of "a clock-making divinity," who is always interfering to carry out the plans of his own administration. Why, it is said, should not all this have been provided for by a single original act through the medium of general laws? Perhaps this may, *Misleading.* after all, have been so. But who shall apply absolutely to the Infinite Mind[1] (when we know so little of our own), notions drawn solely from human experience, and limited by human imper- *Inapplicable to our notions of the Divine Being.* fection; or distinguish in such a case to little purpose between an eternal ordinance and the individual application of it? To Him there can be no measure of time,[2] but as an eternal present; (which, to speak exactly, forms no part of time); incompatible alike with human modes of thought or with secular succession.[3]

[1] See Comte, *Phil. Pos.*, IV. 664, with the quotation from Père Malebranche.

[2] "M. Bayle sait fort bien que l'entendement Divin n'a point besoin de temps, pour voir la liaison des choses. Tous les raisonnements sont éminemment en Dieu, et ils gardent un ordre entre eux dans son entendement aussi bien que dans le nôtre; mais chez Lui ce n'est qu'un ordre et une priorité de nature, au lieu que chez nous il y a une priorité de temps."—Leibnitz, *Théod.*, p. 563.

[3] "Mentis quippe aspectu omnem mutabilitatem ab æternitate sejungo et in ipsâ æternitate nulla spatia temporis cerno. Quia spatia temporis præteritis et futuris rerum motibus constant. Nihil autem præterit in æterno et nihil futurum est, quia et quod præterit esse desinit, et quod

§ 6. The presence in time and place of surrounding phenomena, their relations accordingly to man's action as objects of desire, or as conditions in whatever manner of his conduct, and of the consequences of his conduct; these constitute the field of Providential operation,[1] and lie beyond the compass of any known Law. This is the work in time of the Eternal Spirit. "I have seen," writes the Preacher, "the travail which God hath given to the sons of men to be exercised in it. He hath made everything beautiful in his time: also He hath set the world in their heart, so that no man can find out the work that God maketh from the beginning to the end."[2] What is temptation but the presence or possibility under given circumstances of a presumed object of desire? The desire is uniform, the opportunity of its operation contingent and variable. What, again, is the lesson of

The area of providential operation.

futurum est nondum esse cœpit; æternitas autem tantummodo est, nec fuit quasi jam non sit, nec erit quasi adhuc non sit. Quare sola ipsa verissime dicere potuit humanæ menti—Ego sum qui sum—et de illâ verissime dici potuit—Misit me, qui est."—Augustin. *de Ver. Rel.*, c. xlix. ὁ χρόνος οὐ δοκεῖ συγκεῖσθαι ἐκ τῶν νῦν.—Arist., *Phys.*, IV. x. τὸ δὲ νῦν ἐστι συνέχεια χρόνου.—c. xiv. See Leibnitz, *Works*, p. 615. Compare Dr. Mozley, *B. L.*, p. 157.

[1] "Conditrix ac moderatrix temporum Divina Providentia."—Augustin. "Ainsi le tout revient souvent aux circonstances, qui font une partie de l'enchaînement des choses."—Leibnitz, *Théod.*, p. 530. καιρὸς πάντων γνώμας ἴσχει.—Soph., *Philoct.*, 837. There is a singular passage in Legge's *Confucius* (§ 100) to the same effect: "How does Heaven speak? The four seasons have their course. The hundred things, what speaks He? No; Heaven speaks not: by the course of events He makes Himself understood; no more."

[2] Eccles. iii. 10, 11.

Observable in the course of affairs.

human affairs if not the need of energy, genius, originality, of thought, of moral force; in one word, of individual character; in necessary correspondence, however, with the surrounding circumstances, in order to secure large and lasting consequences?[1]

> Such souls, 'tis true, but peep out once an age,
> Dull sullen prisoners in the body's cage.

For, however superior their powers, they must confessedly be in harmony and relation with their times.[2] Their very greatness, some would hold, comes of their temperament, and that temperament is the result of many antecedents. Mental as well as physical attributes may be transmissible by inheritance;[3] and a "creational law" may be imagined to explain their commencement.[4] Some

---

[1] "The laws," says Bp. Butler, "by which persons born into the world at such a time and place are of such capacities, geniuses, tempers .... are so wholly unknown to us, that we call the events which come to pass by them accidental; though all reasonable men know certainly that there cannot in reality be any such thing as chance."— *Anal.*, II. c. iv. Comp. Augustin., *Civ. D.*, IV. xxxiii. : "Neque hoc temerè ; . . sed pro rerum ordine ac temporum occulto nobis, notissimo sibi ; cui tamen ordini temporum non subditus servit, sed cum Ipse tanquam dominus regit moderatorque disponit." φορὰ γὰρ τίς ἐστιν ἐν τοῖς γένεσιν ἀνδρῶν, ὥσπερ ἐν τοῖς κατὰ τὰς χώρας γιγνομένοις.—Arist., *Rhet.*, II. xv. ; and *Pol.*, V. xii. 8.

[2] Guizot has some just remarks on this subject, *Civ. en France, Lec.* xx.: "The activity of a great man is of two kinds. First, he understands better than others the wants of his time; its real, present exigencies," &c.

[3] See Comte, *Phil. Pos.*, IV. 373, 397.

[4] Comp. Dr. Mozley, *B. L.*, p. 319. Mr. Herbert Spencer, *First Pr.*, p. 123. "These superior powers of reason or fancy," says Gibbon, c. xxxviii., "are rare and spontaneous productions." "Est casus aliquis," says Bacon, "non minus in cogitationibus humanis quam in operibus et factis."—*N. O.*, Aph. cxxii.

would persuade us to believe that with all their capacities, and aspirations, and beliefs, they are still no accident indeed, yet a *product* of their time. But what shall account for the harmony of the given antecedents; for their coincidence and correspondence; for the melody[1] which pervades their combination; for the co-proportions and correlations, for the co-existence and co-ordination of these births of Time? *In the correspondence of occasion and antecedent,*

Non hæc sine numine Divûm
Eveniunt.

Do they not of themselves call for the notion of Divine superintendence and of absolute appointment, even if the expression of interposition be objected to? The method of Nature, even in physical matters, is nowhere the predominance of any single principle, but the joint-presence and self-correcting union of several.[2] We ask not for a world governed by isolated acts of special intervention, of perpetual and arbitrary interference, *and combination of agencies.*

---

[1] " Dieu est tout ordre : il garde toujours la justice des proportions : il fait l'harmonie universelle."—Leibnitz, *Théod.* In *Ver. Rel.*, c. xxii., Augustine works out at length the metaphor of a harmony or strain pervading the administration of the world. Cf. *Prom. V.*, 556, ὁπότε τὰν Διὸς ἁρμονίαν θνατῶν παρεξίασι βουλαί.

When these prodigies
Do so conjointly meet, let not men say
' These are their reasons, they are natural.'
Julius Cæsar.

This argument is carried out by means of an example very ably in *Dialogues on Divine Providence*, p. 111.

[2] " Is not the universe pervaded by an omnipresent antagonism, a fundamental conjunction of contraries, everywhere opposite, nowhere independent?"—Whewell, *Nov. Org. Renov.*, p. 270.

irreconcilable with general laws, and turning history, as has been aptly said, into an almanac. We acknowledge the results of that power of abstraction in the mind of man, which, growing with education, terminates in annihilating all personification of phenomena, and closes what has been called "the mythical period of history."[1] But, on the other side, this view of life and being, which sees in all things the present controlling hand of God, cannot be charged with being incapable of proof. It rests upon and is an illustration of the Method of Residues, so well known in the Logic of Induction.[2] For it represents an element of causation, a surplus of unassigned effect, which survives all analysis or explanation of natural events. But if the element thus indicated enters as a necessary antecedent into a scientific account of things, being one which, though not itself otherwise determinable, is an uniform condition of phenomena; who shall set limits to its operation, or regard any the smallest event as beyond the providential arrangement of the Almighty? True, the natural here merges in the supernatural; a special providence, it has been rightly said, is an invisible miracle; it is of the same order as the miracle of creation.[3]

An element scientifically admissible.

The border line of the natural and supernatural.

---

[1] See Mr. Lecky, *Hist. Eur. Mor.*, I. 375.

[2] See Mill's *Logic*, III. viii. 5; Herschel's *Discourse*, § 158; and Mr. Fowler's singularly clear treatise on *Inductive Logic*, p. 163.

[3] The very preservation of the universe being a continued creation. See Leibnitz, *Works*, pp. 152, 615. "Dieu n'agit que par des lois générales. Je l'accorde; mais à mon avis cela ne suffit pas pour lever les miracles:

But it is not the less real for being miraculous; nor the less miraculous because through simple repetition we cease to see it to be so. "Circumstances," it has been profoundly said,[1] "traced back to their first origins, may be the outcome of strictly miraculous intervention. But the miraculous intervention addresses us at this day in the guise of those circumstances. There is no law of their coincidence, though coincidences rise out of a combination of general laws. They have a character of their own, and seem left by Providence in His own hands, as the channel by which, inscrutable to us, He may make known to us His will." Nor must it be forgotten that we are dealing not only with general laws which may be considered as unvarying in their operation, but with their application to particular circumstances. These may be so arranged as to effect of themselves the greatest amount of good in each individual case. But among these we are entitled to include the decisions of the human will which may or may not co-operate with the arrangements of Eternal Wisdom. In this manner it is true that " all

Application of general laws to individuals.

si Dieu en faisoit continuellement, ils ne laisseroient pas d'être des miracles, en prenant ce mot non pas populairement pour une chose rare et merveilleuse, mais philosophiquement pour ce qui passe les forces des créatures."

[1] J. H. Newman, *Gramm. of Assent*, pp. 422, 424. Comp. Eurip. *Hec.*, l. 958:

φύρουσι δ' αὐτὰ θεοὶ πάλιν τε καὶ πρόσω,
ταραγμὸν ἐντιθέντες, ὡς ἀγνωσίᾳ
σέβωμεν αὐτούς.

things work together for good to those that love God," who ponder the direction of His providence, and leave room for the suggestions of His grace.[1]

<small>Science predictive only of tendencies.</small>

§ 7. On no other supposition does it seem possible to reconcile the apparent fortuity of human affairs[2] with their admitted regularity, and with the observed uniformity of Nature. It is the boasted test of Science to be predictive;[3] to foretell consequences with unerring exactness. Yet, of what is it really predictive? Of tendencies; not of positive results, nor of particular events; but rather that these will take place under given circumstances, *i. e.* under *identical* circumstances. Experience, that is, custom, leads us to expect a repetition of the circumstances. Yet, the *variety* of Nature is as wonderful as is her uniformity: and

<small>Variety and irregularity observable in Nature.</small>

it is a well-known principle in physics that no two individual products agree exactly in all respects.

> No compound of this earthly ball
> Is like another all in all.

Now, this evident irregularity in the case of

---

[1] As to the bearings of a doctrine of Providence upon the practice of prayer Leibnitz shrewdly observes, "Dans le fond, les hommes se contenteront d'être exaucés, sans se mettre en peine si le cours de la Nature est changé en leur faveur ou non. Et s'ils sont aidés par le secours des bons Anges, il n'y aura point de changement dans l'ordre général des choses."—*Remarques sur le livre de M. King* (*Works*, p. 651).

[2] See Isaac Taylor on *Enthusiasm*, p. 129: "But there is a higher government of men," &c. He is needlessly criticised by Mr. Greg, *Creed of Christendom*. See also Mr. Hutton, *Essays*, I. 42: "And this instinctive conviction," &c.

[3] Comp. Whewell, *Phil. Ind. Sc.*, I. xxxix., *Nov. Org. Ren.*, II. v. 10; Comte, *Phil. Pos.*, I. 62; II. 28, 401, 426; III. 10, 304, 407-13; and Mr. Fowler's remarks, *Ind. Logic*, p. 112.

human affairs,[1] is attributed (not indeed very consistently) by thinkers of the Positive school, to special but undiscovered laws, or to the acknowledged intricacy of the antecedents masking the essential relations of the phenomena, to the plurality and composition of causes, to the intermixture of effects, and the like; which is, in fact, no explanation at all. Yet there is surely point in the sarcasm of Pascal,[2] that had the nose of Cleopatra been shorter, the whole face likewise of the world's history might have been changed. Or, again, that a grain of gravel in the person of a Cromwell, sufficed to give peace to a Continent, restoration to a dynasty, and tranquillity to the alarms of Rome. "Accidents of personal character," writes Hallam,[3] "have more to do with the revolutions of nations than either philosophical historians or democratic politicians like to admit." No cycle, indeed, in human affairs,[4] no theory of "social

Importance of personal character.

[1] Mr. Buckle, *Hist. Civ.*, III. 479, observes with some asperity, "Science has not yet explained the phenomena of history. Consequently the theological spirit lays hold of them, and presses them into her own service."

[2] *Pensées*, xix. 7: "Le nez de Cléopâtre, s'il eût été plus court, toute la face de la terre aurait changé." xx. 8: "Cromwell allait ravager toute la Chrétienté," &c.

[3] *Middle Ages*, I. 132: "It is almost appalling," remarks Dean Church (*Univ. Serm.*), "to watch how some vast change in human affairs has hung upon the apparent accident of a stronger or weaker character."

[4] Magnus ab integro sæclorum nascitur ordo. Φασὶ κύκλον εἶναι τὰ ἀνθρώπινα πράγματα.—Arist., *Phys.*, IV. xiv. See Mill's *Logic*, I. 420 (1st ed.). The theory of Vico is well known. Compare Augustin., *Civ. D.*, XII. xi. xiii., and Origen, *c. Cels.*, IV. lxvii.

rhythm," "equilibration," or "recurring oscillation" will solve this mighty mystery; though history, like a circulating decimal of many figures, "should periodically repeat itself," and things revolve in an eternal round. The problem is one into which too many factors enter.[1] There is, indeed, an error which has too often brought contempt on the acknowledgment of a special Providence; which lies in the monopolizing and appropriation of it.[2] In this way

Error of assumption as to the course of Providence.

> Men may construe things after their fashion
> Clean *from* the purpose of the things themselves.

To leave, however, the existence of a controlling Providence an open question subverts the conditions necessary to constitute a religion. But, if the entrance of a supernatural element into the course of human affairs be, indeed, requisite for any really philosophical explanation of them, the incompatibility of general Laws with the wants of the religious sentiment can no longer be urged. The

---

[1] "History," it has been cleverly said, "like the dial of a clock, presents results, but conceals the machinery producing them."

[2] "Historia Nemeseos sanè in calamos nonnullorum piorum virorum incidit: sed non *sine partium studio*."—Bacon, *Augm. Sc* , II. xi. "To him," says Montaigne, *Ess.*, I. xxv., "who feels the hailstones patter about his ears, the whole hemisphere appears to be in a storm." There is a French saying, "La providence des chats n'est pas la même avec la providence des souris." On this subject Mr. Buckle, *Hist. Civ.*, III. 195, has some caustic remarks. Elsewhere (I. 19, n.) he gratuitously confounds the doctrine of Providential interference with that of Predestination. See some just reflections of Mr. Lecky, *Hist. E. M.*, I. 381, and some noble thoughts of Prof. Goldwin Smith (*Study of Hist.*, Lect. I. 31).

"kingdoms of the world" may still "become the kingdom of the Lord and of His Christ"; and this in virtue of an operation determined by no such laws of time as to compel the inference that it was not so fixed from eternity, or is not so arranged at any given moment by an immediate and ever-present disposition.[1]

§ 8. One of the acutest thinkers of our time, who has passed away not many months since, justly lamented, has contended for the special interposition of God by the side of general Laws, on the ground that both are alike conditions of human thought, seeing that we cannot think the general without the special.[2] At present I would dwell rather on the objective side of experience. The importance of distinguishing between the causes and the occasions of events has often been observed.[3]

This conclusion drawn from experience.

---

[1] "Le présent," finely remarks Leibnitz (*Works*, p. 608), "est gros de l'avenir;" or as Schiller puts it, "Im Heute wandelt schon das Morgen." It is an error, however, to assume the *determining* causes of events to be *necessary* in any case where a counter result is conceivable. The will of God is not incompatible either with contingency in things or liberty in the creature. The main argument of this work, however, does not proceed on any forced or fanciful application of special acts of Providence. Christianity is the concurrent result of preceding events and precedent conditions. As such it is a fact in man's history, which goes for much, and implies further consequences in the undoubted pre-arrangement of God.

[2] Dean Mansel, *Bampton Lect.*, p. 193.

[3] Polyb., III. vi. 6, ἀρχὴ τί διαφέρει καὶ πόσον διέστηκεν αἰτίας καὶ προφάσεως. Hence Aristotle's distinction of Poetry from History: τούτῳ διαφέρει, τῷ τὸν μὲν τὰ γενόμενα λέγειν, τὸν δε' οἷα ἂν γένοιτο. Διὸ καὶ φιλοσοφώτερον καὶ σπουδαιότερον ποίησις ἱστορίας ἐστίν.— *Poet.*, c. ix.; a thought expanded by Bacon in *Augm. Sc.*, II. xiii. Hence

The former, rightly deemed the "eternal lessons of History," are occupied with the tendencies, rather than the occurrences of the time: while occasions, exhibiting principles in the garb of events, constitute the web, and not the warp, of human affairs.

<small>The laws distinct from the occasions of events.</small>

But though the effect be proportioned to the cause, and the motor ideas of an age are relative to its position in the course of human progress, (thus, it may be admitted, Bacon and Descartes would have been powerless in the seventh or the tenth century); yet the circumstances which attend their announcement may be favourable or unfavourable, and admit of no uniform analysis. But they are not therefore to be left out of account. Hence, Mr. Mill,[1] (no mean authority), holds the author of the 'History of Civilization in England' to be in error, when "he attributes all to general causes without imagining that casual circumstances, the acts of governments, the thoughts of men of

---

also his conception (*Ib.*, II. viii.) of an Universal History. So Johnson remarked that Shakspeare's characters "are mostly species, not individuals." See Hallam, *M. A.*, I. 66, and Mr. Buckle, *Hist. Civ.*, II. 317, 324, who cites Montesquieu and adds, "the real history of the human race is the history of tendencies, which are perceived by the mind, and not of events which are discerned by the senses." Mr. Pattison remarks, with his usual discrimination, that Mr. Buckle, having begun with defining history as an inquiry into the laws of events, proceeds to a mere narration. Comte, if I remember rightly, somewhere proposes to write a history, without names of individuals, or even of nations. See *Phil. Pos.*, V. 22, 268. He thus delineates the respective destinies of Athens, Rome, Carthage, and even of Christianity itself.

[1] *A. Comte and Positivism*, p. 114.

genius, materially accelerate or retard human progress." Such incredulity gives rise to an opposite exaggeration, when it is maintained that "the history of the world is but the biography of great men."[1] This is, indeed, not to be able to "see the forest for the trees." Doubtless, there have been turning-points in the world's story. At Marathon, at Metaurus, at Tours, the worship of Ormuzd, of Bel, of Mahomet trembled in the scale. Victory hung upon the standards of the strongest, if not the biggest battalions, or on those which were most ably led, or on both combined. Yet, how is it that it has passed into a proverb that "the race is not always to the swift, the battle to the strong: but time and chance happeneth unto all"?[2] It is not then "gratuitous" to assert a Providential element in history; for it has a real ground in experience. Facts suggest it to a serious mind; and though in ruder times this element has had too large scope assigned it, this only warns us to confine it within due limits. There is at present

Appeal to history.

---

[1] Carlyle, *Hero Worship*; though Guizot rightly reckons them as a separate element in the history of civilization. *Civ. en E.*, I. 56: "No one can say why a great man appears at a certain epoch, and what he adds to the development of the world. That is a secret of Providence: but the fact is not therefore less certain." "The riddle of fortune or circumstance," says Coleridge, "is but a form or effluence of the riddle of man."

[2] Eccles. ix. 11. It was no immature thinker who observed upon such facts as these, that

　　　　　This should teach us
　　There's a Divinity that shapes our ends,
　　Rough-hew them how we will. That is most certain.

Personification of general laws by recent writers, an aspect of history much in vogue, in which General Laws are as much personified as in mythical periods of thought. "The Tower of Siloam," says a brilliant writer,[1] "fell not for any sins of the eighteen who were crushed by it: but through bad mortar probably, the rotting of a beam, or the uneven settling of the foundations. The persons who should have suffered according to our notion of distributive justice, were the ignorant architects or masons who had done their work amiss. But the guilty, perhaps, had long been turned to dust. And the law of gravitation brought the tower down *at its own time*, indifferent to the persons who might be under it." Does not such language show that there may be a Fetishism latent in the highest abstractions?[2] For myself, I do not see that the *unphilosophical.* planetary spirits of Origen or Kepler are more

---

[1] Mr. Froude on Calvinism, *Short Studies*, II. Ser. p. 11. Another instance may be cited from a more exact thinker. "The Law of Gravitation," writes Professor Tyndall, *Fragm. T.*, p. 45, "crushes the simple worshippers of Ottery St. Mary, while singing their hymns, just as surely as if they were engaged in a midnight brawl." "J'ai lu," says De Maistre, "des millions de plaisanteries sur l'ignorance des anciens qui voyaient des esprits partout. Il me semble que nous sommes beaucoup plus sots, nous qui n'en voyons nulle part."—*Soirées*, Vme Entret., p. 188.

[2] On this subject there is something noble in the indignation of M. Comte, *Phil. Pos.*, V. 42. "De nos jours même qu'est-ce réellement, pour un esprit positif, que ce ténébreux Panthéisme dont se glorifient si étrangement, surtout en Allemagne, tant de profonds métaphysiciens, si non le Fétichisme généralisé et systématisé, enveloppé d'un appareil doctoral propre à donner le change au vulgaire?" In V. 49 he remarks that an age of metaphor has now succeeded to the Fetishism of an earlier time. Compare Mr. Tylor, *Hist. Prim. Cult.*, I. 264.

unreasonable than Gravitation made into an agent. It may be through general and permanent Laws (to call them immutable, involves an assumption incapable of proof) that the Providence of God presides over the order, better perhaps to say, the endless play, of the universe.[1] But it would be more exact to give them another name. They are the continuously active will of an ever-present God in its exercise upon the world of its creation; for where the laws are, there is the Lawgiver also.[2]

§ 9. We conclude, then, that in the hypothesis of universal Law, and in the fact, if it be a fact, that the history of physical science is one continued revelation of the reign of Law, there is nothing antecedently fatal to Christianity as a religion for mankind. For if otherwise, it must be so in respect either of its special contents, or of the fundamental evidences adduced in its support; I mean of

Natural law not incompatible with the Providential aspects of Christianity,

---

[1] It is a truer instinct which, with Malebranche, sees all things in God. "Whether a dagger," says De Maistre, "pierces a man's heart or a little blood collects in his brain, he falls dead alike. But in the first case we say he has ended his days by a violent death. For God, however, there is no such thing as violent death. A steel blade fixed in the heart is a malady just like a simple callosity, which we should call a polypus."—*Soirées*, IVme Entret.

[2] Guizot, *Méditat.*, Vol. I. p. 33. Newton's Scholium on the nature of God is thus worded: "Eutis summè perfecti idea ut sit substantia una; omnia in se continens tanquam eorum principium et locus; omnia per præsentiam substantialem cernens et regens et cum rebus omnibus secundum leges accuratas ut naturæ totius fundamentum et causa, constanter co-operans, nisi ubi aliter agere bonum est." See in Brewster's *Memoirs*, II. 154. Compare the description of the Koran (Sale, I. c. vi., p. 166).

nor with its evidences, Miracles and Prophecy, "that splendid apparatus with which its mission was introduced and attested."[1] Into the nature of these evidences I am not now called to enter. For the subject of Miracles, the magnificent dialectical effort made not very long since from this place, must deter, while rendering unnecessary, all inferior handling *viz. miracles.* of the same topic. I would remark only in answer to a more recent objection,[2] that if it be true that as men advance from an imperfect to a higher civilization, they gradually sublimate and refine their creed, exhibiting an indisposition, in place of an earlier proneness, towards the reception of the miraculous: it may still be replied, that Christianity, as it has become better understood, has borne this *These admit of discrimination.* test. Already in the long history of the Church, we have learned to distinguish between true and false miracles, evangelical and ecclesiastical, evidential and doctrinal, intrinsic and spurious imitations. The tendency of superstition to multiply miracles does not disprove their probability, much less their possibility: it rather goes to establish the instinctive nature of their recognition. A truer estimate of the position of Miracles in relation

---

[1] Paley, *Moral Phil.*, Bk. IV. sub fin.
[2] See Mr. Lecky, *Hist. Rat.*, I. 160-195. *Hist. Eur. Mor.*, I. 370, 385, &c. Jean Paul Richter acutely remarks, *Vorschule der Aesthetik*, *Works*, xix. 163, that the greatest miracle is our tendency to believe in miracles, surrounded as we are by the mechanical kingdom of our senses: that in spite of continual contact with the world of matter we still believe in an invisible world.

to faith has taken possession of the Christian mind. "The ideal[1] of the Church's life," it has been well said, "is not the predominance of the supernatural: but the intimate and complete union of the human and the Divine." The proof from Miracles[2] Augustine thought was not suited to every age, or to all minds. On the large and important evidence of Prophecy, which to the mind of Pascal,[3] (as previously to that of Augustine and, as it would seem, of the earlier Fathers), superseded Miracles; it may perhaps be said that it still awaits a treatment in unison with the spirit of the time. At present I would only observe that there is nothing in its nature essentially contradictory to experience. On the contrary, it is consistent and according with expectation, so long as there is admitted a Divine superintendence of events passing insensibly into a continuous interposition, and acting in conjunction with fixed and general laws. It is a

The varying cogency of Christian evidences and prophecy.

Their fulfilment a matter of fact.

---

[1] Pressensé, *Apostles and Martyrs*, p. 16.
[2] *Util. Cred.*, c. xiv.; *Ver. Rel.*, c. xxv. "Cur, inquis, ista (sc. miracula) modo non fiunt? Quia non moverent nisi mira essent: at si solita essent, mira non essent."—*Ut. Cred.*, c. xvi. He also argues that miracles are rather a proof to the ignorant than to the wise.
[3] "La plus grande des preuves de Jésus-Christ, ce sont les prophéties."—*Pensées*, Art. X. "Hujus religionis sectandæ caput est historia et prophetia dispensationis temporalis Divinæ Providentiæ pro salute generis humani in æternam vitam reformandi atque reparandi."—August., *Ver. Rel.*, c. vii. 13, xxv. See Pressensé, *u. s.*, tom. ii. Lecky, *H. E. M.*, I. 399. The teleological character of Christianity in relation to the history and prophecies of the Old Testament, as itself a fruit of "the fullness of the time," is a subject wholly in accord with recent philosophy.

different question which has been sometimes asked, whether Christianity has in its career answered the expectations of the old prophecies respecting it. Thus, the kingdom of Christ is by no means as yet universal: "we see not yet all things put under Him:" nor in the history of the Church has Christianity shown itself a religion of peace. But it has been well replied,[1] that it has fulfilled Prophecy far enough to make the portrait like: and by predicting its own future, answers any such difficulties by anticipation. If destined to be universal, Christ's kingdom is still in a manner "not of this world." It is created and established, not by force, but by persuasion; and persuasion must be always gradual and often precarious. It did not engage to abolish sin and irreligion, even within its pale: the tares should still spring among the wheat. Its very progress was to be made through defeat: it was to conquer by sanctity and suffering.

The mysteries of Christian doctrine not liable to physical explanation.

§ 10. Some elements, it must be admitted, when we are considering the progress and permanence of Christianity, within the circle of Christian doctrine must ever be expected to remain stumbling-blocks to the naked intellect; more especially when it surrenders itself to the narrow dogmas of a purely physical philosophy. There are beings, as Bishop Butler has suggested,[2] to whom the

---

[1] J. H. Newman, *Gramm. of Assent*, p. 441.
[2] *Analogy*, Pt. I. c. i.: "Nor is there any absurdity in supposing," &c.

scheme of Christianity in all its details may appear strictly *natural*. But to us it is not so. The coming of the Son of God in the flesh, the Absolute thus becoming relative, the Infinite finite, the Creator a creature; the spiritual import of death a natural phenomenon (*lex non pœna mors*); the relation of sin to its effects; the fall and corruption of man; the necessity of Redemption; the fact of its taking place in a single tiny world, lost as it were in the infinity of surrounding space crowded with kindred orbs;[1] these are and must be accepted as mysteries, "clouds on the mercy-seat," capable perhaps of explanation, yet only of an imperfect one, unpalatable accordingly to a positive school of inquiry. Yet Mysteries are the properties of all genuine religions, in regard to which the believer "walks by faith and not by sight." Thus "the consciousness of a mystery," it has been rightly said,[2] "is traceable in the rudest Fetishism." The economy of Revelation in respect of them, it may be, differences Christianity favourably from other religions.[3] But whatever may be thought as

Mysteries the property of all genuine religions.

---

[1] Chalmers's discourses on this topic are well known. Comp. pp. 54, 98: "Impossible that the concerns of this puny ball, which floats its little round among an infinity of larger worlds, should be of such mighty account in the plans of the Eternal," &c.

[2] See Mr. Herbert Spencer, *First Pr.*, p. 99: "En articles de foi," it has been beautifully said, "il faut se crever les yeux pour voir clair." "La raison," writes Vinet, "a sa foi; la foi a sa raison."

[3] *Viz.* by confining them to truths answering to the deepest wants of our spiritual frame. "Ce qui en nous est contraire aux mystères, n'est pas la raison, ni la lumière naturelle l'enchaînement des vérités; c'est

to this, they are at least no new difficulties, no new grounds of objection. Nothing about them requires to be given up in the present stage of our knowledge as the creed of an ignorant and bygone age. We are still far from the axiom that nothing can be true but what we can fully understand.¹ Rationalism and Mysticism are, indeed, opposite extremes, between which it may well be the human mind will always continue to oscillate, meeting, however, in one common point. Mysteries are not contradictions to reason or to fact. We should else be holding our religious faith on sufferance of ignorance or error. In effect, the old adage, "omnia exeunt in mysterium" is even now the outcome of a philosophy of experience, the justification of a system of nescience. "The world," said Hume, "is a mystery:" and beyond all that science makes known to us lies the mysterious unknown.² But so again the latent error of Mysticism in religion is the aiming at a comprehension of transcendental truth, at the fruition of a mental certainty which it is not given us to acquire or possess;

Understanding not the measure of belief.

Rationalism and mysticism respectively erroneous.

---

corruption, c'est erreur ou préjugé, c'est ténèbres."—Leibnitz, *Théod.*, p. 496. Paley has some good remarks on this point, *Evid.* II. ii., contrasting the reserve of the Bible with the redundance of the Koran.

¹ Comp. Comte, *Phil. Pos.*, V. 66. It is true that there is an exactly opposite error in which *Revelation* itself is confounded with *Mystery*. "Times," says Dr. Dorner, *Hist. Prot. Th.*, II. 255, "unfruitful in theological knowledge, are ever wont to fall back on mystery, and upon the much abused demand of taking the reason prisoner to the obedience of faith."

² See Herbert Spencer, *First Princ.*, p. 223.

just as in practice it is realized in the abandonment of free-will in its devotion to a pre-assumed will of God. It thus really involves the assumption of mental independence, and runs up into the Schoolmen's postulate that reason ultimately obliges to believe all that faith receives.[1] The difficulties occurring in the system of Christianity form part of the Divine administration, the proper subject-matter of Revelation, being confessedly beyond the reach of human investigation. Of these, therefore, we are no judges; yet the existence of them is recognized in itself to be necessary by the limits of our natural knowledge.

§ 11. Nor is the growing conviction that Religion itself falls within a natural order, and may to a certain extent be treated as a positive phenomenon, determined by the mental faculties and the history of their development, any real stumbling-block to the acceptance of the Christian faith. The criticism of some modern schools of thought,[2] *Natural laws not incompatible with the historical sequence of religions.*

---

[1] "It is an error to suppose Mysticism as the perpetual antagonist of Scholasticism; the Mystics were often severe logicians: the Scholastics had all the passions of Mystics."—Milman, *Lat. Christ.*, VI. 263. See Gieseler, III. 292, and IV. 188, E. T., ed. Clark. Lacordaire speaks of "la certitude mystique et transluminouse." In all Mysticism we must distinguish between an intellectual and an ethical tendency. Comp. Dorner, *Hist. Prot. Th.*, I. 52. There is a tendency in Mysticism towards what has been termed Monopsychism, the belief in the mere existence of a single soul. Such a view is the correlative of pure Materialism.

[2] See Mr. Farrar, *Witness of History to Christ*, p. 61, and Dr. Farrar, *Critical Hist. of Free Thought*, pp. 122, 392. Comp. Hegel, *Phil. d.*

commencing with Lessing and culminating in Baur, grows out of this truth pursued into excess. On the Positivist theory Christianity is the necessary result of previous antecedents. It could not but have arisen out of the contact of Jewish Monotheism and Greek speculation and Roman Empire.[1] This explanation (even if true of a system of dogmas) does not, as we have already seen, account for an historic Gospel, that is, for the series of facts on which Christian dogmas depend. But the still larger fact that the announcement of the religion of Christ was in accordance with the spirit and antecedents of its time, the culmination of an Evangelical Preparation;[2] and further, that in its history it has followed the course of laws unreservedly accepted in other departments of knowledge and action, this result should be a confirmation, not an arraignment, of its truth. It is no tenet of the Christian faith to deny that we are the " heirs of all the ages," or, in the expressive words of Comte, that " we who live are ruled by the dead." The continuity and solidarity of human

When the facts are allowed or.

Importance of the doctrine of an evangelical preparation.

Gesch. 3. *Theil*, III. ii. Mr. Buckle, *Hist. Civ.*, II. 21, attributes the first notion of a theory of religious development to the French writer, Charron.

[1] See Comte, *Phil. Pos.*, V. 349, and Prof. Westcott's just remarks (*Comte on Christianity*), *Cont. Rev.*, VI. 404. Dr. Dorner, *Hist. Prot. Th.*, II. 291, traces this view to Eberhard in his *Geist des Ur-Christenthums*, published in 1807.

[2] On this grand theory of Christian development, the contribution of the School of Alexandria to a history of doctrine, see Neander, *Ch. Hist.*, II. 275, E. T., ed. Clark.

history are ideas which lie at the root of the doctrines of Christ. Time has been when, through an unconscious lack of faith in the ordinary providence of God, the progress of Christianity has been too largely assigned to miraculous and supernatural causes.[1] It was narrowed accordingly to false or unimportant issues. The humbler, if safer, road of regular and ordinary causation was deemed unmeet for it. The presence of the Divine message and its efficacy were hailed more readily in the rending earthquake and the great strong wind, and in the devouring fire, than in the still small voice of moral conviction and spiritual transformation, borne slowly down the stream of time.[2] But now men think and see differently, and looking back we seem to catch the breath of a Divine mystery, mingling ever silently with the voices and tones of men, and tempering with a heavenly calm the fevered spirit of the age.[3] It is not now argued that the rise and progress of Christianity are inexplicable: but rather that its results prove

This sometimes lost sight of.

Present tendency of the age.

---

[1] See some good remarks of Dean Merivale, *Conversion of Empire*, p. 20. "The human mind continued to work by its old accustomed methods; but those methods of thought were themselves of God's original appointment. The Holy Spirit had brooded over their creation, and guided them gently to the end which to Him was present from the beginning." Also *Northern Nations*, pp. x. 103; and Dorner's remarks on Lessing, *Hist. Prot. Th.*, II. 303.

[2] See Mr. Lecky, *Hist. Eur. M.*, I. 412.

[3] "Perhaps," says Laud, *Conf.* p. xxiii., "there may be *in voce hominum tuba Dei*—in the still voice of men the loud trumpet of God which sounds many ways, sometimes to the ears and sometimes to the hearts of men, and by means which they think not of."

L

its permanent and catholic character; that it is a religion to take part and co-exist with advancing civilization.

Relation of intellectual progress to civilization.

§ 12. Thus, in an estimate of the value of Christianity as a permanent element in human progress, some preliminary inquiry into the relation of intellectual conditions towards advance in morals and religion must come in. So long as it is maintained that all advance is really intellectual,[1] and that knowledge and civilization tend rather to the extinction than to the promotion of religious sentiment, the situation of Christianity, equally indeed with all creeds, becomes precarious and doubtful.

Its importance to the fact of the permanence of Christianity.

What, then, is meant in such discussions by civilization? Not, surely, one thing, but many; not a simple, but a highly complex fact. It is, I apprehend, the position or degree of education of the human race at any given period, in respect not of knowledge only, but of social and political condition, dependent on circumstances of race, climate, and other special antecedents; further, also, in respect of moral and religious beliefs, acting conjointly with art and æsthetical development.[2] All

Definition of civilization,

---

[1] See Mr. Buckle, *Hist. Civ.*, I. c. iv. (more especially p. 182). His argument is that civilization is indeed the product of moral and intellectual agencies; but that as morality is really stationary and without advance, the intellect is the prime mover and is permanent in its results. In II. 89, he seems after Descartes to ground religion itself on an idea of the intellect. See, on the other hand, Mr. Lecky, *Hist. Eur. M.*, I. 105, 156, &c.

[2] See Mill's *Logic*, Bk. VI., x. 2. "What is called a state of society is

these elements may be present in a varying relation and in different proportions of force. All may together be acting feebly; some vigorously, some scarcely. Industrial and intellectual culture by no means advances uniformly in all its branches. It may, as in Ancient Greece, be far ahead of other elements of true culture, and be before its time.[1] Knowledge may be at a low ebb in a community where religious convictions have a strong hold upon the hearts and affections of a people. Morality may be weakest in respect of the conduct of the masses, while knowledge flourishes, and a spirit of inquiry is widely diffused. Such a result tends directly against true culture. The conditions of intellectual are not generally favourable to moral growth.[2] Meanwhile, the political circumstances may be auspicious or unfavourable, while the social condition of a nation will exhibit the complex result

a complex result of many factors,

including religion.

the *simultaneous* state of all the greater social facts or phenomena . . . the common beliefs entertained on all the subjects most important to mankind, and the degree of assurance with which those beliefs are held," &c. So also Guizot (*Civil. en France*, Lec. i., p. 273), "It is not these two principles of themselves, which constitute civilization: to bring it to perfection, their intimate and rapid union, simultaneousness, and reciprocal action are absolutely necessary." See the whole of the passage. Comp. also Grant's *Bamp. Lect.*, p. 308. Mr. Tylor (*Hist. Prim. Cult.*, I. p. 1) thus defines: "Culture or civilization taken in its wide ethnographic sense is that complex whole which includes knowledge, belief, art, morals, law, custom, and any other capabilities and habits acquired by man as a member of society."

[1] See Mr. Tylor, *u. s.*, I. 24. Comp. Comte, *Phil. Pos.*, V. 252, 257.

[2] See Guizot, *Civ. en France*, I. 348: "When the social relations have been described, are the facts whose aggregate constitutes the life of an epoch exhausted? Certainly not; there remains to be studied the

of the other elements of its civilization. Hence the differences of ancient and modern culture. They are not only distinct stages of a common progress or development, to which man's nature points and tends.[1] They have proceeded from different principles. Ancient civilization started from one alone, as in Athens from intellectual culture, in Rome from the principle of public utility, the submission of individual development to common good, the recognition and creation of law. Then, rapidly advancing, it became soon exhausted and monotonous. In modern times, civilization is with more reason held dependent on the due disposition of all the various powers of human nature under social forms. The soul of man has accordingly been stirred upon a larger number of points and to a greater depth. It has become more accessible to the power of new ideas. In this result the amelioration of social conditions has, no doubt, reacted on humanity. And it may well be that, as man's nature and knowledge rise with culture, his religious sentiment also alters and expands. But, inversely, Christianity by first changing and regenerating human nature, has developed morally,

Ancient distinguished from modern civilization.

Expansion of the religious sentiment.

internal, the personal state of men, the state of souls; that is, on one side the ideas, doctrines, the whole intellectual life of man: on the other, the relations which connect ideas with actions, creeds with the determinations of the will, thought with human liberty." In II. 395 he blames Bossuet for having confined his view of civilization to religious creeds, and Montesquieu to political institutions.

[1] See Tylor, *u. s.*, I. 25.

and even intellectually, the individual man without necessarily varying his external condition. But this change did not come at once; and under the later Empire the world retrograded in its intellectual stage while in possession of Christian ideas. For "advanced ideas," it has been truly said,[1] "when once established, act upon society and aid its further advance. Yet the establishment of such ideas depends on the previous fitness of society for receiving them." There must be a thorough correspondence of external and internal relations. The religion of our present so-called civilization, if it be only or mainly an evolution of intellect, ignoring the claims of conscience, can but exhibit a one-sided, imperfect progress;[2] it does not fulfil the idea, and must fail, as it has failed of old. Such, however, is not the character of the religion of Christ, which is, therefore, "established on better promises" of permanence and progress. But on what grounds is it asserted that all human advance is intellectual, thus necessitating the conclusion that Christianity is itself an effect and not a cause of progress? Because,[3] it is answered, without external interference people will never discover their existing

Civilization must be as wide as the whole nature of man.

Religion a part cause of progress.

---

[1] Mr. Herbert Spencer, *Classification of Sciences*, p. 37.

[2] See Dr. J. H. Newman, *Gramm. of Assent*, p. 391; also *Essay on Devel.*, I. § 3; and particularly Dean Church, *Univ. Sermons* on the relation of Christianity to civilization. "It corrects the narrowing of man's horizon; which civilization cannot do, perhaps fosters." "Christianity affords the only means of cherishing purity," &c.

[3] Buckle, *Hist. Civ.*, I. 254.

religion to be a bad one; and this implies some previous improvement in reason and knowledge. But has religion, it may fairly be replied, only an intellectual side? Is it not so, as Pascal has said,[1] that "the heart also has its reasons, which reason cannot apprehend"? "It is necessary to imbue our faith with feeling, otherwise it will be for ever vacillating." Has the work of conversion been always among races so far advanced in knowledge and mental resources as to be adequate critics, from the intellectual stand-point, of the merits of a new faith? It is conceivable that the belief of barbarous times or tribes may be in some respects simpler and truer[2] than that of periods of culture, just as the moral qualities of savage races sometimes suffer at the first impact of civilization. Again, is it, as a matter of fact,[3] by intellectual convictions chiefly or solely that religions have made their way in different regions of the world? Perhaps the simplest mode has been the acceptance of the faith of the conquering race by the subject peoples. Between different forms of polytheism such an interchange could not have been difficult.[4] "Civilization," it has been aptly said, "is a plant much oftener propagated than developed."[5] This

Marginal notes: Reason of this. Change of religion not due to an intellectual conviction solely or chiefly.

---

[1] *Pensées*, II. 176, I. 155, ed. Faugère.
[2] See Newman, *Gramm. of Assent*, p. 391.
[3] See an example in Mr. Tylor, *Hist. Prim. Cult.*, I. 27.
[4] See Comte, *Phil. Pos.*, V. 180. Hume, *Nat. H. of Religion*, § 9.
[5] Tylor, *Hist. Pr. C.*, I. 48.

has resulted either from direct compulsion, as by the scimitar of Islamism, or from an instinct of inferiority naturally, and not without reason,[1] accompanying defeat. Where a new language can be imposed, no doubt through "the spiritual relationship" of races, religion may pass also. Yet this is not always so; as, for instance, in the Mahometan and British subjugations of Hindostan. Nor is it so generally, where a strong sacerdotal caste exists among the conquered race.[2] But neither, if it were, could it be traced to any law of rational superiority alone in the religion of the conqueror. For then the progress of religious truth, it is to be supposed, would have been simple and continuous; a result which is not borne out by the history of mankind. Other circumstances, therefore, must be taken into account. The guidance, or at any rate the sequence, of events introduces particular religions into the world and into distinct localities. Once received, from whatever causes, they flourish and endure according to the amount of truth which they contain, combined with the fitness of their doctrines for the special circumstances of region and race, including, it is true, as one condition, a certain stage of intellectual

Historical proof of this fact.

---

[1] Comp. Arist., *Pol.*, I. vi.: τρόπον τινα ἀρετὴ τυγχάνουσα χορηγίας βιάζεσθαι δύναται μάλιστα, καὶ ἔστιν ἀεὶ τὸ κρατοῦν ἐν ὑπεροχῇ ἀγαθοῦ τινος ὥστε δοκεῖν μὴ ἄνευ ἀρετῆς εἶναι τὴν βίαν.

[2] Compare the remarks of Comte, *Phil. Pos.*, V. 241, and Sir John Lubbock, *Orig. of Civilization.*

Generalization of the sequence of religious conceptions.

advance. Thus fetishism may be found to precede polytheism, polytheism the belief in one God.¹ And thus even a large admixture of error is long able to maintain its ground by appealing to some of all the religious instincts of mankind, until, by the will of God, the hour arrives for its supersession by a higher and purer faith.

Thus, Christianity an agent in civilization, whence an argument arises for its permanence.

§ 13. Were it unquestionable that the benefits attributed to the Religion of Christ are the results of social laws alone, or of some foregoing intellectual stage of civilization, or again, that Religion, apart from moral teaching, has no proper and special field of action, it would be plainly futile to argue from the effects of Christianity to its permanence and truth as a religious system. It is thus made answerable for all its defects in operation, for those evils, mischiefs, and shortcomings which a narrow philosophy has always too readily set down to its account, while it is allowed no share in the amelioration of man's estate, no force in the influences which have determined the advancement of the race. I shall therefore attempt to show that the progress of civilization has been in successive ages largely promoted by the character and distinc-

To be shown in detail.

---

¹ As held by Hume, *Essays, Nat. Hist. of Rel.* Comte, *Phil. Pos.*, V. 40, 46; Grote, *Hist. of Greece*, I. 462, V. 22; Buckle, I. 251; and, Mr. Tylor, with some modifications. Mr. Mill, *Examination*, p. 307, remarks profoundly that the psychological rationale of this vast generalization is the historical development of the subjective notion of power. Augustine, *Civ. D.*, IV. xi., strives to represent polytheism as a thinly disguised monotheism.

tive tenets of the Gospel, and these not of an intellectual cast. The philosophy of history points definitely to an improvement in human affairs, an improvement with which Christianity is in accord, and of which it has formed a part. In the next Lecture, however, in order to answer certain objections still met with against the originality and importance of the Faith of Christ, it will be necessary to determine within fixed limits the connection and interdependence of Religion with merely moral systems, and to deduce the fair scope of the former as a distinct agent in the formation of human conduct. One further preliminary consideration affecting the conditions of progressive civilization will then remain. Is there any such inherent internecine antagonism between Science and Revelation, the advance of knowledge and the spread of Christianity, as on this ground alone to necessitate or foreshadow the collapse of religious belief? Are we indeed entered upon an era of scientific attainments in which theological faith, already in some quarters subordinated to metaphysical abstractions, is to be trodden under foot by a positive philosophy, that is, by a belief in concrete laws? Is there to be an endless war between our intellectual faculties and our religious obligations? Are we entitled to predict the decline and extinction of all theologies, as a gradual but inevitable consequence of the course of human

Preliminary considerations.

1. The relation of religion to merely moral systems. (See Lecture IV.)

2. The compatibility of intellectual progress with the permanence and advance of Christianity. (See Lecture V.)

Religion attacked as unserviceable and inefficient.

affairs? Must we look forward to a time when the inutility and helplessness of all religious sentiment to advance the well-being of mankind will be universally admitted? And here it may be at once allowed that the sphere of Religion, whatever be its true work and office in respect of the positive benefits which it confers upon mankind, lies wholly outside Science. It was not sent to redress evils which it is the province of knowledge to remove. But is it always kept in mind, when Christianity is thus assailed on the score of inefficiency, how small a part of those ills which "flesh is heir to," Science

Criticism of the services rendered by positive knowledge to mankind.

itself has hitherto availed to abolish? While conferring on mankind large benefits and grand opportunities, can it be said of this new divinity that it alone brings no evils in its train?[1] The mechanical skill which stimulates as it facilitates production, the mighty powers of locomotion by which the fabrics of commerce are made to traverse the furthest regions of the earth, the progress which is making in the labours of the factory and of the mill—have they hitherto increased the sum of happiness and individual comfort for those vast human masses, the slaves of the mine and of the loom, which have, as it were, leaped into being at the call of science? When I walk through our vast

[1] Mr. Lecky, *Hist. Eur. Mor.*, I. 132, has some just and profound reflections on the tendency of industrial progress to sacrifice moral dignity and elevation of character, and on its relation to a utilitarian standard in morals.

manufacturing capitals, and gaze on the squalid tenements, the swarming alleys, the sordid, careworn faces which meet the view, I cannot but ask myself if this is indeed the end of all their being—whether the increase of wealth, of population and production, if these be its conditions, can be worth its own accomplishment; whether the struggle for existence does not outweigh the blessing, or rather the very reasons of life.[1] Is the elevation of the many a true consequence of the increase of wealth? Is it not as in the days of old? "When goods increase they are increased that eat them."[2] "It is a sore travail which God has given to the sons of men to exercise them." "All things are full of labour; that which is crooked cannot be made straight, and that which is wanting cannot be numbered." Surely these words of the Preacher express a profound disappointment at the little effect of wisdom and skilled knowledge on man's physical and moral condition? Are they inapplicable now? Much, at any rate, remains to be done for these toiling millions which as yet has not been done. Brought into the world to eke out, it would seem, the purposes of labour, they live, they work, they die, uncheered by the lamp of knowledge, which assigns their daily task. What has Political Economy, Ethology, or Social Science[3]

Is increase of production or material progress tantamount to social elevation?

Reasons for doubt.

---

[1] "Et propter vitam vivendi perdere causas."—Juv.
[2] Eccles. v. 11; i. 13, 15.
[3] Compare Dr. Mozley's just remarks, *Bamp. Lect.*, p. 192.

as yet done to mend their lot or gild their prospect, amid the gigantic risks and ever-enlarging perils among which they earn their bread? Then in the moment of writhing pain and impending dissolution, the result of unprevented accident, or in the long hours of wasting, incurable sickness, the effect of some noxious employment, to what shall they turn their dying eyes for consolation, for support? Will the long vista of coming generations born like them to suffer, to struggle, and to die, yet making up the sum of that Humanity,[1] that "unity of our race," that "course of evolution," that "subjective immortality" which to some among us seems the very God of all their worship—will the consciousness of an unknown, unknowable reality underlying the world of matter or of mind—will the "infinite nature of duty"—will these close their eyes in peace? or will they not rather, feeling themselves but denizens of a world that passes, yet heirs of an immortal, immaterial spirit, turn with all their hearts towards a Faith which alone explains the present and guarantees the future; which alone lends strength now and gives assurance and peace for ever; which teaches, that

The need of the motives and consolations of religion evident.

---

[1] See Strauss, *Der Alte und der Neue Glaube*, p. 372 ff.; and Mr. Winwood Reade, *Martyrdom of Man*, pp. 535-7. I quote but one passage: "We teach that the soul is immortal; we teach that there is a future life; we teach that there is a heaven in the ages far away; but not for us single corpuscles, and for us dots of animated jelly; but for the One of whom we are the elements, and who, though we perish, never dies."

though the dust returns to the earth as it was, yet there is hope in man's latter end? For the spirit shall return unto God Who gave it, yea, and Who hath redeemed it from sin unto Himself. For "if in this life only we have hope, what advantageth it?" Let us eat and drink, for to-morrow we die. "But now is Christ risen from the dead, and He is become the first-fruits of them that sleep."

LECTURE IV.

OBJECTIONS TO THE PROGRESS OF CHRISTIANITY CONSIDERED.

"C'est mal raisonner contre la religion de rassembler dans un grand ouvrage une longue énumération des maux qu'elle a produits, si l'on ne fait de même celle des biens qu'elle a faits."—MONTESQUIEU, *Esprit des Lois*, xxiv., ii.

LECTURE IV.

"*Not after the law of a carnal commandment, but after the power of an endless life.*"—Heb. vii. 16.

§ 1. THE many forms of Religion which have played their part on the stage of the world's history, have sometimes been held to be but different modes of proclaiming the same moral truths.[1] It is these which are regarded as the true salt of society, the ever-resumed heritage of the whole human race. "All religions," said Diderot, "are but the sects of the one Religion of Nature." I do not now stay to inquire what such a religion is; whether altogether reasoned out, or itself the gift of a primary revelation: whether it exists; whether it corresponds to the actual beliefs of the lower races; whether it could ever become adequate to the moral wants of mankind; whether it be not Christian morality with the omission of all that is Christian, with its proofs

<small>Religion viewed as a mode of proclaiming morality.</small>

<small>Relation of Christianity to a Religion of Nature,</small>

---

[1] See Comte, *Phil. Pos.*, IV. 77. The teaching of the School of Kant regards ecclesiastical beliefs as the vehicle for conveying truths of pure, *i. e.* natural, religion. See Mr. Lecky's remarks, *Hist. Rat.*, I. 329. Compare H. J. Rose, *Hist. Prot. in Germany*, p. 143. Its effect, as Dr. Farrar, *B. L.*, p. 323, has tersely remarked, is "to destroy Revelation by leaving nothing to be revealed." The Gospel thus only makes legible the eternal Law of Nature written in the heart.

drawn from reason, and not from Revelation. What hinders, however, that such a religion, acknowledging, as it needs must, from the side of experience a sense of sin, even points to a remedy which is found only in the revelation of a Mediator?[1] Such a fact, then, and the system of which it is a part, does not supersede or contradict the instincts of Natural Religion. It rather completes and supplements them, and shows the Christian faith to be itself in a manner *natural*. The objection, however, implied is really this: that Christianity, while no doubt "as old as the creation," is unfortunately also no newer. It is no more than a re-publication of the Religion of Nature. For the principles of morality, it is implied, are in effect few and simple, incapable of enlargement or multiplication. Obscured they may have been from time to time in the progress of ages and by the circumstances of mankind. But positive religions, while they have done much to impede the recognition of these principles, have

<small>supplemental, not contradictory.</small>

<small>Implied objection against the originality and usefulness of religion.</small>

---

[1] "The matter of Revelation is not a mere collection of truths, not a philosophical view, not a religious sentiment or spirit, not a special morality poured out upon mankind as a stream might pour itself into the sea, mixing with the world's thought, modifying, purifying, invigorating it; but an authoritative teaching, . . a religion in addition to the religion of nature, not superseding or contradicting it."—J. H. Newman, *Gramm. of Assent*, pp. 382, 479. See Dr. Mozley in *Cont. Rev.*, VII. On the relation of Christianity to natural religion, see Chalmers, *Bridg. Tr.*, sub finem. He concludes: "Natural theology has been called the basis of Christianity: it were better called the basis of Christianization."

succeeded but poorly in exhibiting their truth, or in facilitating their reception.

§ 2. The error in these assumptions seems to lie in the supposition that all the particulars of moral truth have been from the first well known and understood: or that they are in their own nature incapable of further development. Some who have justly seen that morality has really been progressive, have preferred to attribute the result to improved knowledge rather than to the influence of religious ideas. Can it, however, be seriously maintained, with any show of reason, that the whole aspect of moral truths in the history of our race has been stationary? that there is really nothing to be found in the world which has undergone so little change as those great dogmas of which moral systems are composed;[1] or again, to use the words of a powerful though hasty objector, that "to assert that Christianity communicated to man moral truths previously unknown, argues, on the part of the assertor, either gross ignorance or else wilful fraud." "All the great moral systems," he adds,[2] "which have exercised much influence have been fundamentally the same: all the great intellectual systems have been fundamentally different." So, then, all

Error in this assumption.

Morality really progressive.

---

[1] Buckle, *Hist. Civ.*, I. 180, who adduces Kant's authority to the same effect. See, however, Lange's counter-criticism, *Gesch. des Materialismus*, pp. 511, 512.
[2] Buckle, *u. s.*, p. 181.

moral systems are substantially the same:[1] and thus far all religions embodying and enshrining a system of morals. Such would, no doubt, be the case, if Religion contained nothing beyond morality; or if the number of primary moral truths can be shown to be extremely small, and their application in the form of duties simple and obvious.

And systems of religion vary as to their moral value. But, as a matter of fact, is no difference discernible in the moral value of separate religions, of Christianity as compared with Paganism, or of Oriental systems as compared with one another? Are we, then, still to be told that the morals of all nations have been the same, if not as a matter of practice, and in the diffusion of effects, yet in principle and substance; that no improvements have been made in morality for at least three thousand years; and that it admits of no discoveries?[2]

Twofold reply on the part of Christian revelation. § 3. Such objections, containing an implicit criticism of Revelation, allow, so far as we are concerned with them, of a double answer. One, that Religion, recognizing and addressing the spiritual part of man, influences and enlarges thereby his stock of moral truth, supplying new motives of action on the utilitarian side, new

---

[1] Mr. Lecky, *Hist. Eur. Mor.*, I. 103-114, has ably shown that the unity of morals in different ages is a unity not of *standard*, but of *tendency*. In the same work (I. 156, 165) he argues directly against Mr. Buckle's theory on this subject.

[2] See Sir James Mackintosh ap. Buckle, I. 181. The title of his work is, 'A Dissertation on the *Progress* of Ethical Philosophy.'

LECT. IV.] *PROGRESS OF CHRISTIANITY.* 165

sanctions and grounds of duty in each fresh revela- *From its contents as* tion of our relations with God and man.¹ A test *influenc-* is thus supplied which distinguishes the higher *ing and advancing* from the lower religions of the earth, and still *morals,* leaves the Faith of Christ the foremost in the history of civilization. Religion further systematizes moral truths already recognized by concentrating them into one focus of new unsuspected light. Can the doctrine of the brotherhood of mankind, for example, be considered to stand on the same footing now as before the revelation of Jesus Christ? Does the duty of love to God remain the same? True religion, says Pascal, must have for a credential the obligation of *loving* God. Yet what religion except our own has included this among its ordinances?² Another answer (on which I shall not dwell at length) is that in the application of the rules of known ethical systems there is an indefinite field of extension, one strictly analogous to the growth of knowledge in other subjects. In this direction the history and character of Christian teaching, *and from* not to speak of its positive institutions, has had *torical pro-* a marked and lasting influence. It is unnecessary *during the Christian*

---

¹ Compare Butler's *Analogy*, Pt. II. c. i., where he argues for the *era.* importance of Christianity as a distinct publication of natural morality, containing relations which produce new obligations not dependent on the method of revelation.

² "La vraie religion doit avoir pour marque d'obliger à aimer son Dieu. Cela est bien juste: et cependant aucune autre que la nôtre ne l'a ordonné. La nôtre l'a fait."—*Pensées*, Art. III.

to insist on the importance of casuistry as a department of moral science, or on the contributions which have been furnished to it by Christian theologians.[1] Still wider is the field thus opened when it is considered that the analysis of the circumstances of acts leads up to a revision and re-arrangement of already-known principles of duty. Man's moral and spiritual experience enlarges with his history. New grounds of practice are brought to light, as the action is referred to different reasons of rightness or wrongness. In this manner new moral conceptions, new theories of conduct, fresh central principles of action, new standards of merit, and of the relative value of particular virtues, even new faculties,[2] are so far from being impossible of discovery, that they both in fact exist, and are continually recognized in the growth of culture, illustrating the whole

Mode of advance.

---

[1] On this subject see De Quincey, *Works*, Vol. XIV. pp. 22, 24, 69; also some careful and just remarks by Mr. Morley, *Crit. Misc.*, pp. 351, 364. Sir H. Maine, *Ancient Law*, c. ix., too readily condemns casuistry as a species of moral theology, having its origin in the distinction of mortal and venial sins. If, indeed, we adopt his view, that moral philosophy is but a compound of law and metaphysic, we might fairly doubt of the progressive capacities of ethical science.

[2] Thus Mr. Herbert Spencer holds that moral intuitions are the results of accumulated experiences of utility. See Bain, *Mental and Mor. Sc.*, p. 722. "Character," says Prof. Goldwin Smith, "does not remain the same: the character of the man is continually advancing through life; and in like manner the character of the race advances through history."—*Study of Hist.*, p. 37. Mr. Mill, *Comte and Pos.*, p. 112, looks on Protestantism as specially inculcating a distinct moral principle, involving the duty of culture; *viz.* direct individual responsibility to God.

region of duty. The subject of morals as a practical system reacts upon its own scientific base; and the analysis of complex effects and of compound agents observable in other branches of knowledge, advances here also, and with the same results.

§ 4. But, it may be said, the very progress indicated is an intellectual one, and owes nothing to the influences of Religion. It may be explained by an invariable law of progress observable in human affairs. Science depends on improved methods of research, on their application to instances, on the development of the principles thus suggested. So also with moral truth. Ripened by the circumstances of the time, including new modes and lines of thinking due to physical and intellectual causes, it bears unaccustomed fruits.

Objection, that this progress is intellectual, and not due to religion,

> Miraturque novas frondes et non sua poma.

The general sentiment of an age, it is said,[1] is really determined by the intellectual activity, and indirectly by the positive institutions which belong to it; and moral dogmas,[2] as well as the

---

[1] See Mr. Morley's observations on the development of morals, *u. s.*

[2] Mr. Wallace (*Malay. Archip.*, sub fin.) holds that "while civilized communities have progressed vastly beyond the savage state in intellectual achievements, we have not advanced equally in morals ... It is not too much to say that the mass of our populations have not at all advanced beyond the savage code of morals, and have in many cases sunk below it." Sir John Lubbock's researches lead him to the exact reverse of this opinion. The savage, he holds, is destitute of moral feeling, *e.g.* of remorse.—*Orig. Civ.*, p. 265.

immediate sense of obligation, advance along with it. Where intellect stagnates, morality is low. In the unreasoning savage it may be altogether lacking. To reinstate or create the reign of duty, there must take place a revival or awakening of knowledge. The result is seen in new applications, and a simpler interpretation of moral principles hitherto acknowledged. Thus, the sense of duty, generically the same in different ages, varies in amount, and modifies almost in quantity, the shades of conduct over which it is diffused.

but to a revival of knowledge.

The answer to this view lies in a matter of fact. Among the circumstances of an age, determining the general sentiment of the time, can the power and authority of the prevailing Faith count for nothing? If the opinions of a given period are dependent on its intellectual condition, has this also been altogether unaffected by Religion? Though intellect and knowledge have their share in determining the applications of a sense of duty, the *sacredness* of that sense and the sanctions it imposes are due altogether to Religion, and will vary with its purity and power. It has become fashionable to regard great eras in the history of our belief, the Reformation or the commencement of Christianity itself, as simple moral protests against the corruption of the times. Such a view misunderstands the character of the phenomena it seeks to explain. The Reformation began, indeed,

Reply.
The intellectual condition of the period affected by the prevailing faith.

The sacredness of duty due to religion.

The Reformation not a moral protest.

with a moral movement,[1] exhibited in a mystic pietism opposed in its own nature to doctrinal limitations. Its subsequent phases are well known; and the difference in the prevailing moral sentiment, before and after this vast doctrinal revolution, is too marked to be ignored or attributed to any but its true causes. How completely varied were the moral forces introduced by the doctrines of Christianity is evident from the difficulty and slowness with which its standard of duty asserted itself, failing in many parts of the world to become fairly established, even when the recognition of some of its abstract dogmas gave a show of power and predominance to its position.[2] It is thus no valid objection to urge against the truth or importance of Christianity that in its operation it has been constantly limited by ethical conditions. So was it in the East with the false, subtle, contentious natures of the Greek and Asiatic.[3] Religion in

Nor can the origin of Christianity be thus explained,

though dependent in its progress on ethical conditions.

---

[1] For the moral effects of the doctrinal principles of the Reformation, see Ullmann (Vol. I. p. 10, E. T.), Martensen, *Christian Dogmatics*, p. 26, E. T., and on the transition from the moral to the doctrinal movement, Gieseler, V. 216, E. T. On the relation of the Mystics to the Reformation compare Milman, *Latin Christianity*, VI. 379, and particularly Dorner, *Person of Christ*, Div. II., Vol. I. p. 377, and Vol. II. sub init., and *Hist. Prot. Th.*, Vol. I. p. 51, E. T.

[2] So M. Comte views the Byzantine Church as an example of the impotence of dogma, as such, to rule mankind. It lent itself, he thinks, too much to the side of reason. Dorner, *Hist. Prot. Th.*, 1. 18, has some excellent remarks on the purely intellectual character of the Christianity of the Oriental Church.

[3] Cicero's verdict is well known (*De Orat.*, I. xi.), " verbi enim controversia jam diu torquet Græculos homines contentionis cupidiores quam

Oriental Christianity was represented mainly by theology and the theological spirit; it formed no alliance with true morality, and the morals of the time were utterly debased. It was then shown that a compound made up of asceticism and mysticism may produce a faith unaccompanied and untempered by any infusion of really Christian morality. Insufficient, singly, to counterbalance the want of civilization, or to transmute all contemporary error, had Christianity succeeded in taking full possession of the world with the elements which then constituted it, it would but, to

<small>Illustration from Eastern Christianity,</small>

<small>veritatis." Hooker, *E. P.*, V. iii. 3, holds the chiefest cause of the chronic state of schism in the Eastern Church "to have lien in the restless wits of the Grecians, evermore proud of their own curious and subtile inventions: which, when at any time they had contrived, the great facility of their language served them readily to make all things fair and plausible to men's understanding." Hence, Boileau's caustic comment on the "Martyres d'une diphthongue." "Greek Christianity was insatiably inquisitive, speculative; confident in the inexhaustible copiousness and fine precision of its language, it endured no limitation to its curious investigations."—Milman, *Lat. Christ.*, I. 2. Bacon (on the controversies of the Church) remarks on the heretics who moved curious questions and made strange anatomies of the natures and person of Christ. "Illis temporibus ingeniosa res fuit esse Christianum." Mr. Finlay (*Byz. E.*, p. 262) attributes these controversies to the Greek language rather than to the Hellenic temper. "They had their origin in the more profound religious ideas of the Oriental nations, Syrians, Armenians, Egyptians, Persians." Mr. Froude (*Short Stud.*, p. 98) remarks, "We wonder at the failure of Christianity, at the small progress which it has made in comparison with the brilliancy of its rise. But if men had shown as much fanaticism in carrying into practice the Sermon on the Mount as in disputing the least of the thousand dogmatic definitions which have superseded the Gospel, we should not now be lamenting with Father Newman that 'God's control over the world is so indirect and His action so obscure.'" See Mr. Buckle, *Hist. Civ.*, II. 303.</small>

use the words of Montalembert, have reproduced a kind of Christian China.¹ So was it in the West when, after centuries of power, Paganism was found to have corrupted its teacher with the taint of an inbred superstition. The fact was no new one; it had been already observed and commented on in the days of Augustine.² "It was in vain that Christianity had taught a simple doctrine and enjoined a simple worship. The minds of men were too backward for so great a step, and required more complicated forms and a more complicated belief."³ This has been remarked, I am aware, to the disparagement of the efficacy of the faith of Christ. It proves, at least, that Christianity was not dependent on the existing standard of morals for its advance. How, in such case, were the changes, effected plainly through its means in the absence of knowledge and culture, to be accounted for? Further, its morality however estimated, was its own, and its type of character

from the corruptions of the Western Church.

The progress of Christianity due to the spiritual nature of its revelations,

---

¹ *Monks of the West*, I. 275, Eng. Tr.

² August. c. *Faustum*, XX. c. iv. "Sacrificia eorum vertistis in agapes: idola in Martyres, quos votis similibus colitis: defunctorum umbras vino placatis et dapibus: solemnes Gentium dies cum ipsi celebratis, ut Kalendas et solstitia, de vitâ certe mutâstis nihil." On the reaction of Paganism on Christianity in the fourth and fifth centuries, see Beugnot, *Histoire de la destruction du Paganisme*, II. 92, and Merivale, *N. Nations*, pp. 57-74.

³ Buckle, *Hist. Civ.*, I. 259. Prof. Tyndall writes (*Cont. Rev.*, XX. 766), "Christianity varies with the nature upon which it falls. The faith that simply adds to the folly and ferocity of one, is turned to enduring sweetness, holiness, abounding charity, and self-sacrifice by another."

was an advance upon the highest level of heathenism. It presents a difference not of degree merely, but of kind.[1] But Religion, if assumed to be the product of Revelation, may very well be, and, in fact, must be, in advance of existing civilization. It was so when the Hebrews accepted monotheism, whether this be or be not a Semitic tenet. It was so when the Jews rejected the teaching of the Gospel. It has been so in the development of Gentile Christianity. But the fact of the distance between its ideal and the actual, between its code of action and existing practice, between Christianity in the abstract and as displayed in history, "that rich treasury of man's dishonour;" between the lives of men and the spirit of the Gospel;[2] this difference must surely be allowed for under any system. It is the consciousness of this anomaly in the in-

which were in advance of the existing civilization,

and of actual practice.

---

[1] "Nothing," says Mr. Lecky, "can, as I conceive, be more erroneous or superficial than the reasonings of those who maintain that the moral element of Christianity has in it nothing distinctive or peculiar."—*Hist. Rat.*, I. 338. See this subject continued in II. 110.

[2] "Quid si tale quiddam est vera religio? Quid si multitudo imperitorum frequentat ecclesias, sed nullum argumentum est ideo neminem illis mysteriis factum esse perfectum?"—August. *de Util. Cred.*, c. vii. M. Guizot, while depicting the moral aspect of the Middle Ages, remarks finally: "A certain moral idea hovers over this rude, tempestuous society, and attracts the regard, obtains the respect of men whose life scarcely ever reflects its image. Christianity must doubtless be ranked among the number of the principal causes of this fact. Its precise characteristic is to inspire men with a great moral ambition, to hold constantly before their eyes a type infinitely superior to human reality and to excite them to reproduce it."—*Civ. en France*, III. 115, ed. Bohn.

dividual which forms the stimulus of all earnest souls. "As a matter of fact, Christianity has probably done more to quicken the affections of mankind, to promote pity, to create a pure and merciful ideal than any other influence that has ever acted on the world."[1] And yet the Inquisition named itself with the name of Christ. Principles must ever be of more general account than actions. The first value of the Christian, as of any, religion is in the loftiness and purity of its standard; its secondary worth is in the degree in which this operates.[2] Hence, the fallacy of an appeal to periods when the apparent zeal in the diffusion of religion is greater and the moral results less,[3] as proof of its general inadequacy to impart moral truth in any effective degree. If the religion itself be corrupted, its results, in point of moral effect, must needs suffer in proportion, and this in amount corresponding to the power which it wields. Thus, if the Middle Ages be cited as an instance of the smallness of moral results obtained with a large and prevailing profession of religion,[4] it may be replied, without

Hence apparent historical contradictions

and disturbing reactions.

State of morals under medieval Catholicism.

---

[1] Lecky, *Hist. Rat.*, I. 358.

[2] Condorcet, *Œuvres*, VI. 234, quoted by Mr. Morley, remarks that the religion of books and that of the people may so differ that the effects absolutely cease to answer to the public and recognized causes. This is not allowing enough for an average practical influence, which may be compared to the tenor of administration in politics.

[3] Buckle, *Hist. Civ.*, I. 191.

[4] See Dr. Mozley's remarks, *Bamp. Lect.*, p. 115. Mr. Lecky, *Hist. Rat.*, II. 32, does justice to the services of Medieval Catholicism. In

admitting the fact supposed, that it is, on the other hand, the glory of Protestantism to have effected so large an improvement and so marked an impulse with straitened means and slender resources. For it has certainly reacted on the moral code and average practice of the rival creed. Thus, the tacit moral force of Religion, even in sceptical periods, may be unexpectedly large.[1] Religion, and this is specially true of the Christian religion, ever answers to a personal want in the individual man. Its neglect and degradation have accordingly constantly accompanied the want of culture in the general development of the age.

Corruptions in religion correspondent to moral declensions.

§ 5. It has, indeed, been argued[2] that History does not prove that society owes its moral condition to its religion. If, indeed, but only if, religion were the single moral restraint on a community, would the morals of an age, it is insisted, be according to its prevalence higher or lower. But the theological principle, urges the Positivist, has since the Middle Ages been on the decline. It has succumbed to the

Positivist objection that morality has improved, while Christianity has declined.

---

this view he follows Comte (*Phil. Pos.*, V. 233), Mill, Littré, and other leading thinkers. Gibbon (VII. 60, ed. Milman) enlarges on the moral progress effected by Protestantism.

[1] Thus Dean Stanley, *Essays*, p. 465, remarks that "the religious spirit of the time has deeply penetrated those who doubt, misbelieve, and disbelieve. The change is so great that looking at realities, and not at names, we might call the present posture of philosophers, of Jews, of sceptics towards Christianity almost a conversion."

[2] See M. Littré (*Aug. Comte*, p. 217).

opposition of science, to the strength of industrial development, and to the secularization of governments, substituting a different principle to the exclusion of religious interests. Yet morality has improved. There is more humanity in war, more religious toleration; torture has been abolished, social burdens equalized, poverty relieved and ameliorated. But the facts may be admitted without the inference. Religion now is better understood as to its true work and office. Surrendering ill-advised claims, its real influence is strengthened and deepened. And can it be said that any point of morality now reached in theory or practice is *counter* to the teachings of the Gospel? That our own is an age of faith or of scepticism, of operative or inoperative belief, may be matter of opinion;[1] that its moral qualities are independent of its faith, and public opinion of religious belief, would be certainly difficult of proof. *Proceeds on a false inference.* *The power of Christianity has not become weaker in its effects on public opinion.*

§ 6. The attempt often made from the days of Origen[2] to Tindal and Bolingbroke to prove that Christianity, containing no new moral truth, can *Objection that Christianity teaches no new moral truth.*

---

[1] It has been said to be "destitute of faith, but terrified at scepticism." See Mr. Mill, *Liberty*, c. ii.

[2] *c. Celsum*, I. iv., VII. xxviii., lviii., lxi. Compare Mackay, *Rise and Progress of Christianity*, pp. 21, 22, and *Rel. Devel.*, II. 376–7. M. Renan, *Études*, p. 188. Mr. Farrar, *Witness of History to Christ*, pp. 135, 137, has touched this subject with his usual spirit and ability. Saisset, *Essais*, details as strictly Christian conceptions the universality of the love of God and universal fraternity. These ideas, though latent in human nature, are evoked by Christian civilization.

exercise no distinct moral effect, is now again revived. And doubtless if the whole moral furniture of our being is contained in a few short precepts, "to do good to others, to sacrifice for their benefit your own wishes, to love your neighbour as yourself, to forgive your enemies, to restrain your passions, to honour your parents, to respect those who are set over you;" if this be all (as Mr. Buckle alleges),[1] there might not remain much to be said as to the originality of Christian morals. Though some even of these duties, it must be allowed, were but imperfectly known and badly understood before the preaching of the Gospel. Christianity, it might be shown, has added largely to the very vocabulary of morals. Its notion of holiness, not to speak of repentance, is a new and previously unrealized conception, the illimitable character of which guarantees its permanence. It may not be difficult[2] to cull from individual moralists of Greece and Rome, or of East and West, fragments of Christian

Untrue.

Instances of the fact.

---

[1] *Hist. Civ.*, I. 180. Paley, on the other hand, after asserting that "morality, neither in the Gospel nor any other book, can be a subject of discovery, properly so called," proceeds to show how far the morality of the Gospel is above that of its age and antecedents, and not to be accounted for apart from the pretensions of the religion.—*Evid.*, II. ii.

[2] See M. Denis, *Histoire des Théories et Idées morales dans l'antiquité*, I. 104; Wollaston's laborious *Religion of Nature*, &c. Mr. Lecky, *H. E. M.*, I. 161, complains of the appropriation of heathen ideas by Christian moralists. Augustine, *Doct. Christ.*, II. xl.-xlii., gracefully acknowledges the debt, and fancifully compares it to spoiling the Egyptians. "Nonne adspicimus, quanto auro et argento et veste suffarcinatus exierit de Ægypto Cyprianus doctor suavissimus, quanto Lactantius," &c. Comp. Lactant., *Div. Inst.*, VII. vii.

duties—to find in Plato the recognition of repentance and devotion towards God, forgiveness of injuries, or the portraiture of a celestial love; in Cicero the teaching of universal charity, benevolence, and brotherhood. It may even be easy to exhibit under the garb of moral realizations the saving truths of faith; to see in the salvation offered by Jesus the ἀποφυγὴ κακῶν,[1] the effort to be as wise and good as is possible to man, contemplated by the heathen Socrates; to find in his utterance that the gods will give such things as are good, for they know what is best for man, the keynote of Christian prayer; to recognize in the endurance of the martyr the independence of the Stoic mind, with its larger virtue of patriotism; in Christian meekness and resignation towards God a true philosophic constancy and courage; to explain the success of Christ's Religion as "a reaction from effete forms of thought to fresh convictions of conscience," grappling with external calamity by independent resources of soul. This is easy, because, after all, Christianity must have a moral side, and ground itself in human sentiment, and here, accordingly, comes into competition with purely moral systems. Such a view, however, omits to remember that Christianity founds moral practice

Eclectic attempt to compose the morality of the Gospel.

Christian morality based on its doctrines.

---

[1] See Plato, *Phæd.* 107, c., Xen. *Mem.* I. iii. 2, &c. On the relation of Platonism to Christianity, comp. Döllinger, *Gentile and Jew*, I. 328, who justly thinks it to be negative rather than positive.

upon doctrinal beliefs,¹ thus procuring new sanctions and originating fresh ideas within the scope of morals. It thus supplied a pure morality by means of dogma before such was recognized through the medium of ethical science. Nor have its dogmas receded before the advance of scientific morality. The moral progress of modern Europe, while it has found nothing discordant in the type of Evangelical character, has tended to confirm the distinctive tenets of the Gospel.²

<small>Christianity introduced a higher moral type.</small>

§ 7. A more thorough and searching examination has sufficiently demonstrated the advance towards a purer and higher type of character made under the auspices of Christian doctrine, and as a consequence of it, in the absolute embodiment of Divine love which it proposes to all ages for imitation in endless variety. While

---

[1] Mr. Lecky, *H. Rat.*, I. 335-6, considers that dogmatic systems serve only to supply suitable motives of action in the absence of a moral philosophy. Its formation, he thinks, is the first step in the decadence of religions. This is true to this extent, that the most elementary forms of religion seem to afford little trace of ethics (compare Tylor, *Hist. Prim. Cult.*, I. 286). On the other hand, ethics may, as in Confucianism, overpower and extinguish the religious element. "To give oneself earnestly to the duties due to men, and while respecting spiritual beings, to keep aloof from them, may be called wisdom," this was the maxim and practice of its founder.—See Legge, II. 130, 319. But it has been truly said that so-called natural religion, the apotheosis of moral abstractions, exists only in books. Religions which have vital force and influence, are positive religions, *i. e.* they make for themselves a Church and rites and dogmas.

[2] The course of attacks on Christianity from this side has been, first, to separate theology from morals, which, as having a scientific basis, has had some share of success; next, to supersede religion by morality, a much less hopeful undertaking.

doing justice to pre-Christian ideas,[1] to the aims of Stoical and Platonic ethics, and to the practice of an Aurelius and a Julian "lending a passing dignity to the dishonoured purple," it has yet shown how poor was the substitute they contemplated for a faith which appealed courageously, but also triumphantly, to the masses, and was the creed alike of the slave and of the sage. It is often thought enough to remark that Paganism was doomed before Christianity appeared. But why, if this be so, did Christianity alone succeed, alone survive of all the sects and schools which competed for the mastery of mankind? Why not simple monotheism, or some abstract form of thought? "Christianity grew," it has been said,[2] "because it could best make good the blank left by the discredit of the old religions, by the despondency, incredulity, and disgust which made room for it." True; and these were the first results which convinced the world and converted it. It was found to contain all essential verities.[3] The fundamental ideas of Natural Religion con-

It succeeded from its very superiority.

Causes of this superiority.

---

[1] See at length Mr. Lecky, *H. E. M.*, I. 180, 190, 363. "Of the sects of ancient philosophy the Stoic is perhaps the nearest to Christianity. Yet even to this sect Christianity is fundamentally opposite."

[2] Mackay, *Rise and Progress of Christianity*, p. 163. See Neander's reflections at the opening of his history, I. p. 3, and Dean Merivale's *Lectures*, p. xi. "Christianity, in fact, was not simply the resource of a dissatisfied philosophy: it was not accepted as the only refuge from the blank negation of a creed. It was the tried and approved of several claimants to the sovereignty of the religious instincts among men."

[3] Compare Saisset, *Essais*, p. 299.

fessedly belong to it. It inherited all that is true in earlier theologies and systems of philosophy;[1] the unity, the personality, the independence, the energy, the love of the Divine Nature; the grandeur, the littleness, the strength, the weakness, the dignity, the responsibility of man. No philosophical mind would desire to deny the obligations of Christianity to foregoing systems among which it assumes its due and ordered rank;[2] or that its teaching is in a sense progressive, the outcome and result of time. Jewish prophecy and heathen philosophy had in different ways prepared for its reception. Christ came to fulfil the Law and the Prophets; the Law of Moses, it is true; but no less the Law of Nature, and of Gentile morality in its highest and purest conceptions. For these, Jewish Prophecy no less prepared a way, and often antedated their spirit.[3]

In what manner a result of the age in which it appeared.

§ 8. A bold attempt has been sometimes made

to Christian morality as defective.

[1] Compare Prof. Jowett (*S. Paul's Epistles*, II. 204). "The peculiarity of the Gospel is not that it teaches what is wholly new, but that it draws out of the treasure house of the human heart things new and old, gathering together into one the dispersed fragments of the truth." Of course it is not intended to represent Christianity as a mere system of eclecticism.

[2] Compare Comte, *Phil. Pos.*, V. 349.

[3] "Christianity," remarks Neander profoundly, "is the end to which all development of the religious consciousness must tend, and of which, therefore, it cannot do otherwise than offer a prophetic testimony. Thus there dwells an element of prophecy, not merely in revealed religion, unfolding itself beneath the fostering care of the Divine Vintager (John xv.) as it struggles onwards from Judaism to its complete disclosure in Christianity, but also in religion, as it grows wild on the soil of Paganism, which by nature must strive unconsciously to

to disparage the truth of Christianity, by charging upon it the inculcation of defective morality, even in the person of its Founder;[1] sometimes of immoral developments, sometimes of ethical rules untrue without requisite limitations, and impossible in practice.[2] Such accusations may on the whole be left to balance one another, as when it is said by one school that the religion of Christ has never sufficiently encouraged the culture of the intellect, and by another that it gives a factitious and disproportionate influence to what are called "the higher parts" of human nature. If the Altruism of the Positivist be deemed an

Self-contradictory.

---

the same end."—*Ch. Hist.*, I. 240, ed. Clark. Comp. Merivale, *Lect.*, p. 70. "The law is the teaching of the human conscience generally, whether enlightened by a revelation, or any other less special illumination from above; by the habits and ideas of human society," &c.

[1] See Strauss, *New Life of Jesus Christ*, I. 438; and Mr. F. Newman on the Defective Morality of the New Test. "The character of Christ," said Paley, finely and truly, "is a part of the morality of the Gospel."

[2] Thus M. Comte regards the Lutheran preference of Faith to Works, and the Calvinistic doctrine of Predestination, as strictly immoral in their tendency. *Phil. Pos.*, V. 685. Shaftesbury (*Works*, I. 98) charges on Christianity the omission of the heroic virtues: of patriotism and public spirit, and of private friendship. Yet Christ Himself wept over His country. Cf. also Rom. ix. 3, 4. Mr. Lecky, *H. Rat.*, II. 113 (see also *H. E. M.*, II. 149), observes, "that Christianity triumphed only by transforming itself under the influence of the spirit of sect." This means that it transferred men's allegiance from their country to the Church. I do not think this is properly chargeable on the principles of the religion. Yet, if true, it would only be substituting a much larger area of patriotism, and one which coincides with a large advance in civilization. The practice of the early Church ("Nec ulla res aliena magis quam publica," Tert. *Apol.* c. xxxviii., and see Origen, *c. Cels.*, VIII. ii.), in this matter furnishes no proper estimate of the intentions of the religion.

Unpractical. improvement on the morality of the Gospel in living for others without the limitation of loving our neighbour only as ourselves, it seems not unreasonable to require that this level should first be reached.[1] Total annihilation of self, at best an impracticable dream, was far from the thought of Him who "knew what is in man." But Christianity has been charged with other more practical

Further objections from the results of Christianity. failures. Indifferent and injurious to secular progress, to material welfare and industrial development ("infructuosi in negotiis dicimur"), it has been taxed with the custom of religious wars, of persecution for opinion, with the institution of torture, with doctrines pernicious to sound morals, such as absolution, indulgences, the placing ceremonial observance before natural duty, the reprobation of good actions wrought without the pale of the Church, and a benevolence, however well-meaning, yet economically mistaken. It has been blamed for errors in practice fraught with social misery and mischief, yet consequent on Scriptural, or at the least ecclesiastical, doctrine.[2] So also for shortcomings in the enforcement of moral

---

[1] There are, indeed, some good remarks on this point in Comte, *Phil. Pos.*, IV. 553, V. 434. Compare Prof. Goldwin Smith, *Study of Hist.*, p. 3, and Mr. Herbert Spencer, *Study of Sociology*, *Cont. Rev.*, XXI. 318–321.

[2] Compare Condorcet, as quoted by Comte, *Phil. Pos.*, V. 423. Such are the medieval view of the sinfulness of usury, the treatment of witchcraft, the wager of battle, the institution of Monasticism, &c. See Mr. Farrar's remarks (*Witness of Hist. to Christ*), Lecture V.

laws, with an inability, for example, to suppress warfare, to prevent or redress social injustice and economic errors. The importance of such charges lies not only in their imputation on the moral estimate of Christianity, but still more on its value as an instrument in civilization, and as consequently a permanent agent in human progress. Nor can it be denied that the evils in question are in some sort the results of the teaching of Christian ideas. Unless, however, it can be shown that they are the logical consequents of such ideas, their natural fruit and reasonable issue, so that each can be referred to the doctrine on which it rests, forming part of the actual message of Christianity, no vital blow has so far been struck on the armour of Christian defence. Religious wars were certainly not unknown to other times and other systems. All may, perhaps, be more correctly attributed to a political or defensive origin,[1] or to a survival of Paganism, wherein "the kingdom of Heaven suffered violence," and "the violent took it by force." The political effect of a common faith is to react hostilely upon foreign creeds. Persecution for belief, whatever immediate motive is assigned to it, was practised by Pagan rulers in

Their importance.

Such results are not chargeable on the principles of the religion.

Case of religious wars.

Persecution for belief.

---

[1] The wars of Charlemagne may be cited in this respect: the Crusades were actually defensive. See Comte, *Phil. Pos.*, V. 404. Compare Paley's remarks on some supposed effects of Christianity (*Evid.*, II. vii.). The religions of Greece and of Rome, so far forth as State institutions, involved penal consequences and even death. See Döllinger, *Gentile and Jew*, I. 243-5.

pre-Christian times. Yet it may be admitted that both the evils complained of, the custom of warfare on the score of religion, and of persecution for erroneous belief, flow to some extent from the nature of the case, and are due to the action of historical Christianity.[1] Partly, indeed, they were based on a false analogy of Christian duty with the Levitical code. But there is probably a necessary tendency in all dogmatic teaching to condemn error in opinion as a duty, and that too more strongly than immorality itself. Toleration even now is not uncommonly held to involve or imply scepticism. Prior to experience, it is expected that compulsion can procure uniformity;[2] and the golden rule is forgotten, "Religionis non est religionem cogere." The outward confession of faith is not readily distinguished from a saving implicit belief; and in the confusion compulsion is enlisted on the side of a mistaken humanity, whether for the victim or the survivor;[3] but,

[1] The judicial murder of Priscillian dates A.D. 386. It was condemned by Ambrose and Martin of Tours, though not by Leo. The early Christian apologists naturally express themselves on the side of toleration. Lactantius, but fifty years before the death of Priscillian, and himself a resident at Trèves, thus writes: " Religio cogi non potest ; verbis potius quàm verberibus res agenda est ut sit voluntas. Nihil est tam voluntarium quam religio."—*Div. Inst.*, V. xx.

[2] And so indeed, in fact, it has succeeded in doing: but only after the manner of those who, in the words of Tacitus, " solitudinem faciunt, pacem appellant."

[3] See Mr. Lecky's remarks, *Hist. Rat.*, II. 11, *Hist. Eur. Mor.*, I. 420, on the inevitable tendency, if not the moral compulsion, to proselytism which underlies an assumed possession of truth. See Dean Hook, *Lives of Archb.*, N. S., I. 7-9.

however present to the eye of the Founder of our religion as a result of the leaven wherewith He leavened the Church and the world, can this fact be properly urged against His teaching as a fault or a crime? Rather it is the consequence of its historical development, of the tardy course of human affairs,[1] and, philosophically considered, of the imperfection and limitation of the creature. By the union and identification of the Church and Empire, orthodoxy became an Imperial interest, and persecution for opinion was rendered not only possible, but politically incumbent. It is not, then, the words of Christ,[2] which are answerable for the teaching of a duty of persecution. God forbid. But rather the supremacy, in the State, of the Church. Heresy and schism, as ecclesiastical offences, were put on the same footing with rebellion as a civil crime.[3]

Predicted by Christ.

Course of events.

§ 9. But, it may still be said, these evils are chargeable on Christianity as a system, as an historical fact; they have followed in its train. And, no doubt, it is not intended to clear the Religion of

The historical results of Christianity, no doubt, of a mixed character.

---

[1] "For fifteen hundred years after the establishment of the Christian religion it was intellectually and morally impossible that any religion that was not material and superstitious could have reigned over Europe." —Lecky, *H. R.*, II. 227.

[2] "Compel them to come in." See Bayle's famous treatise (*Contrains-les d'entrer*), and Ffoulkes' *Div. Christ.*, pp. 91–2.

[3] There is a remarkable defence in Dr. Draper's *Hist. of the Intellectual Devel. in Europe* (I. 134) of the medieval policy of repression, grounded on a supposed foresight of the fearful consequences of the intellect of a people outgrowing their religious formulæ.

Christ of all its attendant effects, as though the brightest light never cast a shadow. The innocent blood shed by the Churches of East and West is the price paid for the enforcement of dogmas otherwise fraught with good. It is enough to weigh in the balance the acknowledged services of Christianity against its confessed ills; and more especially to examine whether such evils are properly inherent in its frame.[1] If not, they need not, it is clear, overcloud its future. As a matter of fact we have already outlived them. The opinions to which they are due, are now admitted to be elements foreign to the nature of our Religion, antagonistic to its inner life and spirit, and inconsistent with its central ideas.[2] Thus a real distinction has always to be drawn between faulty inferences or erroneous applications of Scriptural language to the subjects of morals, policy, and science, and the actual and eternal teaching of the Bible. The very tendency manifest in the general history of nations to employ religion, outside of its central scheme, as a political engine in matters of social law and civil government, has led to this result. Of this character[3] are the notions of usury being immoral, of

The evils not inherent in the system,

and transient.

Due to Scriptural misinterpretation.

Instances.

---

[1] "Le Christianisme a été intolérant: mais l'intolérance n'est pas un fait essentiellement chrétien." — Renan, *Vie de Jésus-Christ*, p. 412.

[2] See some good remarks on this subject in the *Christian Remembrancer*, No. CXXXI., p. 232.

[3] For the political economy of Christianity, as not being incompatible with historical progress, see Goldwin Smith (*Lect.*, p. 39).

the production of wealth being condemned, of a community of goods, of one absolute, universal form of political government, of the unlawfulness of military defence. Political and economic errors have on these subjects shielded themselves with the authority of Inspiration, and, by rendering scientific progress impossible, have risked the permanence of Christianity itself. But with the advance of knowledge and free inquiry this confusion has been long on the wane. Salmasius,[1] for example, wrote successfully to correct the medieval idea that the Bible condemns usury, and Protestantism found no difficulty in receiving the correction. The true embarrassment lay in the claims of Roman Catholic tradition. Some errors might more properly be regarded as anticipations of truth. Thus primitive Christianity found in a transient communism[2] a natural expression of new-born love and zeal. It never sought to erect a doctrine, inimical to all eco-

And to premature movements.

---

[1] See Mr. Lecky, *H. Rat.*, II. 290, who has pursued the whole inquiry with his usual vigour and in a fair spirit. Mr. Buckle (I. 283) on the contrary declaims, with heat, against "the ignorant interference of Christian rulers," forgetting that other religions have at least made the same mistakes. Thus the Mahometan law prohibits interest altogether, with the natural result. See *Wealth of Nations*, Bk. I. c. ix.

[2] Resting mainly on Luke xii. 33. The rhetorical statement of Tertullian is well known (*Apol.*, xxxix.) : " Omnia indiscreta sunt apud nos praeter uxores." Clement of Alexandria, in his treatise *Quis dives salvetur*, rejects the notion of communism. See also *Strom.*, III. 449, and Augustine, *Haer.*, c. xl. In *Enarr. in Ps.* 124, § 2, he rebukes the opinion that "non debuit Deus facere pauperes: sed soli divites esse debuerunt." On the view of Ambrose as to the right of property in *land* (*de Off. Minist.*, I. xxviii., and *Serm.* 8 *in I's.* 118, § 22), see Schmidt, *Essai*, p. 259 ; also Champagny, *Charité Chrétienne*.

nomical progress into a normal condition of society. "Whenever a great religious movement," it has been truly said, "has taken place in history, the spirit of humanity has beaten in this way against its earthly bars, and struggled to realize at once that which cannot be realized within any calculable time, if it is destined ever to be realized here."[1]

Charges of feebleness and inutility.

§ 10. The charge of feebleness and inutility is, indeed, of a wholly different kind; and will be variously estimated by different persons according to the measure of their previous expectation of the working of Christianity. But it must be borne

Too general.

in mind that we are no judges of its possible or of its proper operation;[2] of the relations or course of affairs which make up the government of the world. Nor can Christianity be fairly accused of failure in these respects, unless indeed

Should be tested by its own predictions of itself.

the result has not answered to its own predictions. But this it is not attempted to show. Thus the continuance of wars among mankind has been deemed in some quarters a strong objection to

---

[1] Prof. Goldwin Smith, *u. s.*, p. 41.

[2] For Bishop Butler's canon is no less true than stern: "Objections against Christianity, as distinguished from objections against its evidence, are frivolous."—*Anal.*, II. iii. For if the natural and moral government of God be a scheme but imperfectly comprehensible, how much more so is the course of revealed religion. "When we argue," says Paley, "concerning Christianity, that it must necessarily be true because it is beneficial, we go, perhaps, too far on one side; and we certainly go too far on the other when we conclude that it must be false because it is not so efficacious as we could have supposed."—*Evid.*, II. vi.

the usefulness and credit of Christianity.¹ But such objectors fail to perceive that the continued existence of warfare is a result of man's moral nature remaining unchanged, and this perhaps by an express provision of nature, wars being a main element in the course of rudimentary civilization at the least. No doubt, it is the work of the Religion of Christ to bring about this change. It does so by substituting larger and unselfish sympathies; by reducing the theory of war to a defensive instead of an offensive basis.² But His kingdom upon the earth in the hearts and spirits of men, though universal, was to be created slowly by suasion, not by miracle.³ There is no engagement on its part to abolish selfishness, passion, sin, speedily or throughout. By slow advances in individual sanctification a higher level was to be reached of moral type, of peacefulness and love. The present comparative rarity of war in respect of former ages is admitted. Little by little, it may be hoped, this scourge is retreating before the march of civilization. Trade, law, diplomacy, literature, political

[margin: These are in course of fulfilment.]

[margin: Increased rarity of wars.]

---

¹ See Mr. Buckle, *Hist. Civ.*, I. 191. Mr. Lecky, *Hist. Rat.*, II. 384, arguing from a general immemorial union between the sacerdotal and the military spirit, infers that no theological agencies are pacific. This is hardly convincing. See also *H. E. M.*, II. 269.

² See Comte, *Phil. Pos.*, V. 82. Mr. Freeman (*Norman Conq.*, I. 33) observes, "the evangelical precepts of peace and love did not put an end to war; they did not put an end to aggressive conquests, but they distinctly humanized the way in which war was carried on."

³ Compare Dr. Mozley, *Bamp. Lect.*, p. 17: "We can, indeed, in imagination conceive," &c.

science, even the invention of fire-arms and improved means of locomotion, have been assigned a share in this momentous change.[1] But has the religious sentiment been altogether without part in it; and among other elements is no effect to be attributed to the spread of a purer Christianity? An under-current of humiliation mixes now with the *Te Deums* of victory; and ministers of mercy claim their place in the ranks of contending armies. A growing sense of the *folly* of war may be due to advancing culture; a conviction of its *wickedness* can only spring from a Religion whose mission upon earth is "peace, good will toward men."

How far due to Christian influence.

§ 11. We have been led more than once in our preceding remarks to the confines of a subject which, in our review of objections to the progress and permanence of Christianity, is the last awaiting examination; I mean, the relations between Science and Religion; their distinctive position and respective consummation. Is this peace or war? Is a *modus vivendi* practicable between them? Or do they necessarily and eternally conflict? As darkness flees at the approach of dawn, must one pale before the other's rising beams; and is this the fate reserved for the time-honoured claims

Relations between science and Christianity.

Whether formidable to the permanence of our religion.

---

[1] See Buckle, *u. s.*, I. 203, 224. Christian efforts in this direction, put forth in the darkest and most violent ages, even where unsuccessful, should not be disparaged. Such were the "Peace of God," the "Truce of God" (the former having the wider scope), and the like. See Gieseler, II. 447. Robertson, *Church Hist.*, II. 504-5; also Lecky, *Hist. Rat.*, II. 115.

of Religion, as hitherto understood; and in especial for the faith of Jesus Christ, under the full light and fierce heat of a noontide civilization? Some, it is true, still hold that a real conflict between Science and Religion is in the nature of things unlikely or impossible. "Not only are the two heterogeneous;[1] but the results of Science, whether physical or human, are part of the data which it is the function of Religion to co-ordinate." "The time is approaching," says a careful and impartial writer,[2] "when it will be generally perceived that, so far from Science being opposed to Religion, true Religion without Science is impossible. And if we consider the various aspects of Christianity as understood by different nations, we can hardly fail to perceive that the dignity, and therefore the truth, of their religious beliefs is in direct relation to the knowledge of Science and of the great physical laws by which our universe is governed." "The natural works of God," wrote Faraday,[3] "can never by any possibility come in contradiction with the higher things which belong to our future existence . . . I do not think it at all necessary to tie the study of the Natural Sciences and Religion together."

In the view of some, no real conflict between them.

On the other hand, a multitude of reasons have been adduced to weaken this position. "Of all anta-

Opposite view.

---

[1] Prof. Westcott, *Cont. Rev.*, VIII. 377.
[2] Sir J. Lubbock, *Orig. Civ.*, p. 256.
[3] *Life*, II. 196.

gonisms of belief," says Mr. Herbert Spencer,[1] "the oldest, the widest, the most profound, and the most important, is that between Religion and Science. It commenced when the recognition of the simplest uniformities in surrounding things set a limit to the previously universal fetishism. It shows itself everywhere throughout the domain of human knowledge, affecting man's interpretations alike of the simplest mechanical accidents and of the most complicated events in the histories of nations. It has its roots deep down in the diverse habits of thought of different orders of minds."[2] Then the tests of history and experience, it is said, prove the uniform undeviating growth of knowledge, and a corresponding decline in the power and spread of Religion. This, indeed, is a matter of fact, and, as such, admits a direct reply. But next, it is added, there are circumstances to explain this alleged result. All advance is intellectual; Religion is of its own nature stationary, conservative, reactionary. This is the very moral of the history of Persecution

Appeals to experience.

Grounds of this opinion.

---

[1] *First Principles*, p. 12.

[2] Prof. Huxley takes up different ground: "The present antagonism between theology and science does not arise from any assumption by the men of science that all theology must necessarily be excluded from science; but simply because they are unable to allow that reason and morality have two weights and two measures; and that the belief in a proposition because authority tells you it is true, or because you wish to believe it, which is a high crime and misdemeanor when the subject-matter of reason is of one kind, becomes, under the *alias* of 'faith,' the greatest of all virtues when the subject-matter of reason is of another kind."—*Cont. Rev.*, XVIII. 457.

for belief. Again, Revelation is incompatible not only with the claims of Reason, but with the results of Science. The advance of knowledge undermines the bases of religious beliefs by impairing the states of mind on which they repose, and the needs for which they exist. By explaining phenomena, by reducing them to universal invariable expressions, by substituting continued for free agency, most existing religions, all in fact but a religion of Nature, if such really exists, are merged in the scale of superstitions unworthy of scientific acceptance. For the sphere of Knowledge is held to be positive; the real is bounded by the realm of sensation; all beyond is chimerical, is vain. Wonder recedes as the antecedents of all phenomena become known; and with wonder fear, and with fear reverence, and with reverence adoration, and with adoration the *caput mortuum* of religious belief.

§ 12. Not to admit a fact is, of course, to disallow the reasons by which it is sought to be explained. If Religion (I speak more particularly of the Faith of Jesus Christ) exhibits no decline, it may be held unnecessary to dispute the alleged conditions of such a catastrophe. It may be well, notwithstanding, to encounter the particular objections against the prospects of Christianity which have been here brought within view. They affect its past as well as its future, explaining its successes by other than spiritual antecedents, and denying it a career in the

The truth of this view denied.

Reasons for meeting it in detail.

ultimate advance of mankind. Let us inquire, then, in the first place, whether it be true that in Religion we find the sole branch of human activity which is of a stationary character, ever looking backward, never forward; bound by the laws of its being to a rigid immobility. What is the conception of its nature which necessitates such inferences respecting it?

Conception of the nature of religious principles on which this view is based.

All Religion, I apprehend, in this view of it, being based on a fundamental Revelation, is assumed to announce truths of a final and unique character, capable of extension by nothing unless a further revealment, conveyed through a special illumination. But such a mode of information is not only beyond and beside, it is in opposition to, the ordinary means and ways of knowledge. For these are tentative and curious of inquiry; so that the position of knowledge in respect of an existing standard of belief or duty can never be guaranteed, neither can it even temporarily acquiesce in any foregone conclusion. It is in this way, then, that while Religion is stationary, Science and Thought inherently progress.

How far admissible.

In reply it may be admitted that a truth of Revelation is not homogeneous with the conclusions of research, experiment, or reason.[1] It is accepted on other and particular grounds; accordingly its sphere of relation is special also. Its kingdom is not of this world. It deals not with that which

Distinct sphere of religious truth

[1] Compare Dr. J. H. Newman, *Essay on Devel.*, c. iii. § 5.

constitutes the real limit of positive knowledge, the present physical condition of the universe; it carries us on to that region of the unseen or supernatural[1] upon which Nature everywhere borders and rests. The phenomena which it explains point to a future stage of being, with which alone it is properly occupied. Its home is in the spirit of man, his conscience, the higher reason and will. "The natural man receiveth not the things of the spirit of God, for they are foolishness unto him; neither can he *know* them, because they are spiritually discerned."[2] The beliefs which these inspire are no affirmations of the intellect only—no products of the logical faculty. Its dry light has here no place or room. They address themselves to the spirit in man, and by a living act of that spirit they are apprehended and appropriated. Psychologically they are instances of that indefinite consciousness which, as has been well said, "cannot be formulated." They are thoughts which, "though impossible to complete, are real, being normal affections of the mind."[3] Nor is there anything on this side of man's nature which is truly reactionary in its relation to mundane knowledge. Industrial development, for example, has been held to be

Why called spiritual.

Their psychological character

---

[1] "In our definitions," says Emerson, "we grope after the spiritual by describing it as invisible. The true meaning of spiritual is real: that law which executes itself, which works without means, and which cannot be conceived as not existing."

[2] 1 Cor. ii. 14.

[3] Herbert Spencer, *First Princ.*, p. 88.

inconsistent with theological beliefs from being in its nature secular, and depending on the fixity of natural laws. But is the earth, we may ask, to be less well tilled, its riches straitened, its secrets less amply communicated, because Revelation unfolds the home beyond, where the "wicked cease from troubling and the weary are at rest"? Surely, as a matter of experience, it is true that "man doth not live by bread alone." The true strength of Religion, then, lies in its allowing all other intellectual activity to be progressive and indefinite; a very "infinite of thought." For itself it claims only a just acquiescence in human testimony for its evidence, and the confluence of the higher instincts with its revelations. It "speaks not in words which man's wisdom teacheth, but which the Holy Ghost teacheth, comparing spiritual things with spiritual." "Thus may we know the things which are freely given to us of God." No antagonism, then, with the tendencies or results of Science is to be feared, but such as renders the existence of a spiritual element in man unlikely or impossible.[1] Around this central fact the battle must be waged of atheism with faith in God, of secularism with theology, of materialism with Christianity. For the rest the discoveries of Science constitute no standing menace to the teachings of Revelation:

marginalia: not truly reactionary; or aggressive.; At what point antagonistic to science or natural knowledge.

[1] Compare Prof. Goldwin Smith's noble reflections, *Lect. on Study of Hist.*, p. 46. "Let true science make what discoveries it will, for example, as to the origin of life," &c.

nor needs Religion perish because Knowledge strides onward. They occupy, in fact, distinct spheres, moving in different planes; nor do they touch each other vitally in one point of their circumference. No doubt, this has not been always, if it be now, understood. There have been eras in human progress when the claims of Theology have been alike extravagant and fatal. There have been martyrs consequently in science no less than for religious belief.[1] Rested upon false and foreign pretentions the very truth of Christianity as a whole has been put on its trial, and has been staked upon impossible or insignificant issues. *Eppur si muove* is the answer to all such disputations. But have not these already, at least in large measure, passed away? The strange passion for balancing the whole structure of Christian truth on isolated and subsidiary questions has well-nigh burnt itself out; while those which still remain are yielding to the gentler touch of reason and of time.[2] In thus speaking, I do not say that it is not good in these latter days to re-read, in some of its portions, the

Foregone conflicts.

These already on the decline.

Past lessons.

---

[1] Though, according to Cyprian, "esse martyr non potest qui in Ecclesiâ non est."—*De Unit. Eccl.* Augustine remarked more justly, "Martyrem non facit pœna sed causa."

[2] Χρόνος εὐμαρὴς θεός.—Soph. It is the more to be regretted that here and there some ill-timed pæan of victory on the side of science seeks to fan the decaying embers of theological jealousies. Thus it is proclaimed that "the gradual destruction of the old theology is everywhere preceded by the growth and diffusion of physical truths."—Buckle, III. 478. "Extinguished theologians," cries another, "lie about the cradle of every science as the strangled snake beside that of

history of the Church: and by its tempered light, chequered with the fortunes of the past, re-adjust the relations of doctrine to the demands of Science and the warnings of experience. Much in days gone by has been assailed, which now we should be careful to accept. Much has been maintained which now we do not care to defend.

> Non tali auxilio, non defensoribus istis
> Tempus eget.

The letter of inspiration, the questionable text, the unwarranted reading or rendering, the long-drawn dubious inference, the uncertain voice of tradition, the arrogant ill-founded assumption of the supremacy of authority over reason, of dogma over conscience, the little-heeded intruded fallacy, at best the poor fabric of human ingenuity imported into a heaven-sent mystery (for *Scriptura non fallit, si se homo non fallat*);¹ all these must pass away, and with them the heats and bickerings, the jealousies and variance of bygone controversies. For never will the work of Christ take root, or the message of His salvation go forward among men, till it is known and felt that "that message is peace, and its effect quietness and assurance for ever." Yet it must be admitted that throughout the past history

Spirit of the Gospel message.

Hercules."—Huxley, *Lay S.*, p. 305. As a matter of fact what essential portions can be named of Christian orthodoxy which have been surrendered or destroyed? Some fancied outwork perchance, some moss-grown battlement: but what vital doctrine of the faith or saving truth?

¹ Augustin. *de Urbis Excidio*, c. ii.

of the Christian Church, in proportion to the intricacy, doubtfulness, and transcendental character of the dogma involved, the passions of men have risen highest, their feelings have been the most deeply stirred,[1] till error has been magnified into guilt, and difficulty of conviction into reprobation. In view of the permanence of the Faith which we inherit, it is important to remember that, while in no wise committed to the errors of the past, Christianity has before it all the promise of the future. A sense of the reality of Christian truth as a spiritual religion, based not so much on logical convictions as on a personal relation of the believer to the "God of the spirits of all flesh," "Who hath spoken unto us by his Son," this it is which is essential to the progress of Christianity among mankind. Hence our safeguard against surrendering the vital elements of an objective faith in mistaken consideration for the doubts and difficulties of a half belief. "He that is not with us, is against us; and he that gathereth not with Me, scattereth

The permanence of Christianity as a religion ensured by its past experience.

Vital doctrines have been ascertained and tested.

---

[1] "Divisions in matter of religion," says Hooker, "are hotlier prosecuted and pursued than other strifes, forasmuch as coldness, which in other contentions may be thought to proceed from moderation, is not in these so favourably construed."—Vol. II., p. 4, ed. Keble. Johnson attributed it to personal uneasiness when our confidence in an opinion which we value is diminished. But Coleridge, with more penetration, has observed that deep feeling has a tendency to combine with obscure ideas; a fact not confined to professed theologians, but exhibited by whole nations.—*Friend*, I. 138. Merivale, *Conversion of North. Nations*, pp. 42, 43, has well shown that "Arianism was but a slightly disguised Paganism: and so no question of a letter," &c.

abroad," speaks surely an eternal warning. The victories of Christianity have everywhere been the triumphs of a definite faith. It has ever given forth to the world no uncertain sound in its conflicts with Rationalism or with the passions and licence of mankind. The *residuum* of a religion from which there has been carefully filtered off all special truths and objects of belief, retaining only some few moral generalities, can but issue in something very dissimilar to a living historic Christianity. To the last, it is true, some differences as to the larger and more intractable problems of man's nature in relation to God and the external world may be expected to remain among Christians themselves. There can, however, be no question as to the disintegrating effects of time and advancing knowledge on the peculiar prepossessions of individual schools of thought and belief. There is a tendency arising from the historical antecedents of Protestantism to undervalue that catholicity of belief which must undoubtedly be held to be the normal and ultimate condition of Christianity, answering to those larger speculations on the continuity and totality of human history which Science now opens out to view. The corrective to this tendency lies in a truer appreciation of the essential spirit of Protestantism.[1] Appealing to reason, without renouncing an authoritative standard, and

Prospects of Christianity in favour of ultimate unity.

Value of the principle of Protestantism.

[1] See Mr. Ffoulkes' remarks, *Divisions of Christendom*, p. 195.

to private judgment fortified by the verdict of historical inquiry, its standing-point fits it expressly for the work of reconcilement between a traditional faith and the rationalizing forces of progress. The anarchy of criticism which marks the process of severance and reunion has been mistaken by Comte [1] and others for the ultimate issue of centuries of unreasoning credulity. Protestantism, it is asserted with much injustice, has made no converts, and nowhere enlarges the area of its conquests.[2] Since the treaty of Westphalia, it is said, no new territory has been added to its sway. But its work lies deeper, and must be traced in a re-animation of the spiritual vigour of Christianity, in a general rehabilitation of its beliefs, and in re-arming it to meet the developments of increased knowledge and

Its adaptation to the wants of the time.

Its true function.

---

[1] See *Phil. Pos.*, V. 354. "L'esprit d'inconséquence," &c. V. 299, 327. He is so prejudiced as to see no difference between Primitive Lutheranism and pure Deism.

[2] Macaulay's remarks are well known, *Essays*, pp. 352, 536 : "During these two hundred and fifty years Protestantism has made no conquests worth speaking of. Nay, we believe that, as far as there has been a change, that change has, on the whole, been in favour of the Church of Rome." So also Mr. Lecky, *Hist. Rat.*, I. 187, who adds, "Whatever is lost by Catholicism is gained by Rationalism." The same writer, however, in another passage makes this important admission, "Protestantism as a dogmatic system makes no converts, but it has shown itself capable of blending with and consecrating the prevailing Rationalism."—*Ib.*, II. 93. Prof. Westcott very justly observes, "However imposing the apparent unity of the religious life of the middle ages may be, it cannot be questioned that socially and individually the principles of Christianity are more powerful now than then. We lose the sense of their general action in the variety of forms through which they work."—*Cont. Rev.*, VI. 416.

advancing civilization. It, at least, has no Syllabus to retract, no Decrees to disannul. Liable, indeed, to an excess of critical bias, its true mean lies in a spirit which, ever ready to give an answer of its faith, still tempers faith with charity, and enlarges to the utmost the bounds of agreement in belief; "made all things to all men," if by any means some may be saved; seeing it is "the same Spirit of God which worketh all in all." Doubtless there must arise out of the limitation of human nature itself an ultimate boundary even to Christian charity. It seems a duty to "mete the bounds of hate[1] and love;" and yet

> As far as may be to carve out
> Free space for every human doubt
> That the whole mind may orb about.

Practical limits to toleration of opinion. It seems practically impossible to grasp truth, the truth of sacred things, firmly and yet not jealously; to be as earnest in the propagation of right belief without asserting its confession to be individually necessary to salvation as with such a creed; to hold fast the convictions of personal assurance, and yet to recognize that to all it is not given "to arrive at the knowledge of the truth."

[1] Ps. cxxxix. 21, 22: "Do not I (should I not) hate them, O Lord, that hate Thee? . . . I hate them with perfect hatred." Dr. Kay in his note on this passage cites Archbishop Trench, "Hatred of evil, purely as evil, is eminently a *Christian* grace," and Dean Stanley (*Lect. on J. Ch.*, p. 253), "The duty of keeping alive in the human heart the sense of burning indignation against moral evil, against selfishness, against injustice, against untruth, in ourselves as well as in others,— that is as much a part of the Christian as of the Jewish dispensation."

Yet this weakness springs really from a want of faith. Toleration, if it is not to be indifference, must be grounded on the perception of counter-views as necessarily complementary and tending to establish the ultimate mean of truth. Thus, He who came among men to found "the everlasting Gospel," may be trusted to work with it to its more perfect reception, according to the light and knowledge of the time. Only, let not "the wrath of man" think "to work out the righteousness of God." Christianity has survived revolutions of opinion, which, beforehand, might not unjustly have been deemed fatal to it. "It is I: be not afraid," is the lesson eternally stamped on the changes through which it has passed, and which now, if ever, is applicable in an age saturated with the idea of continuous and universal development, "stirring all science to its very depth, and revolutionizing all historical literature."[1] Such a prospect, in earlier times, may be thought to have offered the only plausible defence of persecution of unbelief. But if so, it is valid no longer. It has pleased God, by the teachings of experience, to "increase our faith." We have learned to believe in the Religion of Jesus Christ, not as an abstract creed, vulnerable in every article; not as "the law of a carnal commandment," which "decayeth and

Principle of genuine toleration.

Grounds of hopefulness.

Christianity a power.

---

[1] Lecky, *Hist. Rat.*, I. 283. "Filiation and development," says M. Littré, *Les Barbares*, p. 139, "constitute the essence of history."

waxeth old;" but as a power,[1] regenerative of our race, subtle and continuous as the agencies of nature, "the power of an endless life." Faith is reassured; we are no longer "ashamed of the Gospel of Christ;" for it is "the power of God unto salvation to every one that believeth."

[1] Compare the opening reflections of Neander, *Ch. Hist.*, I. p. 2. C. Schwarz, *Gesch. der neuesten Theologie*, p. 43, criticises unduly this view of Neander, who, he says, has given accordingly a history of piety, not of the Church.

LECTURE V.

OBJECTIONS TO THE PROGRESS OF CHRISTIANITY CONSIDERED.

"Naturam hominis hanc Deus esse voluit, ut duarum rerum cupidus et appetens esset, religionis et sapientiæ. Sed homines ideo falluntur, quod aut religionem suscipiunt, omissâ sapientiâ; aut sapientiæ soli student, omissâ religione; cum alterum sine altero esse non possit verum."—LACTANTIUS.

"Meantime it seemed as if mankind in Europe, and especially in England and France, had now for the first time opened its eyes to Nature and to its strict conformity with law: and they who yielded themselves unreservedly to this tendency more and more lost sight of the independence and existence of spirit."—DORNER, *Hist. Prot. Theol.*, II. 258.

LECTURE V.

"There is a spirit in man: and the inspiration of the Almighty giveth them understanding."—Job xxxii. 8.

§ 1. IT is urged by some who look on Christianity as a bygone or a transient creed, that not only are the results of scientific inquiry formidable to the reception of orthodoxy in detail; its method also is aggressive, incompatible with the standpoint of theological beliefs. Inductive science rests essentially on the basis of individual and specific experience, on methodized observation. Its reasoning is that of common sense and common life. It appeals only to matters of fact. It is, therefore, from first to last,[1] from principle to conclusion, from the first individual instance examined to the latest universal law registered for future inquiry, within reach, so to speak; patent to sense, and liable to verification. "The man of science," says Professor Huxley,[2] "has learned to believe in justification, not by faith but by verification." Such a method has in it nothing transcendental, nothing superstitious, nothing supernatural. Moreover, it has on its side, it is said, the results of

Objections to the method of Theology as being not inductive.

Popular demand for verification.

---

[1] Compare Comte, *Phil. Pos.*, IV. 697–9.
[2] *Lay Sermons*, p. 22. Mr. Matthew Arnold remarks, that "the licence of affirmation about God and His proceedings in which the religious world indulge, is more and more met by the demand for verification."—*S. Paul and Protestantism*.

Reasons for its being very commonly entertained, time and experience. Former ages have gone wrong in proportion as they have abandoned or failed to recognize the truth of the inductive spirit. It is now on all hands welcomed; and the era of its triumphs has begun. But Theology, it is urged, alone refuses to be brought within its sway. Its information flows from another source. "In Theology,[1] certain principles are taken for granted; and, it being deemed impious to question them, all that remains is, to reason from them downward."[2] The general truths which bind up and enwrap its conclusions, are the gift of anterior Revelation. They cannot be substantiated by facts, and are accepted with an unreasoning assent. For Religion, "taking its ground on the first conclusions obtained in the process of human reflection, thenceforth obstinately defends what it holds to be Divine revelations. But the supposed revelations inevi- *and Theology and Science being held to be diametrically opposed.* tably come into collision with new ideas and experiences to which Science alone can afford to give a hearing."[3] Thus, while Science is the result of inquiry, Theology is bred of faith; its theory precedes experience and controls it. In

---

[1] M. Guizot, *Civil. en France*, II. 385, points out how early this conflict arose between the scientific spirit and theological deduction, when remarking on the Neo-Platonism of Alexandria, and the kindred views in medieval times of Scotus Erigena. Mr. Mackay, *Rise and Progress of Christianity*, p. 288, prefers to deduce the existing dualism of Theology and Science from the Nominalism of Occam.

[2] See Mr. Buckle at length, *Hist. Civ.*, III. 282-3, 464.

[3] See Mr. Mackay, *u. s.*, pp. 270-1.

the one, doubt, scepticism, originality, aptness to discover, are virtues and the highest of duties. In the other, originality is the parent of heresy, and therefore a crime. Thus in Christianity it is an accepted principle that "there can be no concerning truth which is not ancient; and whatsoever is truly new, is certainly false."¹ Or, as it has been said, "That is true which is first, that is false which is after." Faith becomes thus an indispensable duty, and credulity an honour. "It is impossible to establish the old theological premisses by a chain of inductive reasoning."²

§ 2. I have quoted objections which show pretty clearly the current of thought which is at present setting in on the relations of Theology to Science. In replying to them, I shall not now stay to prove that a fitting measure of scientific scepticism (a term, however, covering very opposite meanings), is by no means out of place in the elements of a religious philosophy. It was a theologian³ to

Scepticism (rightly understood) not incompatible with a religious philosophy.

---

¹ Bp. Pearson, *Expos. of Creed*, dedication. This corresponds to the maxim of Vincentius Lirin., "Dum novè dicitur, non dicantur nova."
² Mr. Buckle, III. 283.
³ Archbishop Leighton, thus declaring himself a Cartesian. The noble maxims, "Intellectum valdè ama"; "Fides quærens intellectum," are worthy of the brightest age of culture. For the meanings and history of Scepticism, see Dr. Farrar, *Bampt. L.*, 592-3. "The best Christian in the world," said Shaftesbury, *Works*, III. 72, "who, being destitute of the means of certainty, depends only on history and tradition for his belief, is at best but a sceptic-Christian." "Scepticism," writes Bishop Harvey Goodwin, "implies only that a man is determined to look into matters for himself; not to trust every assertion, not to repeat a parrot-creed." Leibnitz's golden rule must be

P

whom we owe the remark, "that men that know nothing in sciences have no doubts." That during certain periods in the history of the Church belief was held meritorious in proportion to the doubtfulness of the subject, is perhaps true;[1] but it was not so from the beginning. It will, however, probably be admitted that truths of Religion are of two kinds, primary or inferred, principles or conclusions. The latter have certainly been obtained by reasoning, and reasoning not necessarily of one kind. The theology of the Reformers, for example, showed that careful inductive examination into the sources and history of doctrines, the facts of our religion, and the contents of the Bible, is in no wise alien to the spirit of the Christian faith.[2] The same spirit has survived and dominated later controversies, and is at this very hour invading the precincts of Catholicism. But not only so. The records of our faith, their genuine-

Distinction between primary and inferred truths in religion.

The latter frequently obtained by induction.

---

borne in mind: "Il faut prendre garde de ne jamais abandonner les vérités nécessaires et éternelles pour soutenir les mystères; de peur que les ennemis de la religion ne prennent droit là-dessus de décrier et la religion et les mystères." "Religious disbelief and philosophical scepticism are not merely not the same, but have no natural connection."—Sir W. Hamilton, *Lect.*, I. 394.

[1] Compare Milman, *Lat. Christ.*, I. 439.

[2] Hence the historical labours of the *Magdeburg Centuriators*, and Selden's famous saying, that "the text '*Search the Scriptures*' had set the world in uproar." It would be interesting to inquire how far the impulse was thus given to inductive tendencies which culminated in the Baconian method. On the rule and practice of an "Inductive Exposition," Isaac Taylor, *Hist. Enthusiasm*, p. 314, grounds his expectation of the reunion of all Protestant bodies.

ness, authenticity, and even inspiration, the value of the manuscripts on which they rest, and of the testimonies by which they are supported, all such points lie open to inductive instruments of inquiry; and these are being more and more largely employed by the ablest theologians of the day. And if this be true in the case of the Sacred Volume, which in whatever measure conveys the Word of God, it is still more true in respect of doctrines[1] dependent for their authority on the practice and common tradition of the Church. Here at least the conclusions at issue, affecting the hereditary standing of opinions and usages, are within the range of historical inquiry; that is, of a science of observation, and are of a tentative character. In its inferential portion, then, Theology nowhere refuses to accept the ascending road of a patient and rigorous induction. It stands on the same foot with other branches of historical criticism. And to turn to the principles (for Christian dogmas have been properly termed the principles of Theological Science on which, as upon axioms, the cardinal truths of our Religion must finally turn), are these fairly described as the products of unreasoning acceptance, even if they have some analogy[2] with the maxims or conventional *ultimata*

Theology a science of historical criticism, reaching even to its primary truths.

[1] See Mr. Ffoulkes' remarks, *Divisions of Christendom*, p. 196.

[2] This is the view of Bacon, *Augm. Sc.*, IX. i. "In rebus naturalibus ipsa principia examini subjiciuntur . . . . . aliter fit in religione; ubi et primæ propositiones anthypostatæ sunt atque per se subsistentes;

of legal and political science? As dependent on facts received upon testimony and observation, they stand on historical evidence open to inductive inquiry. Christianity indeed, as an historic religion, has in this respect specific claims upon a Positive school of thought.[1] Miraculous and portentous events, it has never been denied, must be subjected to this test, and stand or fall by its verdict, so that the latest assaults upon these have been directed to the end of discrediting any amount of testimony which may be brought on their behalf. The tendencies of human nature, it is held, in a credulous age are more than sufficient to account for the result.[2] Nor when the facts of the Scriptural narrative have been adequately attested, are its doctrines altogether exempt from the processes of a positive method. The analogy of Nature may be employed in attacking or in defending them. This line of argument may be applied within some extent even to those conceptions of the Divine

Employment of natural analogy

et rursus non reguntur ab illâ ratione quæ propositiones consequentes deducit. Neque tamen hoc fit in religione solâ, sed etiam in aliis scientiis, tam gravioribus quàm levioribus: ubi scilicet propositiones primariæ placita sunt, non posita; siquidem et in illis rationis usus absolutus esse non potest."

[1] Compare Prof. Westcott's remarks in *Cont. Rev.*, VIII. 373. He infers that there is no fundamental antagonism between the Positive method and Christianity; and that the former is no lasting religious power, but a transitional preparation for a fuller faith.

[2] Bishop Butler's warning is here of importance:—"The credulity of mankind is acknowledged: and the suspicions of mankind ought to be acknowledged too; and their backwardness even to believe, and greater still to practise what makes against their interest."

Nature on which the Christian system rests. It is sufficient to overthrow the objection, otherwise a plausible one, that in accepting a scheme of Revelation, we are but hallowing the creations of the human intellect — notions which, being limited, cannot but be inadequate and misleading; thus, as it were, "sacrificing to our net, and burning incense to our drag." Again the facts in regard of human nature and of human history which the system of Christianity assumes, and to which it addresses itself, are capable of independent proof or disproof; and this of an experimental kind. For the field of experience is not confined to material nature.[1] The existence and validity of conscience, the facts of its testimony to spiritual truth, the existence and nature of the spiritual element in man, its inherent instincts, its unconscious but indubitable witness to the need

and of historical evidence.

Of observation

---

[1] See Dr. Mozley's powerful remarks in *Cont. Rev.*, VII. 484. I cannot refrain from quoting the following fine application of this mode of reasoning:—" When, in reviewing the history of the past, you find certain ideas arising in the first known period of the life of humanity and co-existent with it: undergoing transformation from epoch to epoch: but remaining always and everywhere essentially the same, and inseparable from human society, gathering renewed strength from every social upheaval destructive of the temporary ideas of a single people, or a single epoch: when on interrogating your own conscience in supreme moments of deep affection, sacred sorrow, or devotion to duty, you find within your hearts an echo answering to the ideas transmitted by the ages; those ideas are true, are innate in humanity, and are destined to accompany its onward progress. . . . God, immortality, duty, the moral law sole sovereign . . . are ideas of this order."—Mazzini in *Cont. Rev.*, XX. 161.

of Revelation, and to the subject-matter of its announcements; these cannot be characterized as deductions from any *a priori* system, but rather as matters of fact, and not of probability, of immediate experience less remote, indeed, than the proofs of external phenomena.[1] Crucial instances and a doctrine of averages are not excluded from the treatment of them. Theology refuses certainly with scientific sternness to admit "that Religion[2] is to each individual according to the inward light wherewith he is endowed," or that "it consists essentially in an adaptation to the characters, ideas, and institutions of those who profess it." Such an assumption would be as fatal to its own validity as the admission of a sophistical psychology has shown itself in the history of philosophy. It confesses, however, the constraint of adequate and properly unexceptionable generalizations[3] both as regards individual experiences and general results. Thus it yields an experimental explanation of some

(marginal notes: and experiment. Of explanation and verification.)

---

[1] So J. P. Richter observes, *Selina* (*Works*, XXXIII. 223), that the soul or mind is more evident and certain to me than my body: for only by it can I know and feel the body. A similar idea occurs in Augustin. *d. Genesi ad litt.*, V. xvi., "God is nearer, more related to us, and therefore more easily known to us, than sensible, corporeal things."

[2] Buckle, *Hist. Civ.*, III. 477.

[3] In inductive logic every exception should admit of separate explanation, and so "prove the rule." But "the natural-history-sciences," remarks Dr. Rolleston, "do not usually admit of the strictness which says that an exception, so far from proving a rule, proves it to be a bad one."—*Address before the British Assoc.*, 1870, p. 14. The same limit may accordingly be allowed as to generalizations of moral and spiritual facts.

ultimate questions to which Metaphysic from its speculative character furnishes no abiding solution.

§ 3. Theology, as we have seen, has been attacked, and its progressive capacities disparaged, on the score of its being essentially deductive.[1] Such a criticism is, however, conceived in a narrow spirit. So far as it is true, it proves nothing against the general credibility of its doctrines, for it would not be contended that there is anything in the nature of demonstration, as such, vicious or erroneous. Deduction, as a mode of proof, where its premisses are not hastily or arbitrarily assumed, presents a scientific method more perfect, because more truly natural than any other. "In itself more perfect," says Hume, "it suits less the imperfection of human nature, and is hence a common source of illusion and mistake."[2] Accordingly, it is very generally admitted that the progress of Natural Science trends in this direction.[3] But

The deductive method

as truly natural as the inductive,

---

[1] Thus even Whewell, *Bridgew. Tr.*, III. v. vi., and *Indic. of a Creator*, p. 45, considers it a matter of fact that inductive philosophers have readily recognized an intelligent Author of Nature, where deductive reasoners have failed to do so. Mr. Lecky, *H. E. M.*, II. 205, holds that "the growth of an inductive and scientific spirit is invariably hostile to theological interests." He afterwards apparently limits this to Catholicism.

[2] *Essays*, IV. i. Liebig, in his criticism of Bacon, remarks: "In der Naturwissenschaft ist alle Forschung deduktiv oder apriorisch: das Experiment ist nur Hülfsmittel für den Denkprocess."—ap. Lange, *Gesch. des Materialismus*, p. 349.

[3] "A revolution," writes Mr. J. S. Mill, "is peaceably and progressively effecting itself in philosophy, the reverse of that to which Bacon has attached his name.... Deduction is the great scientific work of the present and of future ages."—*Logic*, I. 579–80.

however this be, in deduction we recognize an instrument of science, an ideal type of knowledge, of at least co-ordinate authority, sanctioned alike with its rival method by the constitution of the human mind; a type antecedent perhaps in nature and validity, and certainly more suited to the final relations of Knowledge and Being. Now, the subject-matter of Revelation cannot but be final in its character, incapable of subsequent variation or revision. The gift of the "Father of lights," it "knows no variableness, neither shadow of turning." No succeeding announcements can from the nature of the case contradict the principles which it proclaims or implies. Nor can the ultimate posture of things fail to be in agreement with what has been thus previously declared of the Divine administration. The employment, therefore, of deduction in Religion, as a specific department of knowledge, is not properly liable to exception, even were this, which it is not, a solitary example of its application. Now, the test of the deductive stage of a science (and perhaps of all Science in the strict usage of the term) is the capacity of inferring from primary and fundamental conceptions a mediate system of truths. Space and Numerical magnitude are at once recognized as ideas of this fruitful character.[1]

and more suited to the ultimate condition of science.

Theology necessarily final in its character.

Revelation analogous to the gift of primary intuitions

[1] See some very able remarks on this subject in the *Christian Remembrancer*, No. CXXXI., p. 230; and compare Prof. Westcott, *Cont. Rev.*, VIII. 378, on the narrowness of the purely scientific view, isolating and excluding Religion.

Such, also, are our notions of God and the human Soul, when the further conception is added of an accessory revelation. For it needed something more than the mere action of man's mind to "bring life and immortality to light." But the Christian ideas of the character and work of the Divine Being as the Father, Redeemer, and Sanctifier of mankind, once given, (even as the chief links in the colligation of scientific notions have ever flashed into the minds of discoverers by a power confessedly beyond the teaching of method, 'a vision and a faculty divine'),[1] the legitimate inferences are the property of logical reflection, and can be tested by application to the facts of man's nature and circumstances, as the verifications of Natural Laws already surmised are obtained from the inspection of instances.[2] This constitutes the appropriate *evidence* of truths received at the first "neither of man, nor after man, but by the revelation of Jesus Christ."

and colligation of ideas.

§ 4. But Religion, it is said, impedes knowledge

Objection to the truth of theology as being stationary and reactionary.

[1] So Tennyson speaks of—
　　　The fair new forms
　That float about the threshold of an age,
　Like truths of science waiting to be caught.

[2] Hence Mr. Fairbairn remarks, *Immortality of the Soul, Cont. Rev.*, XX. 29, that "Religion, or rather its philosophic theology, may now become a science as purely *inductive* as any of the physical sciences. The now possible analysis of the faiths of the world, if accompanied by a searching analysis of the faculties of the mind, will hand over to thought our primary and necessary religious ideas, which, as ultimate religious truths, constitute in their synthesis the foundation of the universal and ideal Religion of man."

by leading men to be satisfied with an easy belief, and by making inquiry a crime. All progress is in this manner barred, and there arises a marked and singular exception to the aggressive spirit of all other branches of knowledge. An essential incompatibility emerges between a stationary faith and a progressive philosophy. No doubt, we reply, it is beyond human power to add to the subject-matter of Revelation, though clearer light may, in the course of ages, be thrown upon its obscurer regions. It may, in this view, be compared to all great and organic truths, making up the stock of true human knowledge, and constituting a deposit of belief handed on to succeeding generations. Once discovered, these are not again lost in the history of culture, but become the inalienable heritage of the race in its progress to fuller knowledge.[1] But the application of Revealed Truth to the circumstances of human history, its practical developments in living actual results, its inherent and unsuspected activity, its conformity with unknown powers, and, it may be, principles of human nature; these and other considerations supply a field for the enlargement of our acquaintance with the meaning and potential character of Christianity

Revelation, in what sense final,

but admitting of indefinite application

---

[1] Macaulay, indeed, *Essays*, pp. 536, 537, argues at length that we have no security for the future against the prevalence of any theological error that has ever prevailed in time past. Such a view deprives Religion of all benefit from contemporary light in other subjects of thought, which, *if only free access be allowed*, cannot fail to affect existing religious opinion.

as a scheme of Revelation, which admits of endless advance and indefinite augmentation. "It is not at all incredible," writes Bishop Butler,[1] speaking of the Holy Scriptures, "that a book which has been so long in the possession of mankind should contain many truths as yet undiscerned. For all the same phenomena and the same faculties of investigation from which such great discoveries in natural knowledge have been made in the present and last age, were equally in the possession of mankind several thousand years before." So too, the ultimate verification, and even, perhaps, enlargement of this scheme by the facts of Science (which also has its revelations for mankind,) is a continually growing addition to the bulk of human knowledge. In this view Christianity must not be denied the place even of a progressive science.[2] The laws of

and verification, adding to the bulk of knowledge.

---

[1] *Analogy*, II. c. iii. "It is true, indeed," writes Mr. Rogers, *Essays*, II. 335, "that theology cannot be said to admit of unlimited progress in the same sense as chemistry, which may, for aught we know, treble or quadruple its present accumulations, vast as they are, both in bulk and importance. But even in theology, as deduced from the Scripture, minute fragments of new truth or more exact adjustments of old truth may be perpetually expected." Dean Stanley, *Serm. on the Bible*, p. 112, writes, "Never before our own age has there been so keen, so discriminating a perception of the peculiarities (if I may so speak), the essential, innermost, distinguishing marks of the unapproached and unapproachable Character described to us in the Four Gospels. We have not arrived at the end of it. Far from it. In the very fact of the large traits of His life and character which still remain unexplored, lies a boundless hope for the future."

[2] Compare Butler, *Anal.*, II. iii. "As it is owned the whole scheme of Scripture is not yet understood; so if it ever comes to be understood, . . . it must be in the same way that *natural* knowledge is come at by the continuance and *progress* of learning and of liberty," &c. See some remarks by Dorner, *Hist. Prot. Th.*, II. 4.

Christianity, in what sense a progressive science,

natural development apply to its enouncements equally with those of other departments of truth. The realization of "things not seen as yet;" ulterior applications of acknowledged principles and promises; the laying aside inherited prepossessions antagonistic to the genius of our Religion, and from which the truth alone, when more and more reflected on and assimilated, can set man's spirit free;[1] these are lands in the realm of Christian thought perhaps yet unexplored, and, certainly, not yet taken into possession. The gradual evolution of fundamental ideas, the discovery of new relations involved in them, and new spheres in which they are valid; these are elements of progress inherent and permanent. Such an advance in no way, indeed, impairs the final character of Christian truth as Revealed.[2] And yet in this manner, side

and a theory of development admissible.

---

[1] On admissible developments of doctrine in Christianity, see Archer Butler (*Letters*, pp. 55-8). Dr. Newman's well-known "Theory" is an attempted solution of an admitted fact. See also De Quincey's *Essay on Protestantism*, at length.

[2] In quitting this part of the subject I am anxious once more to insist on the necessity of a fixed and primitive standard of doctrine. It is one thing to hold with Bp. Law (*Theory of Religion*, p. 145) that "though the whole scheme of our redemption was completely delivered, and *all its essential parts* recorded during the extraordinary assistance and inspection of the Holy Ghost, and in some respects the primitive Christians seem to have the advantage of others; .... yet it by no means follows that the true genius, import, and extent of this revelation must be as well understood by the generality of them as it could be by any that came after them." It is another to proclaim with Channing (*Letter on Creeds*) that "the wisest theologians are children who have caught but faint glimpses of the religion; who have taken but their first lessons, and whose business it is to 'grow in the knowledge of Jesus

by side with physical studies and philosophical deductions, Christian Science may still climb the starry heights of Thought and Being, and draw ever nearer the eternal springs of Intuitive Truth.

§ 5. When the wondrous fertility of the present era in discovery and information, physical and historical, is taken into account, undoubtedly a certain alarm lays hold of the religious mind, lest the advance of positive Knowledge, and our familiarity with the facts of Nature, should leave no room for the fears and hopes of a world unseen. The very difficulties for which Religion undertakes to account may, it seems, after all, disappear. Explanations of Laws of Nature may take the place of yearnings of heart and soul after the Ineffable and the Divine. Dim, ambiguous issues may be discounted for present certainty and immediate enjoyment. May it not be wiser to enjoy the pleasures of sense for a season? Fatalism may be found to extinguish the terrors of wounded consciences; and the utterances of Inspiration may be analyzed into vulgar errors and unmeaning super-

<small>Practical alarms from the collision of natural knowledge with revelation</small>

Christ.' Need I say how hostile to this growth is a *fixed creed*, beyond which we must never wander? &c." It needs hardly to be pointed out that the theory (of Hegel, Baur, &c.) which regards Christianity *itself* as a development in the history of Universal Religion, a phase in the evolution of the Universal *Geist*, and capable accordingly of a specific perfectibility, is wholly beside our present point of view. So M. Comte looks on the present form of Christianity as the last and highest type of Monotheism, including within itself the characteristic elements of all the preparatory developments, and due to them.

and of materialistic opinions. stitions. And certainly, if it can be shown that in the universe of things all is material,[1] and bound by Laws of Matter; that Life itself is but a trick of force; that the realm of the Invisible, of Him "Who dwelleth in the light to which no man can approach, Whom no man hath seen, neither can see," is baseless, fictitious, inappreciable; who shall fathom the sadness which should brood over heart and spirit,[2] or fill the aching void which nothing *Their effect upon a belief in immortality.* can make good? To leave this mortal scene, to shift this mortal coil, to "go we know not whither,"

To lie in cold obstruction and to rot;

this has assuredly been through all ages the ruling dread, the master-doubt which haunts the mind of man.[3] What, then, if the sum of all our knowing be to find that he, also, is but the creature of a day, a modification of undying matter, an emanation, the sport of generative forces, a passing type, a sin-

---

[1] Materialism really inverts the true order of existence. Compare Plato, *Legg.*, X. 888, 889. "Il paraît bien," says Leibnitz of Spinoza, "que l'âme ne lui étoit qu'une modification passagère: et lorsqu'il fait semblant de la faire durable et même perpétuelle, il y substitue l'idée du corps, qui est une simple notion et non pas une chose réelle et actuelle."—*Théodicée*, p. 12, a most pregnant passage.

[2] "Prétendent-ils nous avoir bien réjouis de nous dire qu'ils tiennent que notre âme n'est qu'un peu de vent et de fumée, et encore de nous le dire d'un ton de voix fier et content? Est-ce donc une chose à dire gaiement? Et n'est-ce pas une chose à dire, au contraire, tristement comme la chose du monde la plus triste?"—Pascal, *Pens.*, Art. I.

[3] It was this which led Epicurus to say that "if fear of the Gods and fear of death were not, we might well do without Physics;" and compare the effect of the preaching of Paulinus on the Northumbrians in Bede,

gular variety, linked in the evolution of eternal Nature, or "throned in the arms of an Almighty Necessity"? One fact, or set of facts, as yet repels this monster generalization, which would otherwise reduce all specific sciences to an absolute uniformity, and confound them in one undistinguishable identity. One Science holds bravely on through these surgings of opinion, and the buffets of an absolute criticism: the science of God and the Soul, existences essentially different from all material forms, and bound each to other by relations which give to Religion a meaning and a name.[1] Man, it has been finely said, " is alone in nature, a world within a world;" (and yet he is not alone, for his Father is with him;) "he alone of

This doctrine associated with religion,

H. E., II. xiii. Hence the profound melancholy of classic Paganism on this topic.

>Soles occidere et redire possunt.
>Nobis cum semel occidit brevis lux
>Nox est perpetua una dormienda.—Catullus.
>Damna tamen celeres reparant cælestia lunæ.
>Nos ubi decidimus
>Quo pater Æneas, quo dives Tullus et Ancus,
>Pulvis et umbra sumus.—Horace.

Such thoughts are but echoes of the old plaint, "One generation passeth away and another generation cometh: but the earth abideth for ever." —Eccles. i. 4. "Unde enim metuunt mori et malunt in illâ ærumnâ vivere quàm eam morte finire nisi quia satis apparet quam natura refugiat non esse?"—August., *Civ. D.*, XI. xxvii. It may be hereafter found to be true that a spiritual substance, by virtue of its essential constitution, is immortal; but at present our knowledge of the fact must be inferential. See Mill, *Examination*, p. 211.

[1] "Religet ergo nos religio uni Omnipotenti Deo."—August., *Ver. Rel.*, c. lv. sub finem. "Si enim divina aut a Deo data est anima, sine dubio datorem suum novit."—Tert., *Trst. Anim.*, ii.

all the creatures communes with a Being out of Nature; and he divides himself from all other physical life by prophesying, in the face of universal visible decay, his own immortality."[1] The spirit of man, then, protests that it, too, is a fact, a distinct consciousness; it lives, and, living, exists for that eternity of which it alone is cognisant. But, if the spiritual element in man be admitted, it is, at least, not unreasonable that there should exist a Revelation as the supply to its inevitable questionings. Even on a theory of Evolution, Christianity would have most claims to be heard.[2] For it satisfies to the full the native testimony of the soul of man, rising, as it were, by a law of continuity from animalism to rationality, from the rule of the senses to speculative intelligence, and from self-seeking passion to self-sacrificing love.

and satisfied by the Christian system.

§ 6. Thus a true vital antagonism between Religion and Science, fatal to the permanence and progress of the former, alone emerges where, and so long as, the latter recognizing only the validity

The only vital antagonism between religion and science.

---

[1] Mozley, *Bampt. L.*, p. 89. "Immortality is not a doctrine of the schools, but a faith of humanity; not based on the metaphysic or proved by the logic of a given system; but the utterance of an instinct common to the race which has made itself heard wherever man has advanced from a religion of nature to a religion of faith. And there is no article of belief he so reluctantly surrenders even to the demands of system."—Fairbairn on *Belief in Immortality*. This proposition is sustained by the learned author through a large and careful induction of the most ancient religions of the earth.

[2] "Aux yeux de l'histoire," says a Positivist writer, "il n'y a point de fausse religion : il n'y a que des religions incomplètes, qui cheminent dans les temps et se perfectionnent."—Littré, *Paroles*, p. 19.

of *phenomena*, excludes from these all operation of man's spiritual part. In strictness, Science must be held to comprehend the connection of all truths certain from the laws and constitution of the human mind. If, however, it is assumed that in Nature¹ nothing exists but what is given in experience, represented in the forms of time and space and force, under the relation of cause and effect; then, indeed, a principle which originates its own acts, which prophesies its own responsibility, and which explains, out of its own instinctive habit, its existence and destiny, its relations to God and to the universe in which it finds itself, can only be something beside and beyond Nature, even while related to it. It must, then, stand or fall at the caprice of Nature's worshippers.² But, happily (apart from any verbal controversy), the existence

relative to the existence of a spiritual principle in man.

---

¹ Compare Coleridge, *A. R.*, pp. 48, 190. "The ways and proceedings of God with spirits are not included in Nature, that is, in the laws of heaven and earth."—Bacon, *Confession of Faith* (*Works*, VII. 221). In the magnificent passage in Professor Huxley's *Lay Sermons* (p. 37), beginning, "That man, I think, has had a liberal education," &c., there is a total omission of any spiritual element in man capable of culture or expansion. On the importance of the spiritual element in philosophy at the present time, see Janet, *La Crise Philosophique*, p. 7.

² Leibnitz tells a story of a learned chemist, who "avoit fait une prière, qui pensa lui faire des affaires. Elle commençoit: O sancta mater Natura, æterne rerum ordo. Et elle aboutissoit à dire que cette Nature lui devoit pardonner ses défauts, puisqu'elle en étoit cause elle-même."—*Théod.*, p. 605. He seems to have been of the same mind with Lear:

Thou, Nature, art my Goddess: to thy law
My services are bound.

of such a principle in man is capable, as with other psychological facts,[1] of experimental and scientific proof. It is not simply that, as has been said, if all argument is against it, all belief is for it. The grounds of that belief are patent. It is based, not alone on the precarious testimony of individual consciousness, but on a comparison of such consciousness, under many aspects; on a wide generalization of varying ages and countries, and a collection, practically unlimited, of particular instances. The notion of *spiritual action* is admitted by Mr. Darwin to be instinctive in man. "The conception of the human soul," writes the historian of Primitive Culture,[2] "is, as to its most essential nature, continuous from the philosophy of the savage thinker to that of the modern professor of theology. Its definition has remained from the first that of an animating, separable, surviving entity, the vehicle of individual personal exist-

marginalia: This capable of scientific proof / from testimony ancient and modern,

---

[1] The fallacy met with in the writings of Mr. Buckle, as well as of the more purely Positivist school, is to assume that psychology is a branch of metaphysic; that metaphysic does not study phenomena; and that its object-matter is the *individual* mind. The impossibility is evident of accounting for the ideas of God and of man's personality on purely materialistic principles. On the Positivist notions of the soul, comp. Jauet, *La Crise Phil.*, p. 115.

[2] Tylor, I. 453. "The minimum definition of religion is the belief in spiritual beings."—I. 383. In the shadow, pulse, heart, breath, he finds in the rudest tribes a generally apprehended representation or suggestion of the soul. On the mythology of the Soul (a distinct line of proof), see Max Müller on the *Philosophy of Mythology* (*Cont. Rev.*, XIX. 108). On the Hebrew and Indo-Germanic appellations of man and spirit, compare Delitzsch, *Biblical Psychology*, pp. 82, 143, E. T.

ence." The highest efforts of heathen philosophy in East and West culminated in a recognition of its authority and power, its sole or corporate immortality.[1] Moreover, the reality of the personal affections in man, which are the groundwork of most of his acts, and of all which constitutes his true nobility, has never been denied. Yet, under a pure Naturalism, excluding all recognition of a spiritual life, whatever may be demonstrated as to their origin, these must appear both meaningless and void. Their earnestness and simple trust, their rich store of high and unselfish feeling, become fantastic and absurd.[2] The same, also, is

from examination of human nature,

---

[1] It has been maintained, I am aware, that a belief in God is compatible with an ignorance of the soul's immortality; and that this was the state of heathen opinion at the time of the coming of Christ (see Dean Merivale, *Lectt.*, p. 24. At p. 54 he writes, "Belief in a future state is the touchstone of all spiritual conceptions of human nature.") I do not think this has yet been proved. Plutarch's treatise, *Non posse suave v. sec. Epic.*, should be consulted on the differences of opinion among the Stoics. See Döllinger, *Gentile and Jew*, I. 353. It is quite possible, however, for ingenious disputants in all ages to argue against the instincts of common sense. Cicero (*Tusc. Disp.*, I. xvi., xviii., xxxi.) writes: "Sed ut Deos esse naturâ opinamur, qualesque sint, ratione cognoscimus: sic permanere animos arbitramur consensu nationum omnium; qua in sede maneant, qualesque sint ratione discendum est." Herodotus (II. 123) makes it an Egyptian discovery: elsewhere he admits it to have been a Teutonic conception (IV. 94). It is no objection that this conviction is a gradual one (see Fairbairn, u. s. *C. R.*, XX. 374, ff.), any more than that the belief in a God has found recusants. See Harless, *Christian Ethics*, p. 42, E. T.

[2] This line of argument against all systems tending to Atheism is indicated by Shaftesbury in his Enquiry concerning Virtue (*Works*, II. 69). The same topic is powerfully handled by Mr. Hutton, *Essays*, I. 19. "A fully realized Atheism will undermine the worth of personal human affections; not merely indirectly by losing sight of immor-

true of the religious sentiment in man, of which, it cannot be doubted, his nature is capable when developed by culture and improvement. Thus religious biography, exhibiting in various ages of Christianity and at different eras of civilization the same characteristic features and common results, pointing accordingly to a common origin, furnishes an argument of a strictly inductive kind for the determination of a spiritual element in human nature correspondent to influences of the Divine Spirit. Hence that communion of man with his Maker, "the Father of Spirits," whereof he alone is capable, an excellency whereby he is distinguished from the beasts that perish,[1] and is crowned with glory and worship.

from inductive analysis.

Its results.

> Ideo venerabile soli
> Sortiti ingenium divinorum que capaces.

From that fountain flow his highest and purest inspirations; but no less those contradictions and warrings of counter-impulses, the travail and the toil of yearning souls, conscious of Heaven, yet

tality, but still more by cutting off the chief spring of their spiritual life. If that fine wide-spreading network, hidden from all human eyes, the winding crossing blending diverging threads of human affection, which hold together human society, be indeed conceived as issuing everywhere out of everlasting night; as spun, snapped asunder, and again repaired by the mere automatic operation of Nature's unconscious and impersonal energy; the personal affections lose quite the richest and most permanent of the conscious influences at least, which minister to their life and growth."

[1] Compare Lactant. (*Div. Inst.*, III. x.). Thus man, created in the likeness of God, must be essentially a spirit (John iv. 24). Gregory

borne down to earth, unresting,¹ unsatisfied while still the slaves of sense. But with the reality of the spiritual principle in man is inseparably connected the presence of a will which, by its acts, announces its own personality and individual being. As it is impossible to sever in conception the notions of spirit and will, so practically it is by the character of the will developed in act that the spirit itself is differentiated. Thus is it that we know " what manner of spirit we are of." It is for this reason probably that in Holy Scripture² the term itself, as a power or property seated in the human soul, never stands singly, but is always specified. It is the "spirit of meekness," the "spirit of knowledge," the "spirit of fear," the "spirit of love," and the like. The recognition of this principle from first to last, in the Old as in the New Testament, gives unity and consistency to Revela-

Its connection with the existence of will in man,

---

of Nyssa (ap. Delitzsch, p. 197) makes use of the image of a piece of glass, which, although in very diminished proportion, reflects the entire form of the sun, to represent how out of the limited nature of man's spirit shine forth the copies of the inexpressible attributes of the Godhead. Thus Goethe:

> Wär' nicht das Auge sonnenhaft
> Wie konnten wir das Licht erblicken?
> Lebt' nicht in uns des Gottes eigne Kraft
> Wie konnte uns das Göttliches entzücken?

See Sir W. Hamilton, *Disc.*, p. 19.

¹ " Quia fecisti nos ad Te, Domine, inquietum est cor nostrum, donec requiescat in Te."—August., *Conf.*, sub init.

² This remark is made by Coleridge, *A. R.*, p. 42. Compare the teaching of the Homily for Whitsunday, Pt. I., sub fin.

tion.¹ The proof, then, of our spiritual nature, together with the admission of this element in man, may be regarded as the one thing vital to all spiritual religion. It alone suffices to account for the existence, the office, and the success of Christianity. On its reality as a principle, and on the unquestionable character of its testimony rest the bases of our religion, as an enduring and undying faith. Yet now we are called on to believe that it is the function of Knowledge (which is, however, the true image² and mirror of Being) to extinguish the notion of such a spiritual principle in man, and to abolish all faith in the reality and power of its utterances. This, it seems, is to be the latest work of positive Science, its closing service to mankind, the crowning effort of the progress and culture of natural studies.

and relation to the permanence of Christianity,

§ 7. But it is said that in the advance of knowledge we are fast losing the elementary principles, both of divine worship and of religious belief. In surprise, if not in fear, according to the old observation of Aristotle³ (or, more strictly, of

Science asserted to be destructive of religion

---

¹ "I stand before myself as before a riddle: whose key is not to be found in the human self-consciousness, but is given to it by God in the word of revelation."—Harless, *Christian Ethics*, p. 50.

² "Scientia essentiae imago."—Bacon, *N. O.*, Aph. cxx.

³ Διὰ γὰρ τὸ θαυμάζειν οἱ ἄνθρωποι καὶ νῦν καὶ τὸ πρῶτον ἤρξαντο φιλοσοφεῖν ... ὁ δ' ἀπορῶν καὶ θαυμάζων οἴεται ἀγνοεῖν· διὸ καὶ φιλόμυθος ὁ φιλόσοφός πώς ἐστιν.—Arist., *Metaph.*, I. ii. Μάλα φιλοσόφου τοῦτο τὸ πάθος τὸ θαυμάζειν· οὐ γὰρ ἄλλη ἀρχὴ φιλοσοφίας ἢ αὕτη.—Plato, *Theæt.*, 155. D. Compare Mr. Morell, *Phil. of Religion*, p. 202, and Coleridge, *A. R.*, p. 178. Sir W. Hamilton, *Lect.*, I. 37,

Plato), all Philosophy and all Religion found their beginning; in the felt need, that is, of a Being to still the alarms and satisfy the curiosity of the human mind. "Physical wonder," says a recent writer,[1] "is no doubt an *introduction* to the belief in the supernatural. It tends to raise in the mind a larger idea of possibility; the notion of the potential as distinguished from what is actual, the sense of the unknown." But, at the present time, the grounds, it is argued, of physical wonder are disappearing. Under a rigid, unfailing uniformity, each event can be assigned to its appropriate antecedent. *as extinguishing the sentiments of awe and admiration.*

> The world's young ignorance is o'er,
> As Science forging day by day
> Her close-linked chain withdraws
> The once-felt touches of God's hand
> For dumb organic laws.

There is further to be considered the ordinary effect of custom and familiarity upon the mind. Repetition, it has been often observed, diminishes wonder, and in matters of a moral and religious kind sensibly reduces the feeling of awe. It is true, it must be admitted, that the fact of not feeling surprise at a phenomenon which really remains *This doubtful.*

---

comments on the tendency of physical studies to extinguish religious adoration by mechanical views of Nature. He has, indeed, been powerfully combated by Mr. Mill (*Exam.*, p. 544), who seeks to strengthen himself by the united testimony of two eminently *religious* minds, Wordsworth and Faraday. Compare Mr. Darwin (*Descent of Man*, I. 68).

[1] Dr. Mozley, *Bampt. Lect.*, p. 76.

unexplained, is no adequate reason for not seeking to assign the ultimate causes of its existence, even though we are thus led to the confines of supernatural agency. It is, however, unfortunately a characteristic of the present era of thought, that an ascertainment of facts or of a law combining or regulating facts is held sufficient without proceeding to any further explanation of them. Thus an indifference on the part of mankind at large, or of our own generation, towards a religious view of Nature is assumed; it is seldom confirmed, and is certainly not justified. But it is urged that now admiration of the vastness and simplicity of Natural Laws may well take the place of childlike surprise and immature suppositions, and that it is the only sentiment worthy of the philosophical elevation of our time. No doubt, there is a wonder which is the legitimate offspring of scientific knowledge.[1] But there is no admiration in it; enthusiasm does not spring from any intellectual deductions. Admiration cannot really be felt in respect of things, or any arrangement of things. It has regard only of persons; it is the tribute of mind to mind.[2]

Substitution of Laws of Nature for a personal God.

---

[1] Οὐδὲν ἂν θαυμάσειεν οὕτως ἀνὴρ γεωμετρικός, ὡς εἰ γένοιτο ἡ διάμετρος μετρητή.—Arist., *Metaph.*, I. ii. "Admiration," says Mr. Mill, "is a different thing from wonder, and is often at its greatest height when the strangeness which is a necessary condition of wonder, has died away."

[2] "Man," says Carlyle, "cannot *know*, unless he can *worship* in some way." "A man," writes Mr. Picton, "cannot worship a *thing*, however big."—*New Theories and Old Faith*, p. 45. The same writer clo-

And thus if God be excluded from the universe which He has framed, to make room for Law; and if man, through the negation of will and spirit, be degraded to the scale of a mere chattel, and bondsman to the order of Nature; admiration of the wisdom and beauty of creation, together with fear (now denounced as Fetishism) of the power and justice of the Creator, are, it may be admitted, out of place.[1] Now, in proportion to our increasing knowledge of the Laws of Nature, our old superstitions, it is said, in regard to the Author and so-called Administrator of the Universe must totally change. For if all Religion reposes ultimately on fear,[2] and is most marked in those climes and

Its consequences.

Subversive indeed of Religion,

---

quently remarks (p. 52), "When once man could so far stand distinct from and over against nature as to feel wonder, the life of contemplation was begun, and at least the germ of God-consciousness was formed. For the sense of wonder involves the realization of a disturbed unity which the soul struggles to restore. And here we have the beginnings both of Science and Religion, which like highly differentiated organs in the mature animal may very well have been indistinguishable in their germs. The sense of wonder is closely akin to that of awe, and easily suggests some unknown power."

[1] Mr. Hutton, *Essays*, I. 16, has some profound remarks on this great moral want in Atheism. "If you do not believe that 'Good' is living and free—that it is a person—you cannot believe that it will find you out; and you may be truly as incompetent to find it out as to leave the earth for the sun."

[2] Mr. Buckle, *Hist. Civ.*, II. 171. "The origin of veneration is wonder and fear. These two passions, either alone or combined, are the ordinary source of veneration; and the way in which they arise is obvious. We wonder because we are ignorant; and we fear because we are weak."—*Ib.*, III. 272. "The whole system of the theologians reposes upon fear, and upon fear of the worst kind," &c. He thus repeats the notions of Hume (*Natural Hist. of Religion*, § vi. &c.). Shaftesbury (*Works*, III. 36) more truly observes, "We can admire nothing pro-

countries where the grandeur of natural phenomena and the suddenness of physical calamities overpower the resources of man; let this fear be taken away, and the pillars of all dogmatic beliefs, the slow and laboured inventions of a cowed and panic-stricken spirit, will crumble into dust. Such is the line of proof from which it is inferred that as the human race advances in culture; as we mount the scale of causes which link creation by a golden chain with the throne of God¹ and "climb up into Heaven;" no godly fear, no inbred sense of awe, is to hold the spirit captive when, covered with the shadow of His glory, we draw near the ante-

but neither necessary

nor probable.

---

foundly without a certain religious veneration, and because this borders so much on *fear*, and raises a certain tremor or horror of like appearance, 'tis easy to give that turn to the affection, and represent all enthusiasm and religious extasy as the product or mere effect of fear. Primus in orbe Deos fecit Timor. But the original passion, as appears plainly, is of another kind," &c. Compare Bacon, *Augm. Sc.*, II. xiii., de panicis terroribus, and Lucretius I. 102-27. Mr. Lecky (*H. E. M.*, I. 149) remarks, "In a few minds the contemplation of the sublime order of Nature produces a reverential feeling; but to the great majority of mankind it is an incontestable though mournful fact, that the discovery of controlling and unchanging Law deprives phenomena of their moral significance, and nearly all the social and political spheres in which reverence was fostered have passed away." The same writer (*Hist. Rat.*, I. 285) has some exquisite observations on the manner in which "the sense of beauty (and growth of art) has gradually encroached upon and absorbed the feeling of reverence." . . . "Religious ideas," he adds, "die like the sun; their last rays, possessing little heat, are expended in creating beauty."

¹ "Catena illa Homeri decantata (causarum scilicet naturalium ad pedem solii Jovis fixa memorabatur: neque quisquam Metaphysicam et quæ in natura æterna et immobilia sunt tractavit atque animum a fluxu rerum paulisper abduxit qui non simul in Theologiam Naturalem inciderit; adeo paratus et propinquus est transitus a vertice illa pyramidis ad Divina."—Bacon, *Works*, I. 525.

chambers of Deity, and lift "the transparent veil which dimly hides the shrine of an Eternal Being." Well may we agree with a writer who, on his part, also has left his mark on the thought of the time,[1] when he holds that "the character of our troublous era lies even in this; that man has for ever cast away *fear*, which is the lower, but has not yet risen into perennial *reverence*, which is his higher and highest attribute." To degrade Almighty God to the level of His works by making them the substitute for an unknown, unappreciable principle; to confound Nature and the laws and powers of Matter with their Author and Preserver, this is rather to be accounted fetishism, however latent, or in whatever manner modified by the temper of the time. For does not any such theory change the truth of God into a lie, worshipping and serving the creature more than the Creator, Who "is blessed for ever"?[2] Where, however, we may reasonably inquire, is the degradation to the nobility of man, when he lays his hand upon his mouth in the presence of his Maker and Preserver, Who "maketh the winds His angels, and the flaming fire His minister;" and though he confess

Unsuitable to the intellectual elevation of the age.

---

[1] Carlyle, *Sartor Resartus*, p. 173, and *Miscell.* I. 19. We are, in fact, in that state of things described by Shakspeare, where he says, "We have our philosophical persons, to make modern and familiar things supernatural and causeless. Hence is it that we make trifles of terrors, ensconcing ourselves into seeming knowledge when we should submit ourselves to an unknown fear."—*All's Well*, act ii. sc. 3.

[2] Rom. i. 25.

Himself but dust and ashes? Reverence, we may rest assured, will never be analyzed into superstition; nor devotion, the instinctive tribute of man's spirit, into ignorant alarm.[1]

Religion independent of advance in knowledge.

§ 8. In determining, then, the relative position of Theology and Science, it must not be forgotten that the causes for which Religion exists, are not such as to depend on any advance in mere knowledge. The difficulties for which it accounts are such as no perfection of Science can hope to remove. All existing religions have been denominated as "so many modes of manifestation of the unknowable." If so, they must, at least, teach something about God and His dealings with mankind. But, in what way shall Science look to satisfy the strivings of man's spirit, or suppress his sense of sin? When it shall have substituted for conscience and remorse Necessity and Law, will it, indeed, have found the "balm in Gilead" which may "minister to the mind diseased"? But, if the need of a Religion to tranquillize the throes of human nature be admitted, an argument for its permanence will appear in the very inability of all foregone philosophy to frame one.

Attempts on the part of philosophy to usurp its functions,

It is not that the experiment has not been tried, but that it has always failed. If Stoicism,[2] for example, with its grand and lofty

---

[1] This innate feeling of reverence connected with dependence seems admitted even by Dr. Strauss in his *Alter und Neuer Glaube*, p. 146.

[2] Mr. Lecky, in his *History of European Morals*, I. 186-235, has touched the subject of Stoicism with a masterly, if with a partial, hand.

ideal of following God and becoming godlike, its unselfish enthusiasm—

> Non sibi sed toti genitum se credere mundo,

its perfect severance of virtue from expediency, its subjugation of the affections to reason, its recognition of an overruling Providence, and of a system of probation, its high sense of the native capacities of man and the power of his will, of the duty of self-scrutiny and of mental purity; if a system of morals and thought, thus grandly framed, failed in practice through its want of acquaintance with that nature which it strove to elevate, from its suppression of its emotions, from its repression of its desires, from its own austerity and hardness, from its virtual disbelief in a future life; what creed of mortal mould may look to take its place? Neo-Platonism, Eclecticism, tried and failed.[1] Are we now to look to the halting atheism of a negative belief, the "Catholicism without Christianity" of a Positivist Church? Inherent diversities of opinion; want of practical acquaintance with the needs of man's soul and with its boundless capacities of emotion and idealization; the impossibility of building faith upon a speculative foundation; *e. g.* of Stoicism.

Of Neo-Platonism.

Of Positivism.

It had, doubtless, its darker side, over which he casts a veil, in its pæderasty, tendency to suicide, &c. Comp. Döllinger, *G. a. Jew*, I. 357, and for its later development, II. 124-7. "Never," he admits, "was there a system of morality which found so many and such striking echoes in Christianity as does that of Epictetus."

[1] Compare Dean Merivale, *Lectt.*, p. 119; and Pressensé, P. II. tom. ii. p. 60. Eclecticism in morals is represented by Plutarch.

defect of imagination and constructive power to frame any acceptable scheme of worship; these and other hindrances have continually foiled philosophers when charged with the task of putting together a new coherent and purely rational religion.[1] The prospect thus opened should not be disregarded by those thinkers who, while professing themselves favourable to Christianity as a type of religion, as a moral ideal, or even as an abstract rule of faith; nevertheless, in handling it, leave no standing-ground between the admission of critical canons fatal to all genuine belief, or a return to medieval dogmatism. It is thus held not unfair to attack Christianity at large, or some particular article which the Church has *unâ voce* declared to be a Christian doctrine, by arguments which, if valid, are valid against all teaching of Revealed Truth. Some postulates there must be in all systems of religious belief, as the basis of any argument in support of the faith declared. "Let him," it has been said, not unreasonably, "who is too high-minded to beg his ground, and will take it by a strong hand; let him fight it out with the Atheist or the Manichean, but not stoop

Their failure.

Unfair attacks on the spiritual doctrines of Christianity.

---

[1] See Saisset, *Essais*, pp. 24, 25, and some good remarks by the author of *Ecce Homo*, p. 99: "If philosophy undertakes to solve the same problem, what is its method? By what means does it hope to awaken good impulses in hearts that were before enslaved to bad ones? .... The truth is that philosophy has no instruments that it can use for this purpose." Schleiermacher also (*Christlicher Glaube*) insists on this same fact.

to pick up their arrows, and then run away to discharge them at Christianity or the Church."[1]

§ 9. An age of admitted scepticism has not, as yet, proved itself either fatal or, perhaps, even dangerous to the truth of Christianity. By Gibbon it was thought to have been really favourable to the progress of religion, that is, of the Christian religion. It is the modern fashion to predict that it will be its bane. But it may be held for certain, looking to past experience, that a sceptical spirit must sooner or later give way to a state of things in which the yearning after religious belief will vastly predominate. For scepticism, though just[2] within just limits, being the natural resort of the intellect when overweighted by authority, and by no means, therefore, a necessary alien from the household of faith; yet represents, at most, but the negation of implicit belief or of credulity; and is, therefore, in itself, no more than a definite stage, a passing phase in the process of intellectual

Scepticism or a spirit of inquiry not formidable to religion,

being transient

---

[1] Coleridge, *A. R.*, p. 221.

[2] Thus scepticism, considered as a means of arriving at truth, may be coeval with belief itself. For "les conditions de la civilisation," says M. Renan, "sont comme celles d'un problème à données limitées." "Had religion," he justly adds, "been a simple superstition, like astrology, science would long since have swept it away."—*Questions Contemporaines*. On the limits of scepticism Leibnitz observes, "il ne faut point *douter pour douter;* il faut que les doutes nous servent de planche pour parvenir à la vérité. Il ne faut point qu'on puisse reprocher aux vrais philosophes ce que le fameux Casaubon répondit à ceux qui lui montrèrent la Salle de la Sorbonne, et lui dirent qu'on y avoit disputé durant quelques siècles; 'Qu'y a-t-on conclu'? leur dit-il."

growth.¹ True scepticism is often made to do service for positive unbelief, and more especially of theological postulates. But this is to confound cause with effect, a logical aspect of Thought in general with its application to the results of a particular inquiry. If, however, scepticism can issue only in chronic incredulity, the prospect, blank indeed for Religion, whose very soul is faith, might prove equally so for all certainty whatsoever. There is a faith which precedes and lies at the root of all scientific proof. There is a faith which belongs equally to its most cherished triumphs. "We call its discoveries sublime; but the sublimity belongs not to that which they reveal, but to that which they suggest."² And thus the mind of man, the consummate outcome of a practically infinite evolution, would, if deprived of faith, be reduced to the condition of an organ destitute of all objective environment or appropriate function. Such a theory of things is simply inconceivable and disastrous. Perilous times may come, as ere now they have

and preparative.

Negation of belief entails the eclipse of all knowledge.

---

[1] "Though there are many who describe our own time as an unbelieving time, it is by no means sure that posterity will accept the verdict. No doubt it is a sceptical and critical age, but then scepticism and criticism are the very conditions for the attainment of reasonable belief."—Tylor, *Hist. Prim. C.*, I. 253.

[2] Prof. Goldwin Smith, *Lectt.*, p. 48. He adds: "and that which they suggest is that through this material glory and beauty, of which we see a little and imagine more, there speaks to us a Being Whose nature is akin to ours, and Who has made our hearts capable of such converse."

cast a cold shade upon the enthusiasm of religion and the fortunes of mankind. We may "fear as we enter into the cloud," and "the love of many may wax cold." But dark, indeed, must be the prospect which shuts out altogether and always from the soul of man its faith in God, in the reality of its own instincts, in its personal immortality. Such a view of human life and of the universe is mournful, from its very hopelessness, beyond recall, beyond redress.¹ But sometimes it shows darkest the nearest before dawn; and there is good cause to ask whether it be not so now.²

§ 10. For Religion in some shape is a necessity, not a weakness, of the heart. Philosophically viewed, it supplies in Revelation a remedy for that confession of Nescience which constitutes the sum of Natural Religion. In the highest stage of

<small>*Forecast of the reconciliation of revelation and science.*</small>

---

¹ This has been thus exquisitely expressed:—

> Mourn not for them that mourn
> For sin's keen arrow with its rankling smart.
> God's hand will bind again what He hath torn,
> He heals the broken heart.
> But weep for him whose eye
> Sees in the midnight skies a starry dome
> Thick sown with worlds that whirl and hurry by,
> Yet give the heart no home:
> Who marks through earth and space
> A strange dumb pageant pass before a vacant shrine,
> And feels within his inmost soul a place
> Unfilled by the Divine.
>
> D. Greenwell, *Carmina Crucis.*

² Compare Luther, *Ausleg. der Genesis,* c. xliv. 17 (ap. Bunsen, *God in Hist.,* III. 240); and Ozanam (*Civilis.,* I. 31), who says rhetorically, "Providence loves such surprises."

civilization the purest form must ultimately prevail. Such we hold, and even by opponents has been admitted, to be the faith of Jesus Christ.[1] It is not here contended that the influences of civilization and of Christianity are, in fact, identical. Each may owe much to the other: and both something to the mutual alliance of their individual force. It may be that each moves in a distinct sphere, with separate action, and to appearance separate interests. But if it be urged that in the admitted advance of human affairs intellectual enlightenment is the cause, Protestantism or any other form of Christian truth but an effect; it is enough to reply, that thus at least they co-exist; the religion of Christ in its purest form is the religion of civilization. Nor, in saying this, do we undervalue the benefits of Knowledge and Science as true

Co-existence of Christianity with advancing civilization.

[1] " Le monde sera éternellement religieux ; et le Christianisme dans un sens large est le dernier mot de la religion."—Renan, *u. s.* "Deism," he adds, "cannot be the final term of religion; for it is not truly a religion at all: it is a scientific conclusion." The following sentences, written nearly half a century since, are now doubly interesting:—" We confess, the present aspect of spiritual Europe might fill a melancholic observer with doubt and foreboding. It is mournful to see so many minds, noble, tender, and high-aspiring, deserted of that religious light which once guided all such : standing sorrowful on the scene of past convulsions and controversies, as on a scene blackened and burnt up with fire: mourning in the darkness because there is desolation, and no home for the soul; or, what is worse, pitching tents among the ashes, and kindling weak, earthly lamps, which we are to take for stars. *This darkness is but transitory obscuration :* these ashes are the soil of future herbage and richer harvests. Religion, Poetry is not dead; it will never die. Its dwelling and birth-place is in the soul of man, and it is eternal as the being of man."—Carlyle, *Miscell.,* I. 72.

elements of progress; or seek to stem and turn aside the tide of advancing culture. It is folly even to wish to reverse a movement in human affairs which is definite and uniform in operation. It is a question of fact whether Christianity has not or is not moved along with it, mingling with its advance, and assimilating its effects. "It is the peculiarity of the religion of the Bible," it has been well said, "that whatever be the aspect of the past, and of the present; in spite of all glories of what we look back to, and all discouragements in what we see now, it ever claims the future for its own."[1]

§ 11. It is the truer, as it is the heartier, faith to hold that, in the golden age which Science now ranks as to come, and not as gone, Knowledge and Religion must ultimately coalesce and coincide. The one is the science of the visible; the other of that which, though invisible, is no less real, no less truly a phase of Truth and Being. But if both are founded in the reality of things, there must be between them a fundamental harmony. For "it is incredible that there should be two orders of truth in absolute and everlasting opposition."[2] The

Meeting-points of knowledge and religion.

---

[1] Dean Church, *Univ. Serm.*, p. 72. "The tendency," says Sir H. Maine, "to look not to the past, but to the future, for types of perfection was brought into the world by Christianity."—*Ancient Law*, p. 74. "Hopefulness has ever been a note of the Church of Christ. It has been often mistrusted and misapprehended."—Merivale, *Northern Nations*, p. 116.

[2] Herbert Spencer, *First Princ.*, p. 21.

world began, we are now told, with Nature-worship; can we on a theory of evolution believe that at its close it will have developed no higher form? The dangers at present besetting Christianity are twofold. There is an ideal spiritualism abroad devoid of an objective basis. Where current, it brings Religion into contempt. There is also a secularistic Materialism, co-ordinate with a worship of Nature.

Jamjam efficaci dat manus Scientiæ.

Unreal results of science. Extremes thus meet. We have not now the cult of Ceres or Dionysus; but under other names the forces of Heat, Light, and Fecundity have taken their place and rank. But all such ultimate, assumed entities are to be deprecated, even if themselves forms of one Universal Force. They are questionable, unscientific resting-places in the analysis of truth, which must, to be complete, lead on to the source and origin of Force. There is surely a far higher boon in store to be conferred by the increasing light of Knowledge, when it shall be poured not solely on the simpler problems of the physical world, but upon the mysteries of the two voices in man, the microcosm of the universe, those jarring elements of Duty and Passion, of the *Ultimate relations of knowledge and will.* animal and the spiritual, of Nature and Grace. Originally created to be a part of the undivided system of Nature, working in automatic harmony with the constitution of the world around him;

in the exercise of a will independent of Divine Wisdom and of the laws it had imposed, Man fell from his high estate. Only by the reconciliation of his will with perfect reason, by the recognition of foregone perversity, by the confession of the justice and the mercy of his God, and by the submission of mind and spirit to the higher law of Morality and Religion; by these only, as subjective personal conditions of his Redemption, may he hope once more, in "the times of restitution of all things," to find himself in accord with a purified Nature, fulfilling the law of his being, the commandment of his God, and made "partaker of the Divine Nature." So far, if it be no further, may the plummet of finite Thought, led by the indications of Revelation, sound the depths of the nature and existence of evil in the world. Potentially real,[1] a secondary development of things, its very being and action may be but temporary and relative,

Tendency of knowledge to abate moral evil.

---

[1] Cf. Orig. c. Cels., VI. lv. Thus August., Civ. D., XI. 9. Mali nulla natura est; sed amissio boni mali nomen accepit; following the more ancient opinion, τὸ κακὸν τὸ δυνάμει ἀγαθόν. Arist., Metaph. N. iv. οὐκ ἔστι τὸ κακὸν παρὰ τὰ πράγματα. Comp. Plato, Theæt. 176, A. So also Basil (Hexam. Hom., ii.). Leibnitz, Théod., p. 550. "Quant à la cause du mal il est vrai que le diable est l'auteur du péché; mais l'origine du péché vient de plus loin, la source est dans l'imperfection originale des créatures," &c. His own explanation of this is well known. "Dieu a permis le mal, parce qu'il est enveloppé dans le meilleur plan qui se trouve dans la région des possibles."—Ib., p. 601. "Il se peut que tous les maux ne soient aussi qu'un presque néant en comparaison des biens qui sont dans l'univers."—p. 509. Bishop Butler (following August., Conf., II. v.), "There is nothing in the human mind contradictory, as the logicians speak, to virtue."—Anal., I. iii. "There is no such thing as love of injustice, oppression, treachery, ingratitude,'

conditioned by a finite state of existence and knowledge, admitting of ultimate explanation. That which is individual is in its own nature imperfect: and imperfection is a transient form of evil. But the will of man is confessedly individual, personal. The inherent conflict of self-interest with the common good can only be overcome by the conviction that it is through conformity to the universal law, as the expression of the wisdom of the Creator, to the whole constitution of things, that the perfection of the individual is reached.[1] This, if any, must be the lesson of ultimate civilization, and it is a lesson in the accomplishment of which the Faith of Christ may be expected to take a large share. "Christianity," it has been well said,[2] " has been revealed as a social and as a personal power in the richest variety of circumstances. It remains for us to harmonize the idea of society and self as they are seen to be harmonized in the teaching of the Apostles. In this lies the highest problem of philosophy and the most worthy aim of life. 'The prize is noble,' as Plato said of the corresponding problem in his age, 'and the hope is great.'" In this

Requires the co-operation of religion.

Coincident with the work of civilization.

&c.—*Serm.*, I. Mr. Mackay (*Progress of Intellect*, I. 482) has touched this subject with much profundity and learning. Physical evil must of course be distinguished from the moral and metaphysical notions. It may prove to be a necessary tendency of general laws, and to redound in many ways to the formation of moral excellencies.

[1] Compare Mr. Mill, *Exam.*, p. 510, who quotes an observation of M. Réville respecting human freedom. "La liberté complète, réelle, de l'homme est la perfection humaine, le but à atteindre."

[2] Prof. Westcott, *Cont. Rev.*, VI. 417.

law and scale of progress, that which we call evil must itself have been foreseen, and in a manner foreordained and provided for, by the act of Eternal Wisdom. One day "the depth of the riches of that wisdom and knowledge," (now "past finding out,") will be revealed, its ways disclosed; and the sufferings of "a bondage of corruption"[1] will show all unworthy to be compared with the glory that shall dawn upon the world become the kingdom of the Lord and of His Christ.

§ 12. "The Master of all who have knowledge."[2] Such is the title claimed by Dante for Aristotle, the Prince of ancient thought. Shall it not hereafter be given to One greater than Aristotle, who shall rise up in the judgment with the men of this generation and condemn them, as many as have divorced Science from Faith. For in that day secular philosophy, however glorious, will be transmuted into divine. The very course of the integration of human Knowledge may be expected to lead to the

Science inseparable from faith.

Tendency of human knowledge towards perfection.

---

[1] "L'imperfection qui accompagne la solution du corps pourroit donner lieu au sentiment d'une perfection plus grande, qui étoit suspendue ou arrêtée par la continuité qu'on fait cesser; et à cet égard le corps seroit comme une prison."—Leibnitz, *Works*, p. 603.

[2] "Il Maestro di color chi sanno." "La plus forte tête de toute l'antiquité, le grand Aristote," says M. Comte (*Phil. Pos.*, IV. 38), perhaps from an unconscious predilection; for it was very anciently remarked that Plato referred all to Mind, Aristotle to Law. The medieval reputation of Aristotle, whom the Schoolmen placed almost on a level with the Fathers, was according to Mr. Lecky (*Hist. Rat.*, I. 417), due to the early heretics. See Dean Milman, *Lat. Christ.*, VI. 267.

reception of one common, universal Religion, when the relations of Matter to a central Force shall be understood. The latest generalization of the inductive reason will be comprehended, as alone it can be comprehended, through the intuition of Him (for " we shall see Him as He is "), Who is the Author and Cause of all things, " Who is Alpha and Omega," " the Beginning and the End," the " First and the Last." In that day " whether there be knowledge, it will vanish away," because " we know but in part." What is there in the loftiest human speculation which should exempt it from the fate of all finite things? " Positive knowledge [1] does not and never can fill the whole region of possible thought. At the utmost reach of discovery there arises and must ever arise the question —what lies beyond? Science is a gradually increasing sphere, and every addition to its surface does but bring it into wider contact with surrounding ignorance. But if knowledge cannot monopolize consciousness;[2] if it must always continue

Inherent defects of positive knowledge.

[1] Mr. Herbert Spencer, *First Principles*, pp. 16, 17. The same thought that the material world cannot of itself contain a revelation of the Divine, the finite of the Infinite, occurs in Tennyson—

> Forerun thy peers, thy time: and let
> Thy feet millenniums hence be set
> In midst of knowledge dreamed not yet.
> Thou hast not gained a real height;
> Nor art thou nearer to the light,
> Because the scale is infinite.

[2] " Il n'y a que Dieu qui voie, comment ces deux termes *moi* et *l'existence* sont liés, c'est-à-dire, pourquoi j'existe."— Leibnitz, *Nouveaux Essais*, IV. vii 7

possible for the mind to dwell upon that which transcends knowledge, then there can never cease to be a place for that which is of the nature of Religion." For what region can be found in all the realms of Science, which is not relative only to our present living powers and to the world we now inhabit? What necessity[1] can be claimed for the Laws of Nature, as they are known to us, still less for the several facts which represent and engender them, which can resist the sentence of mutability so legibly written upon them? Knowledge then, as alone we now possess it, is of time, not of eternity; it is marred by the imbecillities of man's understanding. "Eye hath not seen, nor ear heard, neither have entered into the heart of man the things which God hath prepared for them that love Him." But "when that which is perfect is come, then that which is in part shall be done away."

Laws of nature devoid of the idea of necessity.

[1] See Sir W. Hamilton, *Appendix to Reid*, p. 971, who quotes Spinoza (*de Intell. Emend.*, § 108); " ideæ quas claras et distinctas formamus ita ex solâ *necessitate* nostræ naturæ sequi videntur, ut absolutè a solâ nostrâ potentiâ pendere videantur: confusæ autem contra." Chalmers's noble argument for the doctrine of immortality from man's capacities for knowledge is well known. " But for the truth of immortality man would be an anomaly in nature . . . . The whole labour of this mortal life would not suffice for traversing, in full extent, any one of the sciences. And yet there may lie undeveloped in his bosom a taste and talent for them all, none of which he can even singly overtake. For each science, though definite in its commencement, has its outgoings in the Infinite and the Eternal."—*Bridg. Treatise*, Pt. I. sub fin.

LECTURE VI.

THE PERMANENCE OF CHRISTIANITY INFERRED FROM THE CHARACTER OF ITS INFLUENCE.

"Ne quisquam nos aliena tantum redarguisse, non autem nostra asseruisse reprehenderet ; id agit pars altera operis hujus."—AUGUSTINE, *Retract.*, II.

"Imperium facile his artibus retinetur, quibus initio partum est."—SALLUST, *Bell. Catil.*, II. iv.

LECTURE VI.

"Who is he that overcometh the world, but he that believeth that Jesus is the Son of God?"—1 John v. 5.

§ 1. THE direct or positive proof originally proposed to be offered in these Lectures in respect of the permanence of the Christian Religion led first to the inquiry, what are the vital forces of any Religion; and next, in what degree are these exhibited in the past history and present condition of Christianity? These forces, common to all systems of Religion, may be compared with the powers of nutrition, reproduction, and growth in organic bodies. Such are the hold exercised by the theory of belief upon the spirit and conscience of its professors; the tendency of the system to extend itself by conversion; and, thirdly, the power of assimilating healthfully the varying conditions of progressive civilization. With the last of these lines of proof we have been indirectly occupied throughout the four preceding Lectures. For the objections which have been considered to the progress of Christianity have been such as belong to the highest stages of culture and scientific research as yet reached by the most civilized portion of mankind. Lastly, since every form of Religion asserts for itself an absolute

Stage of the inquiry.

Vital forces of Religions threefold.

In part already considered.

Concluding argument for

possession of Divine Truth, its announcements are to be considered final, or, at least, as preparative[1] to one complete scheme. A concluding argument will hence arise in favour of the truth of Christianity from the universality of its tenets and their adaptation to the history and circumstances of mankind, warranting in this manner its assumption of doctrinal finality. If its morality is sound and universal; its type of character perfect and complete, not partial, national, local, or generic,[2] but correspondent to the unity of our race; if its revelations, replacing earlier creeds and inheriting all they held of truth, reach on to the horizon of humanity, and assure for ever the destinies of man, we need not greatly fear for the future of a Religion which can only be coeval with our race. We now proceed to examine, in the first place, the character and extent of the influence exercised by Christianity at various periods on the consciences of its converts.

§ 2. It has been asked by a leading thinker of

[1] Such as the Mosaic system; which cannot therefore be properly attacked, as it has been by Kant and others (see *Religion innerhalb*, &c., *Werke*, VI. 301, ed. Hartenstein), as not Divine, because it did not preach immortality. Warburton's proposition on this subject is well known.

[2] "The ceremonial law was succeeded by a pure and spiritual worship, equally adapted to all climates, as well as to every condition of mankind."—Gibbon, c. xv. Compare Palmer (*Treatise on the Church*, I. vii.) on the catholicity of Christianity. "The New Testament," says Prof. Seeley, *Lect. and Essays*, p. 276, "is the text-book of universal or natural morality." On the objection that if Christianity be in harmony with human nature, it may be viewed as a human invention, see Merivale, *Conv. of N. Nations*, p. 3.

our time,[1] "what are the conditions necessary to constitute a religion?" "There must," he replies, "be a creed, or conviction, claiming authority over the whole of human life; a belief or set of beliefs deliberately adopted respecting human destiny and duty, to which the believer inwardly acknowledges that all his actions ought to be subordinate. Moreover, there must be a sentiment connected with this creed, or capable of being evoked by it, sufficiently powerful to give it, in fact, the authority over human conduct to which it lays claim in theory." In other words, the success of a religion may be held to result from the relation of its doctrines to the organ of belief in man, from the convictions which it furnishes to the faculty of Faith. For Faith, the outcome of our spiritual nature in its apprehension of God, is the vital spark of all Religion. If Faith be on the wane, there is a canker at the root of the creed. The external organization, the ecclesiastical arrangements, may look vigorous enough, but the end draws on. In criticising, then, the claims of a religion to acceptance from the side of experience, *i. e.* from its past success and present

Preliminary examination of the elements necessary to the success of a religious system,

viz. the relation of its doctrines to the principle of faith.

---

[1] Mr. J. S. Mill, *A. Comte and Positivism*, p. 133. He adds: "It is a great advantage, though not absolutely indispensable, that this sentiment should crystallize, as it were, round a positive object—if possible, a really existing one—though in all the more important cases only ideally present. Such an object Theism and Christianity offer to the believer." Mr. Lecky, *H. R.*, I. 389, speaking of the first ages of Christianity, remarks that "it was then strictly a religion; that is to say, it consisted of modes of emotion, and not of intellectual propositions."

condition, and in inferring from these grounds its ulterior prospects, regard must be had to the work which lies before it, to the end which it proposes to itself for accomplishment. Now, all positive Religions[1] lay claim to some measure of Divine Revelation; *i. e.* to communications from God to man beyond the ordinary modes of information and knowledge. These it is its province to propagate amongst mankind. Any religion, then, which should altogether divest itself of mysteries, the meeting-points between Nature and that which transcends it; satisfied with the simple proclamation of moral truths, however refined, or with a republication of the so-called Religion of Nature, which is, in fact, the apotheosis of moral abstractions; thus carrying no further message to the spirit and higher reason of man; any such religion may on

All religions properly vehicles of revelation to human nature,

---

[1] It has been said very truly that so-called Natural Religion exists only in books. Religions which have vital force and influence are positive religions; that is, they make for themselves a Church, and rites, and dogmas. These dogmas are the solutions of the great problems which have ever disquieted the mind of man—the origin of the world, the origin of evil, its expiation, the future of our race.

Quid sumus et quidnam victuri gignimur.

Mr. Lecky, *H. Rat.*, I. 182, points out that "Protestant Rationalism regards Christianity as designed to preside over the *moral* development of mankind. . . . In its eyes the moral element of Christianity is as the sun in heaven, and dogmatic systems are as the clouds that intercept and temper the exceeding brightness of its ray." In p. 335, he seems himself to incline to the view that dogmatic systems are a provisional arrangement for semi-barbarous periods, though he admits that Christianity is the solitary instance "of a religion not naturally weakened by civilization." Pietism in the hands of Spener, Francke, &c., as also the Remonstrants, early endeavoured to separate religious morals from dogma. The movement has terminated in Strauss.

these very accounts be suspected. It falls short of the due operation of Religion in itself; which, as a function of human nature, has its own appropriate work by the realization of which it must stand or fall. That work,[1] though the contrary is not unfrequently asserted, is not identical with the inculcation of morality, however high, however pure. The Science of Ethics falls legitimately within the ken of human knowledge, capable of improvement and advance. But when it has led man to the threshold of Religion, a sphere is discovered to him from which he has not borrowed morality.[2] Thus the doctrines of a religious system, while properly in accord with morality, transcend by their nature the limits of its teaching.[3] Morality is present in them, even if as

are not concerned with the inculcation of morality.

---

[1] The most elementary forms of religion seem to afford little trace of ethics. Compare Mr. Tylor, *Prim. Cult.*, I. 386. In Confucianism, on the other hand, ethics overpower and extinguish the religious element. See Döllinger, *Gentile and Jew*, I. 56-8; Legge, II. 130, 319. "To give oneself earnestly to the duties due to men, and while respecting spiritual beings to keep aloof from them, may be called wisdom," was the maxim and practice of its founder. It is not strange to find, from Mr. Cooper (*Pioneer of Commerce*), that his temples at the present day are deserted. Lange, *Gesch. des Materialismus*, p. 537, says, "Die Religionen haben ursprünglich gar nicht einmal den Zweck der Sittlichkeit zu dienen." See Buckle, *Hist. Civ*, II. 303. "The Church," writes Dean Hook, "was not incorporated to inculcate a code of morals. . . . . . The inculcation of morality is an incident of Christianity, and not of its essence."—*Lives of Archbishops*, N. S., I. 3.

[2] Compare Guizot, *Civ. in E.*, I. 87, ed. Bohn. Paley's *Evid.*, Pt. II. c. ii., on the morality of the Gospel. Christianity, strictly speaking, is no new code of morals, but an appeal to the highest moral experience.

[3] "There is a fine line," writes Coleridge, "which, like stripes of light in light, distinguishes, not divides, the summit of religious Morality from spiritual Religion."—*A. R.*, p. 81.

a vital, yet as a rudimentary element. This fact is evident on a comparison of barbarous with civilized races.¹ To condemn a creed on moral grounds is not, therefore, properly conclusive, though it is, no doubt, the case that in proportion to its truth it will encourage a purer and more elevated morality,² which varies in most men in proportion to their practical belief in God and His promises. Its real test on the experimental side lies in the accomplishment of its true specific end. And this would seem to be so to educate, to mould and inform the spirit of man, as to restore it to its divine image, and prepare it for a future continuous existence.³ This work involves, indeed, moral issues. The correlations and interaction between the life that now is and its after-stage very soon become mutually interpenetrated. The spirit, as part at least of the principle of personality in man, is inseparable from those acts or decisions of the will which determine its character, and as Revelation instructs us, its ultimate destiny. Religion then, which occupies itself with the spiritual

Relation of morality to a system of religion.

Proper test of the success of a religion

includes moral influence, but as a secondary element.

---

¹ Compare Mr. Tylor, *Prim. C.*, II. 326.
² Hence the fine lines of Persius:

    Compositum jus fasque animo sanctosque recessus
    Mentis, et incoctum generoso pectus honesto;
    Hæc cedo ut admoveam templis et farre litabo.

³ Mr. Lecky well observes, *H. E. M.*, I. 363-4, "Reverence and humility, a constant sense of the true majesty of God, and of the weakness and sinfulness of man, and a perpetual reference to another world, were the essential characteristics of Christianity, the source of all its power, the basis of its distinctive type."

element in man, cannot be divorced from the morality which it must teach or tolerate.[1] Its converts will act upon the principles of their belief, which supply them with a new series of motives, and these will accordingly become evident in the conduct and disposition of the believer. In this manner a moral test may be applied of the character and efficacy of the Revelation, for it may fail on either side. On the one hand, it may be found to put "bitter for sweet, and sweet for bitter;" it may put "darkness for light, and light for darkness;"[2] that is, its tenets, as in the case of many heathen idolatries, may corrupt the moral sense; its positive enactments or promises may confound the natural law of right. On the other hand, its power of moral suasion, though wholesomely directed, may be feeble and inoperative. Its voice may utter no

A moral test thus applicable

---

[1] Mr. Buckle, I. 425 (after Hallam) traces the *scientific* separation of theology from morals to Bishop Cumberland. Mr. Pattison (*Ess. and Rev.*, p. 256) remarks very truly that those ages in which morality *alone* has been most spoken of have ever been those in which it has been least practised.

[2] Isaiah v. 20. Thus Bishop Butler, *Anal.*, II. c. iii. : "Though objections against the evidence of Christianity are most seriously to be considered, yet objections against Christianity itself are in a great measure frivolous; almost all objections against it, excepting those which are alleged against the particular proofs of its coming from God. I express myself with caution, lest I should be mistaken to vilify reason; which is, indeed, the only faculty we have wherewith to judge concerning anything, even Revelation itself: or be misunderstood to assert that a supposed revelation cannot be proved false from internal characters. For it may contain clear immoralities or contradictions; and either of these would prove it false. Nor will I take upon me to affirm, that nothing else can possibly render any supposed revelation incredible." And again: "It is the province of reason to judge of the morality of the Scripture," &c.

of a practical nature.

uncertain sound, but yet it may fail to nerve mankind for the battle with evil. The standard, then, of the truth, and hence of the permanence of a religious system, apart from its particular evidences, will appear first and properly in the character of the hold gained by it on the spirit and conscience of those who profess it; then, by consequence, but in a secondary degree, in its general moral effects as exhibited in practice. If without marked effect, or if immoral in tendency, a presumption arises against its truth, stronger or weaker in the former case in proportion to the length of date and nature of the circumstances attending its operation. Success upon certain occasions affords, it is true, but slender guarantee for truth, for the result may be differently explained. But when itself the issue of unfavourable conjunctures and contrary to ordinary expectation, or when steadily continuous, however slow the process,[1] it raises in the mind an almost instinctive conviction of its providential character and ultimate triumph.

Different theories as to the original success of Christianity.

§ 3. Very different reasons, as might be expected, have been assigned to the rise and first successes of Christianity, according to the varying temperament

[1] "The Christian body," says Dr. Mozley (*B. L.*, p. 140), " is enlarged by growth and stationariness combined: each successive age contributing its quota, and the acquisition, once made, remaining. . . . . And the same principle of growth can at last convert the world: however slow the process, the result will come, if Christianity always keeps the ground it gets: for that which always gains and never loses must ultimately win the whole."

of particular thinkers. It has been regarded by some in the light of a moral protest against general and overwhelming corruption. By others it is viewed as a stage in the history of superstitions, a phase and a necessary phase of mental enthusiasm. By others it is admitted to have embodied a large moral advance. By some, again, its rapid progress is explained through the advantage of an unrivalled organization. But those who attribute its success to its moral excellences, neglect to take into account its qualities as a religion. They ignore the fact that it is to these, and not to any mere ethical superiority, that its real advance is due. But, if it be regarded as but one among the many superstitions which had preceded it in East and West, the fact of its success, and still more of its continuance, remains yet to be explained. To the liberal zeal of Christianity, freed from the fetters of the Mosaic Law, Gibbon assigns much of the success of its preaching.[1] But other superstitions, in the times of the Empire, were equally yielding, equally

Neglect its qualities as a religion.

View of Gibbon

---

[1] *Decline and Fall*, c. xv.: "Under these circumstances Christianity offered itself to the world, armed with the strength of the Mosaic Law, and delivered from the weight of its fetters," &c. If, indeed, the remarks of this great historian be understood of a comparison between the genius of the Christian religion and the class-interests of previous systems as well as of the existing state of Roman society, they might well be received as a fair tribute to the intrinsic superiority of Christianity. M. Littré (*Études sur les Barbares et le Moyen-Age*, p. 2) has some true and fine remarks on the sterility of the results arrived at by Gibbon, who in recounting the Fall of the Empire, takes no heed of the regeneration of the world by Christianity.

pliant in receiving proselytes, without being equally rewarded. And the intolerance of the simple-minded followers of Jesus for all other forms of belief; their impolitic vehemence against immoral institutions; their somewhat narrow impatience of current philosophical systems; their jealous secrecy as regards the mysteries of the faith, while little in accord with the liberality to which such great results have been attributed, are known to have proved stumbling-blocks to a general reception of the new Religion. It does not seem to have occurred to this writer that the secret of the success of Christianity may well have lain in the harmony of its doctrines with the religious needs of the time, the deliverance which it held forth from impending ruin at the end of the world, by many deemed so near;[1] the inward calm and satisfaction which it wrought on the minds of its converts; the stores of spiritual strength which it instilled under circumstances of much worldly depression. These were its legitimate instruments of triumph.[2] The miracles which it claimed, whatever part they may have had in the

inadequate.

True causes of its triumph.

---

[1] This subject, it is well known, is especially brought forward by Gibbon, *u. s.* But he treats it in the light of a vulgar superstition, which must have been at least as dangerous through the discovery of its fallacious expectation, as powerful in the cogency of the alarm which it created.

[2] "No other religion ever combined so many forms of attraction as Christianity, both from its intrinsic excellence, and from its manifest adaptation to the special wants of the time."—Lecky, *H. E. M.*, I. 419.

persuasion of unbelievers, were shared by it with rival faiths. Its virtues, like its doctrines, were certainly its own. The pen of our great historian, though dipped in gall, does not disallow the moral reformation introduced by Christianity, enforcing, as it did, repentance for sin and blamelessness of life.[1] "He that nameth the name of Christ, let him depart from iniquity," was long the rule and mark of Christian converts. Nor was this a result of which the causes remain unexplained. They are patient in the character of the Religion preached, as well as in the circumstances of the age which received it. The doctrines of Christianity contained within them the core of man's moral regeneration, a supply to his spiritual destitution, motives to repentance laid in the atoning work of God for man; motives to new action, founded evermore on promises of Divine grace.[2] Hence the peculiar characteristics of Christian virtue, issuing in a new moral type built upon the

Testified by the moral reformation effected.

Character of its doctrines.

---

[1] For testimonies to an admitted moral superiority on the part of the first Christians, compare Pliny, *Epp.*, X. 97; Galen (ap. Gieseler, I. 126, ed. Clark); Justin M., *Apol.*, II. i. xii.; *Paræn.*, c. xxxv.; Athenag., *Leg.*, c. ii. xi.; Ep. ad Diogn., c. v. vi.; Tertull., *Apol.*, c. 45; Origen, *c. Cels.*, III. 30; VII. 48, 49; I. 67: τὸ ὄνομα τοῦ Ἰησοῦ . . . ἐμποιεῖ θαυμασίαν τινα πραότητα, καὶ καταστολὴν τοῦ ἤθους, καὶ φιλανθρωπίαν, καὶ χρηστότητα, καὶ ἡμερότητα ἐν τοῖς μὴ διὰ τὰ βιωτικὰ, ἤ τινας χρείας ἀνθρωπικὰς ὑποκριναμένοις, ἀλλὰ παρὰ δεξαμένοις γνησίως τὸν περὶ Θεοῦ καὶ Χριστοῦ καὶ τῆς ἐσομένης κρίσεως λόγον.

[2] "The force which Christianity has applied to the world, and by which it has produced that change in the world which it has, is, in a word, the doctrine of grace."—Mozley, *B. L.*, p. 180.

model of a crucified Saviour; the humbleness; the self-sacrifice; the forgiving spirit; the obligation of remembering the poor; the enforced chastity of a redeemed body become the temple of the Spirit of God; the faith in a life to come, showing itself patient of tortures and of death.

§ 4. The wider yet far more searching analysis,[1] instituted since Gibbon wrote, of the causes which prepared the Greek and Roman civilizations for the infiltration of Christianity, has seen in the new spirit which stole upon the philosophy of the age, in its broader and more eclectic character under the cosmopolitan system of the Empire, in its introspective and subjective tone, a temper of thought not ill-suited to the announcement of Christian morality.[2] But the increasing corruption of the outer world, against which Stoicism spent its strength in vain, despite the wholesome influences of daily duties and domestic intercourse, called for more drastic and intrinsic remedies. The need of a religion which might reconcile and

Analysis of the state of civilization at this period.

Its corruption, and need of restoration

---

[1] See Mr. Lecky's powerful, and in many respects adequate, inquiry into the moral causes which preceded the rise of Christianity in the Roman Empire.—*H. E. M.*, l. c. iii. Compare also Dean Merivale (*Hist. of the Empire*, VI. 356 ff.); and especially Neander's (I. 6-117) masterly review of the religious state of the world at the coming of Christ; together with Döllinger, *Gentile and Jew*, I. 347, 370; II. 284-9.

[2] See Prof. Lightfoot's learned disquisition on the relations of Stoicism to Christianity (*St. Paul and Seneca*), in his Commentary on the Epistle to the Philippians. He shows that Stoicism itself was indebted to Oriental sources, and probably to Christian teaching.

in practice absorb the highest truths of conflicting philosophical systems was more and more felt. Its sanctions secured to the soul of man what centuries of argument and discussion had failed to effect. No closer relation than this needs to be sought between Pagan morality and Christian influence. The fixed idea of the religion of the time was that of a *national* Providence, addressed on the part of man by ceremonial observances.[1] The disintegration of social superstitions was due to their own inability to meet the wants of the period and the tendencies of the age.[2] Credulity gave way before a real and growing anxiety to learn and know the truth—truth which would set men free from many a cruel and degrading practice. The same providential arrangement which, having first created the Macedonian Empire and ordained the Roman Conquest, had prepared, against the promulgation of Christianity, a language common alike to East and West,[3] had reserved for it an era markedly

as to religious ideas.

The circumstances favourable to the introduction of Christianity,

---

[1] It culminated in the Deification of Emperors. For an example of the declining condition of the old state-religion, see Tac., *Ann.*, III. 58.

[2] Thus Chrysostom writes (d. *Babyla*, *Opp.*, II. 540): ὑπ' οὐδένος ἐνοχληθεῖσά ποτε τῆς Ἑλληνικῆς δεισιδαιμονίας ἡ πλάνη ἀφ' ἑαυτῆς ἐσβέσθη, καὶ περὶ ἑαυτὴν διέπεσε, καθάπερ τῶν σωμάτων τὰ τηκηδόνι παραδοθέντα μακρᾷ, καὶ μηδένος αὐτὰ βλάπτοντος αὐτόματα φθείρεται καὶ διαλυθέντα κατὰ μικρὸν ἀφανίζεται. See ap. Gieseler, I. 321. Compare Plutarch (d. *Superstit.*, c. xxxiii.). It was remarked that there were no martyrs for heathen doctrines. "Quis eorum," says August., *in Psalm.* 141, § 20, "comprehensus est in sacrificio, cum his legibus ista prohiberentur, et non negavit?" "Paganism," writes Dean Merivale, "had no tap-root of moral renovation."

[3] "Græca leguntur in omnibus fere gentibus," says Cicero, *pro Archiâ*,

favourable for the introduction of the new doctrines, combining, as they did, a basis of historical facts[1] with an appeal to personal religious consciousness. "No other religion," it has been truly observed, "had ever united so many distinct elements of power and attraction; so much ethical reality with a profound sympathy in human trials; so much feeling with so much truth."[2] This, however, must not lead us to forget that it is in the distinctive tenets of Christianity that we must look for the true causes of this very combination: in the spiritual convictions which it aroused and satisfied; in the religious emotions which it controlled; in the promises which it alone fulfilled.[3]

but answering to its distinctive tenets.

c. x. Plutarch considered it the mission of Alexander, τὴν Ἑλλάδα σπεῖραι. Compare Neander, I. 67, and some remarks by Mr. J. S. Mill (*Positivism*, p. 24). See also Droysen (*Gesch. des Hellenismus*). It must not be forgotten that the tendencies of an age are only the consequences of its historical circumstances.

[1] "Up to this time there had never existed among mankind any historical truth on which a religious faith could be based; nor yet any philosophic faith founded on a personal religious consciousness residing within man's own breast, and finding its credentials and interpretation there. 'What is truth?' asks Pilate. 'What can this barbarian teach us?' exclaims the Athenian."—Bunsen, *God in Hist.*, III. pp. 66, 67, E. T. My line of thought in this Lecture leads me to contrast the permanent change of moral teaching, which accompanied Christianity, with the world as it found it. This was, however, fundamentally due to the miraculous element which was inherent in its enouncements. This course of reflection is most ably worked out by Dr. Mozley (*Bamp. Lect.*, p. 170 ff.).

[2] Lecky, *H. E. M.*, I. 412–414.

[3] If Christianity had been only or principally an intellectual movement consequent on previous phases of thought, it would not have commenced with the poor. Compare Neander, 1. 9. Dean Milman, *Latin Christ.*, I. 451, has some good remarks on the strangeness and originality of the fundamental Christian ideas to the Roman world, and the consequent difficulty of their reception.

In these and not in its moral worth, however highly estimated, lay the talisman of its triumph. The doctrine of salvation by belief, "which, then, for the first time, flashed upon the world," gave the real death-blow to philosophical scepticism.[1] It was the new-born consciousness of sin, which, awakening remorse, lit up the sense of responsibility and turned it inward on the soul, that invested human life with a solemnity and import never before felt; which opened,[2] as they had never before been stirred, the lips of prayer. Pliny had deemed it but a pollution to the Infinite Spirit of God to concern Himself with the petty affairs of men.[3] It was the Christian's privilege of suffering for and with a suffering Redeemer[4] (thus

Instances.

---

[1] "Apud Ciceronem et Platonem aliosque ejusmodi scriptores multa sunt acutè dicta et leniter calentia; sed in iis omnibus non invenio, Venite ad Me."—Augustin., *in Matt.* xi. 28. See *Conf.*, VII. ix. 13. Carlyle remarks: "The old world knew nothing of conversion. Instead of an Ecce Homo, they had only some Choice of Hercules. It was a new attained progress in the moral development of man; hereby has the Highest come home to the bosoms of the most limited."—*S. R.*, p. 136. For individual examples of the manner in which Christianity wrought upon educated minds, see Justin Martyr (*Dial. c. Tryph.*), Augustine (*Conf.*), Synesius, and the *Recogn. Clement.*, I. sub init.

[2] See M. Denis, *Idées Morales*, II. 234, and Döllinger, *Gentile and Jew*, II. 75-7. A true Roman prayer may be found in Cato, *Re Rust.*, c. 41.

[3] *Hist. Nat.*, II. iv., VII. i.: "Irridendum verò, agere curam rerum humanarum illud, quidquid est summum. Anne tam tristi atque multiplici ministerio non pollui credamus dubitemusve?" Comp. Cic., *Nat. D.*, II. ii.; *Invent.*, I. xxix.; and Seneca, *Epp.*, 41, 95. He thinks Providence *sometimes* cares for men.

[4] Compare Clem. Rom., *ad Cor.* I. xlix., and *Ep. ad Diogn.*, c. x. Prof. Lightfoot (*u. s.*, p. 326) well observes: "The moral teaching and example of our Lord will ever have the highest value in their own province; but the core of the Gospel does not lie here. Its distinctive

no mere ascetic truth that pain is good, and no evil); the requital of love for love, of sympathy for man in return for the sympathy of God;[1] which transmuted the dross of universal luxury into the fine gold of the noblest self-sacrifice and heroic self-control. And thus, lastly, it was far more the hope of eternal life than the fear of everlasting torment,[2] which, to the Christian convert, dignified earthly sorrows and levelled worldly enjoyments.

This influence wholly a spiritual one,

§ 5. Thus the spiritual character of the hold exercised by primitive Christianity on the lives and consciences of its converts must be considered a fact beyond dispute. It is attested both by the

---

character is that in revealing a Person it reveals also a principle of life— the union with God in Christ, apprehended by faith in the present, and assured to us hereafter by the Resurrection. This Stoicism could not give, and therefore its dogmas and precepts were barren."

[1] "The great principle of *vicarious suffering*, which forms the centre of Christianity, spreads itself through the subordinate parts of the system, and is the pervading if not the invariable law of Christian beneficence."—I. Taylor, *Nat. Hist. of Enthus.*, p. 162. "The precepts and examples of the Gospel struck a chord of pathos which the noblest philosophies of antiquity had never reached. For the first time the aureole of sanctity encircled the brow of sorrow, and invested it with a mysterious charm."—Lecky, *Hist. Rat.*, II. 266.

[2] In this matter M. Comte takes a truer view than Gibbon or Mr. Lecky.—See *Phil. Pos.*, V. 422. Christianity, he thinks, preserved to itself the advantage of leaving the nature of future pains and rewards open.—See also IV. 190. On the influence of immortality as a Christian motive, compare Lucian, *Mort. Peregrin.*, § 13. On the current views of immortality, see Döllinger, *Gentile and Jew*, II. 143–6. M. Rio remarks that the earliest delineations of Christian art represent ideas of joy and felicity. Conceptions of Hell and Purgatory come much later, and from heathen sources. There were Roman philosophers who erected to their friends tombs dedicated "Somno æternali."—Orelli, I. p. 262.

voice of Christian Apologists, by the unwilling witness of adversaries,[1] and still more convincingly by institutions and social and moral changes which remain as monuments of the influence of nascent Christianity. Testimonies to the active moral force of the new Religion abound, indeed, in the earlier Fathers.[2] Virtues, hitherto little, if at all, recognized, now made rudimentary graces; passive endurance; forgiveness of injuries; resignation under calamity, not as a necessity,[3] but as a duty of the human spirit; humility and meekness; benevolent unselfish effort replacing a narrow Egoism;[4] fortitude under pain and death for the cause of belief; a sense of sin, not as an outward offence, but as an inward stain; a strengthened

but exhibiting moral results.

Instances.

---

[1] As Epictetus, M. Aurelius, Julian. Cf. Lucian, *d. Mort. Pereg.*, XIII.

[2] *E.g.* Justin M., *Apol.*, I. xiv. xxv.; II. xii. *Dial. c. Tr.*, 110, 119, 131. Tertullian, *Apol.*, xxxix. Minuc. F., c. ix. Lactant., *D. Inst.*, III. 26; V. 18. Origen, *c. Cels.*, I. 67. See the temperate statements of Gieseler, I. 298, and Robertson, *C. H.*, I. 274. Compare some vivid remarks of Mr. Allies, *Formation of Christianity*, pp. 269, 270: "The Christian faith had laid its hand on the individual man," &c.

[3] In striking contrast, therefore, to the Mahometan virtue of submission, perhaps implied in the name "Islam." In *Phil. Pos.*, IV. 190, Comte coldly analyzes this quality, which he thinks only compatible with the acceptance of laws of Nature: "Quant à la résignation religieuse et surtout Chrétienne elle n'est, à vrai dire, malgré tant d'emphatiques éloges qu'une prudente temporisation qui fait supporter les malheurs présents en vue d'une ineffable félicité ultérieure."

[4] "Fecerunt itaque civitates duas amores duo, terrenam scilicet amor sui usque ad contemptum Dei, cœlestem vero amor Dei usque ad contemptum sui."—August., *Civ. D.*, XXIV. xxviii. "Le principe qui dominait l'antiquité était l'egoïsme du plus fort, tantôt celui de l'État, tantôt celui de l'individu. La personnalité de l'homme, sa liberté, ses droits naturels, étaient méconnus."—Schmidt, *Essai*, p. 116.

conviction of the freedom and spirituality of the human will; conversion from habits of vice, sudden, yet lasting; the consolations of faith and prayer as the outpouring of the soul to its Redeemer; the renovation of domestic virtues and proprieties, impaired by the vices of Roman society and the evil effects of slavery; the duty of almsgiving and active charity;[1] the recognition of the rights of conscience and of religious freedom; the severance of spiritual from political obligation; a higher estimate of the value of human life; the sense of a real brotherhood among mankind, involving religious equality with slaves;[2] a moral ideal suited to high and low; the replacement of hereditary priesthoods by common religious functions; an operative faith in the reality of another world; these and other kindred ideas, pregnant with fruitful effects, bore witness to the power and originality of the Faith of Christ in regenerating the heart of man, when first it broke, like the light of morning, on the world,[3] as upon men awakened

---

[1] "Ad hanc partem (sc. beneficentiæ) philosophorum nulla præcepta sunt."—Lactant., *D. Inst.*, VI. x.

[2] Comp. Archdeacon Lee's *Lectt. on Eccles. Hist.*, pp. 24–29; and on the operation of the Christian doctrines, Merivale, *Lectt.* pp. 155, 156. On the general services of Christianity at this epoch, Ozanam, *Civilis.*, I. c. i.

[3] ὥσπερ οἱ τὸν ὕπνον ἀποσεισάμενοι εὐθέως ἐγρηγόρασαν.—Clem. Alex., *Pæd.*, I. vi. § 28. Mr. Mill on Liberty, p. 22, has some disparaging remarks on the ease with which Christian precepts may be acquiesced in without their gaining a practical hold on the believer. Lange, *Gesch. des Mat.*, pp. 530, 531, observes truly, that amidst many analogies between the condition of modern society and that of the Roman Empire, the differences induced by Christian ideas are palpable.

out of slumber to renewed and vigorous life. The extinction, gradual but complete, of gladiatorial shows;[1] of exposure of infants, and infanticide;[2] the establishment of orphanages, refuges, almshouses, and hospitals;[3] the emancipation of slavery;[4] the sanctification of the marriage tie;[5] the foundation (at least after the decay of all Imperial institutions) of primary and public schools;[6] are standing proofs of the tendency and influence of Christianity in apprehending and advancing the true welfare of mankind. These are

Vast moral reforms.

---

[1] Compare here Ozanam, *u. s.*, II. c. ii.; and Luthardt, *Apolog.*, pp. 243, 244, E. T.; Lecky, *Hist. Rat.*, II. 264.

[2] τεκνογονοῦσιν ἀλλ' οὐ ρίπτουσι τὰ γεννώμενα.—Ep. ad Diogn., c. v. See Milman, *Lat. Chr.*, I. 547.

[3] See Gieseler, II. 60. Χηροτρόφια and ὀρφανοτρόφια are known to date from the fourth century; so also πτωχοτροφεῖα, νοσοκομεῖα, ξενῶνες, and ξενοδοχεῖα. The Βασιλειὰs was a hospital for lepers. The charitable offices of the Parabolani, Fossani, or κοπιάται ("ultimum illud et maximum pietatis officium peregrinorum et pauperum sepultura," Lactant., VI. xii.), should be added. On the non-existence of hospitals and infirmaries in Pagan times, see Schmidt, *u. s.*, p. 75.

[4] Comp. Robertson, *C. H.*, II. 229. Gregory Naz. and Chrysostom insist largely on the duty; but the first instances are long before : *e. g.* Hermes, Prefect of Rome under Trajan, freed 1250 ; Chromatius under Diocletian, 1400, &c. Under this head fall all measures for the improvement of serfs by Gregory the Great, the laws of Constantine and Justinian, &c. Comp. Guizot, *Civ. en Fr.*, II. 125, III. 137, ed. Bohn. Milman, *Lat. Chr.*, I. 338, 365. Lecky, *H. Rat.*, II. 256-258. The Romans often exposed and put to death sick slaves.—Suet., *Claud.*, c. xxv.

[5] Even with the Jews, marriage was only a political institution. Contrast with this the touching treatise of Tertull., *ad Uxor.*, II. ix., &c. Compare Milman, *Lat. Chr.*, I. 344.

[6] The first mention of Christian primary schools occurs in the fourth century in Chrysostom and Basil. See in Guizot, *u. s.*, I. 351; II. 100. There is a treatise by M. Lalanne on the *Influence des Pères de l'Église sur l'éducation publique*.

its fuller triumphs, the records of a world-wide humanity, new in motive and spirit as obligatory on the followers of Him Who died for all men. Yet it is far more in its action upon individuals, where History leaves no trace; in calm and silent influences shed upon personal character, as generation after generation has worked its work and passed; in the purity of domestic life, in souls attuned to the practice of human charities, to the privilege of suffering, to a departure full of immortality; that the real work of Christianity as compared with other religions must be sought and found.[1] Biography, more than History, is its true record. Never before was the reflection of a Divine Image mirrored so clearly in the human soul or in the practice of mankind. The summits of Christian heroism in martyr, saint, and confessor, first touched with the tints of Heaven, were

Difficulty of following it into private and personal life.

---

[1] See some good remarks in Robertson, *C. Hist.*, I. 363; and Lecky, *H. E. M.*, II. 156:—"Christianity has suffered peculiarly from this cause. The spheres in which its superiority over other religions is most incontestable, are precisely those which history is least capable of realizing." "The record of the spiritual Church," says Isaac Taylor, *Enthus.*, p. 191, "is 'on high,' not in the tomes that make our libraries proud." "The influence of religion," writes Paley, *Ev.*, II. c. vii., "must be perceived, if perceived at all, in the silent course of private domestic life . . . The kingdom of heaven is within us. That which is the substance of the religion; its hopes and consolations; its intermixture with the thoughts by day and by night; the devotion of the heart; the control of appetite; the steady direction of the will to the commands of God, is necessarily invisible. Yet upon these depend the virtue and the happiness of millions." Christianity, as a system of human restoration, works from the individual to the general. See a fine passage in Milman, *Lat. Chr.*, I. 24.

the first to shine out in the full radiance of moral splendour. But the warm rays were not long in winning their way to valley and to plain, shedding abroad their gifts of fruitfulness and life.

§ 6. Thus the hold of primitive Christianity on the minds and consciences of men was both of the strongest and of the highest kind. For it sufficed to effect, through much individual suffering and sacrifice, a moral revolution in the world; and completely changed, by moral force alone, the existing religions. And it must be observed that the changes effected, fraught indeed with very important moral results, were brought about by strictly spiritual convictions. These are to be assigned as the true causes of the movement. Here lies the real point at issue with much of the critical philosophy of our time.[1] It is evidently possible, in reviewing the career of Christianity, to scan it from more than one point of view, provided only that these be not mutually inconsistent. Charges of failure are necessarily incompatible with admissions of success. But the allowed successes may be variously explained. The benefits effected for mankind by the Religion of Jesus Christ can hardly now, as facts, be disputed, though they have sometimes been forgotten by too hasty objectors. At

Superiority and force of the spiritual element in primitive Christianity.

The services of Christianity sometimes assigned to its positive institutions.

[1] Neander (I. 3) remarks: "Because Christianity enters readily into all that is human, striving to assimilate it to its own nature, and to interpenetrate it with its own power, it appears on a superficial view as if it were itself only a product resulting from the combination of the different spiritual elements it had drawn together."

T

present it is more common to attribute them to the influence of consummate positive institutions; or at least to the operation of natural causes in such a manner as to eviscerate all native force and vigour in the supernatural elements of Christianity. Neither the founder of Positivism,[1] nor his most discerning followers, have denied the signal services of Christ's Religion to mankind. They contend, however, that this has been the result of the circumstances of the times, due really to the necessary evolution of ideas in intellectual and social advance. It is important, therefore, to remark how closely the effects of our Religion may be traced to the doctrines of its creed. No philosophical improvements, no uprooting of effete institutions,[2] no craving after moral reforms, no

This view unfounded.

---

[1] Comte remarks, *Phil. Pos.*, V. 328, that Catholicism (with him the embodiment of Christianity) has never been fairly criticised, having constantly been the subject either of unlimited panegyric or boundless detraction. He admits the earliest ideal of the Christian Church (V. 229), *viz.* as an universal spiritual power independent of the temporal, to be the greatest triumph humanity has yet achieved. He regards Catholicism as having done its proper work from the fifth to the thirteenth centuries, placing the acme from the middle of the eleventh to the close of the thirteenth. Of this he writes (V. 326): "Le système catholique du moyen-âge forme le chef-d'œuvre politique de la sagesse humaine." But everywhere he denies (*e. g.* V. 418, 419) that the moral excellence of Christianity is due to its doctrines, but only to its social constitution. M. Guizot (I. 85) more truly observes that it is "by moral life, by internal movement as well as by order and discipline, that institutions take possession of society. The Church mooted all the great questions which interest man: busying itself with the problems of his nature and the chances of his destiny. Hence its great influence on modern civilization."

[2] Thus M. Littré (*Barbares*, p. 231), "Le Christianisme naquit de

agitation for political changes, no mere variation of social conditions, nor all these combined, are sufficient to account for the conversion to the Faith of the Nazarene of the Roman world. The character and history of that change are, if dimly, adequately known and understood. A set of facts and historical circumstances, making up the life, and death, and thoughts of a Galilean peasant, won the ear first of peasants like himself, of women and of slaves;[1] by-and-by, of the men of thought and action; and afterwards of nations and governments. It was found little by little to contain the elements of an universal religion, and to proclaim a Revelation congenial to the wants of mankind at large. In it the ends of the earth met. The leaven of an Oriental mode of faith wrought for the first time in harmony with the genius of the Aryan peoples. But its advance was through personal influences, from heart to heart still more than from mind to mind. Had Christianity been only or principally an intellectual movement, consequent

Its true history.

Its operation, first personal, then public,

l'union du Menothéisme hébreu avec la philosophie grecque." In pp. 65, 68, he draws out admirably the cessation of Polytheism through the "malaise religieux" of the time. Christianity, he adds, supervened, and became for the many what philosophy had been for the few, a religion essentially *moral* (?) and open to all; &c. Compare Mr. Lecky, *H. E. M.*, I. 356, "Combining the Stoical doctrine of universal brotherhood, the Greek predilection for the amiable qualities, and the Egyptian spirit of reverence and religious awe, Christianity acquired from the first an intensity and universality of influence which none of the philosophies it had superseded had approached." This species of Eclecticism assumes everything and proves nothing.

[1] See Origen, *c. Cels.*, I. xxvii., III. ix. lv.

on previous phases of speculation, it could not have commenced with the unlettered and poor. The mine of sympathy, which it opened, with all the deepest wants of man's spiritual nature, never afterward failed in its yield. In the hearts of the multitude it proved a source of moral regeneration. When placed in the crucible of philosophical criticism, it transmuted all baser elements of human Thought, and survived the test. The thinkers of Alexandria, Athens, and Rome, gradually allied themselves with its teaching. When subjected to the rough handling of Barbarian hordes, it still conquered. The example of a Divine Life, the sacrifice of a Divine Atonement, meeting the two fundamental conceptions of all Religion, ancient as well as modern, the need of Sanctification and of Justification, wrought uniformly and universally. It appealed to latent instincts of spiritual belief.[1] Sinful indulgence had, indeed, to be cast aside. Sacrifices, meet to purge the conscience, were demanded of habits, prepossessions, of the ordinary weaknesses and average endurance of mankind. Women faced the pang of separation more cruel than death, the ruin of their homes, the terrors of martyrdom. Men counted the cost of social degra-

called for self-sacrifice,

---

[1] Mr. Lecky, *Hist. Rat.*, I. 389, observes: "Of all systems the world has ever seen, the philosophies of Ancient Greece and Rome appealed most strongly to the sense of virtue: and Christianity to the sense of sin. The ideal of the first was the majesty of self-relying humanity: the ideal of the other was the absorption of the manhood into God."

dation and loss, and set it down for gain. From what motive then, ethical or physical? No doubt from a sense of duty; but of what duty? The instinctive call to love Him, Who "had first loved them," and to imitate His goodness.[1] A new conception of the gift of life, of the value of man's soul, of its responsibilities, of its capacities, of its dangers, and its hopes, was opened out before them in the Incarnation and Intercession of the Son of God, in the abiding presence of His Spirit among men. Who would not now strive after the Eternal, the Divine? *based on the imitation of Christ.*

§ 7. The hour came when Christianity, no longer an oppressed or tolerated faith, was seated on the throne of the Cæsars.[2] Under Constantine it passed from being a set of beliefs into an institution; from a religion into a church, with revenues, organization, an independent machinery of its own. As a moral or spiritual influence only, Christianity, it may well be, could not have survived the conflict with barbarism. The doctrines believed are indeed the true core of a religion; yet there may be times *Establishment of Christianity.*

---

[1] Compare Neander (*Memorials of Christian Life*, pp. 56, 57, ed. Bohn). Thus Ep. ad Diogn., c. x. πῶς ἀγαπήσεις τὸν οὕτως προαγαπήσαντά σε; ἀγαπήσας δε, μιμητὴς ἔσῃ αὐτοῦ τῆς χρηστότητος.

[2] Christianity was first tolerated by Gallienus, A.D. 261. (Euseb., VII. xiii.) Under Constantine Paganism became the tolerated, Christianity the favoured religion. (Gieseler, I. 304.) The word "Paganism" first occurs in a law of Valentinian, A.D. 368. Theodosius suppressed Paganism (A.D. 381), which now wrote its apologies by the pen of Libanius. Lastly, the schools of heathen philosophy were closed at Athens by Justinian. See, however, Gieseler, I. 323.

when it is the organism which preserves the vitality.

Its effects. How did the Church of Christ bear this test? Can we read in its after-fortunes the same traces of a Divine origin and of a Divine Presence? When we look on the marred visage of a divided and dismembered empire; on the warrings of contending sects; on the victories of a rival yet apostate faith; on the social miseries and general immorality of the times, amid which " the old order changing " slowly passed away; can we still see in the Religion of Christ the hold upon the hearts and consciences of men, the moral life and inward working, which are the seal of its heavenly mission?[1] Why, it has been

Why Christianity did not save the empire. sometimes asked, did not Christianity, at a time when its power seemed at the greatest and as yet unimpaired, save the Empire?[2] For our unworthiness, answered Salvian;[3] from its own overweight

---

[1] For the opposite view, see Zeller, *Antiquité et Moyen-Age*, p. 205.

[2] Compare Montalembert, *Monks of the West*, I. 256, E. T. Guziot, *Civ. en Fr.*, Lec. 11ᵐᵉ, points out that Christian *society* is only developed after the invasion of the barbarians, and belongs to modern history. M. Littré gives a different reply; *viz.* that Christianity was at first a spiritual, and not yet a temporal power. Mr. Lecky, *H. E. M.*, II. 151, finds an explanation in the fatal indifference of Christians to " the throes of their expiring country." He quotes the striking words of Chateaubriand: " Orose et Augustin étoient plus occupés du schisme de Pélage que de la désolation de l'Afrique et des Gaules." This view certainly attributes much to the power of Christianity.

[3] See *De Gubern. Dei*, III. i. ix.; IV. v. vii. Taking the Gospel precepts he draws a sad but overstrained picture of Christian declension, adding: " Quid enim dignius aut quid justius? Non audivimus, non audimur: non respeximus, non respicimur." Cæsarius Arelat. takes the same view in his Homilies. From these rhetorical accounts we may still infer the general corruption of the times, and perceive how fatally,

of sins, answered Augustine and Orosius. There was reason in both replies. No doubt, the flame of Christian enthusiasm both rose and fell; it had its seasons of declension and revival. But the Empire itself was the beginning of the end of Roman civilization, which was properly founded on the virtues of the Republic. It was impotent of permanent revivification. Under Theodosius, Justinian, and even Heraclius, it showed an appearance of concentration and force which had no true basis of reality. It offered no new conditions of social and political development; no enduring institutions of liberty or usefulness. The Municipal system, with its rules of freedom; the Imperial ideas of majesty, order, and subordination, were, indeed, legacies to an after-time. But it was the Church of Christ which entered on and took up the inheritance. Meanwhile the leaven of Christian doctrines was working after its proper kind. From the individual outwards to the race, through single personal influences, the restoration of human nature was progressing. Following, we may well believe, a Divine guidance as the enforcement of a Divine

_{What it effected,}

---

both in morals and in other respects, Paganism had reacted on Christianity. Compare Schmidt, *Essai*, III. c. vi. The conditions of its wellbeing thus vitiated, it was only by the infusion of a healthier stock in the rude virtues of the Teutonic tribes that it was enabled to put out its native force. It is interesting to observe that Africa, destined to lose for so long the light of Christianity, is described by Salvian as the foulest of all the Roman provinces (VII., xiii.-xv.). Its vices, he says, had bred a second nature in its inhabitants.

and why it survived. Law, and as a moral power among men, it made to itself a spiritual, not a temporal, kingdom, and thus survived the collision of the Empire with Barbarism. Though powerless to avert the shock, it had in a manner prepared for its arrival. *It became the nucleus of social regeneration;* In the free institutions of the Church, based on the spiritual liberty of man, there existed a nucleus of social regeneration, destined to work out, on favourable soil, a new civilization.[1] Its Councils and Synods, provincial, national, and general, offered a standing example of free assemblies, so congenial to the Teutonic temper. Its election of Bishops and clergy,[2] as later of Abbots and Popes, recognized, at first substantially, the claims of merit. Indeed, the Church has always recruited herself from all ranks, and thus avoided the stagnation incident to hereditary castes.[3]

of new ideas, Coming forward as a source of new ideas, Christianity had, at the outset, no fear of progress, intellect, or Science. It re-invigorated Art by endowing it with new motives;[4] it encouraged industry; it worked with the influences which were

---

[1] See Guizot, *Civ. en Fr.*, I. 339, E. T. Writers on this period of history will perhaps always remain divided as to the proportion of effect due to Roman civilization, to German independence, and to Christian influence. The fact of the latter agency is all that is here maintained.

[2] Guizot, *u. s.*, I. 331. Gieseler, I. 418. The Bishop was chosen ἐπισκόπων συνόδῳ ψήφῳ κληρικῶν, αἰτήσει λαῶν. The person elected by the clergy was accepted by the people crying out Ἄξιος, bene meritus; or ἀνάξιος.—See Bingham, IV. ii. 4, 5, and XVII. v. 3, with the authorities.

[3] Guizot, *Civ. en Eur.*, I. 93.

[4] Comp. Ozanam, *Civil. Chrétienne au Vme Siècle*, I. c. i. See also M. Littré, *Les Barbares et le Moyen-Age.* Introduction.

changing slavery into serfdom, and serfdom into free tenures; and welcomed, in the new races which overran the Empire, the virtues of a rude but uncorrupted Barbarism.[1] Thus it furnished its conquerors with the elements requisite to their social development. In the collapse of the Empire, Christianity was left single-handed to contend with the intrusion of new forces, and to undertake the work of reconstruction. On through the Middle Ages (properly so called) intervening between the decay of ancient civilization and the revival of a new and modern culture under the influences of classical philosophy and literature, Christianity, as an intellectual as well as a moral power, wrought alone.[2] The progress made in physical discoveries; in art, however rudimentary, culminating, notwithstanding, in the sublimest ideals; in language and mental discussion;[3] was the fruit of Christian influ-

necessary to the conversion of the barbarians.

Vast consequences due to Christian influence in these times.

---

[1] Compare Salvian, *u. s.*, IV. xiii., VII. vi. "Inter pudicos barbaros impudici sumus: plus adhuc dico; offenduntur barbari ipsi impuritatibus nostris." He excepts among Christians from his rebuke the *religiosi*.

[2] "All the civil elements of modern society were either in decay or infancy. The Church alone was at the same time young and constituted: it alone had acquired a definite form, and preserved all the vigour of early age: it alone possessed at once movement and order, energy, and regularity; that is to say, the two great means of influence."—Guizot, *Civ. en Eur.*, I. 85. Christianity, it must be remembered, preceded the political re-organization consequent on the fall of the Empire, and may therefore be regarded as the more powerful and necessary element.

[3] See M. Guizot's most interesting comparison of the civil and the Christian literature in the fourth and fifth centuries. *Civ. en Fr.*, Vol. 1. Lec. IV. "Intellectual development," he most truly observes, "the labour of mind to obtain truth, will stop unless placed in the train and

ence on the rough material of the Barbaric stock. In this period were sown the germs of all future social advance. The ubiquity and variety of Christian influence in the period we are rapidly reviewing, from the fifth to the fourteenth centuries, are everywhere apparent. It will be sufficient (and in this Lecture only in part practicable) to mark some instances of it; to briefly assign to other sources of influence their due share in the work of European civilization; and lastly, to notice some results and circumstances which have been alleged to make against Christianity as a successful operative element at this period in the advance of mankind.

<small>Method of the present inquiry.</small>

§ 8. "Never," says M. Guizot, "has any other society made such efforts to influence the surrounding world, and to stamp thereon its own likeness as were made by the Christian Church between the fifth and tenth centuries."[1] It was not, be it re-

<small>Efforts of Christianity from the fifth to the tenth century.</small>

beneath the shield of some one of the actual, immediate, powerful interests of humanity. . . . The Christian religion furnished them with the means: by uniting with it philosophy and literature escaped the ruin which menaced them." Thus the spiritual vigour of Christianity worked by means of education, and enlisted in its cause the highest minds of the time.

[1] M. Sismondi, *Hist. d. Franc.*, II. 50: "Lors de l'établissement du Christianisme la religion avait essentiellement consisté dans l'enseignement moral: elle avait excercé les cœurs et les âmes par la recherche de ce qui était vraiment beau, vraiment honnête. Au cinquième siècle on l'avait surtout attachée à l'orthodoxie, au septième on l'avait réduite à la bienfaisance envers les couvents." This summary does not allow sufficiently for the missionary labours of this period. "The triumph," says Dean Merivale, "of the Church over her Northern conquerors was the greatest, I suppose, of all her triumphs, the issue least to be expected beforehand, most to be admired in the retrospect, of any."

membered, till after the invasion of the Barbarians that a career was opened to the Church of influencing civil society. All institutions hitherto had been laid in Paganism. The government and administration represented only the Imperial system. Slowly, as the Empire fell back in every direction on Rome and Constantinople, these gave way. The mass of the provincial population entered the Christian society. New interests and new influence opened before the Bishops and clergy.[1] Literature, education, the exercise of the learned professions, fell into Christian hands. As a moral instrument to govern the lives of men, endowed with an organization fitted by its fixedness yet pliancy for wide-reaching and varied application, Christianity at the period of the invasion of the Barbarians stood forth in all its power, ready for the work which lay before it. By a natural transition the Bishops resident in the cities and centres of population, the last protectors of all that remained of Roman society and Roman civilization, became the counsellors of the invading leaders; the equals of counts and nobles; enjoining humanity towards the vanquished, acting as mediators in

Its new means of influence,

political and social.

---

[1] The clergy were taken chiefly from the subjugated people who thus acquired a powerful influence over their conquerors. See Canon Robertson (*C. H.*, I. 555). They became the "defensores civitatis," or standing advocates of the rights of the provincials. On the effect of the system of Christianity within the Empire on the Germans, see Merivale (*Lectt.*, p. 102): "Rome abandoned by her Cæsars and her legions was left to the counsel and protection of her Bishop and his priest," &c.

the reconstruction of social relations between two hostile races, and holding out the model of Imperial legislation.[1] Their position soon ensured territorial influence[2] and hierarchical organization; a valuable means of permanence in an age when moral consideration only or religious reverence might have proved short-lived. From this era, the era of Gregory the Great, may be dated the final Christianization of Europe in its full possession of society and of the human mind. The religion and laws of all nations are more or less closely connected: and the Barbaric Codes were framed for the most part after their settlement within the Empire and their submission to Christian teaching. The rise, then, of the Church of Christ on the ruins of the Imperial system; its assimilation of the new conditions under which it was placed; forming a bond of union among the scattered fragments of the Empire;[3] the facility with which it applied itself to the social regeneration of the time, constitute a palmary example of the power and character of its influence, of its capacity for permanence and

Its part in legislation.

---

[1] See Robertson, *u. s.*, and Milman's description of the position of bishops and clergy, *Lat. Chr.*, I 361. "Thus the clergy stood between the two hostile races in the new constitution of society—the reconcilers, the pacifiers, the harmonizers of the hostile elements," &c.

[2] Not indeed to the secular clergy at large.

[3] Dean Milman, *Lat. Chr.*, VI. 207, makes some just observations on the importance in respect of holding together the great commonwealth of European nations against a Mahommedan confederacy of an ubiquitous clergy, speaking a common language, of all countries, under one head, law, discipline, &c.

advance. It is true that in secular matters, such as the confirmation of Bishops in their temporalities, (sometimes even in their election), the Church was subordinated to the royal mandates. But on the side of dogmatic and spiritual authority she remained free, supreme: and thus established herself in the most fertile and perennial source of influence. How large a contrast to the decline of ecclesiastical importance in the Eastern Empire! There from the despotic authority of the Emperors;[1] their traditional policy of reducing the Bishops to dependence; their custom of interference not only with the government and administration, but even with the creeds of the Church by decrees and edicts of doctrine; and also from the fact of the laity taking part in matters of theology, and converting them into instruments of policy; the relations of the ecclesiastical to the civil power were impaired: the influence of the clergy in spiritual affairs diminished; and the authority of the Christian doctrine, both among the Barbarian immigrants and within the bosom of the Empire, was vitally affected. Its consequences were witnessed alike in the sub-

Its temporal subordination, but spiritual liberty.

Contrast in this respect between Eastern and Latin Christianity.

---

[1] See Milman, *L. Chr.*, I. 331. "Theodosius and Gratian define or ratify the definition of doctrines, declare and condemn heretics. Justinian is a kind of Caliph of Christianity," &c. Comp. Giesler, I. 341, 421; II. 59, 119, § 116. The words of Constantine (ap. Euseb., *Vit. Const.*, IV. xxiv.) are well known. See Robertson, *C. H.*, I. 296, 298; III. 137. The Emperor Manuel took part, as an author, in theological controversy. Hence Iconoclasm, which was the Reformation of the Eastern Church, was abortive.

servience of Bishops and clergy, during the rival struggles of Constantinople and Alexandria, and in the Iconoclastic controversies, as also in the fanaticism of the monks of the East, alternately encouraged or compelled by court influence.

<small>Spiritual effects of the religion amid moral corruption.</small>

§ 9. There is ground, then, for asserting the presence during these centuries of high spiritual ideas, notwithstanding the corruption and degeneracy of the times: and that the influence of these ideas produced effects which, with whatever admixture, are characteristic of the Religion of Jesus Christ. One by one the Barbarian Tribes, as they mingled with the Greek or Latin populations of the Empire, were silently subdued.[1] Later, indeed, in the case of the Franks, the compulsion of stern and even sanguinary legislation was brought to bear (partly for political objects) in aid of conversion.[2] Heathenism, it might thus be said,

---

[1] Allusion is here made more particularly to the Moeso-Goths, or, as known later, Ostro and Visigoths, within the Empire; not to the *Gothi minores*, as they were called, won over to the faith by Ulphilas, " que les Grecs appelèrent le Moïse de son temps." Ozanam, *Études*, II. 22. " No record whatever," says Milman, " not even a legend, remains of the manner in which the two great branches of the Gothic race, the Visigoths in France, the Ostrogoths in Pannonia, and the Suevians in Spain, the Gepidæ, the Vandals, the mingled hosts which formed the army of Odoacer, the first king of Italy, and at length the fierce Lombards, were converted to Christianity."—*Lat. Chr.*, I. 255. Niebuhr remarks that the proportion of Christians among the Goths was much greater than among the populations they invaded. *Vorträge*, III. 316. See Robertson, *C. H.*, I. 489. From Sozomen, *H. E.*, II. vi., it would appear that Christianity was first spread by Roman captives in the wars of the third century.

[2] " Germany," says M. Littré, with some scorn, " disputed its con-

waned before it, as Christianity in its turn within the realm of Islamism. But the parallel suggested would be found inexact. For the Faith of Christ, though beaten down, survived in many quarters even under the scourge of Mahommedanism;[1] while Paganism in the far North of Europe altogether, however slowly, disappeared. From first to last in the work of the conversion of Europe it is plain to see that it was an infelt sense of the truth and of the blessings of Christ's Religion, which captivated and retained the homage of the Barbarian tribes: the combination of its deeper mysteries with the purity of its moral code. The Barbarians were open to the influence neither of art nor of knowledge. There remained only the logic of the heart. Here the satisfaction offered by the Faith of Christ to the fears and hopes of our nature with its yearning after the Unseen and Divine; here too the intrinsic and exquisite goodness of its teaching, wrought in the case of the German race on congenial soil.[2] Apart

Examples of involuntary conversion.

True influences of Christianity

version for four centuries, and then yielded to the sword of Charlemagne."—*Les Barbares*, p. 18. Mr. Freeman, *Norman Conquest*, I. 29, points out that in England Christianity made its way without violence and coercion. He quotes Bede, *E. H.*, i. 25.

[1] As, *e. g.*, in Armenia. In Persia, Magism, which had resisted the appeal of Christianity, yielded to the scimitar of Mahomet.

[2] Compare Tacitus (*Germ.*, c. ix.). "Cæterum non cohibere parietibus Deos, neque in ullam humani oris speciem adsimilare ex magnitudine cœlestium arbitrantur: Deorumque nominibus appellant secretum illud quod solâ reverentiâ vident." It has been remarked by Grimm (*D. M.*, pp. 9-11) that certain religious forms and words are common to all the races of Teutonic descent. See Milman, I. 242. Similarly the readiness of the language to frame words for the new doctrinal ideas of

adapted to the character of the barbaric tribes.

from any legendary pretensions to miraculous power, they were its permanent credentials to reception. Amid the tumult and suffering of an age of violence, the piety of the Christian believer was the more conspicuous, and took, it may well be, a more vehement and impassioned character "It was the time," it has been finely said,[1] "for great Christian virtues as well as for more profound Christian consolations: virtues in some points strikingly congenial to barbaric minds, as giving a sublime patience and serenity in suffering, a calm contempt of death. The Pagan admired the martyr whom in wantonness he slew, when that martyr showed true Christian tranquillity in his agony. There was no danger which the better Bishops and clergy would not encounter for their flocks. They would venture to confront unarmed the fierce warrior. All the treasures of the unplundered Churches were willingly surrendered for the

---

Christianity points in the same direction. This topic is pursued by the same author (VI. 347). The same remark had been previously made by Guericke (*Kirchengesch.*, sub init.). On the whole subject, see Guizot, *Civ. en Fr.*, Lec. VII. Ozanam, *Études Germaniques*, I. c. iii. Krafft, *Anfänge der Christlichen Kirche bei den Germanischen Völkern*, and Merivale, *Lectt.*, pp. 88, 130. He remarks on the connection between the Teutonic mythology and the teachings of Christianity, for which it formed a preparation.

[1] Milman, *Latin Christianity*, I. 250. "Le Christianisme fut animé d'un ardent prosélytisme. Le prosélytisme triompha: les barbares furent vaincus et pris: s'ils avaient été inconvertibles, nul ne saurait dire ce qui serait advenu des destinées de l'Occident."—Littré, *u. s.* In a single generation from their conversion the Normans became remarkable for their devotion. See Hallam, *M. A.*, I. 135.

redemption of captives. Even the austerities practised by some of the clergy, and by those who had commenced the monastic life, would arrest the attention, and enthral the admiration of Barbarians, to whom self-command, endurance, strength of will, would appear kindred and noble qualities." Nor must the fact of an elaborate ritual,[1] considered as a means of impressing by symbolic forms, or words, the deep-seated truths of the Christian Faith on an unlettered people, be omitted from a review of the spiritual influences exercised at this period by Christianity. If not religion in the highest sense, such modes of representation were the preparation for it.

Symbolical character of the ritual of the Church.

§ 10. The privilege of asylum or sanctuary, claimed by the Christian Church in the Middle Ages, and recognized accordingly in most Barbaric Codes, though familiar in the history of Greece,[2]

Example of Christian influence in the privilege of sanctuary.

---

[1] "Christianity offered itself, and was accepted by the German tribes as a law and as a discipline, as an ineffable, incomprehensible mystery, ... Ritual observance is a taming, humiliating process: it is submission to law: it is the acknowledgment of spiritual inferiority: it implies self-subjection, self-conquest, self-sacrifice. It is not religion in its highest sense, but it is the preparation for it." Ritter (*Christliche Philos.*, I. 40), ap. Milman, I. 376. Dorner (*Hist. Protest. Th.*, I. 17) makes the same remark as to canonical law. An all-embracing spiritual kingdom was thus opposed to physical force and warlike ambition.

[2] C. F. Hermann (*Gr. Antiq.*, II. p. 44) remarks that this privilege belonged mainly to the oldest Temples; and hence infers that it was a relic of the restraint imposed by religion in the earliest and most savage periods. Similarly the Hebrew Cities of Refuge are connected with the primeval practices of "blood-money," and a "revenger of blood."

was confined by Roman legislation to the protection of slaves.[1] It may be cited and selected as an example of the intrinsic influence asserted by Christianity over the most savage of its converts. While it appealed to the innate reverence[2] for holy places congenial to the Teutonic mind, it exercised a restraint on the most violent and fatal passions, based on a strictly spiritual principle. No crime, it taught, is so heavy that it may not be pardoned by the individual man out of the love and fear of God and in imitation of His mercy.[3] Nor at first was it abused, when sufficiently controlled by the higher law of the community. It was in the same manner that the Papacy itself,[4] despite the vices,

Not at first abused.

---

[1] See Gaius, i. 53. Digest, 48, *Tit.* 19, s. 28, § 7. Gibbon (c. xx.) speaks roughly of "the ancient privilege of sanctuary as transferred to the Christian Temples." But the laws of Charlemagne, as also of the Anglo-Saxons, required the Church to surrender persons convicted of capital crimes. Cf. Robertson (*C. H.*, II. 228).

[2] "How must this right," says Hallam, "have enhanced the veneration for religious institutions! How gladly must the victims of internal warfare have turned their eyes from the baronial castle, the dread and scourge of the neighbourhood, to those venerable walls, within which not even the clamour of arms could be heard to disturb the chant of holy men and the sacred service of the altar! The protection of the sanctuary was never withheld."—*Middle Ages*, III. 302. 12th edit.

[3] Being thus reminded that
  All the souls that were, were forfeit once,
  And He that might the 'vantage best have took
  Found out the remedy.

[4] "No accessory or fortuitous aids could have raised the Papacy to its commanding height, had it not possessed more sublime and more lawful claims to the reverence of mankind. It was still an assertion of eternal principles of justice, righteousness, and humanity. However it might trample on all justice, sacrifice righteousness to its own

ambition, and greed of those who sat in St. Peter's seat, fulfilled, out of the very arrogance of its pretensions, a function of undoubted spiritual benefit in those rude and turbulent ages. It was a tribunal of appeal for the helpless, a refuge from overwhelming tyranny, as the impersonation of the power of the Gospel, before which the crowned monarch and the lawless baron trembled and gave way.[1] "Speaking God's testimonies even before kings it was not ashamed." And the same reflection is suggested when there is taken into account the vast system of spiritual authority exercised in the practice of confession, absolution, excommunication, and interdict, in the recognition of the duty of penance,[2] in the existence and usage of Penitentials as a part of Christian law. However rude, humiliating, harsh the discipline enjoined, however tending to corrupt itself through pecuniary substi-

Analogy of appeals to the papacy.

Of the system of penitentials, excommunication, &c.

---

interests, plunge Europe in desolating wars, perpetuate strife in states, set sons in arms against their fathers, fathers against sons: it was still proclaiming a higher ultimate end. It was something that there was a tribunal of appeal, before which the lawless aristocracy trembled. There was a perpetual provocation, as it were, to the Gospel," &c.—Milman, *L. Chr.*, III. 441.

[1] " The medieval popes almost always belonged to a far higher grade of civilization than their opponents. Whatever may have been their faults, they represented the cause of moral restraint, of intelligence, and of humanity, in an age of physical force, ignorance, and barbarity."—Lecky, *H. Rat.*, II. 155. Christianity, it must be remembered, must be judged by the evils it has prevented as well as by its positive benefits.

[2] On the change from public to private confession and penance, with its consequences, see Gieseler, II. pp. 68–70, and p. 318. In the Western Church this important difference was introduced by Leo the Great. Compare Hooker, *E. P.*, VI. iv.

u 2

tution; it yet exhibited the power and quality of a Religion which would not be defied or evaded, to restrain, out of no worldly considerations, the licentiousness, inhumanity, and lawlessness of men. What no human law could effect, it secured by spiritual constraint and the "terrors of the Lord."

<small>Restraint exercised by spiritual influence.</small> Though unsafely lodged in the hands of a fallible priesthood, in a low condition of culture, and destined later to corruption from their corporate and individual covetousness, it still performed its part; rescuing society from moral anarchy, and bringing home to the ignorant and wanton the direct administration of God. Where conscience, as a restraint, would have been powerless, its authority in

<small>Distinction of temporal and spiritual power</small> the person of the priest was obeyed. The particular influences of medieval Christianity hitherto adduced are instances of its general tendency to detach the spiritual from the temporal power, one of its greatest benefits to mankind; and to operate within the just limits of Religion, the hopes and fears of a future life. In this manner the authority of conscience, freedom of thought, individual independence and accountability, were preserved in ways unsuspected, it is true, by the champions themselves of ecclesiastical privileges.[1] Thus the

---

[1] "Les sociétés," says M. Littré very profoundly, "ne sont pas comme un individu qui en une extrémité peut se dire, que faire? et qui dirige des efforts déterminés vers un but déterminé; mais elles ont des impulsions et des instincts produits par les forces intrinsèques qu'elles se sentent."

Inquisition itself, amid all its iniquities, by holding the civil power to be incapable of pronouncing on religious belief, actually became the advocate of toleration. The importance of this element in medieval Catholicism has been honourably admitted by some who in other respects are no partial judges of the working of Christian institutions.[1] I shall cite (though not in the present Lecture) but two other examples of the true character and intensity of the influence of Christianity during this stage of European progress, which will conclude this portion of our subject. Thus far we have seen the services, the triumphs, the potency of our holy Religion in establishing itself upon the ruins of Paganism, in laying the foundations of our modern civilization. We have seen also that it was destined in the wisdom of an overruling Providence to survive persecution from without, internal heresy and division, the revivals of heathenism, and the flood of barbaric invasion. But not only did it survive: it proved itself indispensable to the advance of mankind, socially, politically, intellectually. Under its shadow learning revived; sentiment softened and became refined; the arts expanded, knowledge and thought progressed.[2]

observable throughout medieval Catholicism.

Actual services of Christianity in the reconstruction of society.

No reason for considering its qualities to have become changed.

---

[1] M. Comte and Mr. J. S. Mill, both indeed after M. Guizot, who has irrefragably established this fact. See *Phil. Pos.*, V. 229; Mill's *Dissert.*, II. 243.

[2] "But still, it will be asked, would not all this result of Christianity have been just the same without the peculiar doctrines?"—Mozley,

The question then remains, is there reason to hold its quality to be changed—has it lost its virtue? Have its principles proved hollow and unsound? Has it wrought its work, has it impressed its influence through a falsehood? Such as we have seen it to be, it overcame the world in its fairest and most highly civilized regions. And none but this, we know and are assured, "is the victory that overcometh the world, even our faith."

B. L., p. 190; who replies that besides the matter-of-fact coincidence between the results and the doctrine, there is the conviction of the agents to the same effect. Would a moral Deism have produced the same consequences? Would Christianity deprived of its revealed ideas exhibit the same fruits?

LECTURE VII.

THE PERMANENCE OF CHRISTIANITY INFERRED FROM THE CHARACTER OF ITS INFLUENCE.

"If we are to calculate the probable extension or extinction of Christian opinions, we must consult the evidence of facts on a large scale; and especially must observe what manifestations of intrinsic power they have given on certain peculiar and critical occasions. This is the only course that can be deemed satisfactory, or that is conformed to the procedures of modern science."—I. TAYLOR, *Nat. Hist. of Enthus.*, p. 264.

LECTURE VII.

"*Ye are the salt of the earth.*"—Matt. v. 13.

§ 1. IT may seem at first sight unjust to cite Monasticism as a specific testimony to the power and character of Christian doctrine, when its prevalence among earlier religions, as that of Buddha, is taken into account.[1] No doubt, sacrifices have been made by other faiths to the principle of Asceticism. All such would by some thinkers be equally and unhesitatingly condemned.

_{Monasticism, how a testimony to the influence of Christianity.}

---

[1] Thus M. Littré observes: "Le Christianisme, quelques tempéraments qu'on y ait apportés, est une religion essentiellement ascétique : et comme l'ascétique Buddhisme il avait enfanté le monachisme."—*Les Barbares*, p. 115. Some have traced the origin of Christian Monachism to the Palestinian Essenes, represented at Alexandria by the Therapeutæ; some, on the other hand, to a doctrine of the Neo-Platonists.—Comp. Gieseler, II. i.; Neander, I. 84; Döllinger, *Gentile and Jew*, II. 311-316. Philo (*de Vit. Contempl.*, § 3) recognized the tendency as one common to human nature under certain conditions. πολλαχοῦ μὲν οὖν τῆς οἰκουμένης τοῦτο τὸ γένος. Ἔδει γὰρ ἀγαθοῦ τελείου μετασχεῖν καὶ τὴν Ἑλλάδα καὶ τὴν βάρβαρον. This principle, however, τὸ μόνον εἶναι πρὸς Θεόν, is a different one from the philosophic ascetic spirit which was early remarked in the first Christians, as a reaction on the immorality of the times. Similarly the doctrine of a higher perfection, which arose out of the asceticism of the monastic life, has no necessary connection with its first principles. Comp. De Wette, *Gesch. d. Christl. Sittenlehre*, I. 340. Chrysostom (*a. oppugn. Vit. Mon.*, c. iii., ap. Robertson, *C. H.*, I. 332) well says, "All men ought to rise to the same height; and that which ruins the whole world is that we imagine a greater strictness to be necessary for the monk alone; but that others may lead careless lives."

Others might be inclined to place them on an equal footing. But, on the other hand, it is not unimportant that the Religion of Christ should not in its past history be without a test of spiritual conviction and personal sacrifice which belongs to other faiths. And certainly when the genius of Western Monasticism is contrasted with that of Oriental Monachism; and this again with the futile iterations, external rites, and debasing humiliations of the followers of Gotáma,[1] the faith of Christian Europe will not be found to suffer by the comparison. The great work of Monasticism has doubtless been to exhibit a high, if one-sided, Christian ideal, superior to surrounding secular influences, and surpassing the conception of mere moral or political institutions. I cannot see with some that the presence of such an ideal tends to reduce the average standard of religious duty. M. Renan[2] has not denied to it a savour of originality, the present loss of which to the human mind he views with a cer-

Analogy of Buddhism.

Its alleged moral defects.

---

[1] Compare Mr. Hardy's *Eastern Monachism*, and for the Buddhist monasteries of Thibet at the present time, Mr. Cooper's *Pioneer of Commerce.* "Undoubtedly," says Dr. Mozley (*B. L.*, p. 187), "the doctrines of false religions have extracted remarkable action out of human nature; especially the doctrines of Oriental religions; *e. g.* the Hindoo doctrine of Absorption. But of what kind? Such as is more allied to phrenzy than morals; gigantic feats of self-torture, and self-stupefaction," &c. Eastern Christianity had indeed its Βόσκοι, Ἀκοίμητοι, Δενδρῖται, and Στυλῖται; but when at the end of the sixth century it was endeavoured to introduce the last-named extravagance in the neighbourhood of Trèves, the Bishops removed the pillar.—See Greg., Turon., VIII. xv.

[2] See ap. Montalembert, I. 27.

tain regret. Some such charm it must have been which in modern days wrought powerfully on the soul of a Pascal and an Arnauld.[1] It is not necessary here to balance the good against the evil of asceticism, its follies with its wisdom; or to admit with Mr. Buckle that "it is the prevailing taint of all clerical teaching, the inevitable issue of the theological spirit if that spirit is unchecked."[2] It may or may not belong to a rude stage of society in which isolation is easier and more accessible; and yet its influences might be the more serviceable in an age which measures the interests of society altogether by an utilitarian standard.[3] Monasticism, in its best form at least in the West, did not represent solely, or even perhaps mainly, the claims of an ascetic life. It was practical more than speculative: it looked more to "the performance of rigid

Whether limited to certain stages of civilization.

Not necessarily ascetic or contemplative.

---

[1] Compare Sainte-Beuve, *Port-Royal*, III. 285–287.

[2] III. 272. This author seems to confound asceticism with self-restraint: and in this way he attacks Christianity itself, by impugning the morality of the Gospel. What he really proves is the danger of investing the clergy with secular power, or of accepting as the commandments of God the inferences of men.

[3] Thus Mr. Lecky, *H. E. M.*, I. 136: "Asceticism—including under this term not merely the monastic system, but also all efforts to withdraw from the world in order to cultivate a high degree of sanctity—belongs naturally to a society which is somewhat rude, and in which isolation is frequent and easy." See also *Hist. Rat.*, II. 399–401. In *H. E. M.*, I. 155, he observes: "The monastic system, however pernicious when enlarged to excess, has undoubtedly contributed to the happiness of the world by supplying an asylum especially suited to a certain type of character; and that vindictive and short-sighted revolution which is extirpating it from Europe is destroying one of the best correctives of the excessive industrialism of our age."

duty; to the alternation of severe toil with the observance of an austere ritual, than to dreamy indolence or meditative silence, broken only by the discussion of controverted points of theology."[1] Labour was part of the rule of even the Eastern monks, although too readily abandoned for contemplation.[2] But the contemplative life, though fraught with its own perils, was by no means necessarily identical with a course of self-torture, foreign alike to the dignity and true mission of man. It is not possible within our present limits to dwell on the services rendered by the monastic system of the medieval times to the cause of civilization and to the progress of mankind. It has been

Its mixed results,

---

[1] Milman, *Lat. Christ.*, I. 382. So Guizot (II. 65), speaking of the monasteries of Lerins and S. Victor, remarks, "It was by no means with solitude or with mortification, but with discussion and activity, that they concerned themselves." See the fine passage on the agricultural industry of the Monks of the West, in Montalembert, I. p. 7. This writer deems, however, the signal service of Monasticism to have lain in its fostering a spirit of prayer, and in the intercessions continually offered to the Throne of Grace for the sins of mankind, I. p. xlviii.

[2] Bernardus valles, colles Benedictus amabat: says an old verse. "The Fathers," writes Mr. Lecky, *H. Rat.*, II. 261, "employed all their eloquence in favour of labour; but it is to the monks, and especially to the Benedictine monks, that the change is pre-eminently due." See also *H. E. M.*, II. 165, where he quotes the rule of S. Paphnutius, "To love labour more than rest," &c., and p. 218, "Scholars, too, adds the old chronicler, are martyrs if they live in purity and labour with courage." At a time when religious enthusiasm was all directed towards the monastic life as towards the ideal of perfection, they made labour an essential part of their discipline. Schmidt, *Essai*, p. 228, remarks that the motto of Christianity at this period was not the rights of labour, but the duty of labour. It was told of Becket that he habitually performed harvest work at the monasteries with the monks. See Hallam, *M. A.*, III. 360, 12th ed.

called the school whence issued great minds and madmen.[1] Certainly, whatever may be thought of the vain attempt to find Christian perfection in ignoring one-half of human nature; in constituting (as was too often done) one long, unbroken penance for the true Christian life; in measuring holiness by suffering, and saintly excellence by prayer and pain: whether it be one stage in the history of thought and feeling through which man's mind and soul pass on to other and nobler things; yet doubtless from the cloistered homes of medieval life went forth the thinkers and workers who should mould the intellectual frame and even the political life of coming generations.[2] For Monasticism led on the one hand through Scholasticism to a vast expansion of the human understanding; on the other, though to itself unconsciously, to the overthrow of hierarchical and sacerdotal influence.

consequent on erroneous elements.

Its undoubted services to medieval Christianity.

[1] "De cette rude école du désert il sortait de grands hommes et des fous."—Villemain, *Mélanges*, p. 356. Comte, *Phil. Pos.*, V. 348, regards the monks as "une milice contemplative." They were called "la Chevalerie de Dieu." He holds that Christian Asceticism tended to abase the passions before the intellectual principle; and that by its monastic orders and property the Church founded an industrial agricultural spirit.

[2] "Monastic Christianity led to two unexpected but inevitable results; to the expansion of the human understanding, even till it strove to overleap the lofty barriers of the established Catholic doctrine; and to a sullen and secret mutiny, at length to an open insurrection, against the power of the sacerdotal order."—Milman, *L. Chr.*, III. 239. "Monastic life in its rise had neither the contemplative nor solitary character; on the contrary, it was highly social and active; it kindled a focus of intellectual development; it served as the instrument of fermentation and propagation of ideas."—Guizot, *Civ. en Fr.*, I. 355.

Its testimony to the spiritual influence of the religion.

But that with which we are now concerned is the intensity of spiritual control exercised by monastic Christianity, and the loftiness of its type compared with over-developments of the ascetic tendency. No doubt, its weak point, the inherent defect of all asceticism, was its real selfishness. Its avowed end was the individual salvation of its votaries: this their dominant all-absorbing thought. The good done was in a large measure incidental, or at least secondary. "Even their charities," it has been truly observed, "went to relieve their own souls: to lay up for themselves treasures of good works, rather than from any real sympathy with the people."[1] Their imitation of Christ began in self, terminated in self: it knew not the truer, humbler self-sacrifice of daily life for parent, wife, and child.[2] And yet it was in many ways a true self-sacrifice: not the mere maceration of the flesh of a fakir. In the older and nobler forms of monastic life the loftier ideal combining active good with personal craving after holiness was still present. From the cloister came the most zealous Bishops: the most devoted and successful missionaries. In later times this spirit revived in the Mendicant and Preaching, and, in a different direction, in the Mili-

Its moral defects.

These qualified.

---

[1] Milman, IV. 156. Compare Neander, *Ch. H.*, VII. 325, and Lecky, *H. E. M.*, II. 99, who remarks on the identity of feeling expressed by Sir T. Brown, *Rel. Med.*, II. § 2: "I give no alms to satisfy the hunger of my brother, but to fulfil and accomplish the will and command of my God."

[2] Cf. Id. VI. 306.

tary Orders. They spent themselves gladly for their brethren. The very capacity which has often been remarked in Monasticism of renewing its youth and reverting to the first principles of its constitution proves the same thing.¹ There was the true salt within: and it had not lost its savour. The spirit of self-sacrifice was working still: and on the intensity of that spirit, it has been truly said, "depends the moral elevation of an age, and upon its course the religious future of the world." The faith which forged this instrument to its use, was no baseless dream: it struck deep into the roots of human nature, and drew upon its most heroic qualities.² Its best enthusiasm became its minister: it wrought its appointed work till "the history of self-sacrifice has become the history of the action of Christianity upon the world."³ The lofty and unworldly conceptions, born of the faith of Jesus Christ, gave it its type and beauty; and so called it into being. To their influence from first to last, while pure and uncorrupt, it has borne its witness of truth.

Its tendency to self-regeneration.

Its spiritual enthusiasm.

[1] Comp. Robertson, *C. H.*, II. 698. See Ranke, *Popes*, II. i. 3.

[2] "The Middle Ages," says Montalembert, "were the heroic age of Christianity." Comp. Lecky, *H. Rat.*, II. 267.

[3] Lecky, *u. s.*, p. 405. Milman, I. 234, thus sums up the benefits secured by Western Monasticism: "It compensated for its usurpation of the dignity of a higher and holier Christianity, by becoming the guardian of what was valuable, the books and arts of the old world; the missionary of what was holy and Christian in the new civilization; the chief maintainer, if not the restorer, of agriculture in Italy; the cultivator of the forests and morasses of the North; the apostle of the heathens which dwelt beyond the pale of the Roman empire." See also Hallam, *M. A.*, III. 301.

The Crusades.

§ 2. In a review, however rapid, of the spirit and efficacy of medieval Christianity, some estimate of the Crusades can hardly be omitted. They have been said to "have revealed Europe as Christian,"[1] and form, indeed, the turning-point of its history from the eleventh to the thirteenth century. Their good and ill, their motive and character, have been variously estimated, and will always be diversely apprehended. Unjust, chimerical, unwise; lavish of blood and treasure, beggaring families and nations: squandering the lives of a Barbarossa and a Saint Louis; the causes and pretexts of misery, immorality, and tyranny at home, of increased ecclesiastical domination in Pope and clergy;[2] yet no less the source of subsequent heresy and revolution: they have been held up to condemnation as the type-instance of the fatality attaching to religious wars. Yet it is probably a truer view which regards them as a defensive and not an aggressive struggle;[3] as entered upon to raise a bulwark against Mahommedanism in Palestine rather than

Different estimates of their results.

---

[1] See Guizot, I. 149.

[2] "The Crusades had made the Pope not merely the spiritual but in some sort the military suzerain of Europe."—Milman, III. 439. On the miseries and ill-effects attaching to the Crusades, comp. Hallam, *M. A.*, I. 36, III. 307.

[3] See a good summary in Canon Robertson's *Ch. Hist.*, II. 644, 645, and compare Gibbon, c. lxi. On the defensive character of the Crusades, comp. De Maistre (*Du Pape*, Liv. IV., *Œuvres*, p. 450). Gibbon, indeed, (c. lviii.) observes, somewhat narrowly, that "Palestine could add nothing to the strength or safety of the Latins." Milman comments fairly that the whole question of the *justice* of the Crusades turns on this point (VII. 185, ed. Smith).

in Spain. If fraught with temporary evils, they yet abounded in ultimate benefits; knitting the nations of Europe in one common sentiment, in one common interest: and that by a holy bond drawing each knight and baron from petty personal strifes to strike for a hallowed cause: educating them in the spirit of chivalry and generous competition with the stranger races of East and West,[1] and borrowing from these their different civilization; navigation and commerce were improved: the wealth of the trading classes increased: the number of fiefs lessened, and the anarchy of the times thus reduced. Many of these results, it is true, may be judged to be incidental to the course of affairs; and this, it may be said, cannot be considered to belong to the framework of the Christian system. They show, however, the manner in which under the Providence of God the operation of Christianity blended with the career of civilization and improvement, till it becomes difficult to assign to either its relative degree of importance. Had Christian zeal in the person of a Bernard never kindled the spirit of the Crusades; while it is possible that Christian Europe might have succumbed in detail to the attacks of Islam, it is certain that the progress of material improvement must have been indefinitely delayed. But, whatever estimate

Ultimate services rendered by them to Europe.

Many of these incidental.

Furnish an example of the operation of Christian influence on the course of civilization.

---

[1] See Guizot, I. 154. Gibbon thinks the advantage wholly on the side of the West. See Mr. Lecky's remarks, *H. E. M.*, II. 266, 267.

be taken of their political or social results, there can be but one view of the religious import of the Crusades.¹ They stand forth, the proud answer of Christendom to the challenge thrown down by the creed of Mahomet. If its votaries were ready-minded to seek death on the battle-field in witness of their faith, so too did the followers of Christ. They wended even gladly on a pilgrimage of martyrdom; and gave joyfully their lives, as they supposed, in the cause of their dear and outraged Lord. Not indeed, as the Moslem, to behold the face of Allah through the blood of the infidel: but to win back from pollution the honoured shrine of Bethlehem and the ever-hallowed Mount of Calvary.²

In themselves a remarkable witness to the power of religious influence,

countervailing Mahometan fanaticism,

---

¹ Speaking of the English Crusaders, Matthew of Paris says, "Indignum quippe judicabant animarum suarum salutem omittere et obsequium cœlestis Regis clientelæ regis alicujus terreni postponere."—*Hist. Maj.*, p. 671, quoted by Mr. Buckle, *H. Civ.*, II. 6, who adds that the first tax ever imposed in England on personal property was in 1166, for the Crusade.

² To chase these Pagans in those holy fields
Over whose acres walked those Blessed Feet,
Which fourteen hundred years ago were nailed
For our advantage on the bitter Cross.

Gibbon's well-known criticism that "the God of the Christians is not a local Deity, and that the recovery of Bethlem or Calvary, his cradle or his tomb, will not atone for the violation of the moral precepts of the Gospel," will be seen to be beside the mark of the present argument, which turns not on the justice or propriety of religious wars, but on their mode of exhibiting the spiritual character of an age and the power of religion as a practical motive. "The Crusades," Dean Milman admits, "are monuments of human folly; but to which of the more regular wars of *civilized* Europe, waged for personal ambition or national jealousy, will our calmer reason appeal as monuments either of human justice or human wisdom?"

It has been hinted that these were, after all, the superstitious efforts of a dreaming age, inspired by an unreasoning enthusiasm; which is past never to return, and indicates accordingly the decline of the spirit of religion. "The Crusader's sword," it is said,[1] "has long been shattered; his achievements idolized by the poet and the novelist. Liberty, and not theology, is the enthusiasm of the nineteenth century." Yet the same writer has elsewhere frankly admitted,[2] that "while ignorance and error have, no doubt, often directed the heroic spirit into wrong channels, and have sometimes even made it a cause of great evil to mankind; yet the power of Christianity to evoke and sustain the highest, the most enlarged conceptions, can cease only with the annihilation of the moral nature of mankind." We may be pardoned, then, if we connect these triumphs of the strength of our holy Religion in less enlightened ages, not merely with man's moral capacities, but with his spiritual insight: if we see in them not only a possible but an actual union of the heroic with the religious virtues, of the patriot with the saint,[3] after the apprehension of those far-off times; if we read in them an evidence of a Faith

and exhibiting the fund of Christian enthusiasm,

according to the knowledge of the time.

---

[1] See Lecky, *Hist. of Rationalism*, II. 244.

[2] *Ib.*, p. 405.

[3] "In the Middle Ages the saintly type being the standard of perfection, the heroic type was almost entirely unappreciated. The nearest approach to it was exhibited by the Crusader, whose valour was nevertheless all subordinated to superstition, and whose whole career was of the nature of a penance."—Lecky, *H. R.*, II. 222.

x 2

ever progressive, working after the measure of the knowledge of the age, even according to the promise of its Founder "overcoming the world;" now "subduing kingdoms;" now "quenching the violence of fire;" now "waxing valiant in fight;" "turning to flight the armies of the aliens;" yet always and in all things more than conqueror "through Him that loved us."

<small>Want of discrimination as to the separate agencies in the construction of modern Europe.</small>

§ 3. Much evil, it must be admitted, has been done to the cause of Christian Truth by indiscriminate laudation;[1] or, at least, through an over-estimate of its effects, by way of answer to censures equally exaggerated. There are some who have seen in Christianity the sole and sufficient agent in the work of civilization, disjoining it, like a fragmentary episode,[2] from the ordinary influences at work upon the face of society. We have seen cause, with stricter and more profound thinkers, to take a different course. Christianity has been, no doubt, a leading and a distinct element in modern civilization; but it has[3]

---

[1] See some good remarks on this point in Comte, *Phil. Pos.*, V. 328.

[2] Οὐκ ἔοικε δ' ἡ φύσις ἐπεισοδιώδης οὖσα, ὥσπερ μοχθηρὰ τραγῳδία. —Arist., *Metaph.*, XIII. iii.

[3] "C'est là le beau rôle de la communauté chrétienne sur la terre : elle est comme un ferment de l'humanité, destiné à lui communiquer le principe fécond et indestructible d'une vie nouvelle sans toucher violemment aux institutions établies. Ardents pour la conversion des individus, les Apôtres attendaient sans impatience le renouvellement des formes sociales. Ils l'abandonnaient à l'action du temps et à la puissance irrésistible de l'Esprit de Jésus-Christ. Toutefois s'ils ont respecté les lois existantes, ils ont indiqué en même temps les principes destinés à les modifier en les conformant à la nature du Royaume de Dieu."— Schmidt, *Essai*, p. 175.

worked in conjunction with other forces. And it is difficult accordingly, in some cases, to award duly the proportions of the resultant effect. We have already seen that Roman civilization left its legacy of complex influences in its Municipal system and Imperial traditions. We have seen likewise that in the physical and psychical elements of the Barbarian stock, in their inherited associations and ideas, fresh principles of reconstruction were added to modern society. As Christianity modified the manners and temperament of the Teutonic race, so was there, in some respects, an inverse action on the form and direction of Christianity itself. No competent thinker will either deny the importance of Feudalism as an element in the general progress of these ages, or seek to attribute its consequences to the teaching or influence of Christianity.[1] It coincided, however, with the spirit of the new Religion in raising the moral tone of society. Feudalism was itself the mingled outcome of German loyalty and German independence. The progress[2] of society from villages and manorial residences to towns

What portion due to the action of Christianity.

Its relations to Feudalism.

---

[1] Mr. Freeman, *Norman Conquest*, I. 97, distinguishes between the elements of Feudalism and a Feudal system. In the former, the Church could have no share, however readily she co-operated in developing the latter. Thus, a vast number of the ancient Charters are in favour of the Church.

[2] "We must distinguish," says Hallam, *M. A.*, I. p. 351, N. xviii., "the corporate towns or communities from the other class called burgages, *bourgeoisies*. The Châtelains encouraged the growth of villages around their castles, from whom they often derived assistance in war, &c." In a former passage, he attributes more to the action of Chris-

and trading boroughs was due, not to any ecclesiastical arrangement of parishes, but to the operation of feudal tenures. They were, in fact, the molecules of Feudalism. Yet the operation and distribution of religious influence was probably rendered more favourable by this condition of things. So the extinction of serfdom, though zealously assisted by Christianity, and not unfrequently assigned to its authority, was mainly,[1] perhaps, due to secondary causes originating in the state of affairs just named. The altered position of woman in modern society,[2] though,

Its joint operation.

---

tianity. "The subjection of a heathen tribe is totally different from that of a Christian province. With the Church came churches, and for churches there must be towns, and for towns a magistracy, and for magistracy law."—*Ib.*, I. p. 121. See Adam Smith, *Wealth of Nations*, III. iii., on the rise and progress of cities and towns.

[1] See Hallam, *M. A.*, I. 197–202. In 1167, Alexander III. declared all Christians exempt from slavery. See Voltaire, *Essais*, tom. ii. c. 83.

[2] Thus, Guizot, *Civ. en E.*, I. 71: "Was it not within the bosom of the feudal family that the importance of women developed itself?" and especially the picture drawn by him of the wife as Châtelaine, *Civ. en Fr.*, III. 91. "This elevated and almost sovereign position, in the very bosom of domestic life, often gave to the women of the feudal period a dignity, a courage, virtues, a distinction, which they have displayed nowhere else, and has, doubtless, powerfully contributed to their moral development and the general improvement of their condition." Too much importance has, no doubt, been assigned to the consideration in which women were held by the German tribes (Tacitus, *Germ.*, xviii. xix.). Mr. Lecky, however, in his elaborate Essay, has pointed out some ingredients in this subject due to the action of Christianity, as the tendency of the religion to the milder virtues, the feminine ideal of the Virgin, the Christian laws of chastity, the part played by feminine martyrs, &c. See also Dean Merivale, *North. Nations*, Lect. viii. Had Asceticism been a strictly Christian virtue, it must have been reckoned as tending to debase the position of women (*H. E. M.*, II. 336, 389; *H. Rat.*, I. 235).

to some extent, due to the preceding efforts and to the co-operation of Christianity, as well as to doctrines immediately connected with its system, has been, with reason, traced to circumstances arising simply out of Feudalism. Chivalry itself, *Its relations to chivalry,* which also has been claimed for a Christian institution,[1] may, with better right, be called the daughter of the feudal system. The estimate of its influence in elevating and refining the tone of modern society can hardly be over-charged. Yet the joint efforts of Christianity to lend it all the strength of a hallowing faith, cemented by religious ceremonies and fostered by religious promises, are too well known to need description or comment. Thus, then, in all these cases it is not contended that Religion has been the only influence at work in eliciting our modern civilization; but rather that it has exercised a continuous and independent function. Even its crowning

---

[1] As by Sismondi, *Hist. d. Fr.*, IV. 201: "At an epoch when religious zeal became reanimated, when valour still seemed the most worthy of all offerings that men could present to the Deity, it is not surprising that they should have invented a military ordination, and that chivalry should have appeared a second priesthood, destined in a more active manner to the Divine service." Guizot, however, finds chivalry to be "the spontaneous consequence of Germanic manners and feudal relations;" and that "religion and imagination, the Church and poetry, took possession of chivalry, making it a powerful means of attaining the ends which they pursued, of fulfilling the moral needs which it was their mission to satisfy." See at length *Civ. en Fr.*, III. Leç. vi.; and Hallam, *M. A.*, III. 395, 396, who traces it to the age of Charlemagne. See the sketch of the relation of chivalry to the Church in Robertson (*C. II.*, II. 507).

benefit of distinguishing between the spiritual and the temporal power is in a measure due to other and secular causes. For while recognized fundamentally by the Religion of Christ, and enforced in its organization, it was no less congenial to that spirit of personal and individual liberty introduced in the Teutonic nature into modern society.[1] The believer was not absorbed in the Deity whom he worshipped or in the Church of which he was a member, nor was the individual man sacrificed, as in the Republics of old, to the citizen.

and to the Teutonic character.

§ 4. The incontestable fact that the course of Christianity has been affected in all its institutions and many of its doctrines by the infirmities of human nature and the historical circumstances of its advance,[2] has led to unfavourable but ground-

Corruptions of medieval Christianity

---

[1] See M. Guizot's excellent summary, *Civ. en Fr.*, tom. i. Leç. vii. sub fin. : " The spirit of legality came to us from the Roman world. To Christianity we owe the spirit of morality, the sentiment and empire of rule, of a moral law, of the mutual duties of men. The Germans conferred upon us the spirit of liberty as we conceive it in the present day, &c." Liberty of thought, indeed, he elsewhere (Leç. xxx.) attributes justly to Greco-Roman civilization. This was received neither from Christianity nor from Germany, but is an idea which is essentially the daughter of antiquity. See Mr. Lecky's remarks, *H. E. M.*, II. 197, on the relation of feudal organizations to the Church. Dean Merivale, *Northern Nations*, p. 127, holds that " patriotism was a Pagan virtue, but loyalty is a Christian grace." " To his own Lord the Christian must stand or fall. And as patriotism was the classical, so was loyalty the feudal principle."

[2] Compare the testimony of Jerome (*Vit. Malch.*, sub init.). " Scribere disposui ab adventu Salvatoris usque ad nostram ætatem, quo modo et per quos Christi Ecclesia nata sit ; et adulta, persecutionibus creverit et martyriis coronata sit ; et postquam ad Christianos principes venerit potentiâ quidem et divitiis major, sed virtutibus minor facta sit."

less criticisms of its authority and value. I have already alluded to causes which, in the Eastern Church, debased the genius of Christianity, corrupted its practice, and arrested its progress. It is plain that as the Religion enlarged its boundaries and established its predominance, its moral effects would decline, for various reasons. There may well be a tendency, under a rigid dogmatic system, for morals to assume the form of positive commands, and thus to lose their spiritual savour. To speak, however, of no other cause of declension, the inducements of temporal advancement were now on the side of conversion instead of being against it. The establishment of a State Christianity led indirectly to the repetition of General Councils, as a ready instrument; these to the inevitable enforcement of often transcendental dogmas; these, by a reaction, to political disputes and to theological intrigue and persecution. Orthodoxy now brought its own reward; and sanguinary contests for pre-eminence usurped that rivalry of love, which had once been the honourable badge of the earliest believers in Christ. "The very scenes," we are told, "of the Saviour's mercies ran with blood shed in His name by His ferocious self-called disciples."[1] The growing necessity of conforming a new faith to the apprehensions and habits of barbarous races

inevitable

from its political position.

Fraught with evils,

[1] Milman, *Lat. Chr.*, I. 213.

led of itself, in many ways, to a direct variation of its standard, both as to morals and religious belief.[1] This, however, it must be remembered is no evidence of intrinsic or permanent declension. It has been truly observed that "the very offences signalized are a token of progress, since it is the strongest proof of the firm hold of a party, whether religious or political, upon the public mind, when it may offend with impunity against its own primary principles. That which at one time is a sign of incurable weakness or approaching dissolution, at another seems but the excess of healthful energy and the evidence of unbroken vigour."[2] It was not, then, to be expected but that in the West also Christianity should exhibit transitions often foreign to the spirit of its teaching. Amidst the barbarian elements among which it had to work, Christianity itself began to barbarize. As the price of its influence on an age dark and superstitious, its doctrines were exhibited in a debased, ambiguous form, productive of lasting consequences on the purity of the faith. As the cost of its power over a warlike aristocracy, and of its establishment by the side of feudal institutions, the higher clergy are seen assuming

marginalia: yet necessary to its persistency and progress; in a barbarous age and nation; Its military character.

[1] See Dean Milman's remark, *Lat. Chr.*, 1. 443: "The historian who should presume to condemn this universal popular religion as a vast plan of fraud, or the philosopher who should venture to disdain it as a fabric of folly, would be equally unjust, blind to its real uses, assuredly ignorant of its importance and its significance in the history of man."

[2] See Robertson, *C. H.*, 1. 143.

the character and pursuits of barons and the employments of a warlike profession.[1] The growing strength of the Mahometan invasion gave rise to wars which, having the defence of religion for their aim, threw a decent cloak over the martial tendencies of Bishops and Abbots, and gave to the Christianity of the age a military and violent aspect. The Crusades, which had proved so serviceable an instrument for extending ecclesiastical and Papal influence, were not readily allowed to cease. They were continued with greater success and more barbarity, in the form of religious wars against heretical and unorthodox sectaries. Nor were these contests confined solely to the aim, however unjustifiable, of establishing uniformity of belief by force of arms. The claims and encroachments of the Papal and sacerdotal systems upon the temporal power of the European monarchies involved grievous and continual conflicts. The questions of Investiture and of the particular relations of the Papacy to the personal rights of sovereigns were urged with varying fortunes, but undiminished persistency, until the close of the thirteenth century. Then came the ebb in the tide of spiritual domination,

Religious wars.

Decline of the Papal power from close of thirteenth century.

[1] Comp. Gieseler, II. 374, ed. Clark; Hallam, *M. A.*, c. II. Pt. ii. They were used by the German sovereigns as a balance of power against the nobles, thus receiving whole counties as fiefs, but with the obligations of feudal tenure, *e. g.* military service, the leading troops in person, &c. This custom may be traced as late as Agincourt. See Lecky, *H. E. M.*, II. 265.

which had overflowed the several kingdoms of the West. "Slowly," says Hallam,[1] "like the retreat of waters or the stealthy pace of old age, that extraordinary power over human opinion, the Papal Empire, has for five centuries been subsiding." But how had its tyranny arisen? Where lay the hidden secret of its power? Where but in the mission it existed to fulfil? In its hold upon ages of anarchy and ignorance, of brute force and dormant intelligence, such as only a common faith, a rigid ceremonial, a priesthood linked in one vast hierarchical confederacy, could effectively control. The right of excommunicating sovereigns for moral delinquencies showed the supremacy of the Church in at least its noblest aspect; even though the implied claim of the spiritual over the temporal power was as indefensible as vague. The attitude of a Hildebrand and an Innocent, and even of an Alexander and a Boniface in rebuking injustice, murder, and lust, is full of moral power; rising, in its appeal to the consciences of men, to the dignity of the Jewish Prophets.[2] Men might seem to see again an Ambrose closing the doors of the Church of

Moral dignity of the Papacy.

---

[1] *Middle Ages*, II. 233, 12th ed.
[2] Compare Dean Stanley, *Sermons on the Bible*, pp. 65, 66. "Il est vrai," says Villemain, "que l'ambition a souvent abusé de cet exemple." *Tableau de l'Éloq. Chrét.*, p. 327. De Maistre (*Œuvres*, p. 370) argues that the influence of the medieval Popes was in the main a spiritual, moral, and beneficial one; and quotes to this effect Voltaire, *Essai*, tom. ii., c. 60, 65.

Milan against the blood-stained hands of a Theodosius; or a Leo arresting, by his sole unarmed authority, the licentious advance of a Genseric to the sack of Rome. But the assumption of the power of the sword by the Vicegerent of Christ was as fatal in its consequences to break this spell, as it was without foundation in the doctrine of Christ's Religion. Who could doubt but that when men had opportunity to examine such monstrous claims there would come that secret working of the leaven of truth, which would break forth into spiritual rebellion against the abuse of a religious despotism? The division of interests between laity and clergy; the price paid for the vast access of influence secured to the Church in Monasticism and the celibacy of its ministers, was destined in its effects to rend the institution it had been created to subserve. Theology became the privileged domain of the clerical order, their instrument of power, which it was not in human nature not to turn into a weapon of persecution. The secular arm tamely executed the censures of the Church; while Catholicism lapsed into a theocracy, siding in all temporal matters with the advocates of absolute power. *[Causes of its declension, and of subsequent changes.]*

§ 5. I have already alluded to the subject of corruptions of worship and doctrine. The creation of Theology, which may be defined to be a scientific or orderly statement of Divine Truth, was the *[Corruptions of doctrine.]*

growth of a natural development of reflection upon the revelations to the human mind, contained in the words of Christ. It was the fruit of the first five centuries of the Faith in East and West. Its substitution for the direct teaching of Scripture was the historical result of circumstances attending the progress and spread of Christianity. The Fathers who had codified, summarized, or expanded the truths of our holy Religion, were to the theologians of after-times what the Apostles and the books of Holy Writ had been to themselves.[1] But with this difference. It was impossible in those times, and in that stage of culture, to forge again the link which bound the utterances of the earlier Fathers of the Church with the fresh living springs of Christian truth, from which they drew the inspiration of their teaching. A Scholastic Theology was the exposition of the thought of the age upon the mysteries of the Faith. It was a poor expression, even in the hands of the devouter Mystics, of the mind of a Chrysostom, an Origen, an Augustine. Little by little the ideas of men on the subjects of religious inquiry were riveted to traditional stand-points, and made to run within

Rise of Theology as a science.

Its inherent defects.

---

[1] See Guizot's remarks in *Civ. en Fr.*, Leç. xxix. He considers the theology of the Middle Ages to have commenced in the ninth century. Gibbon, not unjustly, observes, that "for the five hundred years after Christ the disciples were indulged in a freer latitude, both of faith and practice, than has ever been allowed in succeeding ages." Dean Merivale, *Conv. of N. Nations*, p. 40, says, "the fourth century places the Religion of Christ definitively on the basis of a Revealed *Theology*."

appointed channels. Side by side with this artificial, though scientific treatment of sacred truths, was working in practice the influence of legendary corruptions,[1] constituting a sort of secondary Gospel, and ruling with all the force of poetical imagination the heart and belief of the time. Every Christian man, as well as every department of the Church, had his interceding Saint, himself encompassed with miracle, and the vehicle of miraculous intervention, to the worshipper as necessary a medium of spiritual conception and of Divine influence as the ethers and entities of a corresponding stage in physical knowledge. The consequences of such a state of things, in modifying the effects of the simple tenets of the Gospel, were doubtless very large and difficult of estimate. The compromise thus represented between the essential teachings of Christianity, and the slow advances of the barbaric mind towards a higher point of spiritual culture, affects other regions of the Faith. The prevailing views of evil Angels, magic, and witchcraft; of Purgatory, which, at the beginning of the period we have reviewed, was, to the mind of Gregory the Great,[2] but a probable truth; but

Its false developments,

and practical results,

---

[1] Compare Milman, *Lat. Chr.*, VI. 247, who styles this the age of "the mythic literature of Christendom."

[2] I follow the expression of Dean Milman, *Lat. Chr.*, I. 442, VI. 252. Gregory's words are, "Sed tamen de quibusdam levibus culpis esse ante judicium purgatorius ignis credendus est."—*Dial.*, IV. 39. A stronger passage occurs in Ps. iii, *Pœnit. sub init.* Laud (*Conference with Fisher*, p. 296) says: " As for St. Augustine he said and unsaid it, and at the

was soon fraught with the concomitants in practice of absolution, masses, and indulgences,

> Those massy keys of metal twain,
> The golden opes, the iron shuts amain,

borne by "the Pilot of the Galilæan lake;" and no less also the doctrines of mortal and venial sins, of councils of perfection,[1] and works of supererogation, are instances of similar tendencies. They lent, indeed, a factitious superficial authority to Medieval Christianity[2] in its rough encounter with the temper of the age; an influence, however, more or less unreal, since uncongenial with the true spirit and aims of the Religion itself; and destined, accordingly, to pass away in the hour of account, when "the fire should try every man's work," and "the day should declare it" of what sort it is.

tending ultimately to subvert the authority of the Church.

The Reformation.

§ 6. We know, Brethren, how that hour came, that day of darkness and gloominess, of "clouds and of thick darkness;" yet "as the morning spread upon the mountains." For though terrible with "the

---

last left it doubtful: which, had it then been received as a point of faith, he durst not have done. Indeed, then, in St. Gregory the Great's time, in the beginning of the sixth age, Purgatory was grown to some perfection. For S. Gregory himself is at *Scio*, it was but at *Puto* a little before." See Bp. Browne *on the Articles*, pp. 500, 501.

[1] *Consilia Evangelica*, as distinguished from *Præcepta*. See at length Jeremy Taylor, *Duct. Dub.*, II. xii.

[2] There is a tendency in the Positivist School to exalt the doctrines and institutions of medieval Catholicism, such as Purgatory, Confession, Celibacy, Papal Supremacy; and from their decline to infer the ultimate dissolution of Christianity. Comp. Comte, *Phil. Pos.*, V. 269–348. This criticism, however, does justice to the secondary benefits of the system, flowing, indeed, from the tenets of the Religion itself.

earthquakes of nations," it still rose fraught with hope. It was a movement which convulsed the frame of Europe; one of which, it may well be, we have as yet seen but the beginning; for already men's hearts are set upon a second Reformation. At present we are concerned only to estimate the nature of its testimony to the permanence of Christianity. Has it rendered the prospects of our Religion more hopeful? Has it redressed previous shortcomings? or has it, as in the view of some,[1] opened a vista of religious disorganization leading inevitably to a negative philosophy, and to democracy in Church and State? The Reformation proved, indeed, many things. First, certainly, the presence of corruptions inherited and traditional in the framework of the Faith of Christ; corruptions of belief and practice; of the substitution of man for God; of the Church for the Gospel; of sacerdotalism for the moral sense, as the last religious appeal; of salvation by positive ordinances and ritual observances, rather than by personal holiness and implicit belief of a Faith fast losing its hold on the morality and true dealing of the time.[2] All this it proved. But it proved equally the inherent vigour of a Religion which, thus in the course of

Nature of its evidence to the permanence of Christianity.

It proved to be a searching test of the truth and of the corruptions of its doctrines.

---

[1] This is the view of M. Comte; developed at length in *Phil. Pos.*, Vol. V.

[2] Compare Dean Milman's sketch, *Lat. Chr.*, VI. 379, 380, of the virtual teaching of the German Mystics, the "Reformers before the Reformation."

ages, could purify itself like running water, from the errors and defilements of the past: that it is no system which must lean always on ignorance, despotism, or craft.[1] The great hope for Christianity, the standing witness of its perpetuity and truth, must lie always in this possibility of reconstruction, this return upon itself; in this tendency and capacity of expelling all foreign and unhealthy matters, not of kin with the true elements of the Faith of Jesus Christ. But the Reformation, impartially examined, proves likewise that the history of the Western Church prepared for itself the test which was then applied, and which it has successfully survived. However dormant, there lay within its doctrines and institutions that appeal to reason and to the religious conscience which, in fact, produced those effects. In the Monasteries, Schools, and Universities,[2] themselves the creations and nurselings of the Faith of Christ, arose slowly, yet surely, that spirit of inquiry; that love of reality and truth; that consciousness of spiritual wrong, and of a higher law than the constraint of existing practice; which, slowly ripening,

This a really hopeful symptom.

It is important that this crisis arose out of the nature and history of the religion.

---

[1] Comp. Isaac Taylor (*Hist. of Enthus.*, p. 267).

[2] See Guizot, *Civ. en Fr.*, Leç. v., vi. Dean Milman (*Lat. Chr.*, V. 485–8) shows the relations of the Monasteries to the Universities. Mr. Lecky (*H. E. M.*) remarks too narrowly that "it was not till the education of Europe passed from the Monasteries to the Universities, not till Mahommedan science and classical free-thought and industrial independence broke the sceptre of the Church, that the intellectual revival of Europe begins."

contained the pledge of future amendment and of continuous progress. From knowledge alone, however improved and matured, the Reformation could never have taken its rise.[1] But when once spiritual conviction and enthusiasm were enlisted on the side of reflection and inquiry, the result could be no longer doubtful or precarious.

§ 7. It is ever the misfortune of human effort, whether in politics or religion, that the movements it originates must needs reflect the passions, weaknesses, and shortcomings of their authors and their times. The good which a generous enthusiasm promises to itself, is never altogether realized. The evils expected or exaggerated by unfavourable critics remain at least in part to mar the benefits which, on the whole, ensue. I am not concerned to strike a balance between the estimates of those who see in the theological results of the Reformation nothing but good or unmixed evil. It is time that the violent and unintelligent antagonism between Catholicism and Protestantism, unworthy of the enlightenment of our times, and arising simply from traditional

Shortcomings of the Reformation.

Different estimates of its true character.

---

[1] See Gieseler's excellent remarks, V. 202, ed. Clark. This is a truer view than with Mr. Lecky (*H. Rat.*, I. 284) to refer the causes of the Reformation to an increased acquaintance with Latin classics and Greek philosophy. Dr. Ullmann well observes (*Reformers before the Reformation*, II. 3, ed. Clark), "On only one side did philosophy contribute to the revival of Christian piety and knowledge. We allude to Platonism, which, being naturally akin to the Gospel, now entered into league with the new and living theology, and rose with fresh vigour against the Aristotelianism of the Schoolmen." Luther and Melancthon were however, on opposite sides in this matter; at least after 1529.

causes, should give way before a calmer, a more discerning, a more comprehensive analysis. I desire only to insist on facts now generally admitted by impartial investigators. The services of Medieval Catholicism should, as we have seen, be no longer ignored. Neither must its corruptions be denied.[1] The state of the Church of Christ in the fifteenth and sixteenth centuries was such as to demand renovation both in its theory and in its practice. Let us think only of its immorality, its simony, its superstitions. We have already seen that the evils which then afflicted Religion were in many ways the historical consequences of the circumstances under which Christianity had taken possession of the world; the treasure of a Divine Faith poured into earthen vessels. These evils had grown with the growth of the Church: in some doctrinal accretions they touched its vitality nearly; yet without being inherent in the essential principles of the teachings of Christ. Their removal or amendment could be effected only by practical reforms of a nature to eradicate the immorality of the times, more especially in the case of the clergy. But these reforms depended ultimately for their authoritative reception on a reconstitution of Chris-

Undoubtedly inevitable as a practical reform,

but only possible through a purgation of doctrine.

[1] Comp. Döllinger, *The Church and Churches, Introd.; and Lectt. on Re-union of the Churches*. The necessity of the Reformation is sufficiently shown by the impotence of the General Councils of the fifteenth century to abolish abuses. The episcopal system was wholly subject to Papal domination; a fact which told unhappily on the course of the subsequent movements.

tian doctrine. Had the Reformation been only a moral advance;[1] an improvement of life and manners; as some have preferred to regard it, and as at its outset it undoubtedly seemed to its precursors; practical changes would have sufficed. It was, however, not so; the causes of the movement lay deeper; the spiritual element of disturbance was of more account than the moral; and in this fact and in its gradual superiority over all opposition lies the guarantee of continuous religious regeneration, and so of the permanence itself of Christianity. Had the results of the Reformation been solely of a moral character, the ultimate interests of the Religion of Christ might indeed have been imperilled. The chief cause of the existing corruption lay in the distortion of doctrine through human additions and human institutions. Where, then, stood the remedy, and what led to its adoption? It consisted in a re-examination of the Religion itself; of the traditional developments and actually existing system by the moral and by the spiritual sense of the age. If it survived the test, it was once more

Hence a truly spiritual movement, testing the persistency of the principles of Christianity.

---

[1] The moral movement which preceded the actual outburst of the Reformation (which may be considered to have formally commenced with the Papal Bull, *Exsurge Domine* (June 15, 1520), rejecting Luther's propositions and excommunicating him;) can hardly be distinguished from the religious revival which accompanied it. This exhibited itself in simple apostolical preaching; in fraternities for the encouragement of piety and good works, for the circulation of the Scriptures, and the like. Hagenbach (*Vorlesungen*, I. 18) points out the importance of assigning an historical commencement to the Reformation. This he identifies with Luther's Thesis at Wittenberg (1517).

replaced in its native purity and dignity, as the fulfilment and crown of the aspirations of the soul of man. Such, accordingly, was the character of the witness rendered by this, the most important religious crisis in modern history, to the perpetuity of the Christian Faith. The Christianity of Catholicism had in the main become, (not of course to all, or indeed to the highest natures,) an objective law, an external ordinance, a compendium of statutes,[1] as well in spiritual beliefs as on its moral side. Good and wholesome influences were still abiding in it, but trammelled and overlaid by secular corruptions. There was needed, then, a resumption of its first claims on man's intelligence and spiritual apprehension. The Religion must be seen again to be what it really is: not a set of *formulæ* for action or belief;[2] not a visible Theocracy implicated and involved in political embarrassments by an assumption of temporal power; but rather a personal instinct of love and gratitude,[3] based, indeed, on eternal facts of human interest; the out-

Spiritual declension of Catholicism.

---

[1] Comp. Ullmann, *u. s.*, II. 617; or, as M. Comte has happily expressed it, "too much of an institution, too little of a spirit." It encouraged learning, but sacerdotally; industry, but through guilds; chivalry, through military orders, &c.

[2] "Protestantism, as compared with the other two great Church parties of Christendom, rests content neither with a mere intellectual appropriation of Christianity, whether in a speculative form or in a recollective form that faces a traditional doctrine; nor with a mere subjection of the will to a dogmatic or even practical Church law."—Dorner, *Hist. of Prot. Th.*, 1. 5, ed. Clark.

[3] See Ullmann, *Reformers*, II. 618.

come of a living faith, acting powerfully to regenerate and sanctify man's heart, transforming, as a new Divine element of life, the character of individuals and nations. No doubt, this true Christian spirit manifests itself as a moral law and doctrine in agreement with its nature. But its appeal is to a higher consciousness, both as to Reconciliation with God and Sanctification, than belongs to the performance of moral duties; and rests more truly on an assurance of facts which are bound up with the mysteries of the Faith.

Real import of the Reformation

Such was the real import of a struggle which had been maturing through many generations. Its incidents have often been treated as though they were the simple effects of circumstance. In this view .

obscured by its historical character

Gospel light first streamed from Boleyn's eyes.

Men fought, as it appeared, for a mere dogma:[1] and one, too, on which the more moderate thinkers on either side were practically agreed. But the true issues of the conflict lay deep in the constitu-

---

[1] Luther's language as to Justification by Faith is well known. It is the "articulus stantis et cadentis ecclesiæ. De hoc articulo cedere, aut aliquid contra illum largiri nemo piorum potest, etiamsi cœlum et terra et omnia corruant. Nam in hoc articulo sita sunt omnia, quæ contra diabolum et mundum universum in totâ vitâ nostrâ testamur et agimus." See *Art. Smalc.* 305, and *Form. Concordia*, 683. Yet no attempt at a definition of this article of faith had descended from the Fathers. Melancthon, Bucer, and others, moderated the expressions of Luther. The Tridentine Fathers considered that all Luther's errors were based on his view of Justification.—Sarpi, *Hist.*, II. p. 178. See Bp. Browne on the XXXIX. Articles, p. 285. On the first reception of the doctrine by the Catholics of Italy, see Ranke, *Popes*, II. i. 1.

tion of human nature, and involved the destinies of Christianity itself. A fresh recognition of the work of Christ for man, obscured as to its spiritual efficacy by a blank ceremonial belief, was necessary to secure the renewing of a right relation between Himself and His Church, "the blessed company of all faithful souls." A type of such a doctrinal recognition was sought and found in Justification by Faith only;[1] and belief in it was strengthened, if not suggested, by an examination of the witness of Holy Writ. Its application in practice involved differences, not indeed in themselves insurmountable; yet which have hitherto proved fruitful of dissension and schism. Such are a denial of sacerdotal mediation; a low estimate of ecclesiastical authority; a widely varying interpretation of the Sacraments of the Gospel; a wholly altered relation to the historical Church of Christendom. To these must be added, as fresh sources of embarrassment, the admixture of secular interests; together with imperfections of knowledge and character on the part of the leading Reformers.[2]

and narrowed.

Practical results the most intractable.

---

[1] More properly, Fides sola justificat; sed fides non est solitaria; i.e. in the words of Augustine (*De Fid. et Op.*, c. xiv.), "sequuntur opera bona justificatum: non praecedunt justificandum."

[2] "Luther," says Chillingworth (*Rel. Prot.*, VI. 73), "was a man of a vehement spirit, and very often what he took in hand he did not do it, but overdo it. He that will justify all his speeches, especially such as he wrote in heat of opposition, I believe will have work enough." See Sir W. Hamilton's strictures (*Discussions*, 491–506). "If there have been any wilful and gross errors, not so much in opinion as in fact (sacrilege too often pretending to reform superstition), that is the crime of the Reformers, not of the Reformation; and they are long

§ 8. The Reformation, then, can only be considered a fresh conception of the faith and doctrine of the Gospel, a regeneration of the Christian life and spirit; the fruit, indeed, of the history of the Church, with its attendant corruptions of letter and spirit, practice and doctrine, yet in effect a return to the primary teaching of Christianity. It contained, accordingly, distinct elements wrought out by different agencies, by the men of thought and the men of purpose. The first furnished, out of an advance in Scriptural knowledge[1] due in part to the revival of classical learning, those first principles of doctrine which were the grounds of action to the practical reformers of existing abuses. On these last attention has often nearly wholly, but not unnaturally, turned. As the prime agents, the martyrs and confessors of the

This analysis evident from the course of the movement.

The practical aspect of the Reformation has been the most studied.

since gone to God to answer it; to Whom I leave them."—Laud, *Confer.,* xxiv. 5. In the words of Leibnitz, " Ce sont les défauts des hommes, et non pas ceux des dogmes." The fanaticism of the Anabaptists belongs, as Dorner has shown, not to the principles of the Reformation carried to excess, but rather to the social and religious maladies of the pre-Reformation period. See some good remarks of Hallam, *Lit. of E.,* I. 371, on the passions which were instrumental in the Reformation, and Dean Hook, *Lives,* New Ser., I. 20.

[1] Such, *e.g.,* was Nicolaus Lyranus, a Franciscan monk, who as early as 1330 completed his *Postillæ perpetuæ.* It was of this exposition it was said:—

Si Lyra non lyrasset
Lutherus non saltasset.

See Mosheim, II. 644. On the Biblical factor in the Reformation, noticeable as early as the Waldenses, and traceable through Wycliffe (1380) and the various vernacular translations of the Bible in the fourteenth and fifteenth centuries, see Dorner, *u. s.,* I. 63, 441. Lastly, the labours of Reuchlin, Erasmus, &c., must be taken into account.

movement, they have enlisted sympathy and won admiration. Doubtless at such crises decision and self-sacrifice are of more apparent value than the results of slow and just reflection. Yet, on looking back, it is now sufficiently clear that the doctrines for which men died, the contributions of patient thought and learning,[1] form the abiding results of this great epoch in religion, and were the true preparation for it. If, then, this view be correct, the very essence of the Reformation lay, not in any practical correction of abuses, nor in a moral advance, but in its theology and belief. It has been called the reaction of Christianity, as a teaching of the Gospel,[2] against Christianity, as a declaration of Divine Law. It was, indeed, a free doctrine of grace and faith, of love and spirit, leading to the fulfilment of legal and moral righteousness, as a prompting of the heart restored to fresh union with the God of its salvation, and conscious of its own restoration;[3] ideas once

Its true importance as a crisis of belief.

---

[1] Such were the labours of the Reformers before the Reformation, Johann von Goch, Johann Wessel, who held explicitly the doctrine of justifying faith, Gerhard Groot, Jacob von Jüterbock, &c. Of Wessel Luther said: "If I had read Wessel first, mine adversaries might have imagined that Luther had taken everything from Wessel."—*Werke*, ed. Walch, xiv. 220. He also claimed kindred with the efforts of the earlier Mystics, Tauler, Eckhart, and the Friends of God.

[2] It was a saying of Luther's, that "the law and the Gospel are as far apart from one another as heaven and earth."

[3] Luther thus distinguishes between *fides*, *fiducia*, and *certitudo salutis*. Cf. Dorner, I. 149, 230, who well remarks on the fruitfulness of this principle from a scientific or philosophic point of view, as regards the subsequent history of Protestantism; while the Greek and Roman

familiar to the Christian mind,¹ and at no time excluded from its potential teaching, yet which had long been disused or misapplied. The principles it has secured to mankind are those of faith, of a true spiritualism, of individual accountability for belief and practice, as inherent elements of our common Religion. These are the pledges which it has supplied to Christianity of its future share in the advance of human civilization. *Full of future efficacy.* What has been called the principle of private judgment is, in truth, an element of indefinite, though not as is often urged, of unrestricted progress. It is true that the Reformation assumed essentially the obligation of a continual purifying and perfecting alike of practice and doctrine,² of the Church and of the world, of Religion and of Science. And this *Not indefinite.* is a principle of vital progress. But, then, this advance is always to be made upon the foundation

Churches in no way insist upon personal assurance. Calvin (*Inst.*, III. ii. 6) says: "Cardo fidei in eo vertitur, ut promissiones intus amplectendo nostras faciamus."

[1] Comp. Ep. ad Diogn. c. xii. "Ητω σοι καρδία γνῶσις · ζωὴ δὲ λόγος ἀληθής, χωρούμενος. Under Catholicism the personal yearning after salvation and closer communion with God, had too often to find refuge in conventual retirement. We have already noticed the intrinsic selfishness which lay at the root of this system.

[2] "In our own times there is a constant disposition to consider the liberty of the Reformation as an abstract form; to fancy that any imaginable substance may be put into it; and hence to conceive Protestantism as implying a principle of progress absolutely unrestricted, and it matters not whether beyond the pale of Christianity, or even in direct opposition to it. No such tenet has any foundation upon the idea of liberty as conceived by the Reformers and their predecessors."—Ullmann, *Reformers*, I. xviii.

that is already laid, the testimony of the Gospel, and the rule of strictly primitive tradition.¹

The Reformation presents no break in the continuity of Christianity as a system.

§ 9. It is further evident that the Reformation, rightly considered, presents no interruption of the continuity of human affairs,² no founding over again of the Church of Christ. In its truest and best development there was no breaking with the past. It called for no belief that the Church had been at any time wholly forsaken by the Spirit of her Lord, or disinherited of His promises. It never renounced the historical basis of Christianity.

No phase of negation.

It was no mere phase of negation or of destruction, but rather a reconstruction; a transition apparently spontaneous from beliefs, themselves transitional and relative to new modes of religious thought and belief, limited by the canons of Apostolic teaching. The very idea of a *Re-formation* implies a return to a standard or point of outset already known and fixed.³ It is a spiritual re-edification; and, as such, a recall to primitive Christianity, to the words and examples of Christ. For Chris-

---

¹ Comp. the concluding declaration of the Confession of Augsburg: "Tantum ea recitata sunt quae videbantur necessario dicenda esse, ut intelligi possit in doctrina ac caeremoniis, apud nos nihil esse receptum contra Scripturam aut Ecclesiam Catholicam."—*Syllog. Conf.*, pp. 158, 232.

² "Protestantism in all its movements and antitheses preserved the steadiness or continuity of a historical and growing formation."—Dorner, *Hist. Prot. Th.*, I. 9, and the excellent remarks in p. 50. "The Reformation would lose its historical basis and connection, if, in order to furnish a triumphant justification of it, we were to see nothing but darkness before it."

³ Gal. i. 7, 8, 9. For there cannot be two Gospels.

tianity itself was at the beginning a purely spiritual religion, a strong invincible conviction of renewed individual fellowship with a merciful God and Father, effected by the Incarnation and Sacrifice of His Son. It was no less as the offspring and product of this conviction in the believer; or, in other words, of this living faith, a life of love and spontaneous morality.¹ Its body is, indeed, the Church animated ever by the vital presence of Christ and of His Spirit, yet liable to admixture and deterioration, subject to the conditions of earthly things, the results of time and succession, of political issues, and historical development. The balance of complementary doctrines may, in the course of affairs, become overthrown, without, however, those doctrines being severally contradicted or lost; such, for example, as the parallelism of a dogma of Justification with that of Sanctification; of Christ's Atonement with the need of personal holiness; of subjective faith with objective righteousness; of grace with works; of positive commands with moral obligations; of external symbolism with a living consciousness of its significance; of ecclesiastical constitution with spiritual worship. This balance the Reformation sought to restore. It has left some truths clearly defined as its contribution to future ages of the Church, more especially man's need of individual regeneration; that this cannot

No unfruitful reaction.

The true balance of doctrine restored.

Its contribution to the future career of Christianity,

¹ Compare Ullmann, *Reformers*, I. p. 4.

be wrought out by natural means alone; that by a Divine Revelation, and in a Divine relation with the creature of an abiding and universal character, man's salvation is secured. "Thou wilt keep him in perfect peace, whose mind is stayed upon Thee."

§ 10. Thus, if Christianity be indeed the "salt of the earth,"[1] it must needs be purgative, and is ever tending to throw off the accumulations of worldly impurity; an impurity which reaches to the lowering of heavenly doctrines, as well as to the marring of their realization in practice. The Christian idea, the imitation of Christ, made possible by the Incarnation of the Word, will always, in a manner, protest against the defects inherent and immanent in its manifestation in the world.[2] At varying epochs this antagonism could not but show itself forth. The conflicts to which all human progress seems liable, its corruptions, its hindrances, must needs attend equally the action of Christianity upon mankind. Yet "a little leaven leaveneth the whole lump." And this self-

its protestant element.

---

[1] "It was necessary that the Gospel, which had once already proved the preserving salt for the world, where putrefaction had begun, should again penetrate in its original purity, power, and leavening influence, into the hearts and lives of the people."—Dorner, I. 40.

[2] "The Protestants did not get that name by protesting against the Church of Rome, but by protesting (and that when nothing else would serve) against her errors and superstitions."—Laud, *Conf. with F.*, xxi. 3: viz. at Speier, April 16, 1529; where it had been decreed by the Papal party, "contra novatores, ut omnia in integrum restituantur."

quickening, self-renewing process will not be wanting even to the end, while there remains among men the opposition between truth and error, between holiness and sin, between the kingdom of God and the kingdoms of the world.

LECTURE VIII.

THE PERMANENCE OF CHRISTIANITY INFERRED FROM ITS MISSIONARY CHARACTER AND PRESENT STANDING.

"Ex quo intelligimus Ecclesiam usque ad finem mundi concuti quidem persecutionibus, sed nequaquam posse subverti: tentari, non superari. Et hoc fiet, quia Dominus Deus Omnipotens, sive Dominus Deus ejus, id est, Ecclesiae, se facturum esse pollicitus est: Cujus promissio lex naturæ est."—HIERON., *Comment* in Amos, sub fin.

"Is it possible to expect a further and more perfect manifestation of Religion, as we may expect a further and more perfect manifestation of Art, or Science, or Philosophy? No. Never, either in our days or in the remotest future, can any religious progress hope to rival the gigantic step which humanity made through the revolution effected by Christ."—STRAUSS, *Life of Christ*, Vol. II. p. 49, 3rd ed.

LECTURE VIII.

"*Lo! I am with you alway; even unto the end of the world.*"—
Matt. xxviii. 20.

§ 1. THERE is a growing tendency to regard the results of the Reformation in two very opposite aspects. It has been assailed as the commencement of an era of unbelief, of unsettlement of all authoritative teaching; as the cause of all subsequent fluctuations of opinion on religious subjects.[1] Its historical course has been held up as a warning; as exhibiting the Nemesis of a revolt from traditional doctrine. Strange to say, the Romanist and the disciple of Comte, though from very opposite suggestions, are of one opinion as to the demerits of Protestantism. While the former eyes it with sternness, or, at best, with compassion, as the outcome of human waywardness and rebellion; the latter regards it only with philosophical contempt.[2] To him it is an interruption, a

Tendency of opposite views of the Reformation on the present estimate of the Christian religion.

View of the Positivists

---

[1] Gibbon (VII. 61) struck the first chord of this ill-omened prediction. "The friends of Christianity are alarmed at the boundless impulse of inquiry and scepticism;" &c. He here appears in the unwonted garb of "the candid friend" of the Religion of Christ. "Le Protestantisme le grand réveil chrétien," says M. Renan more truly.

[2] Comte notes as marks of the religious disorganization of the age, the resistance of Catholicism to intellectual emancipation, and the secularization of the ruling classes. These are the results of Protestantism, *i.e.* of the right of private judgment, which leads inevitably to Democracy in Church and State, to a negative philosophy, attacking first

stumbling-block, a logical inconsequence, an issue of mental anarchy, a period of transition, of confusion, of necessary evil, fraught with social and political disturbance. As the introduction to after-changes; the pioneer of Positivism; a main agency in dissolving the older military and hierarchical organizations; the accompaniment of an era of free, metaphysical discussion; it might, one would have thought, have been entitled to passing respect. This is not, it seems, to be accorded. But there is also another view of this great historical movement, one which has affected so largely and so permanently the condition and fortunes of Europe; which is now becoming popular. The Reformation is looked on as the companion, and as itself the result, if not the precursor, of a spirit

of the Rationalistic School.

religious truth, while all other becomes a lesser and included result. He divides Protestantism into *a.* Lutheranism, which is really an attack on Catholic discipline, the dogmatic differences being slight: *b.* Calvinism, an assault on Catholic organization or hierarchy, of the most powerful kind: *c.* Socinianism, a dogmatic revolution of the deepest character, being a protest in favour of Monotheism. See *Phil. Pos.*, V. 680, ff. In V. 353 he speaks of "l'esprit d'inconséquence qui caractérise le Protestantisme," and mourns the intellectual fluctuation, the malady of the age, which has flowed from it. He thinks the recognition of the solidarity of man and the continuity of human life have been lost in the anarchy which has been the work of Protestantism. This era of revolution, of dispersive analysis, began, indeed, from the fourteenth century, continuing to the present time, when it is about to close irrevocably. *Phil. Pos.*, V. 233, 346; *Pol. Pos.*, III. 417, 500. See also Littré, *A. Comte*, p. 223; and *Paroles*, p. 60. Dorner, *Hist. Prot. Th.*, I. 272, points out that the Reformation principle, which has been so often termed disorganizing, and has even been confounded with the spirit of revolution, gave effect, with a power previously unknown, to the *divine right* of civil authority.

of Rationalism;[1] an inevitable consequence, indeed, and one not, therefore, to be condemned; part of the natural progress of human effort, and of the growth of the human mind. This progression, evident in all other departments of social activity, in industrial and secular advance, in national morality, in philosophy and speculation, could not fail to make itself felt in the region of theological opinion. This estimate of Protestantism will be found (however it may be connected with it,) not to be identical with that of Positivism; which regards it either as a pure negation, or as a confused form of theological belief. *Its estimate of Protestantism.*

I have already given reasons for believing that Religion, as to its own evolution, is not dependent on moral progress, and is only indirectly affected by intellectual culture. It remains only to disengage the future of Christianity from the consequences to which it must be liable; if it is to be regarded, (together, indeed, with all religions,) as a thing of the past; a lingering survival of an anterior stage of thought or civilization; or again, as a mere vehicle, though of an exalted and highly commendable kind, for passing on to future generations the gift of an improved morality.[2] *How it affects the future of Christianity.*

---

[1] See Mr. Lecky, *H. Rat.*, I. 181, 288. Rationalism, he thinks, is the totality of the influences of civilization. Continental Protestantism has continually developed towards it.

[2] In this, according to Rationalistic theologians, consists the perfectibility of the Religion of Christ; viz. in expanding the doctrines of Christianity into those eternal truths of reason, which constitute the

Theory of Positivism,

§ 2. The former view regarding the prospects of the Christian Church and more immediately of Protestantism, being that of the Positivist school, forms part of an elaborate but highly artificial criticism of life and history; which must, if at all, be accepted as a whole. It must defend itself along its whole line; if it is to be taken as a true explanation of the world and of the times in which we live. At present we are concerned no further than to inquire whether it offers the only legitimate account of the course of human affairs in respect of Religion, and whether its view is sufficiently confirmed by present facts and actual probabilities. No doubt, as has been already said, the Reformation presents no interruption of the continuity of History.[1] It was itself the slow

whether answering to facts.

universal possession of the race. There is something ominous in Mr. Lecky's language when he says: "Loyalty, patriotism, and attachment to a cosmopolitan cause, are three forms of moral enthusiasm respectively appropriate to three successive stages of mental progress: and they have, I think, a certain analogy to idolatrous worship, Church feeling, and moral culture, which are the central ideas of three stages of religious history."—*H. E. M.*, I. 142.

[1] "The error of Positivism," writes Dr. Westcott, "is in limiting Christianity to the view of Catholicism. Christianity is supremely fitted to mould for itself the organism which is best suited to meet the intellectual, or social, or moral wants of the age. It is manifold in embodiment, though one in essence. It is not a principle of order, but a spirit of life. It is limited not by laws of logical construction, but by laws of free growth. It survives the decay of one organization, to animate another."—*Cont. Rev.*, VI. 415. " Il est incontestable en effet d'après l'ensemble de notre passé intellectuel pendant les trois derniers siècles, sans avoir besoin de remonter plus haut, que la continuité et la fécondité sont les symptômes les moins équivoques de toutes les conceptions vraiment scientifiques."—Comte, *Phil. Pos.*, IV. 269. We claim these also for Christianity.

result of time and previous changes. Similarly also it has in turn initiated changes which are still going on, and are still the subjects of discussion and dispute. The real point is the nature of these changes and of their consequences. The Christian world, it is not denied, is endlessly divided, and shows as yet few signs of ultimate reunion. Is this, then, to be held the beginning of the end? Does it mark a decline in the power and spirit of Religion?—in its hold upon the life and mind and conscience of its professors?—in its capacity of assimilating surrounding conditions of culture and of converting unbelief? I cannot see that it does. I see in these facts rather the evidence of the working of a leaven; which, if it ceased to ferment, might be justly suspected of inefficacy and decay. This leaven (if we have learned any lesson from the past history of Christianity, it is this;) works variously in accordance with the circumstances of the time under review. In Protestantism it has been conditioned by the advance of opinion through intellectual discussion and physical discoveries; by military history; by social and political vicissitudes tending to a multiplicity rather than to unity of form.[1] It has been crushed under

Results of the Reformation still in progress.

Division of sects, whether a symptom of decline.

Historical development of Protestantism.

---

[1] "However imposing," remarks Prof. Westcott, "the apparent unity of the religious life of the Middle Ages may be, it cannot be questioned that socially and individually the principles of Christianity are more powerful now than then. We lose the sense of their general action in the variety of forms through which they work."— *Comte on Christianity, Cont. Rev.*, VI. 416.

the burden of successive revolutions. It has been made the pretext for administrative changes, and thus complicated with political interests; at one time for resisting democratic tendencies; at another as the enemy of all political absolutism.[1] It has alternately been held to be the friend or foe of freedom of thought; the ally or enemy of philosophical opinion; as fearing or welcoming the vast and ever-progressing influences of industrial development. But through all it has worked on; and worked after its own kind. There have indeed been times when, exhausted by its struggles for existence and for toleration, its spiritual powers lay dormant, and might seem well-nigh extinct.[2] During long periods the secularism of court intrigues, the heats of metaphysical controversies, the atheistic intolerance of the French Revolution,[3] appeared to have expelled all interest in the

Periods of dormancy or reaction

---

[1] See Lecky, *Hist. Rat.*, II. 182-186. The internecine struggles of Catholicism and the Reformed Faith in France, Germany, and the Netherlands, may justly be claimed as testimonies to the power of the Religion which was held to be at stake.—Cf. Dorner, II. 3.

[2] Mr. Herbert Spencer, *First Princ.*, p. 331, well observes that "Religion, beside its occasional revivals of smaller magnitude, has its long periods of exaltation and depression; generations of belief and self-sacrifice following generations of indifference and laxity. . . . . When from corruptions accumulated around them, national creeds have fallen into general discredit, ending in indifferentism or positive denial; there has always by-and-by arisen a re-assertion of them, if not the same in form, still the same in essence." See Dorner's remarks on the permanence of the Christian Faith through all assaults of philosophical Deism in England, France, and Germany.—*Hist. Prot. Th.*, I. 207; II. 45, 392.

[3] See Buckle, *H. Civ.*, II. 254. He admits that its leaders committed what he thinks was an involuntary error: "In attacking the

message and prospects of Christianity. Yet the instincts of Religion (and, we may fairly add, the virtue of its specific doctrines,) prevailed. Successive revivals of the missionary spirit super-vened on eras of religious indifference; and the truth of Christian teaching has been both vigorously defended and confirmed by actual results. *followed by revivals.*

§ 3. The question of the direction and degree in which the prospects of Christianity have been affected by its history since the Reformation may be narrowed to the inquiry as to what fresh elements have been introduced into the circumstances attending its progress and with what results. These may be briefly summarized as the principle, or rather the fact, of the Renaissance in sentiment, philosophy, and art; of Positivism in material knowledge; the substitution of inquiry for traditional authority; the doctrines of religious liberty and toleration, including the freedom of the press and the disappearance of religious disabilities;[1] the gradual divorce of religion from politics, with its effects upon the alliance of Churches and States. What is the tendency of *New elements of progress introduced by the Reformation.*

These still in movement,

clergy, they lost their respect for religion. In their determination to weaken ecclesiastical power, they attempted to undermine the foundations of Christianity." Isaac Taylor, *Hist. Enthus.*, p. 269, has some fine and just remarks on the triumph of the Christian Religion at this period.

[1] It will be understood that these are, as Gibbon remarks, the consequences, not the design, of the Reformation.

these changes in opinion and practice, changes which are still ripening into action on every side through the length and breadth of Europe? If there be contained within them nothing really and essentially unfavourable to the growth and well-being of Christianity, there is no ground on this account at least to augur the decline of the Religion. If, indeed, they tend in harmony with its doctrines towards the spread of a simpler and more tolerant Christianity, there is rather reason to infer a larger and lasting measure of success for its tenets. It becomes necessary, then, to enter, although but briefly, on some consideration of their several characters and operation.

whether adverse to Christianity.

§ 4. By some the Reformation has been altogether traced to the importation of the classical or purely human element into Western Europe,[1] which was the result in the first instance of the impact of Mahommedanism upon Christianity, and of the fall of Constantinople. Philosophy and taste were revolutionized by contact with the independence of

The classical or human element in modern civilization

---

[1] See Ranke, *Hist. of Popes*, I. ii. § 3, and Gieseler, Vol. V., § 154, who assigns to this element its due share of result. Herder almost couples Ulric v. Hutten with Luther in the work of Reformation. See Hallam, *Lit. E.*, I. 290–7. At first the progress of literature seemed checked: and Erasmus writes (1528), "Ubicunque regnat Lutheranismus, ibi literarum est interitus." At an earlier stage he had made similar complaints of the Catholic party. "Hæresis est politè loqui: hæresis Græcè scire." See Sir W. Hamilton, *Disc.*, p. 209. Socinianism may be rightly regarded as the issue of the Reformation in Italy, where philosophic and æsthetic culture gained the ascendency over the ethical and religious elements. See Dorner, *Hist. Prot. Th.*, II. 127.

ancient modes of thought and feeling: and quickly sought new outlets of expression. Hence the influence of the so-called Humanists on the direction and character of the Reformation, the success of which was in many minds identified with the progress of classical literature. The proof of so wide an assertion must certainly remain doubtful. For our present purpose the admission is sufficient that the presence of "the new learning" was a fact contemporaneous with the tendencies towards a reformation in religion. The relations of an increased acquaintance with the original tongues to the doctrinal interpretation of the Scriptures are immediately apparent; and their value was accordingly substantially acknowledged by some of the leading Reformers:[1] to whom, both in Germany and England, the improvement, and in some cases the foundation, of public schools is due. The wider influence of classical models in framing new standards of literary, philosophical, and moral conceptions, in loosening the shackles of traditional dogmatism, in transforming religious sentiments by the instrumentality of art, may be differently estimated, but

recognized and employed by the Reformers

not dangerous to Christian tendencies,

---

[1] In 1525 Luther addressed a Treatise to the Councillors of every town in Germany, "that they ought to institute and maintain Christian schools," *i. e.* national schools. Melancthon and Camerarius laboured at the establishment of classical schools, *Lycea*, and *Gymnasia*. Melancthon himself kept for many years a *schola privata*. See Dorner, *H. Prot. Th.*, I. 261-270. Hallam, *Lit. of E.*, 1. 330. For England, comp. Seebohm's *Oxford Reformers*, &c. Colet, Linacre, More, &c. See further Whewell, *Ind. Phil.*, Bk. XII., ix.

will hardly be denied. It would, however, be but a narrow view which regards the tendencies of Classicism as essentially irreligious or un-Christian.[1] Rather may we see in this period of European civilization the introduction to a permanent synthesis of two differing sides of human nature and human history: of the natural with the spiritual: of reason with religion: of an æsthetical apprehension of the Beautiful with the higher aspirations of Christian devotion: a synthesis ever in process of completion yet unfulfilled. Christianity which in its origin had successfully contended with heathen Philosophy and Art in their decline, was inevitably destined, at some future stage of human culture, to encounter the elements of Truth which they enshrined, to adopt them into its own theory of reality, and mould them after its own

representing an aspect of truth,

necessary to their completion.

---

[1] A recent historian (Lecky, II. 322) has endeavoured to trace the influences of Rationalism upon Art, "a chief organ of religious sentiments;" and shows how in the course of secularization the ideal of piety was exchanged for that of beauty; more especially in Painting and Architecture, following the intellectual condition of the times. *Ib.*, I. 263–286. There can be no question as to the immediate and, in some respects, lasting effect of the introduction of classic models, and of the sense of freedom gained at the era of the Reformation. Nothing, however, is proved by it as to the declension of Christian influence. In Architecture, the Gothic style, a conception which, if any, is the creation of the Church of Christ, is once more in the ascendant: and there are indications of a similar tendency in the Poetry of the time. Of Painting I need hardly speak. Schlegel remarks that, of the sister arts, Painting is the most truly spiritual, and, together with Music, has in modern Christendom been most employed to exhibit or suggest the mysteries of Divine Love. Sculpture, and to some extent Architecture, as its attendant, occupied with the development of organic form, attained even in heathen times their richest cultivation.

thought. The result thus far would not appear to have been either the decline or degradation of Religion; much less the contradiction or empoverishment of tenets essential to the sum of Christian Faith; but rather the introduction of a broader yet deeper religious type in the adaptation of Revealed Truth to the abstract conceptions of the mind. No doubt the tendency of a classical revival in Science and in Art has been, in the first instance, towards the separate cultivation of distinct principles of Truth and Beauty. Hence the apparent and temporary divorce of Religion from Science; and during the last century, and partly in our own, from Art itself. The medieval intellect may be said to have been entirely and extravagantly religious; just as in Greece and Rome it showed itself exclusively human.[1] It still remains to develope a type of thought and conception which shall harmonize, after the fundamental idea of the Religion of Christ, the Human and Divine. There is, then, little to suggest that the separation of Art and Philosophy from Christian influence is other than transient and contingent: or to show that Classicism and the entrance of a so-called Rationalistic

Apparent divorce of art from religious sentiment temporary.

---

[1] "In the East intellect is entirely religious; in Greek society it is exclusively human; in the modern world the religious spirit is mixed up with everything, but excludes nothing. Modern intellect has at once the stamp of humanity and of divinity. Human sentiments and interests occupy an important place in our literature; and yet the religious character of man, that portion of his existence which links him to another world, appears in every step."—Guizot, *Civ. en Europe*, Leç. vime.

element have exercised any morbific effect upon the powers of Revealed Religion.

Position of the Positive Sciences.

§ 5. The relations to Christianity of an increased knowledge of the material world, and, as its result, of a Positive system of philosophy, have already been considered in various aspects. The notion that the world through the possession of the Positive Sciences has, since the older classical and medieval periods, entered on a new phase of knowledge and reflection, is plainly not without foundation. If we compare the present condition of the Natural Sciences with times in which Mathematics together with the rudiments of Astronomy, Mechanics, and Medicine constituted their whole domain :[1] when Physics, Biology, and Comparative Physiology existed only in outline; and Chemistry and Geology were wholly unknown; the difference is large indeed. Yet this was all that antiquity could bequeath to after-ages; and all that the industry and penetration of the Arabians, having culled from their intercourse with the Greek Empire, brought into the common stock of knowledge.

Their abeyance in medieval times.

---

[1] "La mathématique et l'astronomie, seul domaine que l'antiquité possédât dans la positivité (la physique et la biologie n'étaient qu'ébauchées, et la chimie n'existait pas)," &c.—Littré, *Etudes sur les Barbares*, p. xvii. Humboldt pronounces the Arabians the true founders of the Physical Sciences, according to the modern acceptation of them. They added to the old Greek conceptions the use of Experiment and Computation. See Lange, *Gesch. des Materialismus*, p. 83. Comte considers Physics to have commenced with Galileo's discoveries on the fall of heavy bodies: and that Geometry almost begins with Descartes; that of the ancients having been of a special and limited character.

There was an absence, whatever may be said of the inductive processes indicated by Plato or by Aristotle, not only of real information, but also of the method to seek it and to use it when found.[1] Is it, then, to be supposed that with these changes the limits or direction of even abstract speculation could have remained modelled only on ancient practice? It is further true that, through the suppression by medieval Catholicism of the critical spirit, the antagonism between the defenders of Revealed and the investigators of Natural Truth, more apparent than real, was largely increased. Nor at first was this doctrine of authority much impaired by the interposition of Protestantism. The Reformation, it has been well said by Hallam,[2] "was but a change of masters," and those great men, who had been really, though unconsciously, contending for a perpetual freedom of belief, were the first to coerce speculation, and to inhibit differences of opinion in matters of faith. But it is forgotten by the leaders of the school of thought, which would substitute positive knowledge for theological beliefs, that the general emancipation of thought effected by the Reformation was posterior

Their revival not unfavourable to Religion, nor was the Reformation hostile to them.

---

[1] See at length Whewell, *Hist. of Induct. Sc.*, Bk. IV. Religion, or rather Theology, being in the Middle Ages the only outlet for human effort and human interests, may seem to have suffered from the very introduction of other fields of inquiry.

[2] *Literature of Europe*, I. 370. Lecky, *Hist. Rat.*, I. 404, pursues this topic with some vehemence.

to the religious revolution and dependent upon it.¹ Religion also during the same period with Science had entered upon a new phase or stand-point of opinion; of which, however, the Reformation was the true cause and spring. Science and Religion may be long in working out upon a common footing the details of their respective systems. But it can be no real argument (although repeatedly urged by M. Comte) against the truth of a Protestant Christianity, that it has revolted from the domination of an unreasoning Catholicism: however imposing in speculation, or even in its historical results, may be the idea of unity.

Protestantism friendly to inquiry.

§ 6. If it were true, as has been alleged, that Rationalism is the legitimate result of Scepticism and Toleration in religious belief;² it might next be

Rationalism not the true consequence of toleration of opinion.

---

¹ Guizot, *Civ. en E.*, Leç. xiime, points out that "while the civil and religious societies have undergone the same vicissitudes and been subject to the same revolutions, resulting in the overthrow of absolute power, the religious society has always been foremost in this career." So, in pronouncing on the English Revolution of 1688, Hallam observes that it "is justly entitled to honour as the era of religious, in a far greater degree than of civil, liberty: the privilege of conscience having had no earlier Magna Charta, and Petition of Right, whereto they could appeal against encroachment."—*Const. Hist.*, II. 324. So also Mr. Buckle, *Hist. Civ.*, II. 138, sees "in the Reformation of the sixteenth century the seeds of those great political revolutions which, in the seventeenth century broke out in nearly every part of Europe."

² Mr. Lecky, *Hist. Rat.*, I. 400, 406, regards Rationalism as the issue of the Reformation; and Toleration as the result and measure of Rationalism in Protestant countries. He nowhere, indeed, in his work, defines Rationalism; but in more than one passage sufficiently describes his notion of it. It is a disbelief in authority (I. 90), a demand for evidence. "The essence of the rationalistic spirit is to interpret the

asked whether Scepticism may not be considered to have been the natural result of the Reformation and of the changes which were then inaugurated. And there are writers of a free and philosophic spirit who seem to see nothing mediate between Roman Catholicism and what they denominate Rationalism. But while admitting that toleration of opinion is the legitimate consequence of private judgment, and that the principle of private judgment was the privilege asserted for human thought in the act of the Reformation; it still remains to be shown that private judgment itself is identical with Rationalism in anything like the current acceptation of the term, or in a sense to be held perilous to the claims of Revelation. Faith, it needs hardly be repeated, is, on the one hand, no unreasoning acceptance of truths, however sacred. Nor again is the admission of Authority in matters of Religion

[margin: Involved in the principle of private judgment.]

[margin: Real sense of Rationalism.]

---

articles of special creeds by the principles of universal religion, by the wants, the aspirations and the moral sentiments which seem inherent in human nature. It leads men, in other words, to judge what is true and what is good, not by the teachings of tradition, but by the light of reason and of conscience." Adopting Dr. Farrar's learned and careful history of the term, "*Rationalism* is properly opposed to *Supernaturalism*, having Reason, and not Revelation, for its formal principle; and stands for a purely philosophical view of religious truth."—*Bampton Lectt.*, pp. 589-592. It is hence of importance to insist that the right use of reason does not tend to diminish faith in the supernatural; nor was there any such tendency inherent in the principles of the Reformation; which gave the occasion only and imposed the duty of free inquiry. Hegelianism (Panlogism, as it has been termed) is the acme of Rationalism, which supersedes or constitutes reality. "Alles, was wirklich ist, ist vernünftig."

2 A

within limits other than a reasonable principle.¹ The English Divines, to go no further than our own country, who have fought the battle of religious toleration,² were neither Sceptics nor, as the word is generally understood, Rationalists. In the Church of Rome Scepticism has indeed at all times shown a direct and dangerous opposition towards Christianity itself:³ because the very truth of Christianity is there staked upon the positive institutions of the Church; and now, as it would appear, upon the infallibility of its visible head. But it has not been so within the domain of Protestantism; in England, America, or even in Germany. Here Protestantism, as admitting toleration of religious opinion, shows itself the hope of Christian doctrine, and the ground of its ultimate permanence. "There is no such thing," it has been truly enough said, "as a theological antiseptic." But Protestantism, by blending with and consecrating the prevailing Rationalistic spirit,⁴ affords a standing remedy for traditional and authoritative corruptions of belief.

Perilous position of Roman Catholicism.

Aid afforded by the principle of Protestantism.

---

¹ See this argued by Hooker, *E. P.*, V. viii., who does not exclude "invincible arguments found out by the light of reason."

² Hales, Chillingworth, Jeremy Taylor: not to speak among laymen of Milton and Locke.

³ Thus, very early in the age of the Reformation, the attempt was made by the Italian Humanists to unite the extremes of sceptical unbelief and passive obedience to the authority of the Church. See Dorner, *Hist. Prot. Th.*, Vol. II.; Lecky, *H. R.*, I. 406, and Mr. Buckle's remarks on the causes of the French Revolution, II. 249.

⁴ Mr. Lecky, *Hist. Rat.*, II. 92, justly observes, "When a country, which is nominally Roman Catholic, is very tolerant, it may be inferred, with almost absolute certainty, that the social and intellectual influence

§ 7. Love of truth may be pronounced to have been the rudimentary virtue of Reformed Christianity. This virtue, in the intensity of its spiritual conviction, lay at the root of the movement; and is still the proper attribute of Protestantism as a system. It is true that fanaticism may sometimes have done it injustice in this respect; and, through intolerance in theory and practice,[1] have raised the doubt as to its preference of an authorized creed to the results of genuine inquiry. Yet it has rarely, if ever, subordinated moral distinctions to positive expediency; the means to the end; or sanctioned pious frauds.[2] In its love of truth it has ever sympathized with the instincts of physical discovery, and the employment of a scientific method.[3] The marked diffusion

<small>Love of truth its rudimentary virtue.</small>

<small>Obscured by prejudice.</small>

of the Church is comparatively small. But England and America conclusively prove that a nation may be very tolerant, and at the same time profoundly Protestant. . . . It is this fact which is the most propitious omen of the future of Protestantism."

[1] Hallam's verdict (*Const. Hist.*, I. 94) is, "the difference as to tolerance in religion between Catholics and Protestants was only in degree, and in degree there was much less difference than we are apt to believe;" and see Mr. Lecky's severe strictures, *H. Rat.*, II. 54–61, and Buckle, II. 51. Yet Hallam (*u. s.*, p. 119) seems to admit that the principle of toleration was early and persistently avowed by Protestants. Certainly, it must be allowed to have lain as a germ in the system, however late in bearing fruit, both in our own and other countries. The principles of Romanism are unfortunately committed to persecution.

[2] On the degree to which the medieval interpolations and forgeries had "blotted out the very sense and love of truth from the minds of men," see Mr. Lecky's just remarks, *H. Rat.*, I. 434–6; *H. E. M.*, II. 225.

[3] In England, we may fairly instance Bacon, Boyle, and Newton. Among the founders of the Royal Society were Wilkins, Spratt, Glanvil, and other Churchmen.

of a truthful spirit, which has been the characteristic of the era of Protestantism, has been variously ascribed to the revival of ancient independent systems of philosophy, to the influence of modern secular thinkers, and to the general results of advancing civilization.[1] It may with equal reason, and with perhaps more probability, be attributed to the reaction of religious inquiry upon philosophical speculation and active life. But in either case its possession by a religious system, as part of its inherent and fundamental principles, is both an element of real progress, and a guarantee of permanence to the Faith which it upholds.

<small>Physical discovery indebted to Protestantism.</small>

§ 8. The doctrine of religious liberty, although it did not immediately bear fruit, is in principle fairly and incontestably due to the Reformation; which did not, however, take its rise in any notions of political freedom.[2] Experience shows, it is true, that, under all systems, persecution for opinion is dear to human nature. But it has never been proved to be a consequence of Christian doctrine. Until the establishment of the Church under Constantine, the testimony of the Fathers is wholly in favour of toleration of belief. It is in practice that the difficulties emerge of working out the

<small>Religious liberty immediately involved in the Reformation,</small>

<small>though not at once secured.</small>

---

[1] Lecky, *H. R.*, I. 440; *H. E. M.*, I. 143.

[2] "Political liberty," says Hallam, *Lit. E.*, I. 352, "in the sense we use the word, cannot be reckoned the aim of those who introduced the Reformation." See also the section (II. 33) on the Political Philosophy of the sixteenth century. Compare Mr. Mill on *Liberty*, Introd.

application of the principle of freedom without disturbance, yet without injustice. The removal of religious disabilities, and the relations of theological beliefs to political government, have, since the Reformation, become of necessity the questions of the age; and once more, after an interval of temporary cessation, loom large on the horizon of public opinion in Europe. But their solution no longer involves the rise or fall of Christianity, its success or decline. The usefulness of Establishments[1] and of National Churches in preserving a just liberty of belief against sectarian or unsectarian tyranny; as also in combating so formidable an opponent as "the close phalanx of Rome;"[2] may be too readily forgotten. On the other hand, there is good reason to augur, from the intrinsically spiritual character of our Religion, that it would, under the most voluntary system, be found the most readily to flourish.[3] But in any case the true interests of Christianity are independent of

Practical difficulties still experienced,

but no longer dangerous to the existence of Christianity,

---

[1] On this side may be claimed so liberal a thinker as Shaftesbury, who quotes Harrington to the effect that "it is necessary people should have a public leading in religion." "Why," he adds, "should there not be public walks, as well as private gardens?"—*Characteristics*, I. 17.

[2] "It is still very doubtful whether the close phalanx of Rome can be opposed, in ages of strong religious zeal, by anything except established or at least confederate Churches."—Hallam, *Hist. Lit.*, I 372.

[3] See Sir G. C. Lewis's observations (*Essay on Authority*, p. 301): Mr. Buckle (*Hist. Civ.*, II. 53) considers that "a religion, not protected by the Government, usually displays greater energy and greater vitality than one which is so protected." He further gives a *rationale* of the fact.

the secularization of politics. They are bound up with the maintenance of the Scriptures, its sole authoritative records, and with the earliest principles of their interpretation, historically ascertained; and these, it must be admitted, are on the side of religious equality, and a reasonable employment of private judgment.[1] It may, however, be remarked, that a belief in the progressive power of the Religion, and of its capacity and value in civilization, seems a necessary part of a theory of religious establishments; for, as representing a system of abstract truth only, few would care greatly to support them.[2] Were the Faith of Jesus Christ confined in its teaching to any one form of political government, absolute or popular; this might, in some quarters, and with some show of fairness, be deemed an evidence of its transient and

nor to its true interests.

Question of religious establishments.

---

[1] On the equality and diversity of particular Churches, it may be remarked that the Primitive Liturgies and even *Creeds* bear evidence of the independence of their several forms, while united by a community of doctrine; see Bingham, *E. A.*, Bk. II. c. vi. Some good remarks on the relation of private judgment to a common standard of authority existing in the Church will be found in Bp. Browne, *Expos. of Arts*, p. 480; in Gladstone, *Church and State*, c. v.; and Palmer, *Treatise on the Church*, II. vi.

[2] The grave question as to the duty of the State to propagate truth is, at the present time, practically superseded by a belief that it is not for the interest of the truth to seek the assistance of the State. Without taking up the high ground of Mr. Gladstone (*Church and State*, c. iii. viii.), it is enough to observe that even Macaulay (*Essays*, p. 487) would maintain the duty of religious instruction on the part of the Government as a secondary obligation from its utility as a *moral* instrument. If, then, its value as a *spiritual* agency be taken into account, the obligation is surely enhanced; as well as the danger of making no provision against false outlets for the enthusiasm undoubtedly natural to mankind.

limited character. Such, however, we know from its own doctrines, as well as from the course of its history, not to be the case. Born under the growing absolutism of the first years of the Roman Empire, the Church, though instinctively leaning to the rights of possession, as the best practical proof of its negation of all claims to temporal power;[1] favoured political progress and liberty. True it is, that the original freedom of its principles has, in the course of human affairs, been limited and arrested by the force of circumstances, and the errors of individual leaders. It has accordingly been reproached with its tendencies to Theocracy; with the alliances it has contracted with despotism; and with the slavishness of its passive obedience.[2] Yet no doctrine of Divine Right can be proved in reality to encumber its system; and

Relations of Christianity as a system of religion to politics.

---

[1] Mr. Buckle treats the distinction of *de facto* and *de jure* with much contempt; and as a quibble invented to save the pockets of the clergy, or to cover Jesuitry. *Hist. Civ.*, I. 413. While acknowledging to the full the high qualities of the Non-jurors, I still regard this view as a narrow one.

[2] Shaftesbury denounced Christianity as incompatible with freedom; and even Mr. Buckle seems to agree in the opinion that, "by being a good Churchman, a person may become a bad citizen." No doubt, medieval Catholicism has neutralized its earlier services of distinguishing spiritual from temporal authority by its later attempts to subordinate the latter to the former. Montesquieu, *E. L.*, XXIV. iii. v., considers the genius of Christianity best suited to a constitutional form of Government; while Mahometanism is the religion of despotism; and that Catholicism has an affinity for monarchy, but Protestantism for a republic. Guizot, however, admits that, historically, the Church has always presented herself as the interpreter and defender of theocracy or despotism, under a religious or civil form. The origin of this fact he

Its independence.

Supposed leaning towards democracy.

the highest supporters of the Papal power have at times maintained even ultra-democratic opinions. Democracy, indeed, in the opinion of many the ultimate form of existing governments; the necessary result, it is maintained, of the conclusions of political economy, of the increase of capital, of the expansion of knowledge,[1] and of industrial movements; is in some respects the truest aspect of the spirit of Christianity as the last and highest expression of the Christian ideal of the brotherhood of mankind.[2] "Unam omnium rempublicam agnoscimus mundum," cries Tertullian in his defence of Christianity; "Omnium Christianorum respublica est," is the echo of Augustine.[3] In this freedom, or, it may be, indifference, of the political stand-

traces to the natural conflict between religious restraint and human liberty.—*Civ. en E.*, Leç. vime. "Le Christianisme," says De Maistre, *Œuvres*, p. 121, "est monarchique; comme tout le monde le sait."—See *Du Pape*, I. 249.

[1] "The state of knowledge," says Bacon, "is ever a Democratie; and that prevaileth which is most agreeable to the senses and conceits of people."—*Works*, III. 227.

[2] Lecky, *H. Rat.*, II. 248. Comp. Schmidt, *Essai*, Bk. II. c. ii. Dean Milman, *Hist. Lat. Chr.*, VI. 210, has eloquently pointed out the liberal elements in medieval Catholicism, their effects on social rank and in proclaiming the equality of mankind. See also Guizot's remarks, *Civ. en E.*, Leç. vme, on the amount of individual freedom which modified the spiritual tyranny of the pretensions of the Church.

[3] Tertull., *Apol.*, c. xxxviii.; Augustine, *De Op. Monach.*, c. xv., xxxiii. The indifference of Christians to political affairs, not unnatural under the circumstances of the time and at the rise of the new Religion, was at first thought a consequence of their doctrines. It was held "doctrinam Christi adversam esse reipublicæ."—August., *Ep.* cxxxviii., *ad Marcell*. Mr. Lecky, *H. Rat.*, II. 108, regards all patriotism as a pagan, and not a Christian, virtue. Even if this view were correct, it would but show the suitableness of the religion to co-operate in the

point, may certainly be discerned no unfavourable augury of the probable operation of Christianity amid future revolutions of public opinion in succeeding ages. Strengthened from within by its own native resources of influence, it may be expected to become gradually independent of all such means of influence as governments are undoubtedly capable of exercising upon religious belief,[1] whether beneficially or not. *Secularization not fatal or unfavourable.*

§ 9. An argument not infrequently urged for the probable decline of Christianity remains to be considered. The principle of private judgment, it is said, in matters of religion, which is more and more asserting itself in reason and in fact as the law of Christian communities, penetrating even the armour of Roman unity, is a principle of dissidence and division, making blunt the true instrument for the conversion of the world,—Christian love and oneness of belief. How, it is objected, is mankind to be brought over to the Faith of Christ, when the principle of religious disagreement is both sanctioned and maintained?[2] Who shall judge whether this disagreement does not extend to matters essential to *Objection from the principle of private judgment as theoretically and in fact incompatible with missionary success.*

largest speculations as to the ultimate federation of mankind. Comte admits that the rise of industrial Republics in the Middle Ages is a proof that Christianity is not incompatible with this form of government.— *Phil. Pos.*, V. 458.

[1] See on this subject Sir G. C. Lewis, *Influence of Authority*, p. 291, and Mr. Lecky, *Hist. Rat.*, II. 2–4.

[2] Comp. Voltaire, *Essai sur les Mœurs*, I. iv. "Le plus grand obstacle à nos succès religieux dans l'Inde, c'est la différence des opinions qui divisent nos missionnaires;" &c.

personal salvation?[1] And, at any rate, if the missionary efforts of the Church, while still united, failed to procure the full conversion of the heathen to the knowledge of the truth, what better prospect can attend the labours of isolated bodies? If it is impossible to secure unity within the Church; what are the chances of succeeding with those "that are without;" of winning to the One Fold the sheep that are scattered abroad? It has been already admitted that, in the tendency of any religious system to extend itself by conversion of unbelief, may be found one of the most real tests of its permanence, power, and, ultimately, of its truth.[2] No objector can deny to certain periods of the history of Christianity the presence of this test. Those periods have already, in the course of these Lectures, come fully under review. We are now led to form, though very briefly, an estimate of the present condition and ultimate prospects of our Religion in respect of its missionary efforts.

A power of conversion an admitted test of the vitality of any Religion,

not questioned as to Christianity in its earlier stages.

This principle and duty inherent in the system of Christianity.

§ 10. But, first, it must not be forgotten, as bearing upon this portion of our subject, that the missionary spirit of Christianity, as compared with

---

[1] This objection, it is clear, may be carried too far. All errors, even in matters of faith, cannot be considered *de fide* and heretical. Roman Catholic divines admit that there may be true Churches without the entire profession of the truth; nor is *actual* unity in all matters of faith a real note of the Church of Christ. See Palmer, *Treatise*, 1. v. § 4. These considerations must largely modify any definition of "Fundamentals."

[2] See Grant, *Bampton Lect.*, vi., sub init.

other faiths, was marked in its very origin[1] by the example and action of its Founder. He came, as He expressly records, "*to seek* and to save that which was lost." One of the grandest miracles of this Religion and of its most important announcements, the descent of the Holy Spirit on the Day of Pentecost, had direct reference to the work of Evangelization.[2] In some respects this eagerness to make proselytes might be considered as traditional with the Jews, and was so remarked by heathen writers before the spread of Christianity.[3] In some respects, also, it has been shared by other Eastern religions, by the faiths of Buddha[4] and Mahomet. With the worshippers of Islam, however, the instrument and end of conversion was conquest; not the moral or spiritual elevation of the believer. They massacred; they did not convert.[5] It has, indeed, been asserted that even in the

How far shared by Buddhism, and the Mahometan faith.

---

[1] On the real and disinterested character of the first missionary labours of the Christians, see Origen, c. *Cels.*, III. ix., VIII. lii.; and on the necessary connection between such efforts and a belief in *doctrine*, comp. Dr. Mozley, *B. L.*, pp. 182-5. "Zeal in missionary enterprise is essentially the child of faith," &c. We may set proselytism to the account of Christianity as against persecution. "Le zèle qui convertit et qui fonde est aussi le zèle qui poursuit et qui détruit."—Littré, *Les Barbares*, p. 150. See Guizot, *Meditations*, II. 143.

[2] Comp. Luke xxiv. 47-49.

[3] Comp. Neander, I. 90-93, ed. Clark: Döllinger, *Gentile and Jew*, II. 181.

[4] See Max Müller, *Chips*, I. 257, 293.

[5] "Concerning the means of procuring unity, we may not take up the third sword, which is Mahomet's sword or like unto it; that is, to propagate religion by wars, or by sanguinary persecutions to force consciences."—Bacon, *Essays, Works*, VI. 383. It is too true that the

present day Mahommedanism still makes its converts:[1] a result, however, obtained by secondary agencies, such as the institution of domestic slavery, rather than by any combined or genuine effort to enlarge the area of its beliefs. But with the Faith of Jesus Christ conversion of unbelief has been from the first an intrinsic and palpable duty. "Go ye and teach all nations ($\mu\alpha\theta\eta\tau\epsilon\dot{\upsilon}\sigma\alpha\tau\epsilon$); baptizing them in the name of the Father, and of the Son, and of the Holy Ghost," was the commission of His Apostles. "Out of all nations and kindreds and tongues and peoples" was His Church to be built up; and "unto them that dwell in all the earth" was "the everlasting Gospel" to be preached.[2] Nor has there ever been any long space in the history of the Church, especially when freed from domestic struggles, during which this work has not been carried on by at least some branch of the Christian Communion. No age has been altogether without some fruit of its labours. At the present hour it is being vigorously and honourably maintained: and an important testimony is thus rendered to the life and activity of our Religion, and to the prospects of its extension and permanence. A few proofs in

Original with the Christian religion,

and persistently carried out.

policy of Ferdinand and Isabella to Jew and Moor was a copy of this example.—Milman, *Hist. of Jews*, III. xxvi.; Gieseler, III. v. § 6.

[1] See W. G. Palgrave, *Essays on Eastern Questions*, p. 124; also Döllinger, *Lectures on Reunion of Churches*. The Church Missionary Society's Report for 1872 says, "In some parts of India Mohammedanism is extremely strong, if not increasing; . . . among the African tribes it continues its onward movement."

[2] Matt. xxviii. 19; Rev. xiv. 6.

connection with this part of our subject are all that can be given here.

§ 11. At the time of the Reformation the geographical limits of the Faith of Christ were for the most part identical with those of Europe. Poland and Lapland had at length received the Gospel;[1] and although Constantinople had admitted within its walls its Turkish conquerors, its Christian population still retained one-half of the churches to their use with liberty of worship.[2] In Asia missionaries had touched China: and Nestorianism had made advances in Central Tartary. But other worlds now opened before the march of Christianity; and as if to meet the fresh demand, the nations of the West rose to a new energy, and became endued with greater intensity of enterprise and purpose.[3] It is true that in America and Western Africa the spread of the Gospel was at first utterly thwarted by the avarice and ferocity of the Spaniards and Portuguese. What else could be looked for from men who had mercilessly expelled from the soil of Spain the Jew and the Moor, with the option of

Sketch of missionary efforts since the Reformation.

Evils of the conquest of America,

---

[1] Begun in the middle and close of the fourteenth century, but it was long before idolatry was extinguished.—Gieseler, *C. H.*, IV. 259; Guericke, *Kirchengesch.*, II. 321; Maclear, *Hist. of Missions in Middle Ages.*

[2] Gibbon, VIII. 180, ed. Smith.

[3] Comp. Grant, *B. L.*, p. 281. Dr. Dorner, *Hist. Prot. Th.*, II. 447, remarks generally: "The *intensive* and *extensive* processes alternate with each other in the Church's history. The latter, though naturally arising from the former, brings the Church into a defiling contact with the world, from which it can only be delivered by a fresh concentration and a recurrence to the purifying and intensive process. Nevertheless, the work of Christianity upon the human race is progressive."

conversion or exile.¹ In vain the Dominicans with righteous rigour refused absolution to the inhuman torturers of the native Indians.² In vain the devoted and venerable, if mistaken, Las Casas lived and died among the heathen of Mexico and Cuba. No one can desire to palliate these enormities any more than the miseries of the Slave Trade, that long and grievous stain on the fair scutcheon of modern Christianity. Yet it must be remembered that then, no less than in our own day, the social element, first brought into contact with savage and aboriginal populations, is that which is, for the most part, least under the control of religious and spiritual ideas. The missionary succeeds the settler, the slaver, and the gold seeker. The reproach cast by Lord Bacon on his contemporaries in the days of Elizabeth would hold good even now. "Surely the merchants themselves shall rise in judgment against the princes and nobles of Europe. For they have made a great path in the seas unto the ends of the world; and set forth ships and forces of Spanish, English, and Dutch, enough to make China tremble; and all this for pearl, or stone, or spices; but for the pearl of the kingdom of Heaven, or the stones of the heavenly Hierusalem, or the spices of the Spouse's Garden, not a mast hath been set up."³

of the slave trade.

Social causes of these results.

---

[1] See the remarkable discussion given in Prescott (*Ferdinand*, III. 430) between Sepulveda and Las Casas. "The Spaniard," says the indignant historian, "first persecuted the Jews, and then quoted them as an authority for persecuting all other infidels." See also Helps, *Las Casas*, c. xi.
[2] Gieseler, V. 204. Prescott, *u. s.*, III. 428. Helps, *Life of Las Casas*, c. ix.
[3] Bacon, *Works*, VII. 19, ed. Spedding.

§ 12. And yet when we compare the three hundred years which have elapsed since the era of the Reformation with the fifteen centuries which had preceded, can we say that little has been done or is doing to fulfil the great Christian duty of propagating the Faith? Little, perhaps, to satisfy the eager expectation which calculates (perchance too fondly)[1] on the universal spread of the kingdom of Christ, ere that kingdom be accomplished; ever crying, "How long, O Lord?" "Wilt thou at this time restore again the kingdom to Israel?" Little, it may be, to answer the cavils at the assumed failure and unreason of all missionary efforts which proceed from some objectors to Revelation and from half-hearted friends.[2] Of the labours of the Church of Rome during this period in the field of missions, I would speak with all respect.[3] That Church, which sent forth a Xavier; which fostered the devotion and noble self-sacrifice of the Jesuit Fathers; which (with whatever errors of conception and execution) has planted missions through

Progress of missions large and real.

Efforts of the Roman Church.

[1] See Archdeacon Grant's observations, *B. L.*, p. 301. See also some good remarks in Isaac Taylor (*Hist. of Enthus.*, p. 183), on the probable evils which would accompany a speedy conversion of mankind.

[2] Paley, in his *Evidences* (*Works*, V. 239), remarks with truth that the slow progress and ill-success of modern efforts only magnify the miracle of the first conversion of the Roman world to Christianity.

[3] The *Congregatio de fide Cath. propagandâ* was "erected" by the Bull of Gregory XV. in 1622. The "Seminarium" dates from 1627. As to the Missions here touched on, Charlevoix's Histories for Japan and Paraguay are well known; H. Coleridge's *Life of Xavier* may also be consulted; and for a general account of Catholic Missions, Wittmann, *Allgemeine Geschichte der Katholischen Missionen*, Vol. III. The most recent account of the Mission in China will be found in Cooper's *Pioneer of Commerce*.

the length and breadth of America, from Paraguay to the snows of Canada; no less than in the far East, in India, Tonkin, China, and Japan, and on the coasts of Western Africa; and still maintains with unabated vigour in much of these regions, as well as in the English colonies, its centres of operation; is no sluggard in this work. Xavier alone, in his heroic faith and zeal, his quenchless love of souls, his entire spirit of self-sacrifice, his earnest piety, and careful wisdom, offers, it has been well said, "all that we can desire, all that we can conceive in the character of a Christian preacher sent forth among the heathen to teach repentance toward God, and faith towards our Lord Jesus Christ."[1] Why should it be held that the light of such an example is perished from the earth, never to re-illume the horizon of Christian enterprise? Surely it cannot any longer be urged with truth against Protestantism that in its hands Christianity has lost its expansive power: that neither the spirit of wisdom nor of self-sacrifice animates its efforts for the conversion of the heathen.[2] Long, it is true, this note of an Apostolic Church was wanting while a reformed faith was struggling for existence or reviving its shattered energies.[3] No

Xavier.

His example capable of reproduction.

[1] Grant, *B. L.*, p. 145.
[2] See in Grant, *u. s.*, p. 183. Thus De Maistre, *Du Pape*, III. c. i.; IV. v. He adds, bitterly: "Les églises sont stériles, et rien n'est plus juste; elles ont rejeté l'Époux."
[3] "The constructive intelligence of the seventeenth century possessed itself of the materials accumulated during the Reformation era, to

doubt, the outbreak of the Reformation "isolated the English Church as well as kindred continental bodies from the vast system with which they had been bound up."[1] They were thrown suddenly on their own resources. But little by little, with the return of strength and the opportunity of reflection, the sense of this duty re-awaked among the Protestant Churches. Denmark established the first mission in Hindostan,[2] and also in Greenland. Holland laboured earnestly in Java, Amboyna, Formosa. Germany, in the missions of the United Brethren, showed an unrivalled pattern of wisdom and self-devotion over an area extending from South Africa to Labrador. I will not now seek to recount the efforts made through the Missionary Societies of our own country to wipe away the reproach of past indifference in this the prime of Christian works of mercy. But I would ask you to compare the present state of British India with its aspect a century ago; to look abroad on the work which has been done during the same period in America, Australia, New Zealand, and Africa,

Of the Reformed Churches.

Germany.

Of England.

---

fashion them into means of offence and defence. . . . Within the citadel a vigorous spiritual life, which gave evidence of its existence chiefly in sacred song and music, was not lacking. But the notion of winning the world to the Gospel, and of the moral expansion of the Protestant principle according to its different aspects, had almost disappeared."— Dorner, *H. Prot. Th.*, II. 99.

[1] Grant, *B. L.*, p. 185. Guericke, *Kirchengesch.*, III. 374.

[2] Having later among its missionaries (from 1751–1798) that truly excellent man, Christian F. Schwarz. A general history of Protestant Missions was first brought out by Wiggers, Hamburg, 1856, in 2 vols.

2 B

and to say whether we can see in it only the expiring embers of a faith all but extinct, incapable of further effort or enthusiasm. Do we not rather mark in it the signs under God's blessing of a revival, pure, and fresh, and heartfelt, of a primitive zeal such as has ever stamped the leading eras of Christian advance? Though much, very much remains to be done to consolidate the empire of Christ even in the regions where His name is named, there is still ground in past and present effort for the highest expectations of success. Is it not so that in these latter days the truest seal of missionary devotion has not been withheld in the constancy of an entire Church, as also of individual Christians? Witness the blood-stained cliffs of Madagascar! Witness the island of the South Pacific, which so lately saw our English Bishop Patteson close with a martyr's death the life of an Apostle! Happier in this his meed than Xavier himself. "If," said that faithful servant of Christ, "I should happen to die by the hands of the heathen, who knows but all of them might receive the faith? For it is most certain that, since the primitive times of the Church, the seed of the Gospel has made a larger increase in the fields of Paganism by the blood of martyrs than by the sweat of missionaries."[1] Surely Mission work will be found the true Crusade of the nineteenth cen-

Present aspect of the work.

---

[1] See Dryden's *Life*, p. 174, ap. Grant, p. 179.

tury. It is not for nought that Christianity, once the civilizer and creator of modern Europe, now puts forth its plastic power to re-mould the religions of the world, and summon to one common shrine the aboriginal races of the earth. It is true that many such tribes, the sad survivors of the infancy of our race,[1] have perished as by an unseen law, and are perishing at the first touch of civilization. The Church of Christ but plants itself on their forgotten graves. Yet, if indeed we believe in civilization as the vocation of mankind, and in nations as specifically gifted for this work, how vast is the future now open to Christian enterprise! For the soul and source of all real civilization we hold to be Religion.[2] Colonization and conquest, intercourse and trade, are its pioneers, and to each of the dominant sections of the Christian world may perhaps, in the Divine councils, be reserved a separate portion of this common work. Each of the three Families of

Favourable conjuncture of circumstances.

Probable field open to each of the leading divisions of the Christian church.

---

[1] "Quant aux races sauvages, ces tristes survivants d'un monde en enfance, à qui l'on ne peut souhaiter qu'une douce mort, il y a presque dérision à leur appliquer nos formulaires dogmatiques, fruit d'une réflexion de vingt siècles."—Renan, *Questions Contemporaines,* p. 361. I have to some extent followed the far-reaching speculations of the same able mind in estimating the future spread of Christianity. Meanwhile philosophy, it must not be forgotten, has done nothing in this work. "Condorcet," writes De Maistre, "nous a promis que les philosophes se chargeraient incessamment de la civilisation et du bonheur des nations barbares. Nous attendrons qu'ils veuillent bien commencer."—*Œuvres,* p. 130.

[2] See Luthardt's remarks, *Apolog.,* E. T., ed. Clark, p. 199.

Christianity,[1] the Latin or Celtic, the Teutonic, the Greco-Slave, (for in accepting this new element the Greek Church also has found its Rénaissance;) has at least a probable appointed area of labour. Russia may yet subdue the realms of Buddhism and of Confucianism. For Latin Catholicism may remain the Turkish and Persian Orient. The Moslems of the East, it is true, fix their gaze on Constantinople as the centre of their hopes,[2] looking to a restoration of the Caliphate, and with it of their former glory. But surely they lean on a broken reed. For Teutonic Christianity and our own English-speaking race[3] lies in store the vast appanage of Hindostan, the continents of Australia and North America, and, as it would seem, of Central and Southern Africa,

---

[1] "Throughout the world, wherever the Teutonic is the groundwork of the language, the Reformation either is or, as in Southern Germany, has been dominant: wherever Latin, Latin Christianity has retained its ascendancy."—Milman, *L. Chr.*, I. 8. "Protestantism," says Mr. Froude, *Short Studies*, p. 131, "is Teutonic; Catholicism Latin and Celtic." As to the Greek Church, comp. Dean Stanley, *Lect. on Eastern Ch.*, p. ix. pp. 345, 492, and Neale's *Holy Eastern Church*, I. 14, 15.

[2] See Grant, *B. L.*, p. 285. W. G. Palgrave's *Essays*, p. 131.

[3] "The spread of the English stock, and language, and literature, over the North American continent, has afforded a distinct and very significant indication of the power of Christianity to retain its hold of the human mind, and of its aptness to run hand in hand with civilization, even when unaided by those secular succours to which its enemies in malice, and some of its friends in over-caution, are prone to attribute too much importance."—I. Taylor, *Enthus.*, p. 271. In the East, the opening of Japan, the adoption, as it is stated, of English as the State language, and the large dimensions of Chinese Coolie migration to America, Australia, and India, tend in the same direction.

"even all the isles of the heathen." As the final term of human religions, susceptible of a progressive application,[1] the Avatar of Christianity has still before it a future, which in vastness may overshadow the history of the past.[2] <small>Room for progress.</small>

§ 13. Let us not, then, the creatures of a day, whose term of earthly life but spans the commencement of an immortal existence, deem that progress slow, that career uncertain. For what shall be our standard of measurement? "The blindness of the greatest men, of the highest races, of wide continents" will not shake our faith, that the Divine purpose revealed in the scheme of our holy Religion shall surely come to pass. There are not wanting indications that, "both in the case of men and of nations, the longest training and the dreariest periods of abeyance of spiritual life are often preparations for its fullest growth."[3] Eras of <small>Conclusion.</small> <small>No true standard of the rate of progress of Christianity.</small>

[1] Comp. Milman, *u. s.*, p. 9; VI. 447.
[2] Want of space forbids me to dwell on the symptoms, now happily universal, of the *intensive* progress of Christianity in our own and other countries. These to some extent compete and interfere with missionary labour. Such are the vast efforts made in England during the last half century, not only by the Established Church, but also by Nonconformist bodies, to overtake, as to spiritual provision, the large and steady increase of population, a task the more difficult from foregone neglect; the building and renovation of churches and chapels; the erection and maintenance of schools, in which the clergy are admitted to have taken so great a share; the growing interest in matters of doctrine and practice often involving much personal sacrifice; not to speak of individual acts of Christian religiousness, the growth of charity answering to the increase of national wealth. In proportion as many of these tasks are remitted to the superintendence of the State, the *extensive* action of the Church may be expected to fill a larger field.
[3] Hutton, *Essays*, p. 122.

apparent retrogression may be designed to act but as goads to discipline the faith which hopes and works unshaken to the end. And certainly the new consciousness now dawning on mankind of spaces of duration, hitherto beyond conception, yet now falling into their rank and place in the scheme of evolution of human existence, may teach us to be wary of hastily determining the future of Christianity and of our race by any previous limits of anticipation. It has probably been one cause of the slowness of the spread of the Gospel, now, happily, very generally felt, where over-hasty missionary efforts have neglected all consideration of previous stages of development, intellectual and moral; and have introduced races hardly reclaimed from savagery to theological controversies, or the acceptance of religious practices, which represent the thought of centuries. But the issue of the work of Evangelization can never be doubtful, so long as we reflect upon the characteristics of the truths which Christianity reveals to mankind, and their position in the history of our race. In this respect we may, without undue assumption, appeal to the internal evidence of truth furnished by the character of its doctrines; their universality,[1] their

Retrogression subsidiary to advance.

Progress in knowledge will facilitate missionary success.

Argument for the progress and ultimate permanence of Christianity,

[1] "There is nothing which to any reflecting mind is more signal a proof of the Bible being really the guiding book of the world's history than its anticipations, predictions, insight into the wants of men far beyond the age in which it was written. That modern element which we find in it—so like our own times, so unlike the ancient framework of its natural form—that Gentile, European turn of thought, so

adaptation to the nature which it is their aim to regenerate; their very presumption of finality in the promises which they hold out to assure the spirit of man. Other religions have been local, temporary, limited, fitted for definite stages of culture, partial in their hold upon particular truths, in accord with the spiritual standing, so to speak, only of the people or race. They have accordingly developed tribes and nations to a fixed line and point of progress, and then their course seems stayed.[1] They have no further message to the soul of man; no onward mission to evoke his Divine capacities, or renew his fallen nature. But Christianity has not only, in its history, shown itself adequate to all the circumstances of its de-*from the cosmopolitan character of its doctrines, which find their fulfilment in the development of the human race.*

unlike the Asiatic language and scenery which was its cradle—the enforcement of principles and duties which for years and centuries lay almost unperceived, because hardly ever understood in its sacred pages; but which now we see to be in accordance with the utmost requirements of philosophy and civilization; those principles of toleration, chivalry, discrimination, proportion, which even now are not appreciated as they ought to be, and which only can be realized in ages yet to come; these are the unmistakeable predictions of the prophetic spirit of the Bible, the pledges of its inexhaustible resources."—Stanley, *Sermons on the Bible,* p. 80. I shall readily be excused for quoting this fine passage at length.

[1] " History shows in many ways that Mahometanism has its root only in the past. There is no growth in the faith; no power of adapting itself to the new ages. Mahomet *as he was* rules Mahometans *as they are.* His word was petrified and crystallized in Mecca, and can assimilate no new truth. But the history of the Christian Church is a history of constant growth in spite of sacerdotal resistance; and I believe that the upward course of that growth has ever been the communion with a living Christ."—Hutton, *Essays,* I. 277.

velopment; its definite announcements permit a judgment on its genius and character as a Religion framed for permanence and finality.[1] If true, it proclaims a scheme for the redemption and improvement of mankind, which is unique, complete, and incapable of repetition. Its overtures to the individual soul, limited to no race, or caste, or class, or set of faculties, extend from its entrance into life to the hour of departure; are adapted to its real wants and failings;[2] and provide for that immortality which strikes an answering chord in the heart of every man. Its type of moral perfection, correspondent to the actual phenomena of human nature, is laid in the union of opposed yet not discordant virtues, of impulsive affections and controlled passions, of self-sacrifice identical with the truest self-love, and terminating in the restoration of real self-respect. "He who saves his life

Its tenets responsive to the highest convictions of civilization,

of Moral Science,

---

[1] Compare H. J. Rose, *Prot. in Germany*, pp. 191, 192.

[2] On these topics see Miller's *Bampton Lect.* on the Adaptation of Holy Scripture to the real state of Human Nature; more particularly Lectures iv. and vii. "There never was any religion as that of Christ; so congenial to our highest instincts; so persuasive, so ennobling, so universally acceptable to rich and poor; so worthy of the intellect, so consistent and uncompromising in its rules for advancing moral excellence. Men could not, would not turn from it if it was properly brought home to them; if it was not tendered to them with some admixture of earth about it, exciting their suspicions and robbing it of its heavenly fragrance."—Ffoulkes, *Div. of Christendom*, p. xiv. "Many, I think, are agreed, that after all the most striking evidence for the Divine origin of our faith lies in the patent fact of its existence; of its growth and diffusion; its proved superiority to all other forms of spiritual thought; its proved adaptation to all the spiritual wants of man."—Merivale, *Lectt.*, p. 6; and *Northern Nations*, p. 28.

shall lose it: but whosoever shall lose his life for Jesus' sake and the Gospel, the same shall save it."[1] The term of man's moral progression is by its means indefinitely extended, and rises into a new and nobler sphere than that of ordinary ethics. It alone assuages the sorrows of existence, (from which ere now philosophy has taken refuge in suicide),[2] hallows and explains the mystery of suffering, and takes away the sting of dissolution. Its revelations, while confessedly beyond intellectual comprehension, are guaranteed by their correspondence with the spiritual intuitions of our race; being acknowledged alike by the richest culture and by the lowest barbarism. Man's wants and weaknesses, his hopes and desires, his powers and aspirations, his personal and social capabilities, are together forestalled. Thus the doctrines of Christianity, uniting the human and Divine, make the only adequate provision for the claims of the human spirit in its sense of sinfulness and need of reconciliation, in its yearning after Divine com-

and to the facts and needs of human nature as hitherto developed.

Scriptural provision for the spiritual wants of mankind

[1] Mark viii. 35. Christianity is plainly in accord with that higher aspect of Utilitarian Morality which teaches that a man is bound to live in harmony with the order of the universe, and contribute his part to the common good. Again, each soul of man is "one for whom Christ died" (Rom. xiv. 15). "Magnum opus Dei es, Homo," says Ambrose, *Serm.* x. in Ps. 118, § 11.

[2] See Archer Butler, *Lect. on Ancient Phil.*, I. 443, 459; (it was practised by Zeno and Cleanthes, the Stoics;) and Mr. Lecky, *H. E. M.*, II. 46, for the history of Christian influence on this point. Buckle, *Hist. Civ.*, I. 26, remarks on the fruitlessness of legislation to stay this evil.

munion.¹ For, by the gift of the Holy Ghost, assured through ordained means of reception, man's spirit is associated with his Maker and Redeemer, and life in time with life in eternity. Thus the Ideal merges in the Actual, the Visible in the Unseen, and Earth in Heaven. Raised above an atmosphere of chill Materialism, the Christian walks and lives in a world where things are no longer what they seem; but glow with a new light, and are suffused with a deeper significance.

<small>a permanent system.</small>

> Largior hic campos æther et lumine vestit
> Purpureo: solemque suum, sua sidera norunt.

A door is opened in Heaven; and he hears the Voice which saith, "Come up hither."

<small>No real decay of the power or benevolence of the Gospel.</small>

§ 13. And it is of this Religion that we are bidden to believe, that it is fraught with the fate of bygone superstitions, stricken with palsy, hastening to decay. Although day by day it gives evidence of the living fruits of faith, and zeal, and charity, of a benevolence well-nigh boundless, of a sympathy universal as our race.² Surely the love which has done so much for man, is no unreal

---

¹ "The Gospel, as mere historical truth, would be something past and dead, like a mere doctrinal system of eternal truths, without life and reference to the living person. It is the nature of the Gospel that it is truly known and apprehended only when the historical Christ is at the same time embraced as the present, as well as the eternally abiding, and therefore also future Christ; as still livingly active to-day, and pointing forward into the depths of an eternity whose vital energies repose in Him."—Dorner, *Hist. Prot. Th.*, I. 232.

² See Mr. Lecky's eloquent testimony, *Hist. Rat.*, I. 204, 205; and compare Lange, *Gesch. des Materialismus*, p. 556.

sentiment; it has its root in the truth of things; it is an effluence from Him, Who Himself is revealed as Love, in the person of Jesus Christ, the express Image of Divine Holiness, the Channel of Divine Grace, the Author and Example of all true self-sacrifice. "They who would deprive mankind of Him, would tear out the corner-stone of the noblest edifice of humanity."¹ But this they can never do. And in the darkest hour of human degradation and depression, the word of promise standeth sure, having this seal: "It is I, be not afraid:" "Lo! I am with you alway, even unto the end of the world."² Amen.

The Church of Christ, based on the fact and promise of His indwelling Spirit, necessarily Eternal.

¹ Luthardt, *Apolog.*, p. 297: "As little as mankind will ever be without religion, so little will they ever be without Christ—an historical, not a mythical Christ—an individual, not a mere symbol. Christ remains to us, as the highest we know and are capable of imagining within the sphere of religion—as He without whose presence in the mind perfect piety is impossible."—Strauss, *Soliloquies*, 67 (quoted by Dean Stanley, *Sermons*, p. 111). See Mr. Hutton, *Essays*, I. 278.

² Matt. xiv. 27, xxviii. 20. So Luther had good reason to liken the Church of Christ to the amaranth, which neither withers nor decays. "Sprinkled," he said, "with water, it becomes fresh and green once more, as if raised and wakened from the dead. Even so is the Church by God raised and wakened as out of the grave. For though temporal empires, principalities, and kingdoms have their changings—and, like flowers, soon fall and fade away—this Kingdom, so deeply rooted, by no power can be destroyed or wasted, but remains eternally."— *Table-Talk*, 172, ed. Bohn. "Wherefore, being Christ doth promise His Presence unto the Church even unto the end of the world; He doth thereby assure us of the existence of the Church until that time, of which His Presence is the cause."—Pearson, *on the Creed*, Art. ix.

INDEX

A.

ADMINISTRATION, Divine, harmony of, 127.
Admiration has a *personal* basis, 232.
Altruism not incompatible with Christianity, 82, 377.
Anabaptists, their fanaticism not due to the principles of the Reformation, 329.
Analogy of Nature, a theological ground of argument, 212.
Antiquity no actual test of truth, 28.
Arabians, their services to physical science, 350.
Aristotle, his medieval reputation, 247.
Art, its early relation to Christianity, 280; its present position, 348.
Asceticism not essential to the theological spirit, 299.
Asylum, privilege of, 289.
Augsburg, Confession of, its concluding declaration, 332.
Augustine, S., his view of miracles as evidential, 139.

B.

BACON, Lord, on religious controversy, 11; his view of missions, 356.
Barbarians readily admitted by the Church, 281; mode of conversion, 286; its true causes, 288.
Barbaric Codes, show the influence of Christianity, 284.
Becket habitually performed harvest work, 300.
Belief, Christian, standard of, in Scripture and Creeds, 31.
Biography, Religious, importance of, 228.
Bishops, popular election of, 280; by royal mandate, 285; their beneficial influence, 283, 288.
Bossuet, his argument against Protestantism lies equally against Christianity, 11.
Brahmanism, stationary, 26, 27, 29; its doctrine of Absorption, 30.
Buckle, Henry T., his obligations to Condorcet, 71; his views on civilization, 146; on theology, 208; confounds asceticism with self-restraint, 299.
Buddhism, 26, 27; once a missionary religion, 29, 363; extinguished caste, 30; favours Monasticism, 297, 298.
Butler, Archer, on doctrinal development, 45.
Butler, Bishop, 14, 20, 188, 212, 219.

C.

CALVIN, his doctrine of personal assurance, 331.
Casuistry, its moral value, 166.
Catholicism, Medieval, its declension, 326.
Causes distinguished from occasions of events, 134.
Chance equivalent to ignorance of design, 77.

INDEX.

Chivalry, its relation to Medieval Christianity, 311; its origin, *ib.*

Christ, Jesus, perennial influence of His example, 35, 334.

Christianity, most vigorous in the most civilized regions, 3; a factor in civilization; 8, 152, 308; a fact of long standing, 9; its durability ascertainable, 23; its antiquity, 28; an historical and documentary religion, 34, 64, 212; the religion of progress, 51, 220; its perpetuity a doctrinal tenet, 52, 56, 57, 264, 379; its assumed failure, 58; as being a phase of religion, 60; not a necessary result only of antecedents, 144, 180; its progress, how far supernatural, 145, 265; natural, 162; limited, 169, 171; in advance of, yet co-existent with, civilization, 172, 242; importance of its ideal standard, 173; did not originate in a moral protest, 169; not eclectic, 177; is not a new code of morals, 257; has not declined in moral effect, 175; its part in advancing morals, 170, 176; its slow progress not due to feebleness, 188, 373; has survived changes of opinion, 203; theories of its origin, 261, 275; true causes of its success, 262, 266, 268, 273; its moral power, 269, 272, 276; its services wrongly attributed to positive institutions, 274; founded on a sense of sin, 276; its early influence on literature, 281; intellectual services in Middle Ages, 193; its political affinities, 359; whether democratic, 360; internal evidence of its permanence, 375, 376; its benevolence, 378.

Christians, moral excellence of the first, 263.

Church, The, temporal supremacy of, 185.

Circumstances, their *coincidence* admits of no law, 129.

Civilization, multiform, not a mere intellectual advance, 146, 147; answers to the whole nature of man, 149; difference of Ancient and Modern, 148.

Classicism, its effects on Christianity, 346, 348.

Communism, early view of, in the Church, 187.

Confucius, his view of Providence, 125; of religion, 178, 257.

Consciousness, testimony of, analogous to perception, 106.

Constantine established Christianity, 277; its consequences, 278.

Controversy a sign of religious activity, 11.

Conversion, power of, an element in religious vitality, 26, 253, 362; essential to Christianity, 363.

Creeds, how connected with Scripture, 37, 38; independent form of, 358.

Cromwell, Oliver, cause of his death, 131.

Crusades, The, criticisms of, 304; really defensive, *ib.*; their services to civilization, 305; their spiritual import, 306; exhibit the heroic type of Christianity, 307; later Crusades, 315.

Cycles, theory of, in history, 131.

D.

Deduction, its character as an instrument of proof, 215, 216.

Design, Argument from, not identical with order, 22.

Development, Theory of, its influence on the perpetuity of Christian doctrine, 42; dubiously admitted, *ib.*; rests on authority, 43; really an historical process, 44; Rationalistic theory of, 46.

Discovery in Natural Science a species of Revelation, 217.

Distance of time necessary to clear judgment, 9.

Dominicans, their humane efforts, 366.

Durability, test of, in religions, 26.

Duration a relative idea, 23.

E.

EASTERN CHURCH, its failings, 170; its subordination to the Greek Emperors, 285; its Monachism, 298; its future, 372.
Effectual Call, sense of, in theology, 101.
Epicureanism, modern, traceable in the view of Laws of Nature, 115.
Erasmus, his complaints, 346.
Error, slow extension of, 15.
Establishments, Church, usefulness of, 357, 358.
Evangelical Preparation, truth and importance of, 144.
Evil, existence of, explained by partial knowledge, 20; nature of moral and physical, 245; mode of its extinction, 246.

F.

FAITH the basis of all scientific acquirement, 240.
Fatalism contradicted by consciousness, 102.
Feudalism, its relation to Medieval Christianity, 309; its origin, 310.
Final Causes, fallacy of assuming, 19, 21.
Free Will, in what respects a theological tenet, 79; compatible with physical uniformity, 80.
French Revolution, its intolerance, 344.
Froude, J. A., his view of Calvinism, 80; of General Laws, 136.

G.

GENERAL LAWS, personification of, by recent writers, 136
Gibbon, his view of the success of Christianity, 261; inadequate, 262.
Gladiatorial shows, extinguished by Christianity, 271.
Greek nature controversial, 169.
Gregory the Great, synchronizes with the final Christianization of Europe, 284; his view of Purgatory, 319.

H.

HEGELIANISM, its essence, 353.
History sometimes confounded with biography, 135.
Hospitals, a Christian institution, 271.
Humanists at the Reformation, 347; their servility, 354.

I.

IDEAS gain credence from repetition, 61.
Induction not excluded by theology, 208; unknown to antiquity, 351.
Infanticide, a Pagan custom, 271.
Inquisition, The, how a means to toleration of opinion, 139.
Instincts, existence and testimony of, 82, 85; imply design, 84.
Investiture, Right of, 315.

J.

JUSTIFICATION by Faith only, Luther's view of, 327; its relation to the Reformation, 328.

K.

KANT, on design in Nature, 23.
Kepler, his view of planetary spirits, 136.
Knowledge being positive, finite in character, 249.

L.

LAS CASAS, his devoted life, 366.
Laws of Nature, wrongly identified with a *theory* of Existence, 103; meaning of General Laws, 115; views as to their nature, 118; not yet proved to be universal, 120; by some held to be the term of knowledge, 122.
Leibnitz, his theory of Parallelism, 93.
Love to God, an essentially Christian precept, 165.

Luther, his vehemence, 328; efforts for education, 347; view of the permanence of Christianity, 379.
Lyranus Nicolaus, his *Postillæ perpetuæ*, 329.

M.

MAHOMETANISM, 26, 27; its present progress, 363, 372, 375.
Man, how superior to the animals, 109.
Mansel, Dean, his view of Divine interposition, 133.
Marathon, religious importance of this victory, 135.
Marriage, Christian view of, 271.
Martyrs in Science as in Religion, 197.
Materialism, its connection with Positivism, 68; incompatible with ignorance of physical causes, 91; its gloomy character, 222; its present aspect, 244.
Matter, not eternal, 90; warrants inference of the existence of God, 95.
Medieval Christianity, its corruptions, 313, 355; inevitable, 314; its military character, 315; corruptions of doctrine, 317; false supports, 320; extravagance, 349; suppression of criticism, 351; its liberality, 360.
Melancthon, 323, 327, 347.
Method of Residues applicable to History, 128.
Middle Ages, their religious character, 173.
Miracles, classification of, 138.
Missions, whether incompatible with Private Judgment, 361; prospects of, 362, 370; early recognition of, 363; continuous, 364; their progress since the Reformation, 365, 366, 368.
Monasticism, Christian, its origin, 297; a remedy to excessive industrialism, 299; involved labour, 300; merits of, 301; its defects, 302; self-regenerative power, 303.
Monotheism, its relation to Christianity, 85.

Morality truly progressive, 163, 164; advanced by Christianity, 165; Christian morality the corollary of its doctrines, 178; distinguished from Religion, 258.
Mysteries, essential to Religion as revealed, 141; economy of Christianity in respect of, 141.
Mysticism, the correlative of Rationalism, 142; its relation to Materialism, 142.

N.

NATURAL SCIENCE, its prepossessions as to Theology, 63; these historically justified, 66; present Materialistic tendencies of, 67, 76; easily passes into dogmatism, 69.
Nature, uniformity of, tends to a First Cause, 88; exhibits also variety and irregularity, 130.
Neo-Platonism, its failure, 237.
Nescience, Philosophy of, often tends, though not necessarily, to Materialism, 97, 117.
Newton, Sir Isaac, on the Nature of God, 137.
Numbers no test of truth in Religion, 27.

O.

ORIGEN, his view of planetary spirits, 136.
Orphanages, when first founded, 271.

P.

PAGANISM, inefficient as a religion, 27; its reaction upon Christianity, 171.
Pantheism, essence of, 96; its antidote, *ib.*
Papacy, spiritual function of, as a tribunal of appeal, 291; decline of, 316; its moral dignity, 316.
Pascal, his view of Prophecy, 139.
Patriotism recognized by Jesus Christ, 81; a Christian virtue, 360.
Patteson, Bishop, his death, 370.
Penitentials, their influence as part of Christian Law, 291.
Permanence, a test of reality, 13.

Perpetuity, a test of religious truth, 6.
Persecution for belief, its origin, 184, 356.
Physical Studies not irreligious where not exclusive, 116; ancient cultivation of, 350; indebted to Protestantism, 356.
Platonism, its share in the Reformation, 323.
Pliny, his view of Prayer, 267.
Positive, history of the term, 67.
Positivism assumes all religious belief to be imaginary, 16; a belief in Laws, 59; negative in its tendencies, 66; defective as an explanation of phenomena, 97; its relation to Free-Will, 108; its failure as a religion, 237; its historical criticism of Christianity, 320; confounds Christianity with Catholicism, 342; its view of the Reformation, 340.
Prayer, its relation to human responsibility, 74.
Prescription, limits of argument from, 2.
Priscillian, his execution, 184.
Progress not limited to advance in knowledge, 168; standard of, 373.
Property Tax, when first imposed in England, 306.
Prophecy, historical character of, as evidence, 139; fulfilled in the progress of Christianity, 140.
Protestant, origin of name, 334.
Protestantism, its defect, 200; its true function, 200; asserted to have made no converts, 201; its duty of toleration, 202; a guarantee of permanence, 354.
Providence, theory of, essential to Christianity, 113; general and special, 123; sphere of, 125; misinterpretations of, 132.

R.

RATIONALISM views Religion as a phase of morality, 256; this error examined, 257; not a consequence of the Reformation, 352; defined, 353.

Reformation restored the individual influence of Christianity, 11; and of the Bible, 41; not a mere moral protest, 168, 326, 327; its theology inductive, 210; in itself a test of the truth of Christianity, 321; spontaneous, 322; not a result of improved knowledge, 323; its defects, 323; its practical changes rested on renewed doctrines, 324; date of its commencement, 325; not indefinite, 331; or negative, 332; restored the balance of doctrines, 333; its permanent effects, 334; how a protest, 334; Roman and Positivist views of, 340; Rationalistic view of, 341; still in progress, 343; introduced new elements of progress, 345.
Reformed Churches, their missionary efforts, 369; and prospects, 372.
Religion, an element in civilization, 149; its changes not due to intellectual progress, 150; its true function, 156; not a mode of proclaiming morality, 161; influences the advance of morals, 168; its tacit force, 174; deals with spiritual truth, 195; not reactionary as to secular knowledge, 196; how related to Natural Science, 225; independent of advances in knowledge, 236; the Science of the Soul, 223; a necessity of human nature, 241; its vital forces, 253; necessary elements, 255; a vehicle of Revelation, 256; assumes Mysteries, 256; test of its success, 258; how far a moral one, 259; its periodicity of revival, 344; foremost in political reforms, 352.
Religion of Nature, its ambiguities, 161.
Religions perishable, 2; historical sequence of, 144.
Religious Disabilities, removal of, 357.
Religious Wars, true character of, 183.
Revelation, how far a natural process, 47.

2 C

Ritual, its influence in conversion, 289.
Roman Empire, its condition at the coming of Christ, 264; why not saved by Christianity, 278; effect of its extinction on Christianity, 283.
Roman Catholicism, its present danger, 202, 354; its missionary zeal, 367; and prospects, 372.
Royal Society founded partly by Churchmen, 355.

S.

SAINTS, Intercession of, general in Middle Ages, 319.
Salmasius, his defence of usury, 187.
Salvian, his estimate of Christian declension, 279.
Sanctuary, Right of, its spiritual character, 290.
Scepticism admissible as to religious evidence, 209; not formidable to Religion, 239; whether a result of the Reformation, 353; its peril to the Church of Rome, 354.
Scholasticism, its effects, 301.
Schools, how far due to Christianity, 271; and to the Reformation, 347.
Science, how far predictive, 130; in what respects ineffectual to human happiness, 154; theories as to its relations to Religion, 191, 192; their assumed incompatibility, 193; their meeting-points, 243.
Scripture, its authority, 38; its power of prolonging personal influence, 39; this an element in the perpetuity of the religion, 40; erroneous interpretations of, 186; its relation to the Reformation, 41, 329.
Secularization not necessarily unfavourable to Christianity, 357, 360.
Sensation, fallacies of, 102.
Serfdom, how far extinguished by Christianity, 310.
Slavery, emancipation of, by Christianity, 72, 271.

Soul, proof of its existence inductive, 226; its immortality, whether recognized at the coming of Christ, 227.
Spinoza, his view of Providence, 117.
Spirit, denial of its existence subversive of all Religion, 225.
State, The, duty of, in propagating truth, 358.
Statistics, defective as a means of showing the operation of the Will, 103, 104.
Stoicism, its incapacity as a system of religion, 237; its sources, 264.
Suicide advocated by heathen philosophy, 377; its true remedy in Christianity, *ib.*

T.

TEMPORAL POWER clearly distinguished in medieval Christianity, 292.
Teutonic character, 309, 312; Christianity, 372.
Theism, its relation to Christianity, 70.
Theology a science of historical criticism, 211; its method how far deductive, 215, 216; whether stationary, 218; or progressive, 219; rashly assumed to be opposed to induction and verification, 207; and to science, 208; includes both primary and inferred truths, 210; commencement of, as a science, 318.
Time, a test of truth, 17; in what sense an agent, 18.
Toleration, its fundamental principle, 203; neglected by the Reformers, 351, 355; not a cause of Rationalism, 352, 354; advocated by the Fathers before Constantine, 356.
Tradition, Christian primitive, its relation to Scripture, 38.
Truce of God distinguished from "Peace of God," 190.
Truth progresses slowly but inevitably, 9; how far an attribute of institutions, 13.

U.

ULPHILAS, the missionary of the Goths, 286.
Unity, present need of, 12; the ultimate prospect of Christianity, 200.

V.

VEDDAHS destitute of a belief in God, 68.
Verification admissible in religious experience, 214, 219.

W.

WAR, increasing rarity of, due in part to Christianity, 190.

Wealth, increase of, no guarantee for real advance, 155.
Will of man essentially motive, 78; homogeneous with the Divine, 99; conditioned in action, 100; spiritual character of, 229.
Women, position of, in medieval society, 310; how far elevated by Christianity, 310.
Wonder, how an element in Religion, 321.

X.

XAVIER, his character and death, 368, 370.

www.ingramcontent.com/pod-product-compliance
Lightning Source LLC
Chambersburg PA
CBHW022118290426
44112CB00008B/724